The New Left, National Identity, and the Break-up of Britain

Historical Materialism Book Series

The Historical Materialism Book Series is a major publishing initiative of the radical left. The capitalist crisis of the twenty-first century has been met by a resurgence of interest in critical Marxist theory. At the same time, the publishing institutions committed to Marxism have contracted markedly since the high point of the 1970s. The Historical Materialism Book Series is dedicated to addressing this situation by making available important works of Marxist theory. The aim of the series is to publish important theoretical contributions as the basis for vigorous intellectual debate and exchange on the left.

The peer-reviewed series publishes original monographs, translated texts, and reprints of classics across the bounds of academic disciplinary agendas and across the divisions of the left. The series is particularly concerned to encourage the internationalization of Marxist debate and aims to translate significant studies from beyond the English-speaking world.

For a full list of titles in the Historical Materialism Book Series
available in paperback from Haymarket Books, visit:
www.haymarketbooks.org / category / hm-series

The New Left, National Identity, and the Break-up of Britain

Wade Matthews

Haymarket Books
Chicago, IL

First published in 2013 by Brill Academic Publishers, The Netherlands
© 2013 Koninklijke Brill NV, Leiden, The Netherlands

Published in paperback in 2014 by
Haymarket Books
P.O. Box 180165
Chicago, IL 60618
773-583-7884
www.haymarketbooks.org

ISBN: 978-1-60846-377-0

Trade distribution:
In the US, Consortium Book Sales, www.cbsd.com
In Canada, Publishers Group Canada, www.pgcbooks.ca
In the UK, Turnaround Publisher Services, www.turnaround-psl.com
In Australia, Palgrave Macmillan, www.palgravemacmillan.com.au
In all other countries, Publishers Group Worldwide, www.pgw.com

Cover design by Ragina Johnson.

This book was published with the generous support of
Lannan Foundation and the Wallace Action Fund.

Printed in the United States.

10 9 8 7 6 5 4 3 2 1

Library of Congress Cataloging-in-Publication data is available.

Contents

Acknowledgements

I have incurred numerous debts during the writing of this book. The book began its life as a Ph.D. thesis, although almost nothing remains from the thesis I defended in 2007. For their help with the thesis, I would like to thank Robert Stuart, whose own work on national identity and socialism provided the original impetus for the thesis, and Eileen Yeo and Hamish Fraser, who helped the thesis toward completion.

Since turning the thesis into a book, I have incurred many more debts. For reading chapters of the book and offering helpful comments, I would like to thank the following: Stephen Brooke, Russell Jacoby, Raymond O'Connor, Bryan Palmer, Joan Sangster, Bill Schwarz, and Robert Stuart.

I must also thank a number of institutions. In particular, I thank the University of Strathclyde, Glasgow for the award of an Andersonian scholarship, Trent University for the award of a Canadian Research Chair Postdoctoral Fellowship, and York University where I undertook a Social Science and Humanities Research Postdoctoral Fellowship. Among the staff of these institutions, I would especially like to thank Eileen Yeo, Bryan Palmer, and Doug Hay.

Most importantly, I would like to thank a number of family and friends. I thank my family, and particularly my parents, John and Jill Matthews, who have always supported my career. Many friends have sustained me through the writing of this book. I thank Bryan, David, Dylan, Joan, and Simon. More recently, I thank Aryn.

Finally, this book is dedicated to Jarratt Hull, Mark Allen and Paul Laffey, three friends who are no longer here, but who fired my historical and political imagination in different ways.

Preface

Historians are interested in ideas not only because they influence societies, but because they reveal the societies which give rise to them.[1]

I

Historical relations between socialism and nationalism have tended towards extremes.[2] Sometimes, socialists have combated nationalism and sought to overcome, rather than nurture, national difference. However, when appealing to categories that transcend nationality, such as 'humanity' or 'class', socialism has appeared bloodless and deracinated, deaf to Sigmund Freud's warning that 'the tradition of the race and of the people, lives in the ideologies of the super-ego ... independently of economic conditions'.[3] Yet, when accentuating national sentiments, socialists have mimed the affective identities of political reaction: the (majority of the) European Left's endorsement of their own national states' response to the outbreak of war in 1914 constitutes just one example.[4] As such, socialists have been caught between abstraction and particularity: either they have sacrificed reason and equality for a celebration of particular identities and finished indistinct from their ideological opponents, or they have combated their adversary's discourse but consigned themselves to political oblivion.[5]

This book investigates how socialist intellectuals in Britain negotiated this dilemma. Specifically, it will explore how socialist intellectuals connected with the New Left responded to the national question after 1956, and how their sense of imagined community exerted an influence on their response. Propelled, no doubt, by nationalist awakenings in Europe and elsewhere in the recent past, and the generalised post-socialist fetish of ethnicity, historians' growing interest in socialist approaches to the national question has generated an

---

1. Hill 1972, p. 17.
2. Wright 1981; Forman 1998.
3. Freud 1932, p. 67.
4. Haupt 1972.
5. Eagleton 1990, p. 34.

impressive literature.[6] This has been most remarkable in relation to continental socialism. Historians of British socialism have contributed to this growth, too.[7] However, in the British case, the historiography has focused almost exclusively on the late nineteenth and early twentieth centuries. The more recent past has generally been neglected. This book aims to repair that neglect.

In this book, I argue that Britain's national and nationalist dilemmas are crucial to explicating the nature of New Left thought. Its focus is debates among New Left intellectuals – E.P. Thompson, Raymond Williams, Stuart Hall, Perry Anderson and Tom Nairn – between the mid-1950s and the fall of communism. These debates do not just include those familiar disputes of the 1950s and 1960s around socialist humanism, classlessness, the origins of Britain's present crisis and the nature of culture and community. These debates are covered in depth in the course of the book. But I also follow the New Left's encounter with the national question beyond 1968. Thus the book explores New Left thinkers' negotiation of European integration, separatist nationalisms, and Britishness in the 1970s and 1980s, and, moreover, their encounter with the national and nationalist implications of Thatcherism, the Cold War and the fall of communism in the 1980s and 1990s.

In brief, a contestatory dialogue is established throughout the book based around different New Left perspectives on what has been called the break-up of Britain. That national questions were pivotal to debates within the New Left should come as no surprise. The New Left's ambition was nothing less than the regeneration of socialism, not just as a British but also as an international project. It was this project that yoked together the thinkers considered in this book. They were also joined by a shared awareness of the limitations of Marxist theory. Alongside these elective affinities, the New Left was conjoined by concrete questions of Britain – a historical climate, that is, characterised by decolonisation, the migration of peoples to Britain from its former empire, Britain's 'decline', the evolution of European integration, the rise of separatist nationalisms in Wales, Scotland and Northern Ireland and processes of capitalist globalisation.

A further impulse behind this enterprise is the historical decline of socialism in Britain – both as a political project and as a picture of social reality. Both 'socialism' and 'nation' were relatively straightforward realities in 1950s Britain. But few words have been more contested in political discourse since, and neither enjoys an uncomplicated or stable relationship with reality today. Complications associated with the one seem to have tracked the path of complications with the other. Indeed, liberalism and conservatism seem to have weathered Britain's

---

6. Connor 1984; Jenkins and Minnerup 1984; Nimni 1991; Benner 1995; Forman 1998; and Stuart 2006 are just some of the contributions to the subject.
7. Ward 1998.

national and nationalist storms rather better than socialism over the last half-century or so, which raises the question of the connection between the two. This study examines the nexus between socialism and nation in New Left political thought, with a view to providing a tentative assessment of this connection.

II

In form, this book connects New Left thought to 'the break-up of Britain'. As such, it has much to do with the prejudices of the author in the present. It is assumptions and preconceptions, as Hans Georg Gadamer argued, that make it possible for us to write history in the first place, and historians, like everyone else, are unlikely to get out of bed without prejudices of some sort – even if only the prejudice associated with the idea that sleeping late is lazy. Part of the prejudices and assumptions that the author brings to his book is his relationship with other interpretations of the past. Chapter One illuminates this interception and provides a brief account of the New Left's history.

Chapter Two explores British socialism's negotiation of national identity before 1956. The primary purpose of this chapter is to provide a sense of the socialist tradition that New Left intellectuals inherited as socialists and social theorists. Much work has been done on the relationship between 'red flag' and 'Union Jack' in the work of socialist intellectuals before 1924. Less work has covered the period between the first Labour government and 1956. We still lack a study akin to Paul Ward's *Red Flag and Union Jack: Englishness, Patriotism and the British Left, 1881–1924* but dealing with the 1930s and 1940s. In the absence of such a study, this chapter will provide a brief overview of the complex nexus between socialism and national identity in Britain before 1956.

Chapter Three provides a reinterpretation of E.P. Thompson's contribution to New Left thought. Commentators have often latched upon 'Englishness' as the key to unlocking the meaning of Thompson's political interventions and his historical work. According to this view, Thompson's attachment to 'Englishness' overdetermined his socialism. I reject this view, and provide a reconsideration of Thompson's Englishness among much else. The chapter argues that Thompson is better situated 'in the provinces' – a sensibility or location that has nothing to do with provincialism or parochialism. I argue that it was from 'in the provinces' that Thompson mounted campaigns against metropolitan power and historical determinisms, including dominant nationalisms. Throughout the chapter, the ramifications of Thompson's standpoint will be considered in relation to key debates within the New Left.

Chapter Four considers the work of Raymond Williams. As with contemporary interpretations of Thompson, recent accounts of Williams's thought have highlighted his enduring national connections, in his case with Wales and Welshness. Oddly, however, there is little consideration in this work of relations between Williams's socialism and his Welshness, most often the last sitting unexplained beside the first. Williams's encounter with national identity needs to be reinterpreted in relation to his socialism. This chapter does this by situating Williams within the context of New Left thought, and by considering his engagement with national identity in relation to that of other New Left thinkers. Williams's Welshness, I demonstrate, had little in common with conventional Welsh nationalism, and was complicated by his commitment not only to working-class community but also to revolutionary socialism. I argue that Wales was not Williams's only homeland, nor even his most important homeland, and that his thought does not require reduction to Welshness in order to demonstrate its enduring relevance.

Chapter Five provides an analysis of Stuart Hall's encounter with national identity. Uniquely among New Left thinkers, Hall knew British imperialism from both the 'inside' and the 'outside'. This standpoint, informed by his direct experience of British colonialism and his migration to the imperial metropolis, generated insights into British national identity that were sometimes lacking in the work of Williams and Thompson, despite Williams's and Thompson's unrelenting anti-imperialism. Hall was alert before most others to the effect that immigration from Britain's former Empire would have on Britishness. Increasingly, questions surrounding Britishness became central to Hall's approach to socialism. This was no less evident in his widely influential analysis of Thatcherism than in the characteristic concerns of *Policing the Crisis*, perhaps the emblematic text of British cultural studies in the 1970s. Indeed, the implications of national identity for socialism, I argue, were an enduring feature of Hall's contributions to debates within the New Left.

The focus of Chapter Six is the work of Perry Anderson. Often described as 'Olympian', Anderson has been at the forefront of disputes within New Left thought, not just regarding the nature of socialism, but also the character of British intellectual culture. However, his contributions to those disputes did not come from nowhere. The 'somewhere' that coloured Anderson's take on the New Left, and on other New Left thinkers, will be the subject of this chapter. This 'somewhere', I argue, was a standpoint that flatly rejected nationalism in favour of a cosmopolitan conception of identity and which stressed the communicative rationality of trans-national (Marxist) discourse. This standpoint was detached and elitist, and among its first premises eschewed any association with populism. The effects of this perspective on Anderson's contributions to debates within the New Left will be chartered throughout this chapter. The insights and limitations characteristic of Anderson's contribution to New Left debates will be refracted through the arguments of other New Left thinkers.

Chapter Seven dissects the role of national identity in the work of Tom Nairn. The relationship between place and social transformation has been crucial to Nairn's socialism, no less in his contributions to the Nairn-Anderson theses than in *The Break-Up of Britain*. Indeed, almost uniquely among New Left thinkers, Nairn embraced, without ambiguity, the moniker 'nationalist' (at least from the 1970s onwards), though his view of nationalism was somewhat unique. But his nationalism, at least before the late 1980s, uneasily co-existed alongside his commitment to socialism. His nationalism has also always had an identifiable object – Scotland and the hope of a Scotland independent from the United Kingdom. Before that, he waved the flag of socialist cosmopolitanism, though this standpoint was no less inflected by place. Nairn is the New Left thinker who has been most associated with theoretical developments in nationalism-studies. But this association, once worked through debates within the New Left, takes on, I argue, a different meaning from conventional accounts of Nairn's nationalism.

To pre-empt a conclusion: debates within the New Left between Suez and the end of communism were co-incident with the process that Nairn dubbed the break-up of Britain. That this process had an effect on those debates should be obvious, though it has not featured prominently in the secondary literature on the New Left. Indeed, one conclusion of this book is that those debates had much to say about, and were a response to, Britain's national questions, and that these questions can help explicate their meaning. More widely, the book also claims that New Left debates can help explain something about the decline of British socialism. The relationship is complex, but it was precisely those things that strained the unitary nation-state of Britain – Europe, mass immigration, capitalist globalisation, and the rise of peripheral nationalisms – that cast a pall over socialism's future.

Chapter One
History and Historiography of the New Left in Britain

I

1956 was something like a 'Year Zero' for sections of the European Left. Sheila Rowbotham, from the perspective of the late 1970s, called it the beginning of 'modern times'.[1] De-Stalinisation, dissident-communist attempts to 'humanise' socialism, the Soviet invasion of Hungary, the gathering strength of Labour revisionism and the Suez crisis: 1956 would prove a tocsin and a touchstone for a revaluation of the socialist principle across Europe.[2] The New Left in Britain was born in relation to these international and national conjunctures. In the familiar story of post-war European socialism, 'new' Lefts emerged on the one hand as a product of discontent with international communism and social democracy, and, on the other, as a response to 'old' and 'new' imperialisms and transformations in the capitalist mode of production. Constituted at the interface of these currents, the New Left in Britain reflected and reflected upon a fractured and uneven geography of politics, culture and interest throughout its history.

In truth, 1956 was not a 'Year Zero'. Like all political movements, the New Left drew selectively on the past.[3] The 'religion of socialism', the Plebs League,

---

1. Rowbotham 1979, p. 21.
2. Sassoon 1997, pp. 241–73; Eley 2002, pp. 329–39.
3. I find Lin Chun's suggestion that the New Left 'seriously neglected or underrated' the 'positive and vital elements in the legacy of traditional English socialism' to be inadequate as a characterisation of the New Left's engagement with socialism's past. See Chun 1993, p. xvi.

G.D.H. Cole's guild-socialism, and the 'creative Marxism' of the 1930s, might all be included among those immediate portents in politics and thought that allowed the New Left to distinguish itself in the tradition of British socialism.[4] Indeed, the degree to which the New Left drew on 'mainstream' socialist ideas should not be overlooked. There was a constant tension between the New Left's ambition to found new socialist ideas and its attempt to rediscover an 'essential' socialism obscured by communist and social-democratic theory and practice. If there was a 'core' to socialism, then the New Left found it in a philosophical anthropology that stressed co-operation, community and human creativity. But if the New Left reinserted a utopian element into socialist discourse it nonetheless argued for steel-nationalisation, an incomes-policy and a socialist national plan.

II

The emergence of the New Left in Britain is conventionally dated from the formation of two independent-socialist journals following the events of 1956: *New Reasoner*, direct descendant of *The Reasoner*,[5] and *Universities and Left Review*. Both journals (eventually) positioned the New Left as an alternative to communism and social democracy, with a stress on the need to remake socialism through an emphasis on moral values, feeling and imagination, and a matched imperative to render it correspondent to transformations in capitalist productive relations. However, the sterilities of post-war socialism and its discord with contemporary political economy were widely remarked upon in the early-to-mid-1950s. From R.H.S. Crossman's 1950 book *Socialist Values in a Changing Civilization* to Anthony Crosland's 1956 *The Future of Socialism*, socialists across the Left spectrum identified political archaism and an absence of 'spirit' as characteristic of socialism's contemporary malaise.[6] The New Left was unique because it argued for socialism's rescue through the recuperation of its moral essence and contended that such redemption could only happen outside socialism's customary political manifestations. Thus the New Left located itself in the awkward position of at once valuing and rejecting the tradition that informed its ambitions.

New Reasoner was established and edited by former Communist Party of Great Britain (CPGB) partisans E.P. Thompson, Dorothy Thompson and John Saville in northern England, home to the industrial working class typically outcast from

---

4. Yeo 1977, pp. 5–56; Miles 1984, pp. 102–14; MacIntyre 1980, p. 181; Coombes 1980.
5. Saville 1976, pp. 1–23.
6. Crossman 1950; Crosland 1956. See Black 2003, p. 12.

the 'Deep England' of conservative visions of national belonging.[7] Immediately consequent on the Thompsons' and Saville's disgruntlement with communist orthodoxy – first publicly expressed in *The Reasoner* – *New Reasoner* was a product of European communist dissent, although it also drew strength from a 'native' tradition of socialist protest and struggle, particularly in Yorkshire.[8] The journal was inspired by a concern to recover the 'humane and libertarian features of the communist tradition'.[9] Other than Ralph Miliband and Mervyn Jones, who joined an expanded editorial board in 1958, the journal was staffed and written by ex-Communists, including Doris Lessing, Ken Alexander and Malcolm McEwen. ✗

If the genesis of the *New Reasoner* can be largely understood in the context of dissident communism, the journal must also be read as a response to (what the editors considered) recurrent and new barbarisms of capitalist civilisation. About the chief forms of barbarism *New Reasoner* was clear: imperialism, the proliferation of nuclear weapons, and the constriction of human potential signalled by the extension of the profit motive into all aspects of life. *New Reasoner* highlighted anti-imperialist struggles in the colonial world and endorsed a socialist repudiation of the remnants of British Empire in Asia, Africa and Cyprus – and, in association, mounted pointed critiques of 'jingoism' and nationalism as they materialised in places such as Notting Hill, Nottingham and at Labour Party conferences. Alongside a consistent focus on communist dissent in Eastern Europe, the journal championed a 'Bandung' view of the Cold War,[10] and was much concerned with outlining a 'socialist foreign policy' based on a repudiation of NATO and the Cold War's 'bloc'-politics. Attention to the concrete attributes of a socialist future were no less in evidence among the journal's contributions than philosophical and polemical skirmishes over the nature of socialist humanism and the springs of human growth.

---

7. More or less the best account of *New Reasoner* can be found in Palmer 2002, pp. 187–216. Ten issues of *New Reasoner* appeared between 1957 and 1959. Among figures who served on the editorial board of *New Reasoner* were Doris Lessing, Ken Alexander, Ronald Meek, Randall Swingler, Malcolm MacEwen, Michael Barratt Brown, Mervyn Jones and Ralph Miliband.

8. Dennis Dworkin has suggested that Thompson and Saville saw themselves 'as reviving an older, uncontaminated tradition of English socialist thought and politics – the tradition of Tom Mann and William Morris'. According to him, Thompson and Saville 'saw a return to this heritage, which as historians they had begun to recover, as central to a socialist revival. They wanted to create an authentic English Marxism'. See Dworkin 1997, p. 51. Dworkin's accent on English socialist thought and practice and English Marxism can be disputed. The two influences that Dworkin sees operating on Thompson and Saville – Mann and Morris – were, of course, committed to socialist internationalism. In *this* sense, they are appropriate forbears of the New Reasoners. Arguably the accent on *Englishness* is Dworkin's, not Thompson's or Saville's.

9. E.P. Thompson 1959a, p. 9.

10. *New Reasoner* 1958.

The Oxford Socialist Club was the incubus for the other journal of the early New Left.[11] *Universities and Left Review*, initially edited from Stuart Hall's Oxford kitchen, found a permanent home in cosmopolitan London, an appropriate location perhaps for a magazine that included a Jamaican, a Canadian and two London Jews among its editors, and a range of political exiles and émigrés among contributors to its early issues.[12] Stuart Hall, Gabriel Pearson, Charles Taylor and Raphael Samuel, all graduates of Oxford, were the founding editors of *Universities and Left Review* and in their varied lived experience, they brought distinct and related sources for a rejuvenation of socialist thought and practice to the journal.[13] Hall provided the journal with a diasporic accent carefully attuned to culture's role in subaltern subordination, whether in metropole or periphery.[14] Not alone, his background, formed and marred as it was by colonial ways of life, ensured early New Left sensitivity to the politics of anti-imperialism in Britain's inner cities and in the larger geography of Britain's Empire. Samuel and Pearson each imparted strengths from more localised socialist traditions that were nonetheless shaped in relation to wider-European developments. Via his 'recovery' of Marx's *Paris Manuscripts*, the Montreal-born Taylor also provided *Universities and Left Review* with a characteristic New Left concern with alienation and community.

Universities and Left Review stood in a tradition of Oxford socialism that went back to Cole's *Oxford Socialist* and *Oxford Reformer*.[15] The journal sought to widen socialism's horizons by analysing the urban environment, the evolution of town-planning, architecture and the mass media. By connecting socialism to 'the total scale of man's activities',[16] *Universities and Left Review* attempted to make socialism relevant to people – whether at work or at leisure, whether in terms of social or familial relations. Transformations within capitalist productive relations associated with affluence and deindustrialisation were constitutive concerns of the journal. In addition, *Universities and Left Review* sought to inform the anger of young men and women throughout Britain, manifest not just in the Campaign for Nuclear Disarmament (CND) but also in more broadly dissident ways of life.[17]

---

11. The Oxford Socialist club, not connected with either the Labour Party or the CPGB, included among its members Stuart Hall, Anna Davin, Partha Gupta and Irfan Habib. The minutes of meetings from October 1956 to January 1957 are now available in *History Workshop Journal* 2006.

12. *Universities and Left Review* appeared seven times between 1957 and 1959.

13. By 1959, the number of editors had expanded to include Michael Barratt Brown, Norman Birnbaum, Allan Hall, Michael Kullman, Alan Lovell and Alasdair MacIntyre.

14. See Schwarz 2007, pp. 45–63.

15. Carpenter 1973, pp. 16–17.

16. *Universities and Left Review* 1957, p. ii.

17. Bentley 2005, pp. 65–83.

They travelled some way down the road with this beat-culture, but sought a socialist humanist end beyond what was considered 'disabled romanticism'.[18]

Much New Left historiography has conventionally highlighted the political, sociological and generational distinctions between *New Reasoner* and *Universities and Left Review*.[19] Good reasons exist for these distinctions.[20] *New Reasoner* was steeped in the Yorkshire labour-movement and was sometimes suspicious of metropolitan modes of thought, which it claimed to spot in the pages of *Universities and Left Review*. E.P. Thompson summed up many of the conventional distinctions between the journals. 'You see', he wrote to Raphael Samuel in 1957, 'we cut different characters: ULR is mercurial, sensational, rides loose to theory & principle (query?), goes for gimmicks and so on: all this is excellent, and the right way to break the crust especially with the younger people. The NR is middle aged & paunchy and strikes a note of political responsibility, and dogged deaf endurance'.[21] Matters of temperament and tone, revealed in opposed emphases around trade-unionism, communist dissent and class-analysis, sometimes divided the journals, too.

But as important as these differences were, perhaps of greater moment were divisions *within* the respective journals, something generally neglected in the secondary literature on the New Left. Attitudes toward the Labour Party, for example, generated significant dissent within the *New Reasoner* collective. John Saville, Ken Alexander and Chris Freeman were keen to further relations with figures within the Labour Left, such as Michael Foot and R.H.S. Crossman, and saw the Labour Party as the only possible vehicle of socialist transition.[22] The Thompsons disagreed. They believed that it was 'impossible' to change the Labour Party and that a Labour government was just as likely to introduce state-corporatism as socialism. The Thompsons repeatedly stressed their dissident-communist origins and were not interested in 'disowning their past' which too close association with Labour Party modes of thought, they believed, would imply. There was also dissension within the *New Reasoner* collective around supporting independent Left candidates in elections, such as Lawrence Daly and his

---

18. Hall 1957a, p. 23.
19. For an example, and review, of this historiography, see Kenny 1995, pp. 1–8 and 15–23.
20. Some of the reasons are set out in Davis 2006, p. 344.
21. E.P. Thompson, Letter to Ralphael Samuel and Michael Barratt Brown, 6 February 1957, Raphael Samuel Archives, University of North London.
22. E.P. Thompson, Letter to Ken Alexander, 23 January 1958, DJS/112 Saville Papers, University of Hull Archives, University of Hull; E.P. Thompson, Letter to John Saville, 2 April 1958, DJS/112 Saville Papers, University of Hull Archives, University of Hull; E.P. Thompson, Letter to John Saville and Ken Alexander, 15 November 1958, DJS/112 Saville Papers, University of Hull Archives; Saville, Letter to Edward Thompson, 15 August 1958, DJS/112, Saville Papers, University of Hull Archives, University of Hull.

Fife Socialist League.[23] Tension likewise characterised relations among members of the editorial board of *Universities and Left Review*. Somewhat different to *New Reasoner*, this found expression within the journal's pages, when Samuel took Hall to task over Hall's interpretation of 'classlessness'. This division – between Samuel and Hall – was taken over into the first years of *New Left Review*, too.

There was, though, collaboration between *Universities and Left Review* and *New Reasoner* from the beginning. Discussions about a merger began in 1958 and a decision to merge the journals was taken in early 1959.[24] In other words, divisions between *New Reasoner* and *Universities and Left Review* should not be overstated. Both journals addressed an imagined and real New Left connection with de-colonising movements in Asia and Africa and with an anti-Stalinist humanism in Eastern Europe.[25] Events in Notting Hill (and Arkansas) received attention, as might be expected from a socialist journal situated in London, but Halifax was no less sensitive to the dynamic of metropolitan racism. Also, both journals made connections with the labour-movement, though each lamented the tenuous nature of these connections. The distinction, often repeated in New Left historiography, between the 'cosmopolitanism' of *Universities and Left Review* and the 'parochialism' of *New Reasoner* should be ignored.[26] A quick glance at the contributors and subject matter of the Halifax journal would establish its 'cosmopolitan' credentials beyond doubt. While both journals attempted to manufacture and narrate a constituency for socialism that reached beyond the organised-industrial working class to skilled professionals, teachers and other educators, technicians and the scientific community. Central, here, was the journals' shared commitment to CND.

---

23. See E.P. Thompson, Letter to Lawrence Daly, 17 August 1959, Lawrence Daly Papers, Modern Records Centre, Warwick University, which registers Ken Alexander's opposition to the support that the *New Reasoner* gave to the Fife Socialist League.

24. This was not universally approved. Both Ralph Miliband and Ken Alexander argued against merger. See Ken Alexander, Letter to Edward Thompson and John Saville, 1 April 1958, Saville Papers, University of Hull Archives, University of Hull. Both Saville and Thompson had agreed that merger was necessary by July 1958. See Saville, Letter to Edward Thompson, 15 August 1958, DJS/112, John Saville Papers, University of Hull Archives, University of Hull. The merger did not proceed smoothly, however. Indeed, it could be argued that merger was a necessity rather than a choice. See Saville, 'Background to Merger Question', DJS/112, Saville Papers, University of Hull Archives, University of Hull.

25. On Hall's early connection with West-Indian anti-imperialism, see Hall 1996a, pp. 484–5. A good overview of Thompson's relationship to India is provided in Palmer 1994. On Saville and Indian self-determination, see Saville 2004, p. 57; and on Peter Worsley's relationship to de-colonisation in Africa, see Worsley 2008, pp. 62–3.

26. For this common view – inspired by comments made by Stuart Hall – see Dworkin 1997, p. 54.

What drew *New Reasoner* and *Universities and Left Review* together was an evolving New Left ideology concerned with the transformation of socialism – indeed, in the New Left's moments of hubris, of human nature itself. This ideology was committed to 'socialist advance in Britain'; to 'expose and destroy imperialism and racialism overseas and at home'; to 'the unilateral renunciation of the H-bomb' and ending Britain's 'participation in the NATO alliance'; and to 'unity with the advance to socialism in other countries'.[27] There were more banal exigencies promoting merger too, not least financial concerns and problems associated with maintaining journals on the basis of voluntary labour. If all this was enough to precipitate consensus, there were nonetheless considerable divisions about what the new journal should look like.[28] Right through the early years of *New Left Review*, there was disagreement about whether the journal should be an intellectual intervention or the organ of a political movement.

By 1959, both *New Reasoner* and *Universities and Left Review* were acknowledging the emergence of a New Left political movement, precipitated by the success of the 1958 Aldermaston march against nuclear weapons. However there was other evidence for the genesis of New Left politics, not least the activities surrounding the *Universities and Left Review* club in London, which spawned replicas all over Britain. The New Left had a presence in the Anti-Apartheid Committee, in Labour's constituency-parties, in CND and in the Fife Socialist League, too. In the final issue of *New Reasoner*, Thompson portrayed the New Left in international colours, as a response not just to apathy and conformism in terms of social democracy and communism, but also as a response to Cold War. Not just in communist dissent in Eastern Europe, the flowers of a New Left bloom had appeared in Italy on the fringes of the PSI and the PCI and in France in the form of the *Union de la Gauche Socialiste* and *France-Observateur*. The New Left was what E.P. Thompson would later call an '"International" of the imagination...detached unequivocally from both Stalinism and from complicity with the reasons of capitalist power'.[29]

---

27. 'A General Statement adopted by a joint meeting of the Editorial Boards of the New Reasoner and Universities Left Review on Sunday April 26 1959', John Saville Papers, DJS/112 Hull University Papers, Hull University.

28. These divisions were set out at a joint meeting of the Editorial Boards of *Universities and Left Review* and *New Reasoner* in 1959. Those present: Stuart Hall, Ralph Samuel, Charles Taylor, Janet Hase, Michael Barratt-Brown, Norman Birnbaum, Allan Hall, Michael Kullman, Alasdair MacIntyre, John Saville, E.P. Thompson, Peter Worsley, Alfred Dressler, Joe Greenald, Derek Kartun, Malcolm McEwen, Ronald Meek, Ralph Miliband, Dorothy Thompson and Joan Welton. See 'Minutes of a Meeting of the Editorial Boards of Universities Left Review and the New Reasoner held at 7 Carlisle Street W.1 on Sunday, 26 April 1959 at 10.30am', Saville Papers, DJS/112, Hull University Papers, Hull University.

29. E.P. Thompson 1978, p. iii.

III

New Left Review was launched in late 1959 and its first issue appeared at the beginning of 1960. Hall was the journal's inaugural editor, while the journal's editorial board included Thompson and Raymond Williams among others. The journal was based in London, though many of the board's members lived in northern England. Like its forebears, *New Left Review* initially saw itself as a channel for dialogue between socialist intellectuals and industrial workers, as a forum for the debate, analysis and 'clarification of [socialist] ideas', and as the incubus for the growth of New Left clubs, what the editorial to the first edition of *New Left Review* considered 'the nerve centres of a genuinely popular and informed socialist movement'.[30] Early issues of *New Left Review* diagnosed labourism's sickness, tracked the sociological source of working-class deference, opened a dialogue on working-class culture, explored the meaning of revolution and provided a close watch over the activities of CND and popular culture.

That socialist theory – 'a new, vital, and principled movement of socialist ideas' – was essential to the reinvigoration of socialism was a founding premise of New Left thought.[31] The New Left operated as a 'movement of ideas' that sought to transform consciousness and inform socialist practice.[32] There was no intention to form a 'break-away party', though there was always an intention to act and operate against the party-political system.[33] The opening editorial salvo of *New Left Review* described the New Left's role as educational. Indeed the foundational stress on dialogue, language and ideas was crucial to the New Left's conception of not only the genetic problems of socialist discourse – bureaucratisation, the commitment to dogma and an unthinking reliance on conceptions of progress and science – but also its diagnosis of contemporary malaise – apathy and intellectual conformity induced by a combination of Cold War routines and the reifications consequent on the expansion of consumer-capitalism.

The New Left was confident that socialism 'made possible the assertion of man's humanity, of his potential nature, of that which is specifically human in man: victim no longer of nature or of himself, but a conscious moral agent'.[34] However, if the New Left often talked of socialism in utopian terms, and this deliberately so, this did not result in a neglect of socialist policy. The projection of an 'ideal to which it is legitimate to aspire', and 'the right and reason to enquire into the aims and ends of social arrangements, irrespective of questions

---

30. *New Left Review* 1960a, p. 2.
31. E.P. Thompson 1957a, p. 32.
32. See E.P. Thompson 1957a.
33. See Saville 1991, p. 28.
34. E.P. Thompson 1957a, p. 124.

of immediate feasibility',[35] was a defining feature of New Left rhetoric, but so were plans for a socialist wages-policy, projects for industrial democracy, and strategies for international relations, global trade and European integration.[36] Common ownership as 'the re-appropriation by the workers of their alienated work' was explored in New Left discourse,[37] but so were the problems of education and health and practical measures by which the steel-industry could be nationalised. New Left socialism was characterised by the attempt to synthesise theory with how theory related to people in the here and now.[38]

For New Left thinkers, the full ensemble of social relations were important to a future socialist society, though gender-relations were mostly neglected or ignored by the socialist formation's intellectuals.[39] 'The material processes of satisfying human needs', the New Left maintained, could not be 'separated from personal relations'.[40] At a systemic level, New Left rhetoric deemed outmoded class-relations a fetter on productive development. But its sense of strangled productive advance included racial tensions in Notting Hill, the state of the 'new towns' and a system of communications ruled by the profit-motive. The New Left held to a vision of capitalist productive relations that went beyond the relations of class to include primary affective relations of family, neighbourhood and society. Indeed, it was within the sphere of those intimate relations manifest in 'community' that the New Left gained encouragement for the realisation of its social vision. A 'sense of common lot' and the 'moral principle of sharing and co-operation' – these defining features of working-class community were not just proletarian survival-strategies against penury and alienation but also evidence of working-class self-making and as such of the kind of social potential within historical development.[41]

There was a more recognisable politics associated with the New Left beyond its ambition to constitute a movement of (socialist) ideas. This aspect of the New Left has perhaps received the least attention from subsequent historians. Among the most important of the New Left's political activities – beside its production of ideas – were the Left clubs in northern England,[42] which had

---

35. E.P. Thompson 1958c, p. 91.
36. Alexander and Hughes 1958.
37. Anderson 1961a, p. 44.
38. For examples, see E.P. Thompson 1959a, p. 10; Samuel 1958a, p. 70.
39. On the New Left and gender, consider Kenny 1995, pp. 46–8.
40. Williams 1983a, p. 68.
41. C. Taylor 1958, p. 18; Hall 1960, p. 4.
42. The activities of these clubs are hinted at in D.K.G. Thompson 1996, p. 94. Also important was the short-lived 'Socialist Forum' movement. Information about this movement can be tracked through its journal originally called *Forum – Journal of the Socialist Forum Movement* (the subtitle was later changed to *Journal of Socialist Discussion*). Contributors to this journal included Ken Alexander, Lawrence Daly and G.D.H. Cole. *Forum* was edited by Roy Harrison and Michael Segal.

close connections with *New Reasoner*, and the New Left clubs, which eventually spread from London to Manchester to Glasgow.[43] These voluntary associations of socialism await their historian.[44] Otherwise we might include among the New Left's more prominent 'activist' moments, the involvement of the *New Reasoner* with the Fife Socialist League, the co-operation of *Universities and Left Review* with tenant-associations and the Caribbean community in London, and New Left mobilisation within the Labour Party. However CND, which has received more detailed attention from historians of contemporary Britain, is conventionally considered the apogee of New Left political action. Initially centred on the Aldermaston marches that began in 1958, CND, in combination with the New Left, played a significant part in the short-lived reversal of the Labour Party's nuclear politics in 1960.[45]

'Socialism', Samuel suggested, 'is not only, as is sometimes said, a society of people – it is also a society they will create'.[46] That socialism would be realised from below rather than from above was a defining feature of New Left discourse on political organisation.[47]

> Where there are CND or Direct Action demonstrations, Left Clubs should be the most active groups. Where there are groups of houses without an active community life, where there are young people without a youth club, where there are responsible rank-and-file strikers being snubbed by Trade Union leaders, or coloured workers being frozen out by Trade Union rank-and-filers, there is work for us too.[48]

Consequently, the New Left invested much in ideas of participatory democracy, voluntary association and workers' control. All these concepts implied 'the extension of the individual's power over the collective forces which shape his life, and the creation of a sense of common purpose'.[49] In this sense, the 'democratization

43. *New Reasoner* 1959, pp. 128–9. According to Ioan Davies, by 1961 'there were 39 New Left Clubs across Britain, with the London Club holding weekly public meetings as well as having a series of discussion groups based on education, literature, new theatre, race relations. The Clubs also acted in many cases as the organizing centres for the Campaign for Nuclear Disarmament, and in many other cases were created out of the local groups of the Workers Educational Association and the National Council of Labour Colleges'. See Davies 1991, p. 325.

44. Little has been written about the New Left clubs. Brief comments on the clubs can be found in Kenny 1995, pp. 19 and 32; Dworkin 1997, p. 69.

45. The historiography of the CND is now quite large. For a start, see R. Taylor 1988. Bess 1993a, Chapter Three; Veldman 1994, pp. 180–200 deals directly with links between Thompson, the New Left and CND.

46. Samuel 1958a, p. 50; E.P. Thompson 1960a, p. 32.

47. *Universities and Left Review* 1957, p. 79.

48. *New Left Review* 1960, p. 1.

49. C. Taylor 1958, p. 17.

of power',[50] as 'The Insiders' put it, rather than the 'dictatorship of the proletariat', constituted the proper telos of New Left politics.

In reality, however, the New Left wavered between two, perhaps antithetical, conceptions of socialist policy. Typically, the New Left argued that socialism was co-existent with a 'possible world in which men and women can find a meaning for their lives through greater control over their work and leisure'.[51] In this register, the New Left was suspicious of nationalisation and rejected planning, which, according to its rhetoric, '[took] no account of the existing meaningful relationships in primary societies'.[52] However other cadences also inflected the New Left's socialism. The impulse toward democratisation, individual autonomy and decentralisation in the socialist formation's rhetoric chaffed against an equally strident impulse toward planned production and nationalisation. 'In order to establish new priorities for our society', Stuart Hall conceded, 'we would have to control "the commanding heights of the economy" '.[53] Public ownership and nationalisation were often endorsed as the best means to transcend private property, while characteristic New Left documents such as 'The Insiders' proclaimed the need for a 'socialist plan'.[54]

Something of this vacillation was also characteristic of the New Left's conception of social agency. Overwhelmingly, the New Left placed the burden of socialist transition on Marx's proletariat. According to Raymond Williams, the institutions of organised labour were not just the working class's definitive contribution to culture, but seeds of the social vision commensurate with socialism. Trade unions, co-operatives and the Labour Party itself – the 'collective democratic institution' – were indicative of a 'human relationship' antagonistic to the profit motive and expedients of social transformation.[55] Stuart Hall argued that organised labour had provided 'a consciously worked-out vision of how the society as a whole could be better, and what we would do to make it so'.[56] However, this confidence in labour's potential sometimes faltered. In *The Long Revolution*, Williams spoke of socialism's 'moral decline' and the failure of organised labour 'to sustain and clarify the sense of an alternative human order'.[57] Ralph Miliband described the trade-union movement and the Labour Party as forces for 'neo-capitalism' not socialism,[58] while Hall pointed to 'a crisis in the psychology

---

50. Hall et al. 1957a, p. 64.
51. *Universities and Left Review* 1958, p. 3.
52. C. Taylor 1958, p. 17.
53. Hall 1960a, p. 4.
54. Hall et al. 1958, p. 64.
55. Williams 1957, pp. 29–32.
56. Hall 1960b, p. 94.
57. Williams 1961, p. 133.
58. Miliband 1958b, p. 45.

of the working class'.[59] Indeed Peter Worsley reckoned that the proletariat in Britain had 'been so influenced by [Britain's] long imperialist history that it is perhaps the most chauvinist working-class in the world',[60] and that 'racial prejudice' was entrenched in British society.[61] Chauvinist, inured against theory, compromised by capitalism – by any socialist measure this was an ambiguous agent of social change.

IV

In its original form, *New Left Review* did not survive beyond 1962, despite the political optimism, impelled largely by CND's growth and the expansion of New Left clubs, which attended its foundation.[62] Following the financial and political breakdown of the original *New Left Review* and the resignation of Hall in 1961, editorship was transferred to a collective, comprised of Raphael Samuel, Dennis Butt and Perry Anderson, that proposed a more theoretical journal, one attuned primarily to the socialist and labour movement – a collective which initially had the support of E.P. Thompson.[63] This proposal was met with opposition from Norm Fruchter and Frances Kelly who argued that such a journal would mean a turning away from the gains of Hall's *New Left Review*.[64] Their appeal fell on deaf ears however. In any case, after one double issue in 1962, the collective was disbanded and financial and editorial control was transferred to Anderson (with editorial assistance from Tom Nairn and Robin Blackburn) and the editorial board was dissolved.[65] This permanent transfer is signified in the secondary literature on the socialist formation as indicative of a shift to a 'second' New Left.

The most obvious basis and widely referenced source for the view that there had been a transposition to a 'second' New Left are the contemporaneous accounts of the chief protagonists. Perry Anderson projected the transfer of editorship to the new team, and the consequent shifts in focus and emphasis in *New Left Review*, as inspired by political, organisational and financial vicissitudes consequent on the dissolution of the historical conditions which structured the

---

59. Hall 1960b, p. 93.
60. Worsley 1957, p. 15.
61. Worsley 1960, p. 118.
62. D. Thompson 2007, pp. 7–10, provides an overview of much of this history.
63. Perry Anderson had been involved with the Oxford New Left journal, *New University*.
64. *New Left Review* 1961, 'Memo from Norman Fruchter and Frances Kelly to Editorial Board', Saville Papers, University of Hull Archives, University of Hull.
65. The Editorial Board was dissolved in May 1963. Perry Anderson was editor by July 1962. See *New Left Review* 1962 'New Left Review: Minutes of the Board Meeting held at Keele University on Saturday and Sunday 7/8 July, 1962', Saville Papers, University of Hull Archives, University of Hull.

journal's genesis in the late 1950s – principally the shortcomings of CND and the New Left's apparent lack of a coherent political imaginary.[66] In more polemical tones, Anderson, along with Nairn, figured the break as a result of the 'first' New Left's derisory theory of contemporary British conditions, its politically damaging accent on morality to the neglect of structure and its parochial rehearsal of national traditions to the obfuscation of international Marxist theory.

Thompson figured the break differently. In equally polemical tones, but with an emphasis on political experience rather than *haute theory*, he interpreted the shift mainly in terms of idiom, interest and consciousness.[67] For him, Anderson and Nairn were elitist, sacrificed history to theory and underestimated the strengths of 'native' socialist traditions in their endeavour to uncover resources for social transformation from other countries. No matter the extent of disagreement, or indeed its exact nature, Anderson and Thompson agreed that a break had happened and, whether for good or ill, that something had ended and something new begun.

Reasons for the dissolution of the original *New Left Review* were multiple. The primary problem, perhaps, was organisational, signalled by repeated breakdowns in communication between the *New Left Review* office in London and Editorial Board members. This led, among other things, to E.P. Thompson's criticisms of Hall's conduct as editor and Saville's conduct as Chairman of the Editorial Board.[68] His criticisms, however, were substantive too:

> Two years ago we were making some attempts to clarify theory: and to bring theory to the point of actual policy. Now, after five years of theoretical debate, we are in a worse mess than before. Then we could publish an anti-NATO neutrality issue: now the Board discusses NATO and agrees to differ. Then the ULR published the 'insiders': now everyone gapes when Raymond [Williams] tells us economics is a 'system of maintenance'. Then we were trying tentatively to examine the Soviet Union: now it is a taboo area. Then our economists had got to the point of offering a wages plan: now wages are never mentioned. Then we were giving the Labour establishment a shaking: now they have borrowed our language to give themselves a contemporary veneer. The Marxists have been edged out (too old fashioned), but the 'Conviction' people haven't been held. We have a narrower range of contributors and committed people than two years ago.[69]

---

66. Anderson 1965a.

67. E.P. Thompson, 'Where Are We Now?', Unpublished Memo, DJS/109, University of Hull Archives, University of Hull.

68. E.P. Thompson, 'Letter to John Saville', 12 May 1961, DJS/112, Saville Papers, University of Hull Archives, University of Hull.

69. Thompson, Letter to John Saville, 12 May 1961, DJS/112, Saville Papers, University of Hull Archives, University of Hull. Evidence like this is neglected in Kenny's suggestion

Stuart Hall interpreted the breakdown differently. Hall would have described the relationship between the *New Left Review* office and the Editorial Board as inevitably difficult because there was no agreement among Board members on theory and politics.[70] This, without doubt, was crucial. The journal eschewed political leadership (and organisation) and there was very little theoretical agreement among key New Left thinkers in the early 1960s. Not just Thompson's criticisms of Raymond Williams's *Culture and Society* and *The Long Revolution* give evidence for this.[71] Otherwise, the journal maintained a silence over a number of significant issues that divided the Editorial Board, such as Marxism, China and the Soviet Union. As Hall, following the New Left's 1961 Stockport conference, lamented: 'NLR is a journal without a brief – and therefore impossible to edit and impossible to defend'.[72]

The reasons for the breakdown of the wider New Left political movement are more difficult to grasp. Obviously, some of the reasons related to problems with the journal since *New Left Review* was the *de facto* centre of the movement. Indeed the journal reflected and sometimes reflected upon the incoherence of the wider New Left political movement. Surely, however, the most difficult issue was the New Left's relationship to the Labour Party. This had been a millstone for independent socialists – including those grouped around *Universities and Left Review* and *New Reasoner* – from 1956, if not before. No clearer idea of this relationship had been established by 1962.[73] At its origins, the New Left sought no 'commitment to any political organisation'.[74] But the Labour Party remained an obvious focus of New Left political activity, demonstrated by its role in the

---

that the primary reason for *NLR*'s breakdown is explained by Thompson's behaviour. See Kenny 1995, pp. 35–7. In a letter to Samuel, Thompson argued that 'The NL was founded with certain political aims, & we should always at least consider personal issues in the light of these, not vice versa' – something that might be said of Kenny's view. See E.P. Thompson, Letter to Raphael Samuel, 27 June 1961, Raphael Samuel Papers.

70. Hall, Letter to Edward Thompson, 1960, Saville Papers, DJS/112, University of Hull Archives, University of Hull.

71. E.P. Thompson 1961a; 1961b.

72. Stuart Hall, Letter to Edward Thompson, 1960, Saville Papers, DJS/112, University of Hull Archives, University of Hull. Referring to the 1961 Stockport Conference, Thompson suggested that the main division was between an 'activist' wing and a 'more intellectual-critical' wing. 'So far from being NR/ULR,' Thompson went on, the tension in the New Left 'could break down in an opposite way (a Saville/NR type theoretical quarterly, as disengaged as Science & Society or Monthly Review at its worst – and an activist Cuba-type ULR, direct actionist, etc etc.' Again, Thompson reported the divisions between those who wanted to turn the New Left into a 'ginger group' in the Labour Party and those who wanted to steer clear of an association with the Labour Party. See E.P. Thompson, Letter to John Saville, 12 May 1961, Saville Papers, University of Hull Archives, University of Hull. For Hall's own comments on this conference, see Hall, Letter to Raphael Samuel, 15 June 1961, Samuel Papers, University of North London.

73. For discussion of this, see Rustin 1985, pp. 46–75.

74. John Saville, 'Background to Merger Question', 1959, Saville Papers, DJS/112, University of Hull Archives, University of Hull.

party's conference at Scarborough.[75] Otherwise the New Left, by its own admission, never established satisfactory links with the labour-movement, despite its connection with various trade-unionists, such as Bert Wynn, Jim Roche and Lawrence Daly.[76] Whatever the reasons for the breakdown – the failure of the journal and the clubs, an inability to prise any segment of the labour-movement away from the Labour Party, the forward march of CND halted by detente – it is ironic – but speaks to a need for care in analyzing some sort of 'global' New Left – that a New Left political movement in Britain came to grief in precisely that year when New Lefts elsewhere, particularly in the United States, were beginning their take-off.

After 1962, a reconfigured *New Left Review* engaged the founding, characteristically Gramscian, project of producing an accurate cognitive map of British society – specifically, the history, condition and probable destiny of British capitalism, the British labour-movement and English intellectual traditions: a historical overview, in the more rigorous de-nationalised Marxist terminology *New Left Review* now favoured, of infrastructure and superstructure. Thus between 1962 and 1967 the pilots of the newly imagined journal steered *New Left Review* for a course dictated by the resolve to explain capitalism's historic malaise and socialism's tendency to corporatism, and to internationalise English intellectual culture, particularly socialist culture. The journal briefly flirted with 'left social democracy' before assuming the function of an intransigent socialist opponent of labourism.[77]

In the mid-1960s, amid rising levels of class-antagonism, *New Left Review* found cause for optimism and potential in the movement for workers' control,[78] but thereafter turned its political antennae to peasant revolution and the student-movement as the principal hope for global socialist advance. By the beginning of 1968, in concert with scene-setting articles by the journal's editors, *New Left Review* had published a series of country studies and the work of a new generation of New Left thinkers. Also, the journal had reprinted the work of important figures in continental theoretical traditions – Althusser, Lukács, Levi Strauss. The work of Thompson, Hall, Samuel, Taylor and Saville, however, was absent in a socialist journal now more at home in the peaks and valleys of Marxist theory.

There was a significant rupture within the New Left between 1961 and 1964, represented best by the transfer of editorial control of *New Left Review*, a transfer which by 1964 had been consolidated into something that Thompson would

---

75. The New Left's involvement at this Labour Party conference included the establishment of an *NLR* newsletter, *This Week*.
76. This included the establishment of a short-lived journal, *Searchlight*, which dealt specifically with industrial issues.
77. Anderson 1977.
78. See Blackburn and Cockburn 1967.

designate a coup and Anderson a necessity. The rift was also signalled by the Nairn-Anderson theses, a series of essays that set out to highlight the paucity of socialist theory in Britain, illumine the present crisis of society and economy and lament the seemingly-immovable corporatism of the English working class – a class whose historical agency Thompson had just finished establishing in his 1963 work *The Making of the English Working Class*.

A further note of rupture was sounded by the decision of Ralph Miliband and John Saville to establish a socialist annual, *Socialist Register* – first published in 1964, which was arguably, in contradistinction to *New Left Review*, more attuned to the tone, nuance and idiom of the organised British labour-movement.[79] It was in *Socialist Register* that Thompson's 1965 riposte to the Nairn-Anderson theses appeared, a condemnation of the direction of *New Left Review* that drew an intemperate response from Anderson the following year. If further evidence were needed to establish the break, then appeal could also be made to the absence of any mention of socialist humanism (or indeed of positive neutralism) in the pages of *New Left Review* after 1962, an absence that can be calibrated in the 'second' New Left's less hostile engagement with orthodox communist currents and its openness to the Trotskyist tradition.

In fact, the nature of the rift was best represented by a shift in sensibility. This shift was marked by the 'second' New Left's turn to continental Marxist theory and its self-assumed leadership role in the project to internationalise British intellectual culture.[80] Engagement with the thought of Sartre, Brecht and Gramsci, and the exchange of ideas with socialists in France, Italy and Eastern Europe had been a feature of the early New Left, particularly of that dissident communist tendency associated with *New Reasoner*. The 'first' New Left also shared the 'second' New Left's concern with socialist theory and the need, as Thompson put it, to 'propagandise' socialist ideas. What separated the two was not engagement with other socialist traditions or with 'international' socialist theory, but the nature of that engagement and the ground from where that engagement took place.

However, while there was a significant rupture in the New Left the traditional story often lacks nuance. A complete break between Thompson and *New Left Review* was clear by 1963. However, other early New Left thinkers initially maintained association with the journal, including Williams, Barratt Brown and John Hughes. Debates over incomes-policy that took place in *New Left Review* in 1965–6, with contributions from Ken Alexander, Roy Harrison and Bob Rowthorn among others, would not have looked out of place in the original *New Left Review*

---

79. For an account of *Socialist Register*, see Newman 2004, pp. 113–24.
80. See Tom Nairn, Letter to Stuart Hall, 6 January 1960, Samuel Papers, University of North London. for early evidence of this intent.

or, indeed, in *New Reasoner*.[81] In addition, *Socialist Register* remained open to the engagement with continental Marxist theory of *New Left Review*. Both *Socialist Register* and the Anderson-led *New Left Review* published the work of Ernest Mandel and viewed developments in Italian communism with quiet optimism. Up until at least 1966, too, the 'second' New Left maintained an ambiguous relationship to social democracy reminiscent of earlier New Left negotiations of the majority socialist movement, something evident in Nairn and Anderson's initial positive identification with 'Wilsonism'.[82]

In fact, the substantial ideological distinction within the New Left emerged during 1967–8 – at the point, that is, when *New Left Review* decided that Marxism-Leninism was the principal solution to socialism's contemporary crisis. The turn to Marxism-Leninism in the 'second' New Left was prepared and informed by the example of Latin American revolution. In 1967 the editors of *New Left Review* championed the writings of Régis Debray, believing they offered a 'relentlessly Leninist focus on making the revolution, as a political, technical and military problem'.[83] Events seemed to point toward revolution, in the terms of insurrection, as the only viable socialist road, whether proved negatively in terms of the record of social democracy in Britain or positively in terms of revolutionary developments in Cuba. Vietnamese resistance to American imperialism was equally important to the 'second' New Left's Leninist turn. Göran Therborn suggested that the lesson of Vietnam proved that 'only such a Marxist-Leninist ideology and organisation can prevail over the juggernaut of American imperialism'; for him this ideology could be favourably contrasted with the 'left-wing liberalism' of the original New Left which had left 'a very moderate inheritance indeed'.[84] The shift to Leninism in *New Left Review*, and the decisive ideological rupture it signalled with the 'first' New Left, was consolidated by the events of 1968 – not just the Vietnamese defeat of American forces in Saigon, but also the eruption of student and worker revolt in Paris. A chief lesson of May 1968, according to the editors of *New Left Review*, was its demonstration of 'the potential of small revolutionary groups in helping to unleash a class storm that shook society to its foundations'.[85] This belief would drive key (second) New Left figures toward Trotskyism in the 1970s.

The language of *New Left Review* was 'militarised' after 1967 too. The journal talked of 'people's war', 'red base strategy', 'combativity', and the 'military

---

81. Rowthorn 1965 and 1966; Barratt Brown and Harrison 1966; Alexander and Hughes 1966.
82. Anderson 1964b.
83. *New Left Review* 1967.
84. Therborn 1968, p. 8.
85. *New Left Review* 1968b, p. 7.

substratum', while the bourgeoisie became 'the enemy'.[86] Emphasis was placed on 'Marxist cadres' and on 'vanguards', whether in terms of specific social groups or specific countries. Reforms were considered 'illusions'. The words 'mass' and 'masses' gained a new proclivity – 'mass mobilization', 'winning the mass', 'student masses' became familiar terms of this revolutionary rhetoric.[87] 'Intellectuals', not working-class self-activity, became the pivot around which the future of revolutionary socialism would turn. Foremost among these intellectuals was Louis Althusser, introduced to a British audience by Ben Brewster with the claim that socialist humanism was now old-hat.[88]

The politics of *New Left Review* in this period deserves better than condescension. There was an element of parochialism about British socialist theory, to say nothing of British intellectual culture, even if this judgment couldn't be made about Thompson, Williams or Hall. The 'alien gaze' of *New Left Review* had other benefits too. The journal's introduction of a range of continental thinkers, not least those from the Western Marxist tradition, reinvigorated British intellectual culture, as both Williams and Hall would later recognise. This project was an unqualified success, as was the creation of New Left Books (later Verso) and the Penguin Marx Library that made the key texts of Marx and Engels available to a wide audience. Equally defensible was the 'second' New Left's support for movements against imperialism and criticism of the British Labour government's support for US imperialism in Southeast Asia – criticisms championed by early New Left thinkers too. Second New Left figures also played a key role in establishing the Vietnam Solidarity Committee (VSC) and organising the mass protests against the Vietnam War in London. Less defensible, perhaps, was the belief that Marxism-Leninism had anything to offer the British labour-movement or that it was intellectuals who held the key to socialist advance. This, at least in terms of the original New Left, was a retreat behind problems already negotiated.

At the same time that the 'second' New Left was investing its socialist cache in a mixture of revolutionary voluntarism and 'scientific' Marxism, the original New Left was regrouping around Raymond Williams' *May Day Manifesto* (hereafter *Manifesto*). The original version of *Manifesto* was written and published by Williams in 1967, with help from Hall and Thompson, and Penguin published an updated version in 1968. Although a document that reflected the thought of the original New Left, *Manifesto* owed much to radical Left thinking in the 1960s. This was clear in *Manifesto*'s approach to the 'new capitalism' and the 'new imperialism'. However,

---

86. See *New Left Review* 1968b; *New Left Review* 1968a; Wilcox 1969.
87. See Fernbach 1969; Revolutionary Socialist Students' Federation 1969; Barnett 1969.
88. Brewster 1967, p. 14.

Manifesto's politics were clearly distinguished from *New Left Review* by its commitment to the traditional labour-movement, despite the author's vehement repudiation of labourism. Very much a document focused on labour as an agent of social transformation, *Manifesto* paid only minimal attention to other sites of resistance and rebellion.

In the words of Mike Rustin, one of the key figures of *Manifesto, Manifesto* was intended as a 'unified programme'.[89] Discussion-groups were established, much in the manner of the original New Left clubs, and a National Convention of the Left was created to hammer out a programme for independent Left politics.[90] No unification, particularly about political organisation, was possible however.[91] The *Manifesto* movement was shipwrecked on the same reef as the original New Left. 'A movement which had managed to sustain a significant amount of left unity', Williams remembered, 'disintegrated over the electoral process – over whether it was permissible to make electoral interventions to the left of the Labour Party. A strategy of common activity could survive anything except an election'.[92]

V

After 1970, the New Left's influence was much dispersed, something that proved a great strength and an enervating weakness. Imagine a family tree extending out from a number of forebears in a bewildering number of directions, meeting up, sometimes incorporating, and sometimes being incorporated by, intricacies and associations along the way. For sure, the influence of the New Left after 1968 can be primarily felt in a burgeoning radical public sphere. However, it is difficult to disentangle the threads that connect the original New Left project with this political culture in the 1970s and 1980s. The influence of New Left thought on the development of the History Workshop movement, on the Centre for Contemporary Cultural Studies (CCCS) at Birmingham University, and on feminism, and feminist history in particular, is clear and direct.[93] Less often

89. Rustin 1985, pp. 53–4.

90. For some of the discussion around the *Manifesto*, see May Day Manifesto, 'The Politics of the Manifesto', 1968, DJS/14, University of Hull Archives. The National Convention of the Left drew some leading figures from both the Labour Party and the CPGB and the trade union movement.

91. According to the 'CP Report on May Day Manifesto Conference: 27–8 April at UC London' most of the disagreements within the *Manifesto* movement revolved around the Labour Party. Most of the younger people, the report suggests, wanted a 'new socialist political party'. 'CP Report on May Day Manifesto Conference: 27–28 April at UC London', Communist Party of Great Britain Archives, Labour History Centre, Manchester, CP/ORG/MISC/10/09.

92. Williams 1979a, p. 375.

93. I discuss the influence of the New Left on CCCS in Chapter Four.

noted, but equally important, is the influence of New Left thought on education, film, social work, architecture and psychology, much of which can be traced, like other contributions to British intellectual history, through 'minor' publications and 'little' magazines. Although dispersed, and sometimes protean, a New Left radical culture extended into the 1980s as 'a network with many separate but interlocking nodes of thought and action'.[94]

Through this contribution to a 'socialist republic of letters', New Left thought exerted an influence over a number of political organisations and social movements too. Here mention could be made of the student movement, the Institute for Workers' Control, the Centre for Socialist Education, the peace movement, the women's movement and a number of Marxist political groups. All these organisations and movements had multiple origins. Still, it is hard to imagine any of them *as they were* without something of the break-through announced by the New Left in the mid-1950s. VSC has already been mentioned, but 'second' New Left figures also played roles in the student movement, above all through the short-lived Revolutionary Socialist Students Federation. Later still New Left influence can be felt in the *Beyond the Fragments* grouping and the Socialist Society of the early 1980s, both of which had brief lives, despite the intellectual energy that went into their promotion. The limited success of such movements, as Mike Rustin later suggested, owed much to 'the contradictions of a particular political movement' – that is, a political movement that deliberately eschewed organisation and 'party' as inevitability bureaucratic and anti-democratic.[95]

Founded by Raphael Samuel at Ruskin College, Oxford, the History Workshop movement can be best understood as 'an alternative historical apparatus'.[96] An organisation initially of worker-historians who sought to take back the past from academic history, the movement sustained the distinctive methodology of 'history from below' which owed much of its impetus to a particular reading of E.P. Thompson's *The Making of the English Working Class*. It sought to change the 'intellectual division of labour' by not just bringing history to the people but allowing the people to write their own history. The centre-piece of the movement was the workshops that took place in Oxford from the mid-1960s. These were followed by a number of publications and a journal, *History Workshop*, in the 1970s.[97]

Perhaps the characteristic feature of the *History Workshop* project was its commitment to 'people's history'. The organisation's interpretation of 'people's history' was derived, above all, from the socialist history of the 1930s (which will

---

94. Rustin 1985, p. 56.
95. Rustin 1985, p. 57.
96. Schwarz 1993, p. 203.
97. Samuel 1981; Samuel 1992.

be discussed more fully in the next chapter) and the historical imagination associated with members of the Communist Party Historians' Group.[98] In the manner of Popular Front-inspired historiography, *History Workshop* sought to recover the 'lost' history of both the British working class and working-class political organisation. There were, however, both limits and gains attached to *History Workshop*'s 'populism'. The limits soon became obvious, with the presence of a very different sort of 'people', including Liverpool dockers, associated with Powellism and antagonism to immigration. The undoubted gains – particularly the creation of an alternative historical imagination outside academia – were no less clear.[99] Many innovative methodologies were developed and a new attention to the relationship between 'theory' and 'history' was nurtured.

In the 1980s, *History Workshop*'s attention shifted to patriotism and the nature of national identity in Britain. The result was three volumes of collected essays that grew out of a History Workshop conference in 1984.[100] These were, no doubt, partly a response to critical examinations of *History Workshop*'s understanding of 'the people' and 'the popular'. But they were overwhelmingly a response to Thatcherism's increasingly belligerent appropriation of patriotism for its project of 'authoritarian populism'. The books, as Samuel suggested, 'were born out of anger at the Falklands War, and consternation at the apparent failure of the anti-war half of the nation (the half which had opposed the Suez adventure and supported the Aldermaston Marches) to assert itself'.[101] At one level, *History Workshop*'s volumes on British national identity pointed to a history of radical patriotism that extended back to the Chartists and the Levellers. There was nothing new about this insight, although it was, perhaps, a useful reminder that patriotism was not the exclusive property of any one political discourse. However, as a collection of essays by those on the Left, the volumes offered no overriding interpretative lens: hopes opened-up about Britain's 'multiple identities' – hopes which threatened to descend toward banal multiculturalism – rubbed rough with a more politicised conception of national identity.

Among the first substantive, theoretical and practical, dissection of socialist history's and socialism's – including the 'first' New Left's – conception of 'the people' came from feminism and the Women's Liberation Movement.[102] Gender and sex, as mentioned, were blind spots in the collective mind of the early New Left. Nonetheless British feminism, and feminist history in particular, began as an offshoot of socialist history. *The Making of the English Working Class* might have

---

98. See Schwarz 1993, pp. 206–9.
99. Yeo 1985.
100. Samuel 1989a; Samuel 1989b; Samuel 1989c.
101. Samuel 1989a.
102. See Rowbotham 1989.

ignored the gendered nature of working-class consciousness, but Thompson's social history provided a framework by which later feminist historians would contest traditional history. As a social movement which sought to overturn the gender-order and oppose hierarchies of thought, the British women's movement drew strength, too, from a range of connected social struggles that took issues of race or nationality, rather than class, as the pivot of their practice, though no less important, as model and inspiration, were those women-workers involved in class-conflicts in Dagenham, London and Hull. It also drew strength from the tradition of extra-parliamentary politics associated with the New Left.[103]

Despite initial (male chauvinist) roadblocks, the eclectic character of History Workshop provided a congenial centre for those feminists re-thinking questions of sex and gender, much more congenial, for example, than *New Left Review* which had summarily dismissed Juliet Mitchell's 1966 'Women – The Longest Revolution'.[104] A number of Britain's leading feminists and feminist historians, including Anna Davin, Sheila Rowbotham and Catherine Hall, were associated with the early *History Workshop* movement from which grew a number of conferences devoted to women's liberation and the specific oppressions associated with gender. New Left ideas, then, played some part in the explosion of feminist ideas and the growth of women's liberation in the 1970s, though they jostled with other influences, including *The Second Sex*, American feminism and the counter-culture. 'The radical movement of the late 1960s in Britain, as in the US and in the French "May Events" – the dramatic student and workers' uprising – held out the promise of a politics of everyday life', wrote Sheila Rowbotham, 'which touched the individual imagination, which abolished hierarchy and did not repeat the Stalinist error of justifying means by the end'.[105] The assimilation was neither easy nor straightforward. Feminism 'developed both in tune with and because of disharmonies in the practice of the new left'.[106]

Much of the New Left's influence in the 1970s can be found in the creation of a radical public sphere, of which the women's movement and feminist ideas played an important part. The growth of this socialist republic of letters can be usefully tracked through the proliferation of a number of small journals and magazines. From the women's movement came *Shrew* and *Spare Rib*, journals of the London Women's Liberation Workshop, *Socialist Woman*, connected with the International Marxist group, *Red Rag*, associated with the CPGB, and *Women's Voice*, linked to the Socialist Workers' Party (SWP). Journals associated with a radical public sphere that sat on the border between academia and politics included

---

103. Reid 2011.
104. Mitchell 1966; Hoare 1967.
105. Rowbotham 1999, p. 77.
106. Ibid.

Screen, Radical Philosophy, Capital and Class and *Radical Science Journal*. Radical educators produced *Radical Education* and *Hard Cheese*, radical social workers *Case-Con*, radical architects *ARse*, and radical psychologists *Red Rat* and *Humpty Dumpty*. More directly political magazines included *Big Flame*, *The Leveller*, *Black Dwarf* and *Red Mole*, the last two connected with a newly buoyant Trotskyism.[107]

Some indication of the influence of this radical public sphere can be gained from the 1977 Gould Report, *Attack on Higher Education: Marxist and Radical Penetration*. Frightened of a 'Trotskyist takeover' of the universities, Gould's report bemoaned the influence of radicalism in general, and a radical sociology in particular, within Britain's polytechnics and universities. 'Like Canute's advisers', wrote Hilary and Stephen Rose, 'Gould and his fellow pamphleteers seek to order back the waves of the new left critique, judiciously hinting at the scope of the traditional administrative mechanisms of restrictions on promotions and appointments, a discreet British version of the *Berufsverbot*'.[108] In its hysterics it was a late flowering of British McCarthyism – what E.P. Thompson, in relation to another of its blooms, called 'a psycho-social class spasm of irrationality, analogous to the displaced sense of "threat" in the neurotic personality'.[109] But it was also an early blast in the culture wars that would consume British public discourse from the 1980s on.[110]

Writing in 1990, Perry Anderson would describe Britain's radical public sphere as 'the liveliest republic of letters in European socialism',[111] pointing to the work of Thompson, Williams and Samuel among others. It provided and proved stiff opposition to Thatcherism too – whether in terms of the Greater London Council, European Nuclear Disarmament (END) or debates over education. However, the strength of Britain's socialist republic of letters led not to united political action, or the emergence of a new socialist movement, and this despite the strength of opposition to Thatcherism, but to fragmentation. This was evident as early as the late 1970s. According to Rowbotham, 'we are without a sustained way of organising beyond our specific oppressions and experiences. We lack the means to develop a general theory and programme for socialist change from these varied experiences. And we do not have adequate ways of convincing people of the wider political changes which need to be fought for if their specific demands and needs are met'.[112]

---

107. See Smith 1977; Fountain 1988; Farrar 1989; Andrews 2004; Crossley 2006 for discussions of these journals and the movements and organisations they were attached to.
108. H. Rose and S. Rose 1978, p. 322.
109. E.P. Thompson 1980a, p. 186.
110. Curran, Petley and Gaber 2006.
111. Anderson 1992, p. 197.
112. Rowbotham 1979.

VI

The relationship between socialism and national identity in Britain's New Left has represented a surprising absence in histories of the socialist formation.[113] However this neglect can be contrasted with contemporaneous verdicts regarding the 'first' New Left's purported surrender to nationalism.[114] Indeed a defining feature of the rupture between the 'first' New Left and the 'second' New Left – at least according to representative figures in the latter – revolved around the 'first' New Left's 'pre-socialist' enchantment with nationalism and populism.[115] This was the position of Perry Anderson and Tom Nairn in their conflict with E.P. Thompson over the 'peculiarities of the English'. Anderson, for example, believed that in addition to a lack of theoretical rigour ('the people' instead of 'the working class'), the 'first' New Left's socialism was warped by 'maundering populism', 'messianic nationalism', and a commitment to 'lofty "moral and national principle"'.[116] New Left politics, according to Anderson and Nairn, not only subordinated socialism to nationalism but also duplicated conservative aspects of the national culture.

This view survived its moment of origin and not just among its original adherents. During the early 1970s, Tariq Ali reprised the 'second' New Left critique of the ideological shortcomings of the 'first' New Left in *The Coming British Revolution*. According to Ali, the defining political drawback of New Left political thought was its 'naïve and semi-chauvinistic belief that an imaginative re-establishment of a purely British radical tradition would provide the necessary answers'[117] to socialism's contemporary problems. A similar judgment appeared in Terry Eagleton's *Criticism and Ideology: A Study in Marxist Literary Theory*, where the literary criticism of Raymond Williams was pressed through an Althusserian mill.[118] Stoking a fire originally ignited by Anderson and Nairn in the 1960s, Eagleton alleged that New Left politics was a debased socialism that not only reflected and reinforced the English working class's 'reformist' consciousness but also the idiosyncrasies of English national culture.

A more recent, and arguably more portentous, interpretation of the New Left's encounter with the national question was advanced by Paul Gilroy in *There Ain't No Black in the Union Jack: The Cultural Politics of Race and Nation* – a book composed amid chest-thumping Thatcherite rehearsals of Britishness and national

---

113. However, note Kenny 1995, pp. 180–1; Kenny 2000, p. 19.
114. Anderson 1992, p. ii.
115. This view has its contemporary advocates. For a recent example, see Hobsbawm 2002, p. 214.
116. Anderson 1964, pp. 34–5; Nairn 1972, p. 6. Anderson would later refine his view in Anderson 1980.
117. Ali 1972, p. 201.
118. Eagleton 1976, p. 27.

belonging in the mid-1980s. This was an account of the nexus between socialism and national identity in Britain that in some ways abetted earlier 'second' New Left renditions of the New Left's founding spirits. From the angle of a postcolonial understanding of Empire's imbrications in domestic British history and politics, Gilroy judged that key New Left thinkers, like Thompson and Williams, fortified rather than torpedoed regnant imperial and racial conceptions of the national inheritance.[119] Indeed in Gilroy's view, the Union Jack in Britain had been superimposed on socialism's red flag from the outset, impeding a critical awareness among socialists of patriotism's reliance on racial conceptions of Britishness. This was no less true of Williams and Thompson, he concluded, than of Marx and Engels.

The remainder of this book will advance a more complex view of the New Left's engagement with Britain's national questions. In order to do that it is necessary to place that engagement within the wider context of relations between socialist intellectuals and the national question – a subject to which the next chapter turns.

---

119. Gilroy 1987, pp. 49–50 and 54–5. The same general view can be found in Viswanathan 1993; Clegg 1998, pp. 419–60.

Chapter Two
Socialist Intellectuals and the National Question before 1956

I

If H.M. Hyndman's chauvinism and support for imperialism represent one pole of socialists' interpretation of the national question, at its opposite pole stand William Morris's socialist internationalism and his unswerving anti-imperialism.[1] These extremes have figured prominently in discussions of socialism's negotiation of nationalism. What has less often been noted is that 'the majority of the British left has laid a claim to patriotism, not only when events such as wars have overtaken it, but most of the time'.[2] It is equally true, however, that sections of the British Left have defended socialist internationalism, too, even during wars and Mafeking nights. Sometimes, indeed, socialists have attempted to reconcile the two – a position not devoid of consistency since internationalism is rooted in the existence of a world of nations and national differences.[3] What has been less in evidence in the life of British socialism is the complete rejection of national identity and the nation-state. The argument for 'world socialism' and 'cosmopolitan fraternity' has represented a minority, and extreme, tradition in British socialism. Nonetheless, even this stance, as will be demonstrated below, has found its advocates.

1. Hyndman could often provide 'hostile' interpretations of Britain's imperial mission. See Howe 1993, pp. 28–9. On Morris's internationalism, consider. E.P. Thompson 1976a, pp. 366, 379, 389.
2. Ward 1998, p. 2.
3. See Calhoun 1997, p. 26, on the distinction between internationalism and cosmopolitanism.

It is not, then, a simple question of whether British socialists have been either nationalists or internationalists. The question, most often, has been what sort of nationalism, especially given nationalism's 'multiple meanings',[4] they have endorsed. Few have championed what might be called conservative versions of national identity, much less reactionary nationalisms, though there have been exceptions. Most British socialists have espoused 'oppositional English-ness' or a democratic vision of the nation supposedly consistent with social transformation.[5] In this way socialists repudiated capitalism (even 'modernity') because of its thoroughgoing deracination, and argued that socialism was the 'true' patriotism. Consequently, this socialist internationalism has been equated with what the Webbs' called 'the maintenance of nationality'.[6] Socialists, too, have often sought to represent 'the people' not just against international capi-tal but also against the state. However, just as surely, and especially from 1918 onwards, socialists associated the state with socialism. At the other end of the spectrum, some British socialists, above all influenced by Marxism, have argued that the world-market implied the doom of the nation-state and national iden-tity and would serve as preparation for socialised humanity.

In Britain, too, the Empire has always been closely tied up with the national question. It should not be assumed, however, that British socialists were always anti-imperialist or that their anti-imperialism always implied antagonism toward the British Empire *tout court*. For much of the early-twentieth century, socialists were as often as not supporters of Britain's imperial mission, although they prom-ised that socialism would effect a more efficient, and kinder, form of colonial rule. Curiously, these colonialist do-gooders could nonetheless be anti-national-ist, arguing that imperialism proved that nationalism and national identity were anachronisms ill suited to modern political economy (this anti-nationalism, it is true, rarely extended to their own nation). Britain's working class, in this view, had an Empire, and the Empire's 'super-profits', to lose along with their chains.[7] Still, British socialists also provided an unqualified assault on imperialism, claim-ing that it was not only immoral but uneconomic and inefficient too. However, it was not until the 1920s that some socialists, following the English translation of Lenin's *Imperialism, The Highest Stage of Capitalism*, developed a 'scientific' interpretation of imperialism and included support for anti-colonialist move-ments as among the duties of socialist internationalism.[8]

---

4. Verdery 1996, p. 228.
5. Yeo 1986, p. 310.
6. B. Webb and S. Webb 1913, cited in Ward 1998, p. 4.
7. See Ward 1998, pp. 62–5.
8. Macintyre 1975.

All these complexities and confusions, refracted through particular political contexts, were a feature of the socialist negotiation of the national question in the early part of the twentieth century, as Paul Ward has demonstrated in *Red Flag and Union Jack: Englishness, Patriotism, and the British Left, 1881–1924*. They were also features of socialist intellectual's encounter with nationalism and national identity in the 1930s and 1940s. Here, though, Britain's socialist intellectuals were not just confronted with imperialist adventure, world war and revolution but also with the rise of fascism, with anti-colonialist nationalisms in the British Empire, and, later, with the onset of the planetary contest between socialism and capitalism. The complexity of the engagement between socialist intellectuals and the national question in the interwar and immediate post-war periods will be tracked in what follows, though, necessarily, it will be both brief and selective.

II

By the mid-1920s, if not before, Britishness was at least as characteristic of the British labour-movement as socialism, hardly surprising given the importance of 'national economics' to workers' standard of living.[9] Indeed, with the rise of the Labour Party, socialism was not just readily, and willingly, assimilated to the national state but also to the institutions of 'Englishness', whether Parliament, Lords, monarchy or Empire.[10] If the immediate post-war years saw the nationalisation of socialism in Britain, this did not automatically suggest the repudiation of socialist internationalism. Indeed, with the horrors of the Somme fresh in mind, it was in these years that British social democracy increasingly looked toward international institutions as a mainstay against interstate antagonism and nationalist belligerency.[11]

G.D.H. Cole, perhaps the most influential socialist intellectual during Britain's interwar years, was initially uninterested in international relations, perhaps a reflection of his southern English middle-class upbringing.[12] It has often been noted that Cole's early socialism was overwhelming parochial, overdetermined by his 'Little Englandism'.[13] Cultural nationalism was certainly a feature of his response to World War I, and it shaded his contribution to guild-socialism after the War and throughout the 1920s. In his first major publication in 1913 *The World*

---

9. Hobsbawm 1990, pp. 131–2; Berger 2006, p. 296. See Szporluk 1988, on 'national economics'.
10. See Sassoon 1996, p. xxii, on the nationalisation of socialism.
11. Consider Douglas 2004, pp. 14–23.
12. See Carpenter 1973, pp. 6–12, for brief comments on Cole's background.
13. Gaitskell 1960, p. 12. See also Cole 1913, p. 165.

of Labour, he spoke of a reformed state, embodying a 'true community', as 'the expression of the national will and the depository of national greatness'.[14] As he further refined his theory of guild-socialism, this sense of national community remained paramount, a product of his respect for national difference and his belief that socialism must be grafted on to national resources. Such respect also explains his initial rejection of Bolshevism and his claim that 'the pure class-conscious cosmopolitan of some Socialist theory is as unnatural and as unreal as the pure "economic man" of the older economists'.[15]

No matter how dominant a role this cultural nationalism played, there were other tendencies in Cole's early socialist writings that pointed away from parochialism. For instance, there was the anti-particularist philosophical anthropology that underwrote his guild-socialism, a theory of human nature that emphasised creativity, self-realisation and sociality rather than ethnicity and difference. If Cole, the Oxford don, could dismiss other (national) socialist traditions, he nonetheless devoted much time to the study of French syndicalism, German Marxism and Russian Bolshevism. There was also his recognition that a sense of belonging was much more readily found in associational life – trade union, chapel, and craft – than the institutions of the nation-state.[16] And, finally, there was his growing, and insistent, emphasis on the shortcomings of British democracy and the British state that suggests no easy assimilation of his socialism to British peculiarities. True, the communitarian ideal that underwrote his guild-socialism was certainly national, perhaps even nationalist,[17] but this did not everywhere denote a consistent nationalism nor prevent a thoroughgoing commitment to participatory democracy and decentralisation.[18]

From the 1930s onwards, and consequent to the growing threat of European fascism, Cole assumed a much more straightforward, resolute, internationalist stance. His briefly held 'gradualist' socialism, developed in the late 1920s, was quickly jettisoned for a socialist programme based on social control of the economy and the rejection of parliamentarianism after 1931.[19] In the process Cole overturned his negative view of Marxism, though, whether then or later, his Marxism could never be described as 'orthodox' or Leninist. As well, he took much more note of international issues and became convinced of the need to transcend what Marx called national narrow-mindedness. In the context of fascism and the likely onset of European war, Cole argued for a 'people's front'

---

14. Cole 1913, p. 26.
15. Cole 1915, p. 21.
16. See Wright 1979, p. 39.
17. Cole 1913, pp. 389–90, 410.
18. See Hinton 1995, pp. 68–90, for the anti-statist, if not necessarily a-national, conception of citizenship in the history of British socialism.
19. See Riddell 1995, pp. 933–57, for an account of these years.

that would 'help build up the League of Nations into a real instrument for the preservation of peace and the furtherance of international justice'.[20] Elsewhere, he argued that 'absolute nationalism' would only be eliminated by the spread of 'international fraternity' and its embodiment in a 'concrete human institution', elements of which he spotted in the Soviet Union.[21]

However, during the 1930s Cole never denied the importance of national peculiarities, whether to an understanding of the international system or to socialist strategy.[22] This recurrent emphasis had some odd consequences though. Short of belligerent nationalism, a stress on national difference might be considered a common good; but surely not when used to justify Soviet Communism, as Cole used it in the 1940s.[23] In the mid-1930s, Cole also embraced national planning as a means of winning a country for British workers. However, he also cautioned against autarky. As he would later write, 'national planning in individual countries involves international planning, unless it is to be perverted into isolationism'.[24] His sense of fellowship nonetheless remained national and his conception of community, a concept of the upmost importance to interwar British socialism, was structured by national feeling. By the beginning of the War, though, Cole had overthrown his earlier Empire Socialism, now advocating the liberation of Britain's various colonies and arguing that post-war reconstruction must be properly anti-imperialist and international.[25]

The war against fascism generated a significant shift in Cole's interpretation of the national question. The change was evident as early as his 1939 pamphlet *War Aims*, published shortly after Germany's invasion of Poland.[26] Here, Cole outlined a proposal for a European federation, based on economic and political cooperation, which sought to transcend the power-politics that, he believed, was responsible for conflict. He now claimed that a system of nation-states was no longer reconcilable with peace and recommended 'the entire abandonment of national sovereignty'.[27] Pre-empting debates that would consume socialist, including New Left, intellectuals in the post-war period, Cole argued that Britain should surrender sovereignty to a European Union. He even claimed, in a moment of what seems like war-induced insanity, that he would 'much sooner see the Soviet Union, even with its policy unchanged, dominant over all Europe, including Great Britain, than see an attempt to restore the pre-war States to their

---

20. Cole 1937, p. 24.
21. Cole 1935, p. 90.
22. See Cole 1935, p. 188.
23. Wright 1979, p. 251.
24. Cole 1944, cited in Carpenter 1973, p. 177.
25. Cole 1937, p. 169.
26. Cole 1939.
27. Cole 1941, p. 17.

futile and uncreative independence and their petty economic nationalism under capitalist domination'.[28]

Many of these wartime predictions came to naught, not least his belief that national sovereignty would disappear as a consequence of international conflict.[29] Nonetheless he continued to maintain, throughout the 1950s, the necessity of cosmopolitan fraternity, not just to democratic socialism but also to international peace. After the War, and as the prospect of global contest between the Soviet Union and the United States grew, he pushed for the establishment of a 'third force' in Europe that would reject both Soviet Communism and American capitalism.[30] He was a resolute anti-anti-communist, describing the Soviet Union, despite his misgivings, as a 'great and glorious achievement'.[31] And his 1956 *New Statesman* pamphlet *World Socialism Restated* argued for a steadfast international, perhaps even cosmopolitan, socialism: 'Socialism cannot be fully achieved', he wrote, 'in one country irrespective of what is happening elsewhere'.[32] An expression of this international socialism was Cole's role in the establishment of the International Society for Socialist Studies (ISSS), an organisation that had a brief life in the immediate years before his death.[33]

As thoroughgoing as Cole's rejection of nationhood and national identity was in the 1940s and 1950s it was far from complete. Not only did aspects of his long-standing commitment to national difference influence his understanding of 'socialist unity' but he also continued to advocate 'popular nationalism in the colonial and semi-colonial countries'.[34] The defence of anti-imperialist nationalism in the 'Third World' was consistent with a robust internationalism. However, it is not clear how this related to Cole's repudiation of national sovereignty, nor if his distinction between the 'nationalism of the masses' and the 'nationalism of the foreign oppressors' can be coherently maintained. Lastly, Cole's socialist internationalism was far from any sort of national nihilism: 'I do feel', he wrote, 'a much greater responsibility for helping to put things right in the country of which I am a citizen than in the world as a whole'.[35]

Harold Laski's encounter with the national question in the interwar period was no less contorted than Cole's. No less influential than Cole, Laski was

---

28. Cole 1941, p. 16.
29. Note Wright 1979, p. 254.
30. See Cole 1947.
31. Cole 1958, p. 894.
32. Cole 1956, p. 33.
33. Cole 1955a.
34. Cole 1956, p. 9.
35. Cole 1955b, cited in Carpenter 1973, p. 213.

likewise attracted to pluralism, and to aspects of guild-socialism, in the immediate years after the Great War, and, like Cole, was relatively uninterested in internationalism and international relations. It would, however, be hard to describe him at any time as a cultural nationalist, no doubt a consequence of his Jewishness and his upbringing in liberal, free-trade Manchester.[36] Unlike Cole, Laski (eventually) was far more favourable to Fabianism and made a unique (socialist) contribution to an understanding of nationalism in the 1920s. This is perhaps unsurprising from a political theorist – Laski was Chair of Government at London School of Economics (LSE) from the mid-1920s – whose chief interest was sovereignty, and who had provided a forceful attack on the (existing) state in the 1919 *Authority in the Modern State* and, in 1921, in *The Foundations of Sovereignty*.[37] *A Grammar of Politics*, in 1925, also advanced a thoroughgoing critique of the sovereign state, counting it, and its conjunction with the nation, an obstacle to international peace, and advocated increased authority for international organisations such as the nascent League of Nations.

Described by Eric Hobsbawm as Laski's magnum opus,[38] *A Grammar of Politics* argued for 'the disappearance of the sovereign nation-state',[39] a common theme of Laski's voluminous writings. An international system constituted by sovereign nation-states, Laski believed, delivered permanent competition and war, particularly when those states were ruled by a small minority (capitalists) who supposed their own interest was the 'national interest'. However, he did not recommend the disappearance of the nation-state, although he rejected the idea that the nation-state 'was the ultimate unit in human organisation'.[40] He suggested, rather, that nation-states should no longer be sovereign when their interests impacted upon other states. 'The problem', he wrote, 'is the equation of nationalism, with right'.[41] And the problem would only be overcome by international organisations that held a conception of the common good that transcended the self-interest of nations. According to Laski, the independence of nation-states, particularly small nation-states, was endangered by the national interest of the 'big battalions', making 'cosmopolitan law-making' absolutely essential to 'the rational desire for self-government'.[42]

---

36. See Kramnick and Sheerman 1993, for details of Laski's early years.
37. Laski 1919; Laski 1921. For an outline of Laski's views on sovereignty and the state see Lamb 1997, pp. 326–42.
38. Hobsbawm 1998, p. 192.
39. Laski 1925, p. 227.
40. Laski 1925, p. 222.
41. Laski 1925, p. 226.
42. Laski 1925, p. 232. These insights are overlooked in M. Taylor 1990.

A Grammar of Politics, however, barely noted the existence of the British Empire. Initially, in the 1920s, Laski had sung the virtues of Empire Socialism, a common chorus among intellectuals attached to the labour-movement. In his dismissal of the sovereign nation-state, he certainly made little mention of the situation in, say, India or Egypt where sovereignty, or the lack of it, was precisely the problem, at least for Indians and Egyptians. Even in the late 1920s, he did not believe, for example, that Indians were ready for self-government and suggested that a precipitate British withdrawal would be disastrous. However, following his involvement in negotiations between Indian nationalists and Mac-Donald's Labour government, his view changed.[43] 'To the degree that we refuse India what is essential in statehood for her national freedom', he wrote in 1932, 'we impoverish the spiritual well-being of the world'.[44] He was, however, not a consistent anti-imperialist. Indeed, he endorsed Jewish colonialism in Palestine, despite knowing what that meant for the Arab population. Here he joined the majority of British socialists who believed that Jewish settlement would promote modernisation and socialism in the Middle East.[45]

By the 1930s, Laski had lost much of his faith in the institutions of Englishness. He no longer believed that socialism could be achieved without overturning Britain's constitution or that class-privilege would simply give way before democracy. The times, particularly the failure of the MacDonald government, the Depression and political shifts on the continent dictated this pessimism. By 1933, Laski, an enthusiast, like Cole, of the Socialist League, had thrown his intellectual weight behind the attempt to establish a 'united front' against fascism, a policy rejected by the Labour Party.[46] He championed this stance in 1935 in *The State in Theory and Practice*, a book that demonstrated Laski's increasing reliance upon Marxist concepts. He also played a pivotal role in the establishment of the Left Book Club – perhaps the Popular Front's most significant achievement – alongside Victor Gollancz and John Strachey.[47] He now softened his attitude to the Soviet Union as well, characterising Russia as a 'land of hope',[48] although this view, never wholly consistent or free of ambiguity, would soon be overturned. Indeed by 1938 he had severed any association with the policies of the CPGB and recognised what he believed were the shortcomings of any sort of united front with communism.[49]

---

43. Newman 1993, pp. 114–21.
44. Laski 1932, p. 209.
45. Newman 1993, pp. 121–31.
46. Among the aims of the SL was something Konni Zilliacus called 'a Co-Operative World Commonwealth'. See Douglas 2004, p. 36.
47. Laski 1935, pp. 269–70.
48. Laski 1934, cited in Newman 1993, p. 166.
49. See Miliband 1995, pp. 256–8 for a discussion of Laski's approach to communism.

Laski's views about the nation-state, nationalism and imperialism stiffened in the 1930s. In a 1932 lecture, *Nationalism and the Future of Civilisation*, he argued that 'exclusiveness' was 'the essence of nationality' and that nationhood, welded to private property, implied imperialism and war.[50] 'A world of competing nation-states, each of which is a law unto itself, produces a civilization', he concluded, 'incapable of survival'.[51] Once again, his solution to inter-state anarchy was a 'world community' constituted by nations that had given up traditional ideas of sovereignty. But such a world community, Laski believed, could only arise when the massive inequalities within societies had been eradicated.[52] The problem, for Laski, was the incongruity between an international mode of production and a political system rooted in national sovereignty. But, despite the insights attached to his account of the relationship between capitalism, nationhood and imperialism, Laski spoke more pessimistically of nationalism as an 'irrational impulse' and as the product of the 'ignorance of the common people'.[53]

After 1939, however, and despite his continuing insistence that capitalism and nationalism were the root of evil, he looked more kindly on national sentiment.[54] '[N]o one', he wrote in 1941, 'who has seen Britain at war, above all since the fall of France, can doubt that there has taken place something like a spiritual regeneration of the people'.[55] Even before the beginning of hostilities, he looked forward to a 'people's peace' that would allow the 'common people [to] assume control of their own destiny',[56] and this hope directed much of his political work during the War. However, he neither relinquished his belief in the limitations of capitalism and national sovereignty nor desisted from his attempt to urge a clear policy of Indian self-determination on the wartime Labour Party. Much of this found expression in his somewhat iconoclastic call for a new Socialist International that would unite forces for social change across Europe.[57] Belying traditional claims about the parochialism of British socialism, Laski kept a close watch on European socialist parties, and he attended, and participated, in a number of these parties' initial post-war conferences.[58] The experience of war reaffirmed his belief in international socialism, but it also reinforced his belief in a peaceful transition to socialism, what he called 'revolution by consent'. Nonetheless, he rejected Cold War politics and opposed the establishment of NATO. Shortly before his

---

50. See Laski 1932, pp. 210–11.
51. Laski 1932, p. 211.
52. Laski 1932.
53. Laski 1932, pp. 214, 227.
54. Newman 1993, p. 206.
55. Laski 1941, p. 26, cited in Douglas 2004, p. 75.
56. Laski letter to Hugo Black, 31 August 1939, cited in Newman 1993, p. 203.
57. Newman 1993, pp. 227–8.
58. Newman 1993, pp. 293–4.

death in 1950, he again rehearsed his rejection of national sovereignty and the need to 'more fully...separate the concepts of nation and state'.[59]

Cole and Laski exerted a far-reaching influence over socialist thought before 1945. Together, they assumed positions on the national question that demonstrate the complexities and confusions that attended British socialism's encounter with nationhood and nationalism in the interwar period. From cultural nationalism to cosmopolitan fraternity, from Empire Socialism to resolute anti-imperialism and support for national self-determination, from the argument that socialism was the true patriotism to the view that patriotism was incompatible with social transformation, the work of these two socialist intellectuals ran the spectrum of socialism's answers to the national question. Indeed, from the 1920s onwards, the ideological discourse of British socialism allowed both the rejection and the celebration of national difference, the repudiation of nationalism as inimical to socialism and the assumption that nationalism constituted the education of socialism's desire.

Interestingly, too, both Cole and Laski envisaged the 'break-up of Britain'; or, perhaps more exactly, they imagined 'the submersion of Britain' in a 'world government' or a federated Europe. Indeed, they supposed, that Britain had no future as an independent sovereign nation-state. This was perhaps a normal response to a Hobbesian international system seemingly devoted to war and imperial exploitation. But the belief also derived from a reading of contemporary capitalism. Pre-empting debates about globalisation in the 1990s, Laski, for example, argued that the world 'has become an inescapably interdependent unit' and predicted 'the end of sovereignty of the state in international affairs'.[60] Both Cole and Laski believed that an international mode of production and a political system of independent nation-states were a contradictory, and conflicted, aspect of social reality that could not coexist forever.[61] They hoped, at different moments, that cosmopolitan tendencies associated with socialism would eventually overwhelm the atavism characteristic of certain forms of national belonging.

III

British Communist intellectuals in the interwar years were no less consumed by the national question, and provided no less complex and confusing answers to it, than socialist intellectuals outside the CPGB. Before the 1930s, there were few

---

59. Laski 1948.
60. Laski 1932, p. 215.
61. Laski 1933, p. 502; Laski 1942, p. 10.

intellectuals in the CPGB and they were generally unwelcome *as intellectuals*.[62] The Party's leading theoretician, Rajani Palme Dutt, perhaps put this best: 'First and foremost', he wrote, '[the bourgeois intellectual] should *forget that he is an intellectual* (except in moments of necessary self-criticism) *and remember only that he is a communist*'.[63] Harry Pollitt, the Party's general secretary, was a notorious philistine too. It was not until 1933 that intellectuals were more warmly received.[64] From that time onward a significant number of intellectuals, for varied reasons, became communists, though not all joined the CPGB or remained communists for long.[65] In their negotiation of the national question, communist intellectuals faced an added complexity to socialists outside the Party, namely defence of the socialist Motherland and the need to adjust their views to the twists and turns of Soviet policy. Indeed, there is little doubt that most communists suffered from what George Orwell called 'transferred nationalism', with the object of their 'love of country' being the Soviet Union.

This was true of John Strachey, who did not join the CPGB. In a series of books published in the early-to-mid-1930s – *The Coming Struggle for Power, The Menace of Fascism* and *The Nature of Capitalist Crisis* – Strachey played an important role in popularising Marxist ideas.[66] A former Labour parliamentarian, Strachey was a recent 'convert' to communism following a brief association with Mosley's New Party. After the denouement of MacDonald's Labour government, Strachey's faith in parliament, gradual social reform and social democracy quickly dissipated.[67] So, too, did his assumption that capitalism could be reformed. Alongside this, and his belief that intensified colonial exploitation and war were automatic consequences of capitalist crisis, Strachey provided a polemical assault on nationalism as a form of false consciousness inimical to the values of socialist internationalism. 'The propagandists of the capitalist class', Strachey suggested, 'feel that it is vital that the workers should be made to forget as much as possible that they are workers and to remember every minute of the day that they are Britishers, Frenchmen, Germans, Americans, or Japanese'.[68] National sentiment, in other words, was a ruling-class ruse designed to divert 'the attention of the workers ... from the blatant inequalities of capitalism'.[69]

---

62. McIlroy 2006.
63. Dutt 1933, p. 422 cited in Ree 1984, p. 90 (original emphasis).
64. Wood 1959, Chapter Four.
65. Hobsbawm 2011, pp. 261–313.
66. Strachey 1932; Strachey 1933; Strachey 1935.
67. See N. Thompson 1993, Chapter Four.
68. Strachey 1932, p. 254.
69. Ibid.

This interpretation of nationalism was set out in *The Coming Struggle for Power*, a book that has been called 'the most influential application of Marxism to British conditions in the 1930s'.[70] Strachey, however, did not leave his analysis of nationalism there. He not only considered nationalism a barrier to socialist advance; it was also an obstacle, he believed, to 'the successful working of the capitalist system'.[71] His reasoning was almost algebraic: capitalism produced monopoly that in turn engendered economic autarky whose inevitable consequence were imperialism, international conflict and depression, an unholy cycle of declining rates of profit, intensified colonial exploitation and the war of all against all. In this *The Coming Struggle for Power* mirrored the common, and perhaps complacent, early 1930s Marxist view that private property induced imperialism and war, though the view was widespread outside Marxist discourse too. Less conventional, especially in 1932, was Strachey's argument that it was capitalism, not communism, 'which outrages, ravages and despoils the motherland of every race of men; and that it is communism alone which can bring national liberation to the peoples of the earth'.[72] Pre-empting the Comintern's Popular Front strategy, Strachey argued that love of country was an important ally of communism and this despite, and in a sense because of, communism's irreducible internationalism.

No doubt, Strachey's engagement with nationalism was tainted by confusion – national sentiment was false consciousness for proletariat *and* bourgeoisie; nationalism was characteristic of contemporary capitalism *and* it was the profit motive that trashed real national feeling; and love of country was both an obstacle to *and* an accomplice of socialist revolution. Nonetheless, his analysis of nationalism was not completely without worth. He reinforced Lenin's view about the efficacy of the marriage between national and social liberation in the colonial world, a key feature of the struggle for decolonisation after 1945. He also foreshadowed the kinds of argument that would become increasingly prominent in the discourse of British socialism after 1940, when socialists increasingly envisioned patriotism as among those forces that could help precipitate social transformation. As he suggested in 1935 in *The Theory and Practice of Socialism*, 'socialists and communists do not question the right of men to defend their country; but we do recommend that they should fight first to acquire a country to defend'.[73]

Ralph Fox was among those Party intellectuals who considered *The Coming Struggle for Power* heretical, though Fox would rehearse many of Strachey's

---

70. Pimlott 1977, p. 40.
71. Strachey 1932, p. 334.
72. Ibid.
73. Strachey 1936, p. 259.

arguments about nationalism.[74] Born in Halifax, Fox had joined the CPGB in the early 1920s. He travelled extensively throughout Russia and China, was a novelist and literary critic, and became a Party journalist before his death during the Spanish Civil War. *Communism and a Changing Civilization*, a book Fox published in 1935 in Krishna Menon's Twentieth Century Library project, argued that socialism 'not only does not deny national culture, but it presupposes it and fosters it'.[75] Fox, too, wanted to refute the charge that socialism was insensitive to national feeling and this before the Comintern had accepted the political value of national peculiarities. At the same time, however, he wanted to reassure his readers of socialism's full-blooded commitment to internationalism. 'In a world riven by national hatreds and national oppression', he wrote, 'in which the vilest forms of jingoism and militarism are being erected in all countries into a state religion, it is of the greatest importance that the working class should preserve its international character, putting class solidarity and unity of the oppressed above all others'.[76] Nonetheless, like Strachey, he warmly welcomed a 'nationalism of the oppressed' in the colonial world and identified communism as the true form of national liberation. But he emphasised that communism was a world movement too whose terminus was 'world society' and that 'the revolutionary struggle of the workers [was] hopeless, unless it can eventually conquer on a world scale'[77] (though with a nod to Stalin, and as a gift to inconsistency, he also supposed that it was possible to build 'socialism in one country').

Perhaps alone among communist intellectuals, Fox also envisaged 'the break-up of Britain', a vision, no doubt, encouraged by Fox's lived internationalism.[78] 'The Soviet Republic of Britain', he argued, 'will in fact be a federation of Scotland, England and Wales, to which Ireland will probably join itself voluntarily when socialism is victorious there also'.[79] This was no doubt a touch utopian: James Connolly would have baulked at the idea of Ireland willingly transferring its sovereignty to Britain, even a Soviet Britain. In any case, Fox supposed that a unitary British state, among much else, was a break on the development of capitalist productive forces. 'The four nations, their energies released, working in complete harmony, will be able to perform miracles of creative work that in a few years will put to shame the blundering performances of the imperialist clique which at present rules'.[80] Indeed, a federated Soviet Britain would,

---

74. Fox 1933a, p. 4 cited in N. Thompson 1993, p. 73.
75. Fox 1935, p. 81. The book was completed in 1934 – that is, before the CPGB's shift to a Popular Front strategy.
76. Fox 1935, p. 79.
77. Fox 1935, p. 84.
78. See Fox 1937 for biographical details.
79. Fox 1935, p. 146.
80. Ibid.

Fox supposed, 'mean something else to the world than violence, oppression and terror'.[81] It would be a 'new country', home to both a universal socialist culture and the peculiarities of the English, the Scots, the Irish and the Welsh.

Still, Communist intellectuals in the mid-1930s considered a 'world state' rather than balkanisation the more likely result of capitalist modernity.[82] This belief derived from their political economy. 'The productive forces at the present stage of technique and development', Rajani Palme Dutt wrote, 'raise the possibility and the necessity of an all-embracing world economic organisation for their most effective utilisation. But they thereby sound the doom of the existing system of independent sovereign States and imperialist groupings'.[83] According to Dutt, the 'base' – the world-market, or the interdependence between nations it supposed – was inconsistent with capital's political 'superstructure' – a world-system of nation-states. It was only 'the international working class in alliance with subject peoples throughout the world' that could realise humanity's economic and political unification.[84] This was also Stephen Spender's hope during his brief, and undistinguished, flirtation with communism. He claimed, somewhat portentously, that humanity was more important than nationalities. 'The love of humanity', he wrote in 1937 in Forward from Liberalism, 'rather than separate nationalities, of justice for all men rather than class privilege, of universal peace rather than imperialist competition and war – these are the features of disinterest',[85] by which he meant scientific enquiry and objectivity. The metropolitan Spender had no time for 'regionalism' or 'local culture', which he supposed concerns of the 'bourgeois individualist'.[86]

Nonetheless, Communist intellectuals in the mid-1930s did pay attention to Welsh and Scottish nationalism, especially following the Comintern's shift from 'class against class' to 'popular front' in 1935.[87] The CPGB's stress on 'native radical-democratic traditions', associated with the establishment of a Popular Front, allowed a potentially more favourable assessment of national questions, though it should not be forgotten that intimations of this shift can be found in the pre-1935 writings of communist intellectuals, to say nothing of the past of British socialist discourse more generally. According to the Comintern, communists should seek to 'acclimatise' proletarian internationalism in 'each country in order to sink deep roots in its native land' – a view that Blatchford and Hyndman

---

81. Fox 1935, p. 147.
82. See Douglas 2004, p. 4, for a discussion of this widely held view among socialists and non-socialists that some sort of world-state was a solution to inter-state relations.
83. Dutt 1936, 151.
84. Ibid.
85. Spender 1937, p. 202.
86. Spender 1937, p. 269.
87. See Eley 2004, pp. 261–77, for the shift in Comintern policy; see D. Jones 2010, for the relationship between the CPGB and Welsh nationalism.

among others would have applauded.[88] But the situation in Britain was somewhat unique. If British communists were now being urged by the Comintern to appropriate 'national symbols' the question was '*which* nation's symbols'?

Interesting, in this respect, was the debate on Scotland that took place in a 1937 volume of *Left Review*.[89] The background to the debate was an earlier discussion in the *Communist Review*, which decided that there was no national question in Scotland and that the call for independence was an extraordinary diversion from class struggle.[90] The ostensible purpose of the *Left Review* debate was to throw 'light on the question how far an independent cultural tradition can be used in the fight against imperialism, and how far the concept of nationalism is today purely romantic'.[91] Responding to James Barke's earlier assessment of Lewis Grassic Gibbon, Neil M. Gunn, the novelist and Scottish nationalist, retorted that 'the nation is still the instrument of social experiment'.[92] Puncturing communist illusions about a 'vision of Cosmopolis', an illusion whose realisation, he believed, would amount to a 'beehive tyranny', Gunn argued that the nation was the only possible or realistic framework of 'proletarian theory' and that Scottish communists' repudiation of Scottish nationalism was an instance of their subordination to the English.[93]

The Scottish communist James Barke, predictably, refused Gunn's nationalism, though he was cautious about defending the idea of a Cosmopolis. Indeed Barke had to hold a fine line, since he had earlier rejected national sentiment *tout court*, but now, following the Party's shift away from 'class against class', had to reconcile his repudiation with a Popular Front strategy. Easily enough, he refuted the idea that 'the English' in any way oppressed Scotland, though this was hardly an answer to the existence of a nationalist movement or to the reality of centralisation.[94] He also had strong claims, no doubt, when reminding his nationalist interlocutors that 'there is no line of demarcation between English and Scottish capital'.[95] Unsurprisingly, however, he was not subtle enough to maintain any fine line. On the one hand, ostrich-like, he simply denied that Scotland had a national question, and, on the other, he argued that it was Scottish workers who were 'the real custodians of Scotland's cultural heritage and of Scottish nationalist traditions'.[96] This left unanswered Gunn's contention

88. Dimitrov 1935, p. 71.
89. See Young 1983; Young 1985, for broader overviews of the relationship between Scottish nationalism and British Marxism.
90. McLennan 1932; Crawfurd 1933.
91. *Left Review* 1936a, p. 729.
92. Gunn 1936, p. 736.
93. Gunn 1936, p. 738.
94. Barke 1936, p. 741.
95. Ibid.
96. Barke 1936, p. 742.

that nationhood or nationalism could not simply be wished away, and seemingly proved the nationalist suspicion that British communism was a bulwark of Britishness.

Edgell Rickword attacked the question of nationalism in the same debate from a more abstract position, using Stalin's writings on the national question as his touchstone. Noting the 'alleged arson in Wales',[97] he argued that communists needed to discuss 'these national or minority questions [because they] are bound up with the future of democracy'.[98] Although he acknowledged nationalism's 'seductive' appeal, Rickword did not imagine that 'political independence' would solve anything on its own, especially when 'final control still remains with the large groups of international finance-capital'.[99] Like Marx, Rickword did not believe that oppressed nationalities could free themselves from imperialism without the help of the working class of the oppressor nation, and he also reiterated the standard Marxist view that class questions should always trump national questions when they conflict. 'It is only through participation in the working-class struggle', Rickword concluded, 'that the national characteristics can revive and flourish, and this is no less true for English culture than for those national cultures at present subordinate not so much to the Mother of Parliaments as to the Old Lady of Threadneedle Street'.[100] For most communists national subordination – and the problem of national minorities – was principally a matter of economics rather than politics.

The awakening of 'national characteristics' was just one objective of *Left Review*. Established by the British Section of the Communist Writers' International to promote a 'people's culture' as a stronghold against fascism, *Left Review* was initially edited by Amabel Williams-Ellis, Tom Wintringham and Montagu Slater (Edgell Rickword, Alick West and Randall Swingler were later editors). The journal also hoped to affect 'the mobilization on the cultural front of a People's Movement to out the National Government and call a check to the advance of Fascist barbarity'.[101] There was nothing parochial about the journal however. Indeed, for C. Day Lewis a Popular Front would involve 'throwing off our parochialism and political apathy in the interest of the civilization we have helped to build and can help save'.[102] Mayakovsky, Brecht, Gide, Rolland, Silone and Malraux were among the contributors, while the journal, in various issues, focused upon India, China, Spain, Ireland and, of course, the Soviet Union. This

---

97. This was a reference to the 1936 (nationalist) bombing of the Pennyberth School.
98. Rickword 1936, p. 746.
99. Ibid.
100. Rickword 1936, p. 749.
101. *Left Review* 1937.
102. Day Lewis 1936, p. 674.

internationalism was a matter both of outlook and politics, but it was also reflected in the number of the journals' contributors who fought and died in Spain.

But *Left Review*, perhaps following Moscow's instruction, did seek to reclaim England's revolutionary past, especially from 1936 onwards. Randall Swingler thought William Blake was a touchstone in this respect, 'first, because being the arch-mad-man, we may presume he was considered the arch-revolutionary of literature; second, because his characteristic "Englishness" is admitted by all critics; third, because his "Jerusalem" is probably the most widely sung and best-known of English poems'.[103] Considerations of other English literary figures followed: Rex Warner on Jonathan Swift, Samuel Mill on Tom Paine and T.A. Jackson on Dickens.[104] Derek Kahn argued that 'we are sincerely anxious to draw on the best in our own past'.[105] He recommended 'common law' and the 'concept of Parliament' as among those English institutions that communists should defend and preserve.[106] 'The realization of the ideals, so simple, so human, which are the core of the English, as of every popular tradition', wrote Rickword, 'is only possible if the productive forces of the country are in the hands of the producers themselves'.[107] True Englishness was thus coterminous with the social ownership of the means of production, that is to say, the nationalisation of *British* capital.

This 'oppositional Englishness' could, undoubtedly, take a nationalist turn, as in Jack Lindsay's poem 'Not English': 'No others have the thews / to make this earth, this England, breed to her desire / The disinherited are restored, our mother / England, our England / England, our own'.[108] However, it would be wrong to interpret 'Englishness' in the *Left Review* as only some sort of nationalist deviation or as a simple reflection of Moscow's call for a Popular Front. For example, there was much to admire about some of the discussions that took place around the concept of culture. Derek Kahn could describe culture as much a matter of 'tanks and guns' as 'paintings and poems'.[109] In a definition that pre-empted Raymond Williams' well known discussion of the concept, Kahn considered culture as 'co-extensive with the whole method of living of a given society, and reaches right down to the material foundations of its social existence'.[110] Indeed, the 'defence of culture' for most communist intellectuals meant less the

---

103. Swingler 1937, p. 22.
104. Jackson 1937, pp. 88–95; Mill 1937, pp. 202–7; Warner 1937, pp. 266–72.
105. Kahn 1936, p. 894.
106. Ibid.
107. Rickword 1978, p. 97.
108. Lindsay 1936, p. 357.
109. Kahn 1936, p. 892.
110. Kahn 1936, p. 891.

celebration of English peculiarities than a critique of 'the fetishism of money' and an attack on 'currency cranks and credit fans'.[111] When communists sought to defend 'culture' against modern capitalism, culture was understood as 'eternal' and 'human' not a matter of particularity and ethnicity.[112] And 'Englishness' could be the site of a 'premature revisionism' too. As E.P. Thompson noted, the 'return to national cultural resources' could be evidence of 'the struggle for vitality and for actuality against the *déracineé* uniformity and abstracted internationalist lingua franca of the Stalinist zenith'.[113]

A *Handbook of Freedom* gives some weight to Thompson's argument. The collection of historical documents, with an introduction by Edgell Rickword, was first published in 1939, and published again in 1941 under the title *Spokesmen for Liberty*. The book took the reader from Alfred the Great and the fight for 'national independence' to Siegfried Sassoon and the 'struggle for peace and social justice'. A *Handbook of Freedom* was characteristic of the Party's Popular-Frontism. The book was perhaps distinctive for its careful refusal of anything like 'social patriotism'. It is true, however, that Rickword claimed that a nation's independence was 'an essential guarantee of social freedom'.[114] It is also true that the book summoned up a radical-democratic past in the interests of contemporary (socialist) politics. But Rickword was careful to refuse the idea that freedom was 'some quality inherent in our race'.[115] He also rejected the idea of 'some folk-memory of an original state of freedom'.[116] And he applauded 'the heroic resistance of Welsh, Scots and Irish to the encroachments of the English Crown, of the many nations of Asia and Africa to that of the capitalists'.[117] The tone of this essay points definitively away from the language most often found in *Communist Review* and *Daily Worker* – a language T.A. Jackson associated with the 'Inquisition Complex'.[118] 'Experience, too, bitter experience', wrote Rickword, 'has weaned us from over-much enthusiasm for freedom in the abstract, for the freedom which is the climax of the politician's oratory'.[119]

It was not only literary critics, poets and novelists who were recovering England's lost revolutionary tradition. Communist historians contributed to the project too.[120] A.L. Morton wrote A *People's History of England* in 1938, which is often recognised as the crowning achievement of this attempt to write the 'Eng-

111. Rickword 1978, p. 94.
112. Strachey 1934.
113. E.P. Thompson 1994, p. 238.
114. Rickword 1941, p. xvi.
115. Rickword 1941, p. vii.
116. Rickword 1941, p. xii.
117. Rickword 1941, p. xvi.
118. Jackson 1929, p. 133, cited in Ree 1984, p. 121.
119. Rickword 1941, p. ix.
120. Slater 1935, p. 127.

lish people' back into English history.[121] But there were other, perhaps better, examples. Hymie Fagan's *Nine Days That Shook England* appeared in 1938, and reinterpreted the English peasants' revolt of 1381 as a theatre of incipient communist revolution, while Christopher Hill, Margaret James and Rickword provided a different picture of social transformation in 1942 with *The English Revolution, 1640*.[122] Henry Holorenshaw (Joseph Needham) returned to the Levellers and the beginnings of 'English democracy', while Allen Hutt provided an overview of more recent class struggles in 1937 with his *The Post-War History of the British Working Class*.[123] Gollancz's Left Book Club published many of these, and all were written as useable pasts. The quality of the emphasis varied, but it was not always the case that these histories were examples of Stalinist apologetics and the imperatives of a Popular-Front-inspired compromise with English or British nationalism. They could be read other ways too, not least as a challenge to ideas of British exceptionalism. 'The importance of the Levellers' movement for British socialism to-day', wrote Joseph Needham, 'lies in the fact that the ideals of Socialism and Communism are not, as so many people think, something of foreign origin, French or Muscovite, alien to the genius of the English people. The truth is exactly the opposite'.[124]

But the new emphasis perhaps came at a cost. It has often been argued that after 1935 the CPGB neglected colonial issues,[125] the attention given to 'Englishness' – to the English past and English literature – is one of the reasons given for this neglect. Certainly, the Comintern, when proclaiming the political value of Popular Fronts, made no mention of how France or Britain could be defended without defending the French or British Empires.[126] In addition, from the mid-1930s, and particularly after June 1941, the Party is said to have subordinated colonial freedom to the exigencies of anti-fascism, politely overlooking the evils of British and French imperialism in order to focus the immediate evil of Hitler.[127] *Left Review*, perhaps, might be emblematic, in this respect. It did at one point argue that communists could not 'hope to defend democratic rights here [in Britain], whilst the political aspirations of the Indian and African millions are suppressed not only by every sort of "legal" disability, such as indefinite detention without trial, but by political violence and armed force'.[128] Nonetheless, this warning went largely unheeded and the Empire received little attention in the

---

121. Morton 1940.
122. Fagan 1938; Hill et al. 1942.
123. Holorenshaw 1939; Hutt 1937.
124. Needham in Holorenshaw 1939, pp. 93–4.
125. See Redfern 2004; Sherwood 1996.
126. See Redfern 2005, p. 78.
127. See, for example, Redfern 2004, p. 117.
128. *Left Review* 1936b, p. 2.

journal. Unfortunately, contributors to *Left Review* failed to draw attention to the relationship between English culture and British imperialism; or, the more promising insight, make the connection between colonialism and fascism.

There were some exceptions, and Fox was among them. His approach to the colonial policy of British social democracy – what Fox called 'practical socialism' – in 1935 in *The Colonial Policy of British Imperialism* was sardonic: 'The workers of the Indian State Railways in particular', he wrote, 'will rejoice to know they are living under conditions of socialism and will cease to strike against intolerable hours, wretched wages and bullying foremen'.[129] He agreed with Lenin that a 'socialist colonial policy' was nonsense. 'It is interesting to know', Fox wrote, 'that the next Labour Government will prohibit slavery (the last two apparently overlooked it) and that forced and contract labour will only be allowed on the best "socialist" principles, and not abolished altogether'.[130] Like the majority of British communist intellectuals, Fox argued that the only true socialist policy toward the colonies was unconditional 'national freedom'.[131]

This might be considered the 'orthodox' communist interpretation of imperialism in the early 1930s. Like Fox, communist intellectuals charged that imperialism was a distinct, though inevitable, stage of capitalist development associated with monopoly, the predominance of financial capital, and intensified competition for profit (both resources and markets) between capitalist nation-states. In this sense it is probably true that the most significant communist intellectual in Britain between the wars was Lenin. However, like the majority of communist intellectuals after 1928, Fox also endorsed the 'Stalinist' view that imperialism under-developed colonial economies and that it was the 'native' working class and peasantry, rather than bourgeois nationalists, who would achieve independence.[132]

There was also little sign of oversight in the work of Palme Dutt.[133] The English-born Dutt – his father was Indian and his mother Swedish – wrote extensively on the colonial question throughout the interwar period.[134] Perhaps the most impressive example of Dutt's attention was his *India Today*, described, later, by E.P. Thompson as 'the most thorough and influential political work by any English Communist leader'.[135] *India Today* was both a 'scientific' and a moral argument for national liberation that figured imperialism a burden on the development of

---

129. Fox 1937, p. 175.
130. Ibid.
131. Fox 1937, p. 177.
132. Howe 1993; Macintyre 1975.
133. See Dutt 1936.
134. Dutt 1936.
135. E.P. Thompson, 'Where Are We Now?', Unpublished Memo, 1962, DJS/109, University of Hull Archives.

India's productive forces. Of more interest, perhaps, was Dutt's claim that there was a 'community of culture' in India forged by a combination of the common experience of exploitation and a horizon of liberation. For Dutt, 'nationness' was a matter of the actions of the Indian nationalist movement rather than simply a by-product of imperialism. Thus Dutt understood that nationhood was an imagined community, though one, he believed, primarily imagined through political action rather than the awakening of some submerged ethnicity.[136]

India Today, for perverse internationalist reasons, also described Britain's war against Germany as imperialist.[137] Indeed, if by default rather than design, the CPGB's wrongheaded internationalism suited well the rhetoric of Indian self-determination, the view that Britain could not fight a war for democracy while denying India freedom. Dutt was, if nothing else, a loyal Stalinist, prepared to change his views to suit the needs of international communism as defined by the Comintern. But the book was nonetheless consistent with his earlier view that 'the epoch of imperialism or monopoly-capitalism becomes the central question of foreign politics and war, since each monopolist grouping strives to secure exclusive domination of the maximum area of exploitation, for the control of raw materials and markets, and for the export of capital'.[138] However, by 1942, Dutt was lamenting Britain's inability to mobilise the Indian masses, and India's resources, for the fight against fascism, and arguing that fascism, rather than British imperialism, was the 'colonial peoples'... deadliest and most dangerous enemy'.[139] The chief conceit of this position was the comparison. According to Dutt, 'in the existing types of colonial regime the mass struggle has already won in the majority of cases a varying measure of rights of organisation and political expression'.[140] Ralph Fox might have considered this view akin to the Labour Party's 'practical socialism'.

Not all communist intellectuals in the 1930s, then, overlooked colonialism, or felt the need to obscure Empire by emphasising the virtues of Englishness. This was certainly true of C.L.R. James and George Padmore. Padmore joined the Communist Party of the United States (CPUSA) in 1927 and was sent to London in 1932 by the Red International of Labour Unions (Profintern), following stints in Moscow and Hamburg. The Trinidad-born Padmore made a unique, and impressive, contribution to anti-imperialist thought and practice, not least through his writing for *The Negro Worker* and his 1931 *The Life and Struggles of Negro Toilers*. However, his major contribution to an understanding of British

---

136. Dutt 1940.
137. See Morgan 1989, for an account of the CPGB's initial war-policy.
138. Dutt 1938.
139. Dutt 1942, p. 104.
140. Ibid.

imperialism came following his expulsion by the Comintern in 1934, though he remained in some sense a communist long after that. In his 1936 work *How Britain Rules Africa*, he elucidated the similarities, in ideology and method, between imperialism and fascism, and argued that colonialism was a 'breeding-ground for the type of fascist mentality which is being let loose in Europe to-day'.[141] Although he demanded 'national freedom' for the colonies 'regardless of their social and cultural development',[142] Padmore did not think independence a sufficient response to imperialism. 'We are internationalists', he wrote in the Independent Labour Party's *New Leader*, 'and, as such, want to see a World Federal Union, with colonies as free units, part of such a union'.[143]

The Trotskyist C.L.R. James was no less critical of British imperialism than Padmore. He did, however, offer a distinct, class, interpretation of 'Englishness' during his first years in England. 'I could forgive England all the vulgarity and all the disappointment of London', he wrote, 'for the magnificent spirit of these north country working people'.[144] Like many socialist intellectuals, James made a distinction between a state-inspired Englishness and an oppositional Englishness rooted in the culture of the common people. Alongside Padmore, he established the International Friends of Ethiopia and, later, the International African Service Bureau. However, James could nonetheless be critical of aspects of Padmore's thought. In a review of *How Britain Rules Africa*, James argued that Padmore's appeal to ' "enlightened far-sighted sections of the ruling classes of Europe with colonial interests in Africa" ' was 'madness'.[145] 'Africans', James concluded, 'must win their own freedom'.[146] Before leaving Britain for the USA in 1938, James published *The Black Jacobins*, which demonstrated how this had been done in the past and how it might be done again.[147]

In the interwar period, communist intellectuals responded to the national question from a series of tight political corners. The context – economic crisis, the rise of fascism, colonial exploitation, the imminence of world war – did not allow the kind of dispassionate analysis of nationhood and nationalism that these thinkers would have perhaps liked. They lived the national question as an immediate reality, in terms of the bombing of Madrid, Barcelona and Guernica, of the massacre of Addis Ababa, of the Nuremberg Laws, of the Spanish Civil War, of appeasement and of imminent world war. This urgency coloured the tone of their response, a tone that has since become unfamiliar 'to current habits

---

141. Padmore 1936.
142. Padmore 1940.
143. Padmore 1941.
144. James 2003, pp. 124–5.
145. James 1936.
146. Ibid.
147. James 1963.

of thinking which emphasise the equivocal, the ambivalent and the contingent'.[148] In any case, these intellectuals were communists rather than Marxists, and hardly Marxist 'theorists' at all. Eric Hobsbawm has put the general point well. Communist thought in this period 'was not primarily a gateway to academic theory. It was in the first instance a matter of political action, policy and strategy'.[149]

IV

'This war', claimed the Socialist Clarity Group in 1940, 'which originated in capitalist and imperialist conflicts and began under capitalist leadership, is now assuming the character which was implicit in it from the outset – that of a people's war for liberty and social progress against the forces of reaction and monopoly power'.[150] This view – 'that in the special circumstances of 1939–45', as Geoffrey Field put it, 'an intensification of patriotism coincided with a growing assertion of working-class class identity and solidarity'[151] – has become conventional historiographical wisdom.[152] But the rhetoric of a people's war – the majority of British socialism's embrace of patriotism – was prepared sometime before, not least throughout the 1930s, and an attention to 'the people' hardly constituted a transformation or major shift in socialist rhetoric.[153] Indeed, as we have seen, something like the amalgam of national identity and class-consciousness was long an option as a response to the national question within the ideological discourse of socialism.

Even before the rhetoric of 'people's war' became ubiquitous among British socialists, E.F.M. Durbin had set out the case for reconciliation between patriotism and social democracy in 1940 in *The Politics of Democratic Socialism*.[154] In many ways, the book was iconoclastic, not least because of its reliance on psychoanalysis. But it also went against the grain of British socialist thought in other ways – in the book's repudiation of class-conflict, in its interpretation of Britain's class-structure, and in its relatively up beat assessment of private property. This was evident also, no doubt, in the book's almost heretical claim that 'the loyalty predominant in social life is the nationalism of the working man – then

---

148. Schwarz 2003, p. 135.
149. Hobsbawm 2011, p. 300.
150. Calder 1993, p. 80.
151. Field 1992, p. 20.
152. This view, of course, has been challenged. For a response to this challenge, consider Hinton 1997.
153. See Ward 2002, pp. 174–5.
154. Crossman 1952, p. 6. An even earlier example is Dalton 1935. A good overview of Durbin's contribution to socialist thought can be found in Brooke 1996, pp. 27–52.

and now'.[155] It was individuals' 'passionate loyalty to the geographical and racial groups in whose culture they have been educated'[156] which, above all, explained their political behaviour.[157]

Durbin's was hardly a form of oppositional Englishness. In one sense, *The Politics of Democratic Socialism* did recall elements of the oppositional Englishness summoned up by communist intellectuals in the mid-1930s. However, where those, like Tom Wintringham, claimed that 'there is a tradition of freedom and the struggle for freedom that is fundamental in the development of this country, built into lives and minds',[158] Durbin argued that co-operation rather than conflict was characteristic of the British tradition of democracy. Indeed, most often, Durbin rehearsed dominant, conservative, visions of national identity. Despite the book's social-scientific tone, Durban could wax pastoral when his thoughts turned to England: 'as I move about this island', he concluded *The Politics of Democratic Socialism*, 'in its quiet lanes and in its crowded streets, meeting people of all classes and persuasions, I feel the life of a strong and quiet people about me; more deeply united than they realize, more creative than they ever suspect'.[159]

Durbin's appropriation of the British tradition for socialism pre-empted the similar and more famous argument of George Orwell's *The Lion and the Unicorn: Socialism and the English Genius*. Unlike *The Politics of Democratic Socialism*, Orwell's book was both a celebration of Englishness *and* an argument for socialist revolution.[160] However, whether deliberately or not, Orwell's treatment of Englishness was ambiguous, perhaps even contradictory, as indeed was his treatment of socialism. In any case, his ostensible purpose was not consistency. He sought to demonstrate that national feeling always and everywhere trumped class-consciousness and that only a socialism allied with patriotism could be an effective opponent of Nazi barbarism. This is why he considered communist and socialist intellectuals so excretable, since, Orwell believed, it was precisely they who had torpedoed patriotism's foundations throughout the 1930s. Socialists, Orwell claimed, must 'bring patriotism and intelligence into partnership',[161] not only because this was the only chance of making socialism, but also because the War had demonstrated that capitalism *'does not work'*.[162] 'An English Socialist

---

155. Durbin 1940, p. 185.
156. Durbin 1940, pp. 184–5.
157. See also Durbin 1942.
158. Wintringham 1935.
159. Durbin 1940, p. 334.
160. See Claeys 1985, pp. 186–211, for a discussion of *The Lion and the Unicorn*.
161. Orwell 2000, p. 174.
162. Orwell 2000, p. 159.

government', Orwell concluded, 'will transform the nation from top to bottom, but it will bear all over the unmistakable marks of our own civilisation'.[163]

The Lion and the Unicorn was less cautious, and less substantial if not less influential, than other arguments for the socialist confiscation of patriotism. Like Orwell, R.H.S. Crossman argued that internationalism was a nefarious 'cult', and that socialist intellectuals' attacks on patriotism were not just 'high-minded' and 'superior' but also disastrous.[164] Indeed, a hatred of the 'left-wing intelligentsia' was a common trope among socialist intellectuals. *Contra* so-called rootless cosmopolitans, Crossman counted Englishness a genuine socialist commitment and declared that a socialist movement must 'recognise that its primary responsibility is to its own countrymen'.[165] He reckoned nationalism a 'civilising instrument' and both a cause and effect of democracy, an argument that would become the common fodder of later scholars of nationalism. 'The earlier democrats realized', Crossman wrote, 'that the political institutions necessary to guarantee the rights of private conscience and enterprise could only grow in a community inspired by a deep sense of unity; and they saw in the nation precisely the community they desired'.[166] Marx was both mischievous and misguided – workers did have a country and, in the case of English workers at least, it was a country, according to Crossman, worth defending.

This was hardly news to Marxists. Already in 1940, T.A. Jackson's *Trials of British Freedom* had championed the rituals of British liberty and paid tribute to the working class's role in the making of British democracy. Although the proletarian philosopher was far more likely than Crossman to acknowledge the debt of past class struggles, Jackson also saw no reason for socialism to give up those 'fine and honorable English words',[167] nationalism, democracy, and patriotism. 'We (communists)', Jackson argued, 'affirm it as a fact for which historical record stands as warrant that the true patriotic and nationalist tradition in England, Scotland and Wales, and therefore in Britain, is identical with the true democratic tradition – the tradition of militant, self-reliant, resistance to oppression and unremitting endeavour towards liberation which is the historical heritage of the proletariat in Britain'.[168] At least in the case of Jackson, this was not a strategic or instrumental love of country, but a deeply-felt belief that socialism was the logical terminus of liberty and democracy. National identity, for Jackson as for other communists in the 1930s and 1940s, was a way of fighting for socialism under another name.

---

163. Orwell 2000, p. 181.
164. Crossman 1940, p. 92.
165. Ibid.
166. Ibid.
167. Jackson 1940, p. xx.
168. Ibid.

There is little doubt that 'community' overshadowed 'class' in the rhetoric of British socialism during the war-years.[169] This shading had long been emblematic of R.H. Tawney's picture of socialism. Indeed, the idea that socialism was commensurate with a 'community of culture', a 'functional society' which subordinated economics to a higher social purpose, was a feature of Tawney's major works, including his 1920 *The Acquistive Society* and his 1931 *Equality*.[170] In the 1938 edition of *Equality*, Tawney claimed that socialism must 'wear a local garb' and '[adapt] to the psychology... of the workers of a particular country at a particular period'.[171] And, he went on, it must be 'related... to the mental and moral traditions of plain men and women', which, in England, meant a 'national psychology' associated with liberalism and democracy. This, he argued, could be contrasted with the 'half-tribal conception of national unity' characteristic of Germany and which he associated with 'a form of political primitivism born in the mist of pre-history'.[172]

After June 1941, community outranked class in the discourse of communist intellectuals, too, though, once again, this did not necessarily constitute any sort of mutation.[173] The priority often informed the rhetoric of *Our Time*, a communist cultural journal established by Randall Swingler among others that appeared between 1941 and 1947. *Our Time* encouraged the 'creation of an army of the British people which reflects the aims and aspirations of the people',[174] and counselled 'the full mobilization and control of all our individual resources in the national interest, with a fair and adequate return to all engaged on production – whether owners, managers, or workers'.[175] Indeed, *Our Time* sought to become the voice 'of all efforts to build a national people's culture'.[176] However, it also agitated for a second front in Europe. There were a number of other spiky exceptions to the populist rhetoric of *Our Time* – whether editorials about wartime class-divisions, articles by Nehru on Indian independence, or attacks on the Atlantic Charter and the 'colour bar'.[177]

The idea of a 'people's war' took on a more pragmatic meaning in the wartime writings of Tom Wintringham, a communist, who had fought in Spain, but was expelled from the CPGB in 1938. He played an important role in the establishment of the Home Guard and, through various publications, such as *New Ways of War*

169. See Brooke 1992, p. 273.
170. Tawney 1921; Tawney 1928.
171. Tawney 1938.
172. Tawney 1964, p. 192.
173. See Roberts 1997, for an account of the CPGB during the War.
174. Stevens 1941, p. 15.
175. *Will Mr. Morrison Ban The Times*, p. 9.
176. *Our Time* 1942, p. 2.
177. *Our Time* 1945.

published in 1940 and *How to Reform the Army* appearing in 1939, advanced the idea of an *anti-fascist* war and offered a unique socialist meditation on military strategy.[178] He turned *Picture Post*, briefly, into a newspaper for social transformation. His expulsion from the CPGB also provided him with the freedom to pen a withering critique of the Party's imperialist war stance in 1941 in *The Politics of Victory* – a book, according to David Fernbach, which stands comparison with any other British Marxist text.[179] His slogan 'victory by democracy' was a call not only for socialist reform in Britain but also for Indian self-government and support for revolutionary uprisings in occupied countries on the continent – what Frank Thompson named 'the spirit of Europe'.

Socialist intellectuals did much to promote national unity during the War. But there were some, especially in the early years of war, who supposed this was being undermined by another version of 'Englishness'. *Guilty Men*, the wartime broadcasts of J.B. Priestley, the intemperate pamphlets of George Orwell, the writings of 'Cassandra' in the *Daily Mirror*, and the CPGB's People's Convention all suggest Britain's distance from a unified imagined community.[180] Nonetheless, the war-years crowned the nationalisation of British socialism, its final reconciliation to the British state (this was even true of the CPGB) and to the objective of 'socialism in one country'.[181] This was perhaps a result of the unique role that Labour played throughout the War (Labour was the only European socialist party in government, albeit in a national coalition). It was also a function, particularly after 1941, of the increasing fusion of socialist ambition with national, sometimes nationalist, sentiment.[182] This fusion had long been imagined in the rhetoric of socialist intellectuals, both communist and anti-communist.

V

Our Time welcomed the 1945 Labour Government but it also offered a caution which looked forward to the Cold War: 'We have to find, or rather create, a true internationalism to control our latest weapon ['the bomb'], and this world sense based on realistic understanding of regional opportunities, needs and differences, must also inform our cultural life'.[183] The prime initiatives of Labour socialism reinforced socialism's Britishness as much as its commitment

---

178. Wintringham 1942.
179. Wintringham 1941. See Fernbach 1982, p. 78.
180. See Baxendale 2001, pp. 87–111, on Priestley. For the general point, see Field 1992, p. 23.
181. Sassoon 1996.
182. McKibben 2010, pp. 124, 137.
183. *Our Time* 1945, p. 27.

to social transformation.[184] Indeed, Labour's 'British variant of "socialism in one country"'[185] left the institutions of Englishness untouched.[186] Most revealingly, perhaps, Labour made no effort to institute any sort of 'socialist foreign policy'.[187] In terms of international relations, social democracy served the national interest as Britain's traditional ruling class defined it. Thus Britain was transformed into a Cold War warrior, eager to maintain its international prestige through membership in NATO, commitment to Altanticism, war in Korea and the (mostly secret) development of a nuclear weapons' programme.[188] The warnings of *Our Time* went unheeded.

Perhaps as a consequence of success, particularly the insularity and complacency which success reinforced, Labour intellectuals produced few new ideas until after 1950, when Croslandite revisionism increasingly filled the pages of *Fabian Essays*.[189] The other major contribution to socialist thought in the 1950s came from the now ex-communist Strachey, particularly his *Contemporary Capitalism*. But neither *The Future of Socialism* nor Strachey's thought offered any resistance to hegemonic ideas of Britishness. Revisionism largely endorsed Labour's Atlanticism, its anti-Europeanism, and traditional conceptions of national sovereignty too.[190] The Empire, as opposed to the Commonwealth, was mostly ignored, while intimations of Britain's economic decline were absent in a strangely complacent, and ahistorical, vision of capitalism.

Discordant notes to Labour's Atlanticist tune, though, could be found in the thought of Cole and Laski, as we have seen, and in the writings of Crossman. Each of these thinkers imagined various middle roads between 'actual existing socialism' and 'actual existing capitalism', though, it must be said, none met with any success. Unlike Cole and Laski, Crossman did endorse the Atlantic alliance, though he also admitted Britain's diminished role in world politics and recommended an early version of socialist Europeanism. Crossman prescribed a brake on Labour's virulent anti-communism too: 'The socialist', he wrote, 'must remain sceptical of plans for combating communism which really involve the suppression of national and social revolution among the colonial peoples'.[191] Looking forward to America's war in Vietnam, though surely with Malaya and Korea in

---

184. See Paul 1992; Francis 1995.
185. Morgan 1985, p. 93. See also Hinton 1995, p. 77.
186. McKibben 2010, p. 144.
187. See Schneer 1984, for the opposition to this within the Labour Party, and the opposition's vision of a 'socialist foreign policy'.
188. See Black 2001, pp. 26–62.
189. See N. Thompson 2006, Chapter Twelve. Of course, the history of revisionist ideas extends back, at least, to the 1930s. See Brooke 1996; compare Jackson 2005.
190. See Douglas 2004, Chapter Seven, on Labour's anti-Europeanism.
191. Crossman 1952.

mind, Crossman claimed that 'the spread of communism may be a lesser evil than the containment of it by a ruinous colonial war'.[192]

It is in the context of the Labour government's adherence to Atlanticism and the extreme pressures exerted by the Cold War that we can understand the militant anti-Americanism of British communists after 1945. No doubt this nationalist reflex had something to do with American economic and political hegemony in Europe, evidenced by the Marshall Plan and the Anglo-American intervention in Greece.[193] However, before King Street squashed its limited autonomy, *Our Time* also became increasingly anxious about American cultural imperialism. According to one contributor, 'there is more fun and games to be got out of singing our own songs and dancing our own native dances than in listening to Frank Sinatra or watching jitterbugs'.[194] In the immediate post-war years – and preempting the CPGB's *British Road to Socialism* – *Our Time* sought the 'revival of a great and flourishing national culture . . . as the most sure and effective resistance to the danger of centralized and monopolistic "conditioning" '.[195]

Forebodings about the 'American threat to British culture' were common among post-war communist intellectuals. But they were careful, sometimes at least, to make a distinction between 'the America of Emerson and Whitman' and 'the American trusts' which 'aim to destroy . . . the national independence of all peoples, British as well as Soviet'.[196] This last America, Sam Aaronovitch argued, was associated with racism, Hollywood, comics and gangsterism and was supported by 'British monopolists and right-wing Labour leaders' who were 'engaged in selling British interests, lock, stock and barrel to the Americans'.[197] In such circumstances, he concluded, 'the idea of world government becomes an argument for war against countries that will not give up their national independence'.[198] Not for Aaronovitch the 'world state' associated with British communism in the 1930s. Rather, communists, the 'true patriots', were charged with defending 'the interests of the people which are the true interests of the nation'.[199]

The British Road to Socialism and the cultural nationalism of communist intellectuals were, in one sense, an extension of the radical patriotism associated with people's war and national reconstruction. Communists' cultural nationalism might also be seen as an attempt, an increasingly shrill and unsuccessful

---

192. Ibid.
193. See Eley 2004, pp. 301–3, for a good overview.
194. Mais 1946, p. 235.
195. *Our Time* 1946, p. 27.
196. Aaronovitch 1950, p. 3.
197. Ibid., p. 13.
198. Ibid., p. 21.
199. Ibid., p. 21.

attempt, to salvage the radical potential of patriotism against the dominant conservative and labourist association of the national interest with Atlanticism and
the Cold War. 'Now that Toryism and Right-wing Labour are selling our country
to the American imperialists', wrote the communist historian Rodney Hilton,
'it is a task of prime political importance to mobilize the patriotic instincts of the
people against this betrayal'.[200] It was simply a matter of replacing an old generation of 'guilty men' for a new generation (and Ernest Bevin was considered
most guilty of all). Whatever its origins, it does demonstrate how distorted and
bruised communist intellectuals had become by the early 1950s. Zhandonovism,
controversies over the Marxism of Christopher Caudwell in *Modern Quarterly*,
and a newly-militant British nationalism morphed into anti-communism, and
did much to close the communist mind.

However, this is not all that can be said about communist intellectuals' stress
on national cultural resources. Among certain intellectuals, not least those historians associated with the Communist Party Historians' Group, this emphasis was
associated with a 'creative Marxism' more at home with a literary imagination
than *Inprecorr*. 'Marxism', as Victor Kiernan put it, 'also has much to learn, that
it has not yet learned, from poetry' – an uncommon view among contributions to
Daily Worker. The cultural vitality that had been associated mostly with communist literary critics in the 1930s and throughout the War was increasingly transferred to historians after 1945. E.P. Thompson, who had connections with both
groups, might stand as a bellwether of this change. His biography of William
Morris was initially designed in the tradition established by Swingler, Slater and
Rickword in the 1930s and 1940s. But from the late 1950s onwards, he increasingly
placed himself in the tradition of British Marxist historiography. Thus, cultural
nationalism seems a less fitting way of seeing certain communist intellectuals,
especially those, like Thompson, John Saville and Christopher Hill, who would
leave the Party following the Soviet invasion of Hungary. It was their 'mature
revisionism', of course, that would form one strand of a New Left.

VI

Cosmopolitan fraternity took a series of knocks after 1945, from which it proved
difficult to recover. Atlanticism and Stalinism were deformed examples of internationalism and alternative manifestations existed only in stray colonies of the
mainstream labour-movement, in the increasingly ignored views of Cole and
Laski, in the small Trotskyist movement, and, perhaps, in 'minor' magazines such

---

200. Hilton 1954.

as *Politics and Letters*. An internationalism that held fast to socialism's revolutionary traditions but remained hostile to Soviet socialism and capitalist imperialism was a shamefaced, underground, view in the era of *The British Road to Socialism* and *Fabian Essays*. But following 'Suez' and 'Hungary' an internationalist critique of communism and social democracy from a position of 'rebellious humanism' emerged in the form of a New Left.[201]

The New Left inherited what it believed was a broken socialist vocabulary. For the most part, the British socialist tradition repudiated nationalism, but it did not reject nationality or national identity. It sometimes associated 'Englishness' or the 'British tradition' with socialism and identified this association with a commitment to internationalism – manifest in anti-fascism, in support for anti-imperialist movements and in the refusal of 'two camp' Cold War politics. Englishness was imagined as a product of working-class struggle, thereby scouting the tricky question of the nexus between class and national identity. On the question of national sovereignty, socialist intellectuals hesitated between refusal and espousal. Some would willingly transfer Britain's sovereignty to transnational powers, such as the League of Nations or a European federation, and, in perhaps less defensible cases, to the Comintern. Others understood national sovereignty as crucial to the making of socialism and the nation-state as the framework of any future socialist society. The origins of these conflicted positions were multiple, a reflection of historical and political context and a social reality that was composed of national and cosmopolitan tendencies.

Thus the New Left inherited a conflicted and sometimes confused tradition. Like socialist intellectuals before 1956, New Left thinkers would be forced to engage a series of national questions, from the break-up of Britain's Empire to the existence of peripheral British nationalisms, from the effects of capitalist globalisation to Britain's apparent decline, from the political consequences of national identity in the context of international conflict to the historicity or otherwise of nationhood. The remaining chapters of this book will provide a narrative of this engagement in the form of a dialogue between the New Left's key thinkers.

---

201. E.P. Thompson 1978, p. 242.

Chapter Three
E.P. Thompson in the Provinces

I

What was E.P. Thompson's country? According to some, his country was England, and he was English above all else. The association is sometimes versed with approval, as when he is described as a 'thoroughly English dissident',[1] though more often Thompson's Englishness has been associated with Empire, provincialism, and an outmoded empiricism, as when Stuart Hall refers to him as being 'too English'.[2] During the New Left's birth pangs, Thompson's homeland was considered Marxism, and he was described as a foreign Marxist weed spoiling the irenic idealism of England's radical youth.[3] Shortly after, a younger generation of the New Left was identifying his political thought with 'messianic nationalism', evidenced, above all, they supposed, in his aversion to contemporary European thought.[4] Uniformly hostile, if contradictory, these assessments, whatever their character, miss most of what was important about Thompson's sense of allegiance.

Thompson called a spade a spade, so it is not surprising that he was called a spade in return. But spades, no matter how finely chiselled, and though good for digging, are rarely sophisticated instruments of analysis. It is not strictly for this reason that many critical assessments of Thompson's country are beside

1. Webb 1994, pp. 160–4.
2. Hall 2009, p. 675.
3. E.P. Thompson 1960a, p. 20.
4. Anderson 1966.

the point. Much of it, also, has to do with the lack of feeling for political and historical context of such assessments. If looked at with sufficient care, Thompson's imagined political community will not be found in England, especially not metropolitan England, and not in Marxism, no matter how important the tradition of British Marxist historiography was to his historical consciousness.[5] Rather, it will be found 'in the provinces'. By 'in the provinces', I do not mean to imply any association with provincialism. The phrase is borrowed from Thompson, and he used it, at least in one place, to describe an approach to historical enquiry.[6] In the provinces, however, is not just a place where history could be written. It was a perspective or location, more exactly a sensibility, associated with human agency and political initiative and where both metropolitan power and historical determinism could be opposed. It was, in short, Thompson's country, the somewhere he positioned himself in order to say or write anything at all.

This chapter seeks to make good that claim in the course of an account of Thompson's contribution to New Left thought. Writing from in the provinces, or 'nowhere land' as he rendered this location in his poetry, involved a certain awkwardness. The only other option, Thompson believed, was assimilation. 'For one must, to survive as an unassimilated socialist in this infinitely assimilative culture, put oneself into a school of awkwardness. One must make one's sensibility all knobby – all knees and elbows of susceptibility and refusal – if one is not to be pressed through the grid into the universal mish-mash of the received assumptions of the intellectual culture'.[7] Thompson consistently opposed the dominant culture, whether that culture was socialist, English/British, or academic. He opposed those hegemonies with the values he found in life-experience and minority traditions. From 'in the provinces' he became an international carrier of dissent.

The first section of the chapter will briefly outline Thompson's biography, highlighting moments crucial to his intellectual development.[8] The second section will concentrate on his political interventions in the decade or so after 1956 and the debates they sparked within the New Left. The next section touches down, and this lightly, on Thompson's historical work, with a focus on his elucidation of the 'tradition of free-born Englishmen'. Critiques offered by Tom Nairn, Perry Anderson and Stuart Hall will be discussed. The fourth section of the chapter concentrates on Thompson's political interventions in the 1970s. The final section, bearing the weight of a lifetime's engagement with the mentality that

5. See E.P. Thompson 1978, p. 333, for the importance of this tradition.
6. E.P. Thompson 1994, p. 23.
7. E.P. Thompson 1978, p. 393.
8. Thompson's biography has been the subject of many books and articles. There are some good contributions, most obviously Palmer 1994. However, I would suggest that there is still much that remains to be explored.

informed the proliferation of nuclear weapons, will cross Thompson's anti-war writings in the era of Thatcher and Reagan. A brief conclusion will tie together Thompson's negotiation of national sentiment after 1956.

II

E.P. Thompson was born in Oxford in 1924, the second son of Edward and Theodosia Thompson.[9] His English father, Edward John Thompson, was a poet, literary critic, historian and, at least initially, a Methodist missionary who spent time in India and the Middle East. E.J. Thompson served in Mesopotamia in the chaplain service during the Great War, where he met Theodosia Jessup, whose family was involved with the American Mission in the Levant, and he spent a number of years, both before and after the War, in Bengal, teaching at Bankura College. Following his marriage to Theodosia, and the birth of their first son, Frank, Thompson took up a position at Oxford as a lecturer in Bengali, a position he would hold until his death.[10] In India E.J. Thompson made contact with leading Indian literary and political figures, though his attitude to British imperialism remained ambivalent, and though critical of British treatment of the subaltern, he stopped short of championing Indian independence.[11] Shortly before his death in 1940, however, E.J. Thompson moved to a position on the relationship between England and India that led him 'to question and reject totally the fact and concept of Empire'.[12]

An idiosyncratic product of that great sociological muddle, the English middle class, E.P. Thompson was thus born into a family constituted at the nexus between 'west' and 'east', and that lived the problems of power, imagination and culture. The familial influence on Thompson's later development, if unquestionable (few historians have devoted three separate books to members of their family), is deep and complex, something he admitted when he turned toward the end of his life to investigate the relationship between his father and the Bengali poet, Rabindranath Tagore.[13] A key aspect of that familial influence was India. The fight for Indian independence was among a number of internationalist reasons that would draw Thompson toward a socialist tradition that was

---

9. The best account of Thompson's family background will be found in Palmer 1994, pp. 11–51. There is, however, now a biography of Thompson's father: see Lago 2001.

10. This was never a full-time position, and E.J. Thompson made his principal living from writing.

11. E.J. Thompson's relationship with India has attracted much attention. See, for a sample of this literature, Greenberger 1969; Said 1994, pp. 206–7, 209.

12. Parry 1972, p. 166.

13. E.P. Thompson 1993. The other books which Thompson wrote about his family are E.P. Thompson and D.K.G. Thompson (eds.) 1947; E.P. Thompson 1994.

'revolutionary, rational, democratic'[14] in the early 1940s.[15] In addition to internationalism and anti-imperialism, another probable familial influence was Methodism and Methodism's association with duty, dissent and suspicion of authority.[16] As Thompson later remarked, he 'grew up expecting government to be mendacious and imperialist and expecting that one's stance ought to be hostile to government'.[17]

Karl Deutsch once argued that national sentiment was primarily reproduced through the family.[18] Thompson was socialised into internationalism, but of a specific, some might say English, kind. Nonetheless, the 'tough liberalism'[19] that Thompson believed characteristic of his family's internationalism was hardly a sufficient response to fascism – or, at least, that was what Thompson's brother, Frank, believed. The influence of Frank Thompson on his younger brother was profound, though it neither began nor ended with E.P. Thompson's decision to follow his brother into the CPGB in 1941.[20] Above all, Thompson's debt to his brother would be revealed in his commitment to what Frank Thompson called 'the spirit of Europe',[21] a spirit that both brothers encountered and lived through the war-years. A Classics scholar at Oxford, Frank Thompson joined the CPGB immediately before the War, and volunteered for military service in September 1939.[22] He was no orthodox Communist though, preferring Greek poetry to the *Daily Worker* (perhaps because the former said more about what communism was for). Frank Thompson first served with a communications and intelligence-unit, later with the Special Operations Executive, in the Middle East, Sicily, Serbia and Bulgaria, the last where he, alongside partisans, was captured, interrogated, and shot by fascists in 1944.[23] He died a major and a hero of the Bulgarian partisan-struggle, his mission, in E.P. Thompson's view, undermined by Allied Command. In 1943, Frank Thompson wrote to his brother that there was 'a spirit abroad in Europe which is finer and braver than anything that tired continent has known for centuries, and which cannot be withstood.... It is the confident will of whole peoples who have known

---

14. E.P. Thompson 1978, p. 311.
15. See E.P. Thompson 1978, p. ii.
16. For Thompson's own comment, see E.P. Thompson 1994, p. 52. On Methodism and its influence on the members of the tradition of British Marxist historiography, see Samuel 1980, pp. 52–5; Rowbotham 1993, p. 15.
17. Merrill 1981, p. 11.
18. Deutsch 1953.
19. Merrill 1981, p. 11.
20. Hobsbawm 1995a, p. 142; E.P. Thompson 1997a, 79–86.
21. E.P. Thompson and D.K.G. Thompson (eds.) 1948, p. 169.
22. See Conradi 2001, pp. 90–4, for more on Frank Thompson.
23. E.P. Thompson 1997a.

the utmost humiliation and suffering and have triumphed over it, to build their own lives once and for all'.[24]

This spirit would soon be crushed, but not before E.P. Thompson experienced it during the War in Italy, where he served as a tank troop-commander in the British Army, and, immediately after it, as a member of a Communist volunteer youth-brigade in Yugoslavia.[25] Thompson's commitment to a certain experience of the years between 1940 and 1948 would endure. Indeed, Thompson would continue to defend that generation of communists – his own – that came of political age during the 1930s and 1940s, refusing to reduce their activities or their beliefs to Stalinism, long after he broke with the CPGB in 1956. Thompson joined a communist movement that believed it was 'making history',[26] whether 'in the sierras and on the banks of the Ebro',[27] or alongside partisans in Bulgaria and Serbia. This was not nostalgia, since Thompson would also see much that was wrong with that generation, not just its innocence but also its complicity with mendacity. However, he would always recommend their heroism, and he refused to second-guess their commitment to socialism and internationalism. Thompson knew that Stalinism bred crimes, but he also knew that under the banner of communism, during the 1930s and 1940s, men and women had put their bodies between fascism and freedom. Much of Thompson's politics, over the next four decades, would be dedicated to honouring their sense of commitment, a political commitment that led them to perceive their own deaths as insignificant when compared to the freedom of others.

E.P. Thompson joined the CPGB in late 1941, while he was studying at Cambridge – a time and place when 'almost the only subject of discussion [was] contemporary politics and [when] a very large majority of the more intelligent undergraduates [were] communists'.[28] For Thompson, communism was rooted in 'anti-fascist contestation'[29] and in a 'shared faith and an internationalist fellowship'.[30] But it was also about political judgment and active initiative. This sensibility was further cultivated during the War. When Thompson later recalled the war-years, he remembered 'a resolute and ingenious civilian army, increasingly hostile to the conventional military virtues, which became ... an anti-fascist

---

24. Frank Thompson cited in E.P. Thompson 1994, p. 102.
25. For E.P. Thompson's reflection on aspects of his experience during the War, see E.P. Thompson 1985, pp. 183–202. For reflections on the railway-building experience in Yugoslavia in the immediate aftermath of the War, see D.K.G. Thompson 1993, p. 24.
26. E.P. Thompson 1978, p. 264.
27. Frank Thompson cited in E.P. Thompson 1997a, p. 71.
28. Julian Bell cited in Hopkins, 1942, p. 22.
29. E.P. Thompson 1997a, p. 56.
30. E.P. Thompson 1997a, p. 103.

and consciously anti-imperialist army'.[31] He also remembered the spirit of Europe as it appeared in partisan-resistance to fascism, the battle of ordinary people to establish a common life on the basis of common participation.[32] When Thompson later defended the 'national tradition' it would be that tradition of national sentiment established during the war-years, and which, after the War, was expressed in the election of a Labour government and the creation of a National Health Service – a vision of national sentiment that he opposed to nuclear Britain, the Britain of Chapman Pincer, and the Britain of Perry Anderson and Tom Nairn, too.

Immediately after the War, Thompson received his undergraduate degree and met and married Dorothy Thompson (née Towers), who would become his lifelong intellectual and political collaborator. In 1948, following their participation in a Communist Youth Brigade project rebuilding a railway in Yugoslavia, they moved to Yorkshire, where Thompson took up a teaching post in the Leeds Extra-Mural Department.[33] Not enough can be said about the intellectual and political comradeship established between Edward and Dorothy Thompson.[34] Richard Hoggart would later call it a 'model' intellectual and political partnership.[35] Both were active in Yorkshire Communist activities, particularly the Halifax Peace Committee; and were influenced by Dona Torr and her idea of 'collective intellectual work'.[36] They were also members of the Communist Party Historians' Group, though E.P Thompson's association was passing, while Dorothy Thompson's was more substantial. E.P Thompson's limited involvement with the Group was partly due to the distance between Halifax and London (where the majority of the meetings of the Group were held), partly because he was busy with adult education teaching and his communist activism, which included membership of the CPGB's Yorkshire District Committee, and it was partly due to the fact that Thompson did not think of himself as a historian at this time.[37]

Indeed, Thompson mostly thought of himself as a writer, a thinking that survived his biography of William Morris first published in 1955.[38] Having said that, his work in Adult Education after the War was important to his later development as a historian, not least the impetus it provided to the research for *The Making of the English Working Class*. Blake and the romantics, and their

---

31. E.P. Thompson 1980a, p. 131.
32. Merrill 1981, p. 11. See also E.P. Thompson 1978, p. 160.
33. On Thompson's Adult Education teaching, consult Searby, Malcolmson and Rule 1993.
34. Palmer 1994, p. 54, makes the comparison.
35. Hoggart cited in Palmer 1994, p. 54.
36. E.P. Thompson, Letter to John Saville, 1957, Saville Papers, University of Hull Archives, University of Hull.
37. On Thompson's limited involvement, see Walker 2000, pp. 143–4.
38. E.P. Thompson 1976a. Before *William Morris*, Thompson published two pamphlets: E.P. Thompson 1947; 1952.

particular repudiation of industrial capitalism's reduction of man to things also moved Thompson, as well as Morris, who sought to bridge the gap between the romantics' desire and reason in terms of revolutionary socialism.[39] 'We must', Thompson wrote in 1951, 'change people now, for that is the essence of our [communists'] cultural work'. He went on to suggest in the same piece on Morris that 'all the forces of health within our society are on our side: all those who, in whatever way, desire a richer life, all those who have warmer ambitions for Britain than those of tedious insolvency and rearmament, all those, indeed, who desire any life at all, can be won to our side if we take to them the message of life against that of the slaughter-house culture'.[40] A job begun by Morris, it was a task that Thompson would see as his own throughout the 1950s and beyond.

The immediate years of the Cold War were ones of intense political pressure for communists in Britain, even though Britain escaped the extreme McCarthyism that disfigured American radical politics. 'Vitalities shrivelled up', Thompson later put it, 'and books lost their leaves'.[41] It was not just that creativity and the moral imagination suffered from the poison of dogmatism characteristic of international communism in those years. They also wilted in an 'exterminist' milieu, where abnegation from communist commitments implied acceptance of capitalist imperialism. There were also the ghosts of those who had lost their life fighting fascism to contend with, ghosts ill-served by both local Zhdanovs and nascent congresses for cultural freedom. According to Thompson, 'by the 1940s the stream of "apostates" was so full that all of us were apt to recoil, willfully and unthinkingly, from the brink of any heresy for fear of toppling into the flood'.[42] To be a revolutionary socialist in those years was to be placed between a rock and a hard place, between the bomb and Emile Burns.[43]

Thinking, if muffled, nonetheless went on, not least within the Communist Party Historians' Group and the more tightly (Party) controlled writers' group, a group that Thompson had connections with through friendships with Arnold Rattenbury and Randall Swingler during and after the War. It went on in Yorkshire too, though it was more likely to take place in Adult Education classes than in the Yorkshire Communist bureaucracy.[44] Sometimes the thinking took place undercover. Under the protection of certain people, such as Dona Torr, for example, who acted as a buffer between King Street and the Historians'

---

39. On Thompson's link to the romantic tradition, see Löwy and Sayre 2001, Chapter Five.
40. E.P. Thompson 1951, p. 30.
41. E.P. Thompson 1994, p. 235.
42. E.P. Thompson 1994, p. 236.
43. Emile Burns – a much hated 'cultural' figure at King St., at least by the Thompsons.
44. Nonetheless there were a number of Yorkshire Communists, such as Howard Hill and Bert Ramelson, whom the Thompsons respected. Indeed, the decision of the Thompsons to stay in the CPGB for so long was a product of their respect for figures such as Hill and Ramelson.

Group.[45] Thinking also took place under the cover of Englishness, something ill-understood by Thompson's later detractors. A 'return to national cultural resources' was one way to rebuff the perverse internationalism of British Communism, especially as the CPGB was in the process of committing itself to the 'British road to socialism'. Englishness, in other words, acted as a kind of socialist-humanist *samizdat*. For Thompson, neither *News from Nowhere* nor 'Jerusalem' was easily reconciled to the ABC of communism. The recourse to Englishness also helps explain Thompson's contribution to various CPGB cultural conferences in the early 1950s,[46] and also, in part, his *William Morris: Romantic to Revolutionary*, a sprawling biography of the English revolutionary that was marred, to some degree, as Thompson would later admit, by 'Stalinist pieties'.[47] There was more to the Morris biography than that, and more that was important to Thompson as he took leave of the CPGB, including Morris's attention to the 'moral critique of capitalism' and his belief that socialism must involve a change of heart.

Thompson would call upon Englishness throughout 1956 too, not least after Khrushchev's secret speech.[48] 'Thank God,' he wrote to Bert Ramelson in May 1956, 'there is no chance of this E.C. [Executive Committee of the CPGB] ever having power in Britain: it would destroy in a month every liberty of thought, conscience and expression, which it has taken the British people 300 odd years to win'.[49] Despite the CPGB's best efforts, some communists were aware of the content of Khrushchev's speech well before it was published in the *New York Times* and *The Observer* in June. Thompson's response, prepared no doubt by a 'premature revisionism' learnt at the feet of Torr, Christopher Hill, Swingler and Rattenbury, was swift. In a series of letters to the Communist press, and personal pleas to various representatives of King Street, such as James Klugman, he urged the CPGB leadership to open up the Party and its press to discussion and dissident views.[50] Indeed, throughout most of 1956 Thompson believed that Communism in Britain could be reformed, and this belief inspired *The Reasoner*, the journal of Communist dissent which he edited alongside John Saville and Dorothy Thompson from June.[51]

That all changed after the Soviet invasion of Hungary in October. *The Reasoner*, in any case, had received a hostile reading from British Communist apparatchiks. They found its critique of democratic centralism and the Party leadership, its

45. See E.P. Thompson 1980a.
46. E.P. Thompson 1951a, p. 2.
47. See E.P. Thompson 1976a, p. 769.
48. For a narrative of the CPGB's 1956, see Saville 1976, pp. 1–23; Saville 1994, pp. 20–31.
49. See E.P. Thompson, Letter to James Klugman, May, 1956, CP/IND?KLUG/01/06, Communist Party of Great Britain Archives, Labour History Centre Manchester.
50. Ibid.
51. On *The Reasoner*, see Saville 2004, pp. 105–10.

expression of dissent and its exhibition of liberty of thought, not just unhelpful, but also heretical. However, Thompson, his fellow editors, and many of the
journal's contributors, such as Ken Alexander and Lawrence Daly, believed in
the need for discussion, polemic and theoretical confrontation – as a communist
duty and for the good of international communism. 'We started publication',
Thompson wrote at the time, 'because we believe there is now a crisis in theory
in our movement without precedent, which necessitates the fullest and frankest
discussion, which may have to include critical aspects of our past history'.[52] *The
Reasoner*, nonetheless, was styled as a responsible form of dissent, taking place
wholly within the CPGB, and with respect for the pressures then operating on
British Communists.

The Party disagreed, and the editors were instructed to stop publication after
the journal's first issue. For a time, *The Reasoner* became the Party's most important topic, with numerous branches delivering resolutions to have it banned
(only a few, including the Halifax branch, resolved that it should continue).
Before the Soviet invasion of Hungary, the Thompsons and Saville were willing
to negotiate and compromise, even offering to suspend, with conditions, publication of *The Reasoner* before the upcoming (1957) Party Conference.[53] After
Hungary, however, they were in no mood for negotiation, much less for compromise. Along with seven thousand others, including most Reasoners, they left the
Party. 'Scores of people are leaving already: if the Party can't be changed from
inside, it will have to be changed from outside', Thompson wrote to Howard Hill
in early November 1956. 'If we keep together and do our damndest to prevent
recriminations and bitterness arising, then there is bound to be a reconciliation
on a much better level later on: and if the old gang won't see reason, then we
shall have to go on without them'.[54]

The old gang was not concerned with reason, even after mass exodus, and
one way that Saville and the Thompsons attempted to keep Yorkshire socialists
together after 1956 was through *New Reasoner*, a journal of 'creative Marxism'
that, if still very much concerned with the state of international communism,
was mostly uninterested in the reform of the CPGB. *New Reasoner*, a product of
northern England, did not, however, start out as a journal of the New Left. A voice
of dissident communism, *New Reasoner* was designed as a journal for discussion;
it was committed to keeping communication open between socialists in Britain
and communist dissidents in Eastern Europe; between industrial organisers and

52. E.P. Thompson, Letter to Adrian Ganther, 1956, Communist Party of Great Britain
Archives, Labour History Centre, Manchester.
53. E.P. Thompson, Letter to Howard Hill, 1956, CP/CENT/ORG/18/04, Communist
Party of Great Britain Archives, Labour History Centre, Manchester.
54. Ibid.

students, and between disgruntled ex-communists and the labour-movement. The idea was to 'nourish the development of socialist theory',[55] as Thompson put it in a letter to Saville in 1957. Thompson's own contributions to the journal ranged from a long disquisition on the meaning of socialist humanism to an exploration of Britain's role in Cyprus.

But, arguably, *New Reasoner* did not have a political line, not beyond the intention to explore new socialist ideas and values. Indeed, there was dissension among the editorial team about what the political purpose of *New Reasoner* was. Both Saville and Ken Alexander wanted to establish close contacts with the Labour Left, and each maintained the importance of the Labour Party to any transition to socialism in Britain.[56] There was even talk of formalising these relations. The Thompsons had different ideas, though they also recognised the importance of maintaining contacts with people in the Labour Left and the constituency parties, not least in Yorkshire. They preferred, however, to maintain the extra-Party origins of *New Reasoner*. It was not just a difference of politics, but also one of tone. The 'chief thing I want in this journal is attack', Thompson wrote, 'and I want specialists who write in such a way that serious non-specialists can not only understand what they mean, but (if the subject requires it) can be stimulated, roused or moved by what they say. This is NOT the learned or academic tradition: it IS the tradition of a certain sort of politico-journalism (Swift and Hazlitt) in Britain'.[57]

There were also differences surrounding Lawrence Daly and the Fife Socialist League's election campaign in 1959. The Thompsons were immediately enthusiastic about Daly's campaign.[58] Alexander and Saville, though, were more cautious, with Alexander, in particular, arguing that *New Reasoner* should not support a Left alternative against Labour and the CPGB.[59] The Thompsons worked hard to win over *New Reasoner* and a nascent New Left to the importance of Daly's election bid. Although unsuccessful, at least in terms of winning the vote (the Fife Socialist League did, however, outvote the CPGB), Daly's campaign had an important affect on the Thompsons. 'We talk a lot about the potentialities of working people, in the abstract', E.P. Thompson wrote to Daly, 'but here one felt

---

55. E.P. Thompson, Letter to John Saville, 1957, DJS/107 Saville Papers, University of Hull Archives, University of Hull.

56. E.P. Thompson, 'Letter to Ken Alexander', DJS/112, 23 January 1958, Saville Papers, University of Hull Archives, University of Hull.

57. E.P. Thompson, 'E.P. Thompson to John Saville', DJS/107 1957, Saville Papers, University of Hull Archives, University of Hull.

58. E.P. Thompson, Letter to Lawrence Daly, 17 August 1959, Lawrence Daly Papers, Modern Records Centre, Warwick University.

59. Ibid.

it in the concrete, and it has given me added faith in the real meaning and force of socialism, when people start acting for themselves below'.[60]

Already before the 1959 General Election, the editorial boards of *New Reasoner* and *Universities and Left Review* had entered discussions about pooling resources and establishing a merged journal. *New Left Review* first appeared in January 1960. Thompson had high hopes for the journal, believing it could constitute a broker between popular and theoretical discourse on socialism.[61] Thompson's time as a member of the editorial board was not a happy one though. Just three months after *New Left Review*'s foundation, he attempted to resign from the editorial executive, and he made another attempt in May 1961.[62] The central issue in the latter case was *New Left Review*'s evidence before the Pilkington Commission on British television, though he had long felt uncomfortable with aspects of the conduct and policy of the journal.[63] Indeed, by this time Thompson considered 'the merger [between *New Reasoner* and *Universities and Left Review*] a failure'.[64] The failure, as Thompson saw it, was primarily a result of the journal's unwillingness to offer leadership on politics or theory.

New Left Review struggled on between 1960 and 1962, an initial optimism giving way to sometime cantankerous dispute. Thompson, having been persuaded not to resign from the board, continued to write for the journal, and he played an important role in the first *New Left Review* book, *Out of Apathy*, published in 1960, contributing the book's conclusion, 'Revolution'.[65] But his misgivings about the journal's working methods, and its political positions, went unresolved.[66] 'On a rough calculation', he wrote to Saville in 1961, 'we are publishing no more than and perhaps less now per annum than either journal was publishing two years ago. Where the people around the journals then initiated activities, now we pant along behind activities or (worse) fashions which others initiate. All our committees are dissolved or inactive – pamphlets, industrial, East Europe, Left Clubs, books (never once met), international'.[67] As this list suggests, Thompson was particularly concerned about the journal's neglect of international issues. He ended a letter to Saville in 1961 with the sad lament that *New Left Review* 'doesn't

60. Ibid.

61. Ibid.

62. E.P. Thompson, Letter to John Saville', 12 May 1961, DJS/112 Saville Papers, University of Hull Archives, University of Hull.

63. *New Left Review* 1961, pp. 28–48.

64. E.P. Thompson, Letter to John Saville', 12 May 1961, DJS/112 Saville Papers, University of Hull Archives, University of Hull.

65. *New Left Review* 1960.

66. See E.P. Thompson, Letter to John Saville, 12 May 1961, DJS/112 Saville Papers, University of Hull Archives, University of Hull for this critique of the journal.

67. Ibid.

seem to me to matter much, since it has ceased to be an engaged political journal, and to that degree is not central to the struggle for socialism'.[68]

Hall resigned from *New Left Review* in late 1961. In April 1962, and following Anderson's ascension to sole editorship, with support from Tom Nairn and Robin Blackburn, Thompson resigned from the board, and eventually cut off all association with *New Left Review*, citing a change in the journal's tone, and irreconcilable theoretical and political differences as among his reasons. 'The new Review', Thompson wrote, 'is not cultivating more carefully ground which was broken over-hastily in the past. It is simply evacuating old territory and pitching its tent elsewhere'.[69] Thompson signed off with a 15,000-word letter to the editors and the New Left Board, and a stinging rebuke in *Socialist Register*, which had been established by Saville and Miliband in the wake of the breakdown of the original *New Left Review*.[70] Although he removed himself from direct participation with the journal, he no more readily accepted other positions. For example, he rejected Lawrence Daly's appeal to 'Labour unity' in September 1963, believing that Daly should keep the Fife Socialist League going as an alternative to Labour.[71] Though disappointed by the failures of the New Left, Thompson did not believe that the Labour Party would solve anything much of importance, continuing to maintain the centrality of voluntary association from below evidenced in CND.

Edward and Dorothy Thompson, however, did join the Labour Party in 1962, primarily because of their association with Peter Shore (they had supported his election campaign in 1959), who was committed to nuclear disarmament and who had been an early supporter of CND. As Thompson later put it, he joined the Party 'without enthusiasm'.[72] His association with Raymond Williams' *May Day Manifesto* (hereafter *Manifesto*), a socialist critique of the Wilson Labour Government, revealed a better guide to his engagement with the Labour Party in the 1960s, however. He joined with Williams in editing *Manifesto* during 1967, often visiting Williams in his Cambridge rooms.[73] In a letter to Lawrence Daly, he explained the purpose of the Manifesto. It was designed, Thompson said, 'to inject a theoretical component into current argument and reappraisal', and he believed its 'strength is that it offers an overall connected analysis and it is tough

---

68. Ibid.

69. E.P. Thompson, 'Where Are We Now?', Unpublished Memo, 1962, DJS/109, University of Hull Archives, University of Hull.

70. E.P. Thompson 1965. See Newman 2002, pp. 113–26, on the early history of *Socialist Register*.

71. E.P. Thompson, 'Where Are We Now?', Unpublished Memo, 1962, DJS/109, University of Hull Archives, University of Hull.

72. See Bess 1994, p. 25.

73. Williams (ed.) 1968.

in some of the right places'.[74] 'The thing is', he went on, 'the Left is so incredibly fragmented and demoralized now that I welcome Raymond's initiative very much as an attempt to put things together – from someone who is outside some of the old rows'.[75] But, despite *Manifesto*'s promise, and despite its herculean attempt to make connections between politics, society, economy and international developments, the document failed to produce a coherent movement that could reform socialism 'beyond the fragments'.

In 1965, Thompson agreed to head-up the Centre for Social History at the recently established Warwick University (very much 'in the provinces'). It was a significant change of pace and direction for Thompson and also an indication, perhaps, of his assessment of socialism's contemporary doldrums. It also involved, the Thompsons' move from Halifax to Worcester, which enabled Dorothy Thompson to take up a (full-time) position at the University of Birmingham. Edward Thompson remained at Warwick for five years; the experience was among one of the leading spurs to an extraordinary historical output in the following decade or so. By the mid-1960s, his reputation as Britain's leading social historian had been established by *The Making of the English Working Class*, though this reputation was more likely to be recognised in the North American 'provinces' than in metropolitan England.[76] Research begun at Warwick would yield a number of influential historical essays, an edited book with former students on eighteenth century crime, and *Whigs and Hunters*, a book that mined the field of class-relations in the 1720s. Unlike *The Making of the English Working Class*, much of this was written with an academic audience in mind, though it was no less irreverent and oppositional for that. By the late 1970s, Thompson was master of two historical fields, and a social historian with a genuinely international reputation and range of influence.

But he was very much alienated from political activity during these years, despite his contribution to *Manifesto*, and no matter the extent of his growing reputation as a historian. Student radicalism left him cold, though he did defend student radicals at Warwick during 1970, joining with some to edit *Warwick University Ltd*.[77] His overall assessment of these years, however, was unambiguous. 'Expressive activity was raised above more rational and open political activity', he later said, 'and simultaneously a number of highly sophisticated Marxisms developed, particularly in Western Europe, which increasingly, it seemed to me, became theological in character – however sophisticated – and therefore broke

74. E.P. Thompson 1967.
75. Ibid.
76. Doug Hay, Bob Malcolmson, Barb and Cal Winslow, and Peter Linebaugh – all students of Thompson's at Warwick – were Canadian and American. Herbert Gutman, David Montgomery, and John Beattie were early visitors to Thompson's Centre, all came from North America.
77. E.P. Thompson (ed.) 1970.

with the Marxist tradition with which I had been associated'.[78] Much of his political activity in the 1970s would go into the attempt to highlight and defend what
he considered the 'humane restraints' in British society, from the 'rule of law' to
the jury system, from the National Health Service to the right to strike.[79] And
then in 1978 appeared his philippic against Althusser and British Althusserians,
'The Poverty of Theory', an essay testifying not only to his commitments as a
historian but as a historian concerned with the relationship between structure
and human agency above all. Thompson, however, would soon take leave of this
argument for what he considered a greater danger than Theory – the prospective
end of civilisation.

Thompson's return to anti-nuclear politics began with the resumption of old
fraternities. From an article in *New Left Review* grew a continent-wide movement,
European Nuclear Disarmament (END). 'In this movement', Eric Hobsbawm later
wrote, 'he [Thompson] was to occupy a position of extraordinary prominence,
somewhat analogous to that occupied by Bertrand Russell in the early stages of
the Campaign for Nuclear Disarmament (CND) after 1958'.[80] In one sense, END
was imbued with all the characteristic affirmatives associated with Thompson's
politics since 1956. In another sense, it brought about a widening of Thompson's connections, especially his international connections. For Thompson, END,
among other things, reaffirmed his belief that collective praxis revealed those
human potentials so often constrained, or worse, by power, bureaucracy and
capital. 'The art of the possible', Thompson wrote in 1971, 'can only be restrained
from engrossing the whole universe if the impossible can find ways of breaking
back into politics, again and again'.[81] By the early 1980s, nuclear war had become
a part of politics' 'art of the possible', and END was Thompson's way of breaking
back into politics in order to stop politics from ending the world.

But political activity had its costs – on Thompson's historical work, and, not
least, on Thompson himself. Between 1980 and 1985, in particular, Thompson's
time was completely given over to political activity as he crisscrossed the globe
with his message 'protest and survive'.[82] Others have claimed that it would be
no exaggeration to suggest that this intense period of engagement with 'exterminism', contributed to his early death in 1993.[83] After 1985, he returned to the
various historical projects that had been put aside in the cause of peace, including his Blake book, his book on the romantics and the long-overdue *Customs*

78. Merrill 1981, p. 10.
79. See, in particular, E.P. Thompson 1980a, pp. 39–48, 77–84.
80. Hobsbawm 1994, p. 527.
81. E.P. Thompson 1980a, p. 63.
82. E.P. Thompson 1980b.
83. Rattenbury 1997, pp. 12–3.

in Common. All these projects had their origins in the 1970s or earlier, and all were hampered by bouts of ill health.[84] He had lived with Blake and the romantics for a long time, and his analysis of eighteenth century English society went back to the unfinished business of *The Making of the English Working Class*. New projects, such as his work on Occam Sampson, were barely begun and would remain unfinished at his death. Though he did finish the book on Blake, and the book on his father's relation with Tagore, as well as a series of lectures based on his brother's war experience and *The Romantics* that appeared posthumously in 1994.[85]

'Much of the best in our intellectual culture', Thompson wrote, 'has always come, not from the Ancient Universities nor from the self-conscious metropolitan coteries, but from indistinct nether regions'.[86] Thompson never hid his affection for 'indistinct nether regions', and he always favoured 'provincials,' among them Tom Maguire, C. Wright Mills and Thomas McGrath, all of who opposed and objected to what Thompson would call, somewhat intemperately, 'intellectual metropolitomania'.[87] Thompson's sympathy for the provinces extended to include those fighting British imperialism, and to those Bandung powers that refused to take sides in the Cold War. Thompson also wrote history from 'in the provinces'. The sources that constituted *The Making of the English Working Class*, for example, came mostly from the West Riding not London, while the action of *Whigs and Hunters* occurred mainly in rural England. The moral economy that marked a break on political economy was founded outside metropolitan modes of thinking, in villages and labourer's fields. Not only did Thompson write and think from 'in the provinces', but he also thought (and often struggled) alongside and with those 'in the provinces' too.

III

'It is very easy for us,' Thompson wrote of the British, 'to fall into insular, parochial attitudes, and therefore necessary that we should commence any discussion of the future of socialism by reminding ourselves of the larger facts of our time'.[88] This sentence appears in the introduction to E.P. Thompson's 'Socialist Humanism: an Epistle to the Philistines', and among those facts he recalled was decolonisation and technological development leading to the prospect of human annihilation. Addressing British socialists, Thompson argued for 'the creative

---

84. E.P. Thompson 1987.
85. E.P. Thompson 1992; 1993; 1997a.
86. E.P. Thompson 1965, p. 332.
87. E.P. Thompson 1965, p. 330.
88. Thompson 1957b, p. 105.

part of man' as the key around which the revolutionary perspective of socialism turned, and, consequently, as the combination which had unlocked the mind forg'd manacles of Stalinism in Poland and Hungary. The essay portrayed communist dissidence – the movement it sought to illuminate and of which it was a part – as a revolt against anti-intellectualism, immorality and inhumanity in the name of the 'individual conscience', moral judgment and human agency.[89] Like many of Thompson's other early post-1956 writings, the essay championed a humanist socialism committed to 'respect for man,' moral values and 'the common weal'.[90] Thompson's essay proclaimed humanist socialism an international-ist desire. 'We must', Thompson characteristically suggested, 'do what we can to dismantle the Hydrogen bomb'.[91]

Thompson later lamented that he had written 'Socialist Humanism' too quickly.[92] The confusions of the article are obvious, (ideas are picked up and then dropped, and much of the argument fails, finally, to hang together), but there was arguably little time for some of these niceties in 1957, even though much of the essay's insights had been gathered through the writing of *William Morris*, and during 1956. 'Socialist Humanism' was, nonetheless, the product of intense political activity (Thompson would speak about its themes up and down the country, from the Sheffield Forum at Wortley Hall to the *Universities and Left Review* club in London); it was an immediate and precarious moment of international socialist dissent. The essay was supposed to capture – and be a record of – the moral and political revulsion felt among (some) communists fol-lowing Khrushchev's secret speech, and the Soviet invasion of Hungary. It was a product of dissident winds from the east, and equally of oppositional currents within the British labour-movement. It fit, albeit awkwardly, into its immediate political context. Thompson made an argument for the 'revolutionary perspec-tives of socialism' against both Stalinism (with which the essay was primarily pre-occupied), and those who believed that Stalinism was the true, if extreme, embodiment of communism.[93]

This is all to say that 'Socialist Humanism', as angry as many of its parts were, was a document that reaffirmed love as a central concept of politi-cal theory. 'Socialism is the expression of man's need for his fellow men, his undivided social being, and hence it must find expression in love'.[94] Human-ity's need for cooperative social relations would also find expression through

89. Thompson 1957b, pp. 106–7, 121.
90. Thompson 1957b, p. 106.
91. E.P. Thompson 1957b, p. 138.
92. E.P. Thompson Letter to Raphael Samuel, 1980, Samuel Papers, University of North London.
93. Thompson 1957b, p. 106.
94. Thompson 1957b, p. 128.

ideas and intellectual inquiry too. Thinking, Thompson claimed, could liberate humanity 'from victimhood to blind economic causation'.[95] If there was a chief enemy of socialist humanism, it was anti-intellectualism, a fox that Thompson would hunt throughout his life's work. 'Socialist Humanism' was a statement of international solidarity. On the one hand, Thompson appealed for solidarity between communist dissidence in the 'East' and anti-Stalinist socialism in the 'West' and, on the other, he argued that reform within communist societies was dependent upon the Cold War's termination.[96] Many of these concerns coalesced in the distinctive argument for a new 'socialist foreign policy', which appeared in *New Reasoner*.[97] In *New Reasoner*, Thompson would credit the gathering momentum of the anti-nuclear movement as an expression of 'a new internationalism, which is not that of the triumph of one camp over the other, but the dissolution of the camps and the triumph of the common people'.[98]

In 'Socialist Humanism', Thompson sought to 'make explicit the true, humanist content of "real" Communism'.[99] 'It is my contention', Thompson wrote, 'that the revolt within the international Communist movement against "Stalinism", will, if successful, confirm the revolutionary confidence of the founders of the socialist movement'.[100] Charles Taylor, for one, wondered whether it might be too late for all this. In his response to 'Socialist Humanism', Taylor argued that communism could not be so easily isolated from Stalinism. He also queried whether or not much of the inhumanity of Stalinism would not be found in the ambiguities of Marx. 'Marxist Communism', Taylor concluded, 'is at best an incomplete humanism'.[101] Elsewhere, and in response to much the same argument, Taylor suggested that Thompson was 'too quick' to reaffirm the humanism of communism, and not alert enough to the evidence which brought the two into conflict. Stalinism, Taylor reminded Thompson, was not an alien graft upon Marxism but one result of its development into a 'philosophy of practice'.[102]

These were good arguments, and Thompson admitted as much.[103] Taylor was surely correct about Marxism's connection with anti-humanism, and he was also right to count Stalinism as an 'unbridled voluntarism', against Thompson's emphasis on Stalinism's automatism and economic determinism.[104] Thompson

---

95. Thompson 1957b, p. 115.
96. Thompson 1958c, p. 106.
97. See *New Reasoner* 1958a, pp. 3–10; Thompson 1958b, pp. 49–51.
98. Thompson 1959a, p. 7.
99. Thompson 1957b, p. 120.
100. Ibid.
101. C. Taylor 1957b, p. 98.
102. C. Taylor 1957c, p. 19.
103. E.P. Thompson 1958c.
104. C. Taylor 1957b, p. 93.

was wont to think of Stalinists, like Godwinians, as 'disinterested rationalists' when it would be closer to the truth to name them 'interested irrationalists'. There might be good reasons to rebuke disinterested rationalism, though among them cannot be included the criminal history of Stalinism. Yet Thompson was right to call for a more complex view of recent communist history, against Taylor's elisions. It was no doubt Thompson's experience of the immediate communist tradition that helped form his view of 'positive neutralism', his critique of Stalinism and his support of anti-imperialist movements in Africa and Asia. All were central to Thompson's contributions to *Universities and Left Review* and *New Reasoner*.[105] 'This tradition [the communist tradition], the tradition of Morris and Mann, Fox and Caudwell, is also part of our own socialist tradition'.[106] In other words, if Thompson's humanism was valid – support for decolonisation and antagonism to both sides of the Cold War – then a good part of it derived from the communist tradition.

By early 1959, Thompson was recording the emergence of a New Left, and beginning to see his task, along with other editors of *New Reasoner* and *Universities and Left Review*, as the construction of a political movement committed to the 'principles of socialist internationalism' and 'the socialist vision of a society of equals within a co-operative community'.[107] This was a significant shift. *New Reasoner* was a journal of the 'democratic Communist opposition', even if it also provided the springs of a new socialism. *New Left Review*, on the other hand, was a merger between that tradition of communist dissent and a younger generation of socialists moved as much by *Culture and Society* and CND as the socialist humanism of Fox and Mann. Thus Thompson's contributions to early issues of *New Left Review* would be written in a different register and context, and under different pressures than his contributions to *New Reasoner* and *Universities and Left Review*. His early *New Left Review* articles were felt as contributions to the establishment of a political movement, not just as goads to a revaluation of socialist ideas.

This was true of Thompson's 'Revolution', published in 1960 as a conclusion to *Out of Apathy*. The essay sought to think a possible socialist transition that abjured traditional models of socialist change, and was a deliberate attempt to outline the strategic asymmetry between the New Left and its Left opponents. 'Revolution' rejected what Thompson called 'the fundamentalist model of socialist transition' without, however, fudging the nature of social transformation – the overthrow of capitalist relations of production and their replacement with

---

105. See Saville and Thompson 1958–9, pp. 1–11, for an example.
106. Thompson 1957b, p. 22.
107. Thompson 1959a, p. 6.

a society of equals.[108] 'It is the business of socialists', Thompson wrote, 'to draw the line...between the monopolists and the people – to foster the "societal instincts" and inhibit the acquisitive. Upon these positives, and not upon the debris of a smashed society, the socialist community must be built'.[109] Yet, while he repudiated the need to storm any winter palace, he also maintained that social democracy was an obstacle to social transformation. Thompson did not ignore the international dimension (that 'larger context of nuclear diplomacy and imperial retreat'),[110] and he recommended Britain's withdrawal from NATO and compared the possible consequences of such an action to that which had faced the British people in 1940. 'Events themselves would disclose to people the possibility of the socialist alternative; and if events were seconded by the agitation and initiatives of thousands of convinced socialists in every area of life', Thompson concluded, 'the socialist revolution would be carried through'.[111]

'Revolution' inspired much criticism.[112] Most of it, since it came from those hostile to the New Left, was beside the point. But some of the hostility was an immanent growth. Thompson accepted Charles Taylor's suggestion that his argument about British withdrawal from NATO was a means of readmitting the 'cataclysmic' model through the back door,[113] though he refused to retreat from his claim that withdrawal was a necessary condition of socialist advance.[114] 'Revolution' was baptised by others as 'utopian' and its argument as being removed from the real movement of 'classlessness'. Thompson rejected both claims, and argued they were joined by a common commitment to a static definition of class. Class, for Thompson, was historical and relational, the product of an 'ever-changing and never-static process in our political and cultural life in which human agency is entailed at every level'.[115] Nor did Thompson count 'affluence' a significant riposte to his argument.[116] Thompson was alert to the changing composition of the working-class, but he was not prepared to admit there was anything inevitable about classlessness. Since the factory-system had not produced Peterloo, it was the job of socialists, he suggested, to create a '*new* class-consciousness, consonant with reality'.[117]

---

108. E.P. Thompson 1960b, pp. 6–7.
109. E.P. Thompson 1960b, p. 8.
110. E.P. Thompson 1960b, p. 9.
111. Ibid.
112. Immediate responses – from Charles Taylor, Peter Marris, John Saville, and Sol Encel – to Thompson's article appeared in *NLR*, 4 (July–August 1960).
113. C. Taylor 1960, pp. 3–5.
114. E.P. Thompson 1960a, p. 18.
115. E.P. Thompson 1960a, p. 24.
116. See Hanson 1960, pp. 10–16, for this argument.
117. E.P. Thompson 1960a, p. 27.

These arguments remained inconclusive, largely untested by political practice. 'Defeats', as Thompson wrote in 1965, 'happen'.[118] Indeed, the arguments did not even remain on the page long, since a younger generation of New Left thinkers would swiftly confine them to socialism's archive. Indeed, part of re-establishing *New Left Review* after Hall's resignation, was the argument that the original New Left was politically and theoretically bankrupt. According to Anderson and Nairn who issued the charge, the original New Left, and Thompson in particular, had been infected with parochialism, that parasite which, they argued, repeatedly debilitated British socialism. Thompson's contributions to New Left thought, Anderson and Nairn judged, were tarnished by a *'messianic nationalism'*[119] and by an unproblematic conception of 'the people' consistent with an unhealthy populism. 'Instead of a systematic sociology of British capitalism', Anderson wrote in 1965, '[the New Left] tended to rely on a simplistic rhetoric in which the "common people", "ordinary men and women" were opposed to "interests", the "Establishment", etc. Described as "humanist"', Anderson concluded, 'the idiom [of the New Left] was, in fact, populist and pre-socialist'.[120]

Anderson's characterisation of Thompson's thought as nationalist was off track, as Anderson later admitted in *Arguments within English Marxism*. 'Thompson is absolutely entitled to claim', Anderson wrote there, 'the standard of socialist internationalism. The record of solidarity he cites [in *The Poverty of Theory*] – Yugoslavia, Bulgaria, Korea, Egypt, Cyprus, Algeria, Cuba, Vietnam, Chile – speaks for itself'.[121] Anderson's amended view of Thompson's sense of allegiance was not a simple reversal, however. He argued that Thompson had retained a commitment to the communist internationalism of the 1940s, which allowed a 'unique fusion of *international* and *national* causes on the Left'.[122] 'Unconditional devotion to the international goals of communism', Anderson continued, 'could be combined with intransigent leadership of the fight for national liberation from German occupation'.[123] This fusion could be counted as progressive in the case of Yugoslavia and Albania. It was more ambiguous in England, where, Anderson believed, 'far more traditional [nationalist] over-tones' were 'preserved' – and was presumably preserved in the internationalism of Thompson, too.[124]

In other words, Anderson's new view was less reformed than might appear at first sight. Anderson's recognition of Thompson's untarnished commitment

---

118. E.P. Thompson 1965, p. 348.
119. Anderson 1966, p. 35.
120. Anderson 1965, p. 17.
121. Anderson 1980, p. 141.
122. Anderson 1980, p. 142 (original emphasis).
123. Anderson 1980, pp. 142–3.
124. Anderson 1980, p. 143.

to socialist internationalism was uncontroversial, but his assessment of Thompson's 'Englishness' was less so. Thompson's 'Englishness' was certainly neither nationalist, nor gestural, Anderson's most recent view.[125] Rather, it was wrapped-up, at different moments, with certain historical and political contexts. Anderson himself noted the anti-Stalinist antecedents of Thompson's Englishness in *Arguments within English Marxism*, though not as cause for approbation.[126] Thompson's Englishness was, indeed, in part an anti-Stalinist reflex. 'Since the conditions of CP intellectual life discouraged controversy', Thompson wrote in 1962, 'the form which our "premature revisionism" took was to accentuate the "Englishness" of our preoccupations. One reason', he went on, 'some of us turned to the field of English history, sociology, and economics was in an effort to connect Marxist ideas with British contexts, and to humanize and make concrete the abstract schema of Communist orthodoxy'.[127] Thompson was also to talk of 'an excess [of] international preoccupation' on the British Left, and to suggest that his, and others',[128] accentuation of 'Englishness' was supposed to put a 'brake' on some of these preoccupations.

But Thompson also supposed his 'Englishness' compatible with what he described as 'the traditionally anti-imperialist stance of the labour movement, reinforced by the particular dedication of the Communist and ultra-left groups'.[129] He believed this was 'a deep and authentic tradition', and that it 'has existed not only as a moment of conscience, a protest: it has also been historically *effective*'.[130] This much *Arguments from English Marxism* could not accept. Anderson was also unable to merit Thompson's definition of internationalism, and he failed to explore the difference between Thompson's internationalism and that of *New Left Review* in the mid-1960s. Thompson believed that internationalism was constituted by a discourse or relationship between different peoples, one leading to 'reciprocal *action*,' and not 'intellectual abasement'.[131] 'If we allow the intellectual left here to become so transfixed by the overwhelming problems of the Third World that it ceases to be responsive to British realities', Thompson warned the new editors of *New Left Review*, 'then we may glide into a pharisaical self-isolation, which defeats our own intentions'.[132] For Thompson, in other words,

---

125. Anderson 2005, p. 185.
126. Nor did he note the potential, and in the case of Thompson, real, contradiction between anti-Stalinism and 'communist internationalism'.
127. E.P. Thompson, 'Where Are We Now?', Unpublished Memo, 1962, DJS/109, University of Hull Archives.
128. Ibid.
129. Ibid.
130. Ibid.
131. Ibid.
132. Ibid.

internationalism could lead to alienation from 'immediate solidarities', and the reduction of 'British realities' to parochialism, *pace* Anderson, was absurd.

In truth, Anderson and Nairn did not neglect what Thompson called 'British realities', even if they did lose contact with popular movements. Indeed, among the charges Thompson levelled at them in the course of his 'The Peculiarities of the English', his sometime-intemperate response to the Nairn-Anderson theses, was that they had lost this contact. 'The Peculiarities of the English' offered a rebuke to Nairn and Anderson's analysis of British history, but it also offered a qualified defence of the 'bourgeois-democratic tradition' and the 'English intellectual tradition'. In doing the latter, it is true, Thompson was prompted into 'gestures of Englishry', but he also wished, and this was far from a simple gesture, to make a point about socialist politics. 'England', Thompson wrote, 'is unlikely to capitulate before a Marxism which cannot at least engage in a dialogue in the English idiom'.[133] Though Thompson sometimes worked hard to obscure the point, there was nothing particularly *English* about the 'English idiom'. What Thompson was offering, more to the point, was a reaffirmation of Gramsci's thesis of cultural hegemony (that socialists must work in the culture they find and to some extent with that culture), something that Anderson, strangely enough, would second in his 'Problems of Socialist Strategy', written in the same year as 'The Peculiarities of the English'.[134]

There is a sense, however, in which Anderson and Nairn were vulnerable to Thompson's charge that *New Left Review* evaded 'British realities'. The analysis of British history found in the Nairn-Anderson theses was disembodied, assuming a formal, abstract relation to the subject under analysis. It was this sense of disembodiment that invited Thompson's indictment of evasion. Thompson's antipathy was also generated, no doubt, by the Nairn-Anderson theses' lack of 'affective attachment', manifest, above all Thompson believed, in Nairn's analysis of British labourism.[135] 'We should address ourselves as socialists to the context and people we find about us',[136] Thompson wrote in 'Socialist Humanism'. Scorn was a skewed form of address, he maintained, and attending to context and people was precisely what Nairn and Anderson had neglected to do. Thompson put the essential difference between himself and Anderson and Nairn, much later, in *Witness against the Beast*. Anderson and Nairn saw British history 'from without as a "spectacle"', while Thompson suffered British history as a native,

---

133. E.P. Thompson 1965, p. 337.
134. Anderson 1965a.
135. Nairn 1964a, pp. 38–65; Nairn 1964b, pp. 33–62.
136. E.P. Thompson 1957b, p. 140.

conceiving Britain's past as a 'unitary experience' rather than 'as a theatre of discrete episodes'.[137]

Yet a prospective view has its value, too. At other moments, Thompson could agree with Anderson and Nairn that Britain was a hostile culture, immune not just to theory, but ideas of any sort. Nothing should be taken from Thompson's alternative historical account of bourgeois revolution or British state and society, nor from his telling critique of the Nairn-Anderson theses at the level of concepts – class, agency, model – but none of this required Thompson's more than implied animus against Nairn and Anderson's awareness of the shortcomings of English culture. Anderson and Nairn left themselves vulnerable to Thompson's alternative, and more nuanced, account of British socialism and trade unionism, but their point that Britain's Left was far from anti-capitalist was, nonetheless, fair. Perhaps this judgment required the distance implied by the anthropologist's extra-territorial view.

At its best, 'The Peculiarities of the English' was an exercise in historical dialectics, capable of seeing Britain as *this* (supreme example of a social formation defined by imperialism and the profit motive) and *that* (limited achievement of democracy, trade-union rights, working-class power and civil liberties). At worst, and in some part only, it could read like a displaced and delayed critique of British communism. It is hard not to read Thompson's defence of British liberties in the light of 1956, since these had been at the forefront of his critique of the CPGB. However, this is where Thompson's critique of the Nairn-Anderson theses went off the polemical line. By suggesting that Anderson and Nairn, their Paris-derived idiom, their disregard for 'grand facts', were enemies of '1956', it was Thompson who had 'loosened emotional control'.[138] Thompson was more assured when defending aspects of the British intellectual tradition, and when he provided a defence of British labourism, based on an appeal to the control of historical context. But this did not require – in Thompson's words – '[minimising] their characteristic limitations'.[139]

If the charge of nationalism against Thompson misfired, Anderson's imputation of populism was closer to the target, though with a number of caveats. Responding to a similar argument of Nairn's in *The Break-Up of Britain*, Thompson entered a 'plain repudiation': 'At no time have I ever held up a banner of "populist socialism"'.[140] In *Arguments within English Marxism*, Anderson characterised his

---

137. E.P. Thompson 1992a, p. 190.
138. E.P. Thompson 1965, p. 312.
139. E.P. Thompson 1965, p. 331.
140. E.P. Thompson 1978, p. iii.

initial claim 'prejudicial', but he remained unconvinced that it was completely unfit.[141] Anderson was surely right about this. Indeed, Thompson himself would describe his New Left politics, as it appeared in 'Revolution' and 'Revolution Again!', as 'populist' in a letter sent to Anderson and others in 1962. Talking of a possible socialist transition in Britain, Thompson wrote that a younger generation of the New Left had lost 'the dialectic by which the rhetoric of "opportunity" and classlessness might prefigure the emergence of a new type of "class consciousness", in which it is not inconceivable that salaried, professional and wage-earning strata might discover a common sense of identity as between "the people" and as against isolated centres of financial power and "vested interests": i.e. a "populist" or Jeffersonian radical consciousness, but on a higher level, and within a context in which a socialist resolution alone is possible'.[142]

Populism is not an easy concept to hold steady. Like a freshly caught fish, it always seems to slip from the conceptual grip of political theorists.[143] Something of this ambiguity was no doubt registered in Thompson's use of the term 'populist'. He cannot have been unaware of the uses populism had been put during the 1930s and 1940s. Indeed, Thompson was well aware that even the 'good' populism of the war-years, whether British, Bulgarian or Yugoslavian had nationalist – and, in the case of Britain, imperialist – inflections. But this is no doubt why Thompson was critical of the 'Third World populism' of a younger generation of the New Left. Thompson not only pointed to the way 'populism' could be a means of 'diverting attention from internal contradictions',[144] but he also suggested that nationalism, no matter how progressive, must give way before socialist humanism. 'We have at one and the same time to see', he wrote, 'the great liberating impulses of the Soviet and Chinese revolutions, and of the emergent nationalisms of Asia and Africa; and to adopt a critical and at times uncompromising stand as to certain socialist principles and humanist values'.[145]

The Break-Up of Britain offered a different perspective on Thompson's so-called populism. Defining the 'Anglo-British state' as a 'non-populist structure', Nairn counted Thompson's historical work as part of a fresh 'left-nationalist popular culture', among whose branches could be included the History Workshop movement and Raymond Williams' 'Left-Leavisism'.[146] For Nairn, Thompson

---

141. Anderson 1980, p. 141.

142. Thompson, 'Where Are We Now?', Unpublished Memo, 1962, DJS/109, University of Hull Archives.

143. For recent attempts to catch it, see Canovan 2004; Laclau 2005.

144. E.P. Thompson, 'Where Are We Now?', Unpublished Memo, 1962, DJS/109, University of Hull Archives.

145. Ibid.

146. Nairn 1977, pp. 303–4.

and his populist-socialist comrades were akin to the intellectuals of the radical-nationalist movements of the nineteenth century, movements constituted by 'empiricism' and 'romantic excess'.[147] Although deemed 'progressive and generous' too, Thompson's 'cultural nationalism', according to Nairn, sought to recover and demonstrate, in a typically populist way, the agency and initiative of 'the folk'. This was a bizarre volte-face given the argument of the Nairn-Anderson theses, though there were certain continuities as well, not least the reduction of Thompson to a representative of Young England. However, in reality, by reducing Thompson to an intellectual of Britain's lost nationalist ark, Nairn had radically de-contextualised Thompson's work. The attempt to shunt Thompson's dissident communism into a holding, designated 'normal' historical development (that is, nationalist), was no more successful in *The Break-Up of Britain* than it had been in the original Nairn-Anderson theses.

There was nothing straightforward about Thompson's 'populism', if indeed this is what it should be named. Later, Thompson assented to a definition provided by Raymond Williams. 'To stay with the existing resources', Williams wrote, referring to the New Left, 'to live the contradictions and the options under pressure so that instead of denunciation or writing-off there was a chance of understanding them and tipping them the other way: if these things were populism, then it is as well that the British Left, including most Marxists, stayed with it'.[148] Thompson stayed with it too, but never at the cost of his commitment to socialist internationalism.

IV

Thompson remembered writing *The Making of the Working Class* through the years of the early New Left.[149] It was not written for an academic audience, as suited the time and Thompson's politics. It is perhaps now hard to remember, given the book's later influence, that many within the academy reacted with such hostility to its appearance. This was not just a Cold War reflex, but an anti-socialist reflex with a much longer history in Britain. Nonetheless, as much as Thompson crossed swords with academic sociology, the ideology of *Economic History Review* and the empiricism of a supposedly anti-ideology history tradition, the primary audience of *The Making of the English Working* were the New Left, adult-education students and political activists like Dorothy and Joe Greenald, to whom the book was dedicated. The popularity, and widespread influence, of

---

147. Nairn 1977, p. 304.
148. Williams 1980, pp. 241–2.
149. E.P. Thompson, Letter to Raphael Samuel, 1980, Samuel Papers, University of North London.

the book – it remains in print – perhaps speaks partly to these extra-academic origins.

'History', Thompson wrote in 'The Peculiarities of the English', 'does not become history until there is a model: at the moment at which the most elementary notion of causation, process, or cultural patterning, intrudes, then some model is assumed'.[150] To suggest that the model, which informed *The Making of the English Working Class*, was 'Marxism' would not be false, but hardly illuminating. As Thompson well knew by the early 1960s, there were many Marxisms, and he belonged to an imperilled tradition he dubbed 'creative Marxism'. This was Marxism, Thompson believed, fired by moral imagination, by respect for creativity, ideas and debate, and by a commitment to the recovery of human agency. A Marxism sensitive to values and human need too. Obviously, in this sense, the Marxism that had petrified, and petrified within, Communist Parties, whether in Eastern Europe or Britain, was among the book's targets. Another, surely, was the kind associated with *New Left Review* after 1962, a Marxism, at least Thompson believed, committed to 'system', and employing a static conception of class and a notion of class-struggle deprived of human agency. Important too, no doubt, as among the book's touchstones, were understandings of culture associated with the work of Raymond Williams, which Thompson had earlier engaged in *New Left Review*.[151] *The Making of the English Working Class* reiterated the point of Thompson's review of *The Long Revolution*, that culture was a matter of class-power and conflict and had nothing to do with consensus.

Indeed, according to *The Making of the English Working Class*, culture was those resources that 'the people' employed to understand, experience and, sometimes, struggle against the social and economic changes (another opposed culture) concomitant with the Industrial Revolution. Thompson argued that 'the changing productive relations and working conditions of the Industrial Revolution were imposed, not upon raw material, but upon the free-born Englishman – and the freeborn-born Englishman as Paine had left him or the Methodists had moulded him'.[152] Suspicious of authority, whether secular or other-worldly, steadfast in the protection of free speech, a free press and other civil liberties, the freeborn Englishman – a concept akin to Benedict Anderson's 'imagined community' – constituted a crucial cultural tradition, Thompson argued, by which 'the people' made over nineteenth century English social history. For Thompson, working-class consciousness was as much a matter of imperilled custom as the factory system or the steam engine. The historical lesson for English revolutionary socialists was clear: 'If the tree of Liberty was to grow, it must be grafted to

---

150. E.P. Thompson 1965, pp. 349–50.
151. E.P. Thompson 1961a, pp. 24–33; E.P. Thompson 1961b, pp. 34–9.
152. E.P. Thompson 1968, p. 213.

English stock'[153] – a lesson Thompson directed as much to the editors of *New Left Review* as to former comrades within the CPGB.

Thompson's illumination of the tradition of the freeborn Englishman whether in his histories or in his polemics, would soon be turned against him as evidence of his submission to dominant versions of the national tradition. However, *The Making of the English Working Class* demonstrated that the ideology of the freeborn Englishman was a contested 'cultural artifact', called upon by Church and King mobs *and* radical reformers.[154] Reform cast the tradition in a vision of the English past that flattered its political objectives by closing off opposed meanings of freedom and liberty. Just as Old Corruption had appropriated the language of patriotism during the Napoleonic Wars against the radical patriotism of English Jacobinism, so Reform used the same language against Old Corruption in debates over a free press and the vote.[155] But Thompson also demonstrated the limitations of this imagined community.[156] Luddites showed little regard for property. English Jacobins ignored the rights of Englishmen in their appeal to 'the rights of man'. Paine showed no respect for precedent or constitution. The cooperative mood that sponsored Owenism had little time for notions of sturdy individualism. Thompson's point, nonetheless, was that the tradition had informed modern socialism: 'the champion defending his individual rights passed imperceptibly into the free-born citizen challenging King and Ministers and claiming rights for which there was no precedent'.[157] As such, a socialism informed by long traditions of dissent, of self-autonomy and self-government, even rule of law, offered a rebuke to state socialism and to Cold War dismissals of socialism as akin to tyranny.

In *Arguments within English Marxism*, Anderson suggested that Thompson's book had received something like a warm response from *New Left Review* – 'the admiration and seriousness of its [*New Left Review*'s] approach to [Thompson's] book can scarcely by doubted'.[158] This was to play loose with the truth. Nairn's review of *The Making of the English Working Class* was surely ambivalent, at best. Nairn did refer to Thompson's 'great account of the origins of the English working class',[159] and he did celebrate the book's attention to 'the role of the working class as maker of history'.[160] However, Nairn's object was a complete repudiation of Thompson's argument. When he was not using the book's evidence to

---

153. E.P. Thompson 1968, p. 495.
154. E.P. Thompson 1968, p. 85.
155. E.P. Thompson 1968, p. 717.
156. E.P. Thompson 1968, p. 96.
157. E.P. Thompson 1968, p. 91.
158. Anderson 1980, p. 132.
159. Nairn 1964c, p. 48.
160. Nairn 1964c, p. 49.

reach conclusions antithetical to those of Thompson's, Nairn was referring to the English working class's lack of reason and 'corporative outlook' and the 'integration' of working-class consciousness 'into an entire system of false consciousness'.[161] As well, Nairn rejected those 'pre-industrial traditions' as worthless that Thompson had spent much of *The Making of the English Working Class* explicating. Nairn's reference to English provincialism, backwardness and traditionalism was also meant to bite, just as his reference to 'the immemorial rights of the "freeborn Englishman"' as a form of 'backward-looking traditionalism' was meant to cast Thompson's working-class as 'pathological'.[162]

Anderson's engagement with *The Making of the English Working Class* was more assured and less strident, and appeared much later than Nairn's. Though somewhat antiseptic, and though elusive about the book's immediate context, Anderson provided the most sustained engagement with the 'meta-historical concepts' – agency, experience, class – which underpinned Thompson's history. Much could be said about Anderson's account of these issues in *Arguments within English Marxism*, beginning with Anderson's characteristic concern with concepts. Perhaps of most importance, however, was his suggestion that Thompson had overlooked the nationalist inflections of English popular culture, those 'ideological bonds' that ensured the English working-class's subordination for much of the nineteenth and twentieth centuries.[163] The claim was at the heart of Anderson's critique of Thompson's thesis of historical agency, and was one part of a more general rebuke of Thompson's socialist politics.

Thompson returned to this issue in one of his final essays, a review of Linda Colley's *Britons*. There, Thompson admitted the persuasiveness of Colley's central claim that national sentiment played as great or even a greater role in the genesis of working-class identity as class-consciousness. Yet he also registered doubts about Colley's thesis, not least the degree to which *Britons* neglected the English working-class's conflicted allegiance. Beyond this, Thompson's question 'which Britons?' sums up much of his sense of unease with Colley's book.[164] Indeed, Thompson believed that Colley's argument concealed an alternative Britain. 'I cannot find one univocal nation of Britons',[165] he wrote. He suspected that Colley's resurrected Whiggism hid any expectation of conflict in the nineteenth century sources. 'There are times', he concluded, 'when the patriot must also be a revolutionary',[166] which points toward much of the evidence on which *The Making of the English Working Class* was based, and the sense, overlooked

---

161. Nairn 1964c, p. 54.
162. Nairn 1964c, p. 49.
163. Anderson 1980, p. 37.
164. E.P. Thompson 1994, pp. 319–29.
165. E.P. Thompson 1994, p. 326.
166. E.P. Thompson 1994, p. 329.

by Anderson no less than Colley, that patriotism was unlikely to have only one meaning.

Thompson's objections to *Britons* hardly constituted a complete response to Anderson's critique of *The Making of the English Working Class*, though they point in the direction that such a response might have taken. No doubt, Thompson would also have recalled the argument of *The Making of the English Working Class*, not least the distinction drawn there between 'the people' and the state. Figured in Cobbett's phrase as 'Old Corruption', the 'state system' in *The Making of the English Working Class* was rendered a 'parasitic complex' reliant upon the 'continental spy system' and the (sometime) exercise of coercion to secure consent.[167] The imprisonment of reformers, the suspension of *habeas corpus*, the events of Peterloo, the Combination Acts and the censorship of the radical press assured some incongruity between Old Corruption and 'the people'. Against this class-state, Thompson argued, people mobilised constitutional argument, generated mass meetings for Reform and sometimes took up arms. A parasitic state that alternately allied itself to capital and privilege, could hardly expect deference from the nation, as radicals understood it. Indeed, Thompson claimed, it was in figures like Paine, Cobbett and Hardy that 'the people' found 'those images of independence in which the freeborn Englishman delighted: a firm and dignified commoner, defying the powers of the state'.[168] In other words, with a 'thick' popular culture at their backs, 'the people' marshalled a democratic conception of the nation in their struggle against the arbitrary powers of the state.

This narrative was central to *The Making of the English Working Class*, and, in particular, to Thompson's contention that the Industrial Revolution was experienced as a catastrophic social process. 'The process of industrialization', Thompson wrote, 'was carried through with exceptional violence in Britain. It was unrelieved by a sense of national participation in communal effort, such as is found in countries undergoing a national revolution'.[169] This highlights a context of Thompson's book that Anderson and Nairn had overlooked – contemporaneous struggles for national liberation in the 'Third World'. Given the potency of the discourse of national liberation during the 1950s and early 1960s, it is hardly surprising that Thompson read nineteenth century English working-class history in this way. The book's 'Preface' pointed to this conjunction: 'the greater part of the world today is still undergoing problems of industrialisation, and the formation of democratic institutions, analogous in many ways

---

167. E.P. Thompson 1968, pp. 49–50.
168. E.P. Thompson 1968, p. 149.
169. E.P. Thompson 1968, p. 487.

to our own experience during the Industrial Revolution'. 'Causes which were lost in England', Thompson hoped, 'might, in Asia or Africa, yet be won'.[170]

This suggests that the historical process of decolonisation shaped *The Making of the English Working Class*. Thompson was not suggesting, *pace* the Eurocentrism of modernisation theory and some interpretations of Marxism, that the tricontinental world would inevitably follow the trajectory of Europe. He hoped, via struggle from below, that it would not. He was suggesting that there was nothing inevitable about industrialisation, and that the potentials of human agency were not restricted to Europeans. Thompson's warnings about the 'condescension of posterity' travelled easily across borders, to be picked up by historians from India to South Africa.[171] His warnings received such good reception in the world's 'nether regions' precisely because *The Making of the English Working Class* set its tone against those who would argue that 'modernity' was an inescapable unconscious process with a determined outcome, rather than something involving the active capacities of people. Experience, agency, class – no matter how contentious these terms, they would be invaluable to 'subaltern' historians recovering the pasts of peasants, women and the lower orders. 'India is not *an* important country but perhaps *the* most important country for the future of the world', he wrote sometime later. 'Here is a country that merits no one's condescension'.[172]

Thompson returned to themes of revolution and counter-revolution, and the part of patriotism or nationalism in both, in an essay on Wordsworth and Coleridge, published in 1969 as 'Disenchantment or Default? A Lay Sermon'.[173] Here, again, Thompson showed his awareness of nationalism's power to contain revolt, even if the essay's focus was England's former Jacobin intellectuals. The essay is a far less heroic account of the period between 1789 and the Reform Act of 1832 than *The Making of the English Working Class*. It charts not the making of working-class consciousness but the disenchantment and apostasy of poets, the defeat of 'large political affirmatives of humanism'.[174] Whereas in France the Revolution could be looked back on with 'national pride', Thompson wrote, in England the French Revolution recalled the defeat of 'fraternity or liberty or *égalité*'.[175] But Thompson refused to view the 1790s, despite the decade's shortcomings, 'as no more than a museum for the moralists', much as others considered the communism of the 1930s and 1940s. That meant recalling a 'love

---

170. E.P. Thompson 1968, p. 12.
171. See, for example, Chandavarkar 1997, pp. 177–96.
172. E.P. Thompson 1980a, p. 148.
173. E.P. Thompson 1997a, pp. 33–74.
174. E.P. Thompson 1997a, p. 70.
175. E.P. Thompson 1997a, p. 71.

of country' associated with 'universal visions' and 'egalitarian principles'.[176] He ended the essay by imagining Wordsworth in Lower Saxony in the winter of 1799, 'pitting himself against all inclination to thresh the grain of humanism from the chaff'.[177]

A different conclusion was reached in his essay on Thelwall, published posthumously in *Past and Present*.[178] There Thompson's view had hardened. Thelwall, Thompson concluded, 'stands as yet one more example of the hazards which descend upon reformers who allow their political hopes or strategies to become too much involved with the outcome of developments in other countries. We have seen sufficient examples of this in our own time'.[179] The sting in the tail of this conclusion is unnecessary to the subject that precedes it, however. It is all the more surprising from the pen of Thompson. Of course, it is easy to see how this conclusion fits with Thompson's assessment of *New Left Review*'s supposed uncritical support of 'Third World' nationalisms and a Marxism derived from the continent. It jars, however, when one remembers Thompson's own faith in socialist humanism in Hungary and Poland, and his belief that socialism in the West could advance only in the wake of communist reform in the East. It is a conclusion that not only forgets Wordsworth in Germany, but also Thompson in Yugoslavia.

In the 1970s, Thompson abandoned the nineteenth century, scene of revolution's making and unmaking, of government spies and Peterloo, for the supposedly more placid landscape of England's eighteenth century. It has now become common for historians to find evidence of national consciousness, perhaps even nationalism and nationhood, in just about every age, including England's eighteenth century. According to Liah Greenfeld, England was the 'model' nation, and English nationalism's origins would be found in the sixteenth and seventeenth centuries.[180] Indeed, for Greenfeld, long before the English Revolution, 'nationalism was the basis of people's identity, and it was no more possible at this point to stop thinking in national terms than to cease being oneself'.[181] Nairn had made much the same argument in *The Break-Up of Britain*, though he spoke of a failed English nationalism and a proto-type 'national' state that was weirdly, though necessarily, deformed.[182] Thompson found a different people in the eighteenth century, and an English society far removed from Greenfeld's vision of a 'one class society'.

---

176. E.P. Thompson 1997a, p. 70.
177. E.P. Thompson 1997a, p. 73.
178. E.P. Thompson 1994, pp. 156–217.
179. E.P. Thompson 1994, p. 217.
180. Greenfeld 1992.
181. Greenfeld 1992, p. 87.
182. Nairn 1977.

Thompson despised the modernisation theory, which has informed much nationalism theory in his time and ours. The historical sociology of Nairn or Gellner left Thompson cold, particularly its reduction of human agency to learning lessons and filling in forms. The inevitability of modernisation theory with all its various roads leading to something called 'modernity' was anathema to Thompson's historical consciousness. Opposed to the 'one class society' thesis of many eighteenth-century historians, Thompson would talk of 'antithetical cultures' constituting the 'field-of-force' of Georgian England. Writing of the eighteenth century's 'vigorous self-activating culture of the people', Thompson would suggest that '[this] culture . . . constitutes an ever-present threat to official descriptions of reality; given the sharp jostle of experience, the intrusion of "seditious" propagandists, the Church-and-King crowd can become Jacobin or Luddite, the loyal Tsarist navy can become an insurrectionary Bolshevik fleet'.[183]

The last was hardly possible in the eighteenth century, as Thompson well knew. Class-struggle-without-class was Thompson's characterisation of eighteenth century English society, a characterisation that implied no vision of 'affirmative rebellion'.[184] But rebellion in these historically constricted terms was not without sense. *The Making of the English Working Class* explained that the Industrial Revolution was not imposed on raw material, 'but upon the freeborn Englishman'.[185] Much of Thompson's eighteenth century studies reconstructed this culture of dissent, struggle and opposition, whether in terms of Blacks in Hampshire's forests, the writers of seditious letters, the moral economy of the crowd or the participants in rough music. Dissent did not exhibit the organisation or consciousness he, however, considered consonant with class. But this, according to Thompson, was no reason for describing Georgian England as a 'polite and commercial society', at least not only. Thompson did not deny the place of a reactionary patriotism in the actions of the common people.[186] Yet he was not convinced that this was always sincere, nor unmediated evidence of national loyalty.[187] The mind of the crowd owed more to popular consensus than nationalism, and was part of the folklore of 'the people' rather than the 'fakelore' of the nation.

The presence of class or class-struggle is, of course, no barrier to the growth of national sentiment, even nationalism. Thompson's eighteenth century studies were not *directly* concerned with the relationship between class and national identity, principally because this was not an issue of the historiography when

183. E.P. Thompson 1978, p. 164.
184. E.P. Thompson 1974, p. 388.
185. E.P. Thompson 1968, p. 213.
186. E.P. Thompson 1978, p. 140.
187. The ruling class's means of cultural hegemony in the eighteenth century, according to Thompson, was law rather than national sentiment.

Thompson was writing in the 1970s. Indeed, it is not altogether clear how Thompson's concerns with gentry-pleb relations, with crime and the law or with popular riot – the principal issues dealt with in *Whigs and Hunters* and what became *Customs in Common* – might have fit or complicated a vision of English nationalism's birth in Georgian England or earlier. One thing for certain, however, would have been Thompson's discontent with accounts of English national identity's past in terms of consensus, and the characteristic teleological reduction of identity to any one thing. Thompson found in the eighteenth century evidence, not just of class-struggle but also of a different human nature. This human nature was neither 'traditional' nor 'modern', but an eventuality that Thompson believed could be found in the struggle for use-rights, in the moral economy of the crowd, and in resistance to enclosure. As Thompson suggested at the beginning of *Customs in Common*, this was a human nature constituted by 'alternative needs, expectations and codes'.[188] Forged 'in the provinces', this human nature had yet to describe itself in market terms or in the metropolitan terms of belligerent hostility, always partly constitutive of nationalism.

V

Thompson repeatedly referenced 'democratic liberties' in his skirmish with communist theory and practice. The 'British democratic tradition' was much on Thompson's mind following Khrushchev's 'secret speech', and he was awkward enough to remind the Communist hierarchy the extent to which their thoughts and actions constituted the antithesis of Britain's working-class history.[189] 'Bourgeois democracy', he complained to one correspondent in 1956, 'is a different thing altogether from [those] definite democratic rights and liberties – right to publish, right to organize, rights at law etc'.[190] These things were not delivered by any ruling class, Thompson argued, but wrested from them; 'in fact the British working class have proved on a hundred occasions that they consider intellectual liberty to be their own concern. Many hundreds of labourers were imprisoned, in the time of Bunyan and before, for liberty of conscience'.[191] The CPGB, he concluded to his correspondent, was not just an enemy of democracy and civil liberties but of the British working class, too.

---

188. E.P. Thompson 1992, p. 15.
189. E.P. Thompson, Letter to James Klugman, May, 1956, CP/IND/KLUG/01/06, Communist Party Archives, Labour History Centre, Manchester.
190. E.P. Thompson, Letter to Joan Maitland, 1956, CP/CENT/ORG/18/05, Communist Party of Great Britain Archives, Labour History Centre, Manchester.
191. Ibid.

Thompson returned to questions of civil liberties in the 1970s, this time under the shadow of what he considered Britain's increasing 'statism'. The state's galloping authoritarianism, Thompson believed, was instanced by increased police powers, the elimination of checks on government prerogative, and political and judicial attacks on the jury system. His interest in the 'rule of law' was longstanding, but that interest had been deepened by historical investigation. Indeed, the final chapter of *Whigs and Hunters* anticipates many of Thompson's political concerns in the late 1970s. Although in part mystification designed to shore up ruling class power, and although in part rhetoric which secured ruling class hegemony, the 'rule of law', *Whigs and Hunters* concluded, was also an 'unqualified human good'.[192] The law was not simply a mask, and was not just a sham. It was also, Thompson claimed, a constraint on ruling class power and thus a 'forum' of class conflict.

Thompson's polemical writings on 'law and order' in the late 1970s – which through the auspices of *New Society* reached a wide readership – telescoped his long-standing antipathy toward the British state and the British ruling class. In a series of articles, Thompson protested increased police power without democratic control as evidence of 'statism'; criticised attacks on the jury system as attacks on justice and democracy; defended civil liberties against those who would reduce them to 'bourgeois democracy' or would deny them in support of national security; bemoaned the reduction (or sometimes plain absence) of Parliament's power; and lamented the press's subordination to the police and the security services. His attack on the 'law and order brigade' was no less oppositional.[193] In combination with the state's 'unaccountable administrative rule', the 'law and order brigade' augured not just a new era of relations between 'the people' and 'the law', Thompson argued, but something akin to a new 'national identity' or 'political culture'.[194] 'Take the jury away', Thompson wrote, 'and I would face a crisis of identity. I would no longer know who the British people are'.[195]

Thompson did not just offer a series of refusals and oppositions. He defended the jury system, for example, because he believed that it was 'the last place in our institutions where the people – *any* people – take a hand in "administering" themselves'.[196] While he took issue with the 'law and order brigade', because it was they, he counter-claimed, who were destroying the law and promoting social disorder. These reasons were underpinned by the distinction which Thompson

---

192. E.P. Thompson 1975, p. 267.
193. E.P. Thompson 1980a, pp. 238–9.
194. E.P. Thompson 1980a, pp. 246–7.
195. E.P. Thompson 1980a, pp. 235–6.
196. E.P. Thompson 1980a, p. 109.

drew between 'civil liberties' and 'statism', between the tradition of the 'free-born Englishman' and authoritarianism. Thompson offered a vision of an alternative country, an imagined community rooted in a conception of rights as the common inheritance of all. He envisioned a sense of national identity based upon a certain political culture – a political culture where the rights of the state or the national interest gave way before the 'civil rights of the "freeborn Englishman"', and where the 'nation's rulers' were subject, at all times and in all contexts, to 'rule of law'.[197]

Anderson celebrated Thompson's essays on law and order as 'perhaps the most effective *political intervention* by any socialist writer in England in many years'.[198] However, he also refused certain of Thompson's conclusions. Anderson questioned, in particular, Thompson's interpretation of parliament, and parliament's supposed subordination to the needs of the 'secret state'. 'The English Parliament is not a bastion of civil liberties against the state, temporarily deactivated, but an essential and integral part of the British capitalist state'.[199] Here, Anderson seemed to be suggesting that civil liberties were incompatible with a parliament subordinate to capital, a suggestion that seems to mock the historical record and condemn any struggle for civil liberties under existing conditions. Anderson might have been right to question Thompson's sometime-abstracted conception of 'rule of law', but he was on less secure ground when he argued that civil liberties could only be the product of an overall socialist programme.[200] Thompson would have considered that argument an admission of political quietism.

Anderson was on safer ground when he alluded to the potential problems socialists faced in defending a negative conception of liberty, in a context where conservatism itself was vociferously 'anti-statist'. Thatcherism had its own conception of the 'freeborn Englishman' and was precisely concerned – in rhetoric if not future practice – with (selectively) asserting 'the people's' freedoms against a supposedly bloated state. Anderson did not suggest, however, that Thompson's defence of civil liberties could be elided with Thatcher's assertion of the inherent rights of individual entrepreneurship. His point was that absent the framework of socialist struggle Thompson's libertarianism risked assimilation to 'liberal politics'.[201] 'The full potential of the political issues of democracy raised by Thompson', Anderson wrote, 'can only be realized by persistent and public demonstration of their convergence in socialism'.[202] Thompson might have

---

197. See, in particular, E.P. Thompson 1980a, pp. 153, 178.
198. Anderson 1980, p. 201.
199. Anderson 1980, p. 204.
200. Anderson 1980, pp. 200, 204.
201. Anderson 1980, p. 205.
202. Ibid.

agreed. However, he would have added that conservatism's anti-statism was spurious (this was his position during the course of the so-called Second Cold War), and that Thatcher's attempt to attach a meaning to 'liberty' made it all the more necessary for socialists to offer their own.

Somewhat surprisingly, Anderson only hinted at the potential populism that underlined Thompson's distinction between 'the people' and 'the state'.[203] Thompson's supposed populism was a concern of Stuart Hall's though. Hall disliked Thompson's continued rhetorical gesture toward the tradition of 'freeborn Englishmen', and he found Thompson's use of 'the people' to be innocent at best, mendacious at worst. For Hall, there was 'no fixed content to the category of "popular culture", so there is no fixed subject to attach to it – "the people". "The people" are not always back there, where they have always been, their culture untouched, their liberties and their instincts untouched...'.[204] After all, who were the 'law and order brigade' if not some part of 'the people'? One response to this would be to suggest that Thompson had never argued that any fixed content attached to 'the people', and that his political intervention over 'law and order' was precisely about trying to fix a content to that rhetorical figure which favoured civil liberties. Thompson held no romantic expectations about the inherent 'goodness' of 'the people', even if he was not willing to automatically cast them in the role of the devil.

Civil liberties constituted the main concern of Thompson's political interventions in the 1970s, but they were not his only concern, not even his only main concern. Indeed, Thompson fought on what he believed were two, though related, fronts in the 1970s – against what he claimed was the anti-democratic core of the British political elite, on the one hand, and against certain intellectual tendencies within the British Left, on the other. In the latter case his chief target was the Marxist structuralism of Louis Althusser, which he judged ahistorical, a solvent of socialism's identification with human agency and the moral imagination. Thompson's war against structuralism can be dated as early as his 'Open Letter to Leszek Kolakowski', and was resumed in the conclusion to *Whigs and Hunters*.[205] However, the mature form of Thompson's argument with Althusser and Marxist structuralism appeared in his essay, 'The Poverty of Theory', published together with a series of Thompson's other political and historical interventions in 1978.

'The Poverty of Theory' is among Thompson's most controversial writings. Because of that controversy, it is worth dispatching some less than illuminating clichés that have settled around the essay at the beginning. First, 'The Poverty

---

203. Anderson 1980, pp. 202, 204.
204. Hall 1981, p. 239.
205. E.P. Thompson 1978, p. 352; E.P. Thompson 1975, p. 258.

of Theory' does not constitute an argument against theory *tout court*. In fact, Thompson patiently draws attention to the value and necessity of theory, in both historical investigation and political practice.[206] Second, in no way did Thompson neglect the importance of an analysis of structures, either in the past or the present. Just as he rejected empiricism, though defended the need for empirical study, so he rejected structuralism while asserting the necessity of coming to terms with what he called 'structural actuation'.[207] Finally, Thompson's dismissal of Althusser's Marxist structuralism did not constitute some sort of knee-jerk (typically English) ideational xenophobia. There is no evidence for this reading. Thompson may have considered the work of Althusser and Balibar nonsense – and nonsense because it was ahistorical, and *not* because it was French – but this was not his judgment of the work of Giambattista Vico, Sebastiano Timpanaro (another contemporary critic of Althusser's), Maurice Godlier, Karl Korsch and Walter Benjamin.

Others have wondered at the useless 'violence' of Thompson's attack on structuralist Marxism. From another angle, and given that Thompson had long defended the actuality of human agency, the importance of subjectivity in history, and the centrality of the moral imagination (humanism) to any socialist project, it is no surprise he reacted with such vehemence against structuralism's own 'violence' against these things. Others have suggested that Thompson's response was disproportionate to the actual influence of Althusser's structuralism, or that Thompson's *animus* was out of season because structuralism had already entered the winter of its discontent. However, Althusser's structuralism did exert an influence on socialist history (Gareth Stedman Jones), socialist political theory (Barry Hindess and Paul Hirst), Marxist literary criticism (Terry Eagleton), and it had a favoured orbit within the Birmingham Centre for Cultural Studies (from Richard Johnson to Stuart Hall), too.[208] It is true that, in retrospect, debates over Althusser appear a storm in an academic teacup, since most of these thinkers from Stedman Jones to Hall would (eventually) turn their backs on structuralist Marxism. But structuralism's denouement was hardly obvious in 1978. And, given that Althusser was a stepping-stone on which a significant number of intellectuals rested on their way to 'postmodernism', it is perhaps arguable that the essay retains more than merely historical interest.

In any case, Thompson's particular argument against Althusser's structuralism was not the most important aspect of his overall purpose in 'The Poverty of

---

206. E.P. Thompson 1978, p. 19.
207. E.P. Thompson 1978, pp. 98, 110.
208. Hindess and Hirst 1975; Eagleton 1976; Johnson 1978, pp. 79–100; Stedman Jones 1979.

Theory'. A good deal of it, with whatever extent of success, was devoted to an explication of the historian's craft. Here, Thompson can be taxed on many points, but not that he was some sort of theory-blind empiricist. Some part of his essay was also given over to an explanation of the manifest gap 'between intellectuality and practical experience (both in real political movements, and in the actual segregation imposed by contemporary intellectual structures)'.[209] Thompson's response to this 'grand fact' might have been inadequate, but some gain was nonetheless registered in his suggestion that 'thought' abstracted from 'reality' presented all sorts of problems. Perhaps even more important – and here one finds an echo of the argument of 'The Peculiarities of the English' – Thompson sought to remind his readers that knowledge was not only produced in Paris (or London for that matter). The argument is subtle and can easily be mistaken for a defence of parochialism. However, it speaks to Thompson's respect for a certain kind of knowledge, manifest in his attack on modernisation theory and Althusser's theoretical practice. This, it should go without saying, had nothing to do with any sort of anti-intellectualism or activist populism.

There were, nonetheless, a series of rocky moments in 'The Poverty of Theory'. Most treacherous of all was Thompson's suggestion that structuralist Marxism was identifiable as Stalinism 'theorized as ideology',[210] an argument which Anderson scored a number of points against in *Arguments within English Marxism*.[211] More than this, Thompson's association of Stalinism with abstraction undermined his discussion of the theory/practice nexus, since Stalinism, whatever else might be said about it, had been a form of political practice. Thompson was also wrong to equate Stalinism with determinism and Godwinism, for reasons already explained. Where Thompson was on more solid ground among these pitfalls was his recognition that Marxism – at least in Britain, and soon to be the case in Europe as a whole – no longer retained any meaningful relationship with a mass political movement. Marxism might become more sophisticated, Thompson suggested, but it was unlikely to become more relevant, especially now its highlights were books like *Reading Capital*. The continuing relevance of 'The Poverty of Theory' is not so much as an illumination of the absurdities of Britain's Althusserian moment, though it is that too, but as a eulogy for Marx*ism*.

Perry Anderson was right to see *New Left Review* as one target of 'The Poverty of Theory', and right, in response, to take the measure of Thompson's thought rather than Althusser's. Specifically, Anderson rejected Thompson's reading of Marx, claiming, with some justice, that the '*Grundrisse* and *Capital* are in no

---

209. E.P. Thompson 1978, p. 3.
210. E.P. Thompson 1978, p. 182.
211. Anderson 1980, pp. 116–30.

sense mere works of an "anti-political economy"'.[212] It is true that Thompson could often be too dismissive of economics, as though the problem with capitalism were the fact that it produced steel rather than poetry. Anderson was also right to raise a number of questions about Thompson's understanding of experience and agency and class. 'The Poverty of Theory' was a failed example of the sociology of ideas too, characterised by a clumsy notion of historical context and attended by a narrow range of reference uncommon in Thompson's work (compare Thompson's discussion of Caudwell written almost at the same time).[213]

Hall was equally critical. At a 1979 *History Workshop* conference, which provided an epilogue – often described as 'dark' – to debates surrounding 'The Poverty of Theory', Hall argued that Thompson had overlooked the theoretical advances associated with Althusser's thought.[214] But these advances could have been found elsewhere, as Thompson demonstrated. Hall also drew attention to convergences between Althusser and Thompson – relative autonomy, a rejection of economism and a refusal of reductionism – and contrasted this potential convergence with Thompson's polemical binaries.[215] Thompson's point, however, were that these uncontroversial concepts had no meaning unless they could be demonstrated in historical practice, something that Althusser had not done and could not do. Like Anderson, Hall engaged problems associated with Thompson's conception of experience and what Hall considered an illicit reduction of Marxism to 'History'. These points were well made. However, less appropriate was Hall's suggestion that 'The Poverty of Theory' neglected important issues of both 'theory and politics, today',[216] especially the question of the 'populist socialism' associated with 'people's history'. Hall erred here, since 'The Poverty of Theory' had argued that socialism was 'guaranteed by NOTHING'.[217] Soon, Hall would make 'Marxism without guarantees' his intellectual banner.

Much of the tension between Thompson and Anderson, and between Thompson and Hall were hangovers from the early 1960s. Thompson, with some justice, was irked by the association of his work to 'culturalism', especially given his critique of the 'culturalism' of Williams and Hall in the nascent years of the New Left. Hall, for his part, was still critical of what he believed was Thompson's uncritical invocation of the tradition of the 'freeborn Englishman', something that not only derived from the argument of *Policing the Crisis* but also from Hall's critique of the New Left's conception of 'working-class community'. Central to Hall's argument in both places was the question of the meaning attached to 'the

---

212. Anderson 1980, p. 63.
213. For Thompson's essay on Caudwell, see E.P. Thompson 1977.
214. Hall 1981, p. 379.
215. Hall 1981, p. 382.
216. Hall 1981, p. 385.
217. E.P. Thompson 1978, p. 171.

people', and whether the endorsement of any identity from Britain's past was adequate to the multicultural society that Britain had become. Anderson sought to defend *New Left Review*'s record from the 1960s onwards. He also sought to defend a certain form of intellectual practice – detached, scholarly, political, at constant contest with the inadequacies of British socialism, past and present. Thompson, for his part, remained unrepentant. He refused Hall's charges, and later referred to the contest between himself and Anderson as a draw.[218]

Its shortcomings aside, the final word on 'The Poverty of Theory' perhaps belongs less to Anderson or Hall, than to a theme of Thompson's essay on Caudwell, written shortly before his critique of Althusserian Marxism. What was living in Caudwell's thought, Thompson claimed, was his avowal of *dialectical* materialism (the constant to and fro of 'being' and 'consciousness') against mechanical materialism and idealism, his attempt, though not without ambiguity, to hold in one hand 'brute nature' and 'active subjectivity'.[219] At its best, Caudwell's purpose or ambition – like that of 'The Poverty of Theory' – was to demonstrate the tension, imbrication and mutual interaction between social being and social consciousness, and to illuminate, also, 'a way of seeing coincident and opposed potentialities within a single "moment" and of following through the contradictory logic of ideological process'.[220] This was a view of political reality that Thompson believed was absent among the Althusserians. Absent, too, among the Althusserians was an awareness that knowledge could be made 'outside the academic procedures'.[221]

VI

'Civil liberties and 250 Cruise missiles cannot coexist in this island together',[222] Thompson wrote in 'The State of the Nation'. This was a premonition of Thompson's primary concerns throughout the 1980s – the proliferation of nuclear weapons and the relationship between militarism and democracy. The hope was that a Europe-wide peace movement, and the termination of superpower confrontation, would usher in a new (Left) politics, with the self-determination of societies as its first premise.[223] That was the wager that Thompson invested in European Nuclear Disarmament (END). Alongside his peace activism, Thompson produced a raft of anti-war writings that limned the present danger of human

---

218. E.P. Thompson 1981, pp. 396–408; E.P. Thompson 1994, p. 360.
219. E.P. Thompson 1977, p. 241.
220. E.P. Thompson 1977, p. 238.
221. E.P. Thompson 1978, p. 8.
222. E.P. Thompson 1980a, p. 250.
223. See, for example, E.P. Thompson 1985, p. 117.

extermination and the hope that extermination could be avoided by popular activity against nuclear weapons from below. The primary intent, and indeed virtue, of these writings was to demonstrate that the peace movement had a mind.

'Exterminism: The Last Stage of Civilisation' was Thompson's initial attempt to comprehend the deep structure of the Cold War. Neither an explanation of the Cold War's origins nor a means to apportion sin to one side or the other, the concept was employed to grasp the 'inertial thrust',[224] the superpowers' nuclear-weapons systems. For Thompson, exterminism explained the Cold War as 'an irrational condition'.[225] Indeed, when viewed through the 'exterminist' lens, the Cold War, Thompson claimed, would be understood as an 'addiction' and 'a self-reproducing system'.[226] Mode of production, class-struggle, and imperialism – the traditional concepts of Marxist analysis – were not adequate to the task of explaining either the irrationality or reciprocity of the nuclear arms race. The Cold War, according to Thompson's exterminism thesis, was fixed in ideology and bureaucracy, whose primary consequence was the 'militarization' of politics.[227] But it was not ideological and bureaucratic alone. It had an institutional basis in 'the weapons-system, and the entire economic, scientific, political and ideological support-system...the social system which researches it, "chooses" it, produces it, polices it, justifies it, and maintains it in being'.[228]

Whatever determinist tendency might be spied in 'exterminism', Thompson's words and actions pointed in another direction. He considered only a 'truly internationalist movement against the armourers of both blocs' an appropriate countervailing force to exterminism.[229] END was established in 1980, and Thompson considered the emerging anti-war movement as the wellspring of a third force in international politics.[230] He imagined END as a political link between anti-war activists in the West and communist dissidents in the East, at the same time that he hoped it would forge 'alliances with existing, anti-imperialist and national liberation movements in every part of the world'.[231] Thompson's vision of END recalled not just the internationalism of the New Left, but also the 'spirit of Europe' that informed anti-fascist struggle in the 1940s. By the mid-1980s this was no utopian expectation. 'For the first time since the wartime Resistance',

---

224. E.P. Thompson 1980c.
225. E.P. Thompson 1985, p. 56.
226. E.P. Thompson 1982, p. 56.
227. E.P. Thompson 1980c, pp. 6–7.
228. E.P. Thompson 1980c, p. 7.
229. E.P. Thompson 1980c, p. 26.
230. See E.P. Thompson 1982, pp. xv–xxii, for a brief account of the beginnings of END.
231. E.P. Thompson 1982, p. 74.

Thompson wrote, 'there is a spirit abroad in Europe which carries a transcontinental aspiration'.[232]

The word 'exterminism' proved a distraction, and Thompson perhaps came to regret it. Exterminism, however, did have a rhetorical effect, and perhaps a theoretical and political one too. The term skirted blame and was meant to show up – and this unusual in Thompson's oeuvre – an 'accumulating logic of process' which occurred beyond human intention.[233] The contrast was deliberate. Exterminism, Thompson believed, demonstrated the length that separated technology and ideology from reason. There was a zeal, almost evangelical, invested in the concept because Thompson wished to make plain much that had been obscured, whether by the 'immobilism' of the Marxist Left or the militarism of the Right.[234] In this sense, Raymond Williams' claim that exterminism was a species of determinism was beside the point.[235] Nuclear weapons put human agency in the shadow of their menace, and 'exterminism' was intended to show how. But Thompson also believed that 'exterminism' was a product of its time and had been proved wrong – his wager – not so much by intellectual argument as by the actions of the Europe-wide peace-movement.[236]

In any case, Thompson had a potentially more interesting, if more conventional, explanation for the rigid grooves of Cold War rivalry: nationalism. 'Patriotism', Thompson explained, 'is love of one's own country; but it is also hatred or fear or suspicion of others'.[237] Hatred and fear of the Other, he believed, explained the Cold War's dark heart, a belief no doubt coloured by the appearance of a revenant – he called it 'atavistic' – nationalism in Thatcher's Britain.[238] Hatred of the Other in both 'capitalist' America and 'socialist' Russia secured the bonding that Thompson believed constituted a 'necessary part of the human condition'.[239] But whereas bonding could inspire genuine love, the bonding characteristic of either side to the Cold War inspired fear alone. 'The threat of the Other', Thompson believed, 'legitimates every measure of policing or intellectual control'.[240] In Thompson's use, nationalism explained the Cold War in terms of ideology, provided a rationale for how the Cold War could escalate to a moment where human extinction became 'reasonable', and illuminated its reciprocal logic in terms of the anatomy of human need, no matter how deformed.

---

232. E.P. Thompson 1982, p. 177.
233. E.P. Thompson 1980c, p. 17.
234. E.P. Thompson 1980c; E.P. Thompson 1992, p. 12.
235. Williams 1980, pp. 25–6.
236. E.P. Thompson 1982, p. 135.
237. E.P. Thompson 1982, p. 171; see also p. 39.
238. See E.P. Thompson 1982, pp. 189–96.
239. E.P. Thompson 1982, p. 170.
240. E.P. Thompson 1982, p. 173.

At times, nonetheless, we seem to slosh around among the 'isms' without getting much closer to either the Cold War's origins or – Thompson's purpose – its contemporary nature. This might be unsurprising in a series of polemics against an immediate threat. In another sense, we might wonder what it was about nationalism that was adequate to explain superpower rivalry that was lacking in the concept of imperialism. Perhaps even more unlikely was Thompson's claim that only internationalism could repair the damage wrought by nationalism, a claim that overlooked the historic affective imbalance between national sentiment and international fraternity. At one point, Thompson argued that only internationalism could defeat the nationalist demagoguery that underlined Cold War divisions.[241] But this skirted Raymond Williams' suggestion that bonds of internationalism were too 'thin' to provide an adequate affective response to the 'thick' ties of nationalism. In some moods, Thompson could agree with this. For example, writing in the wake of Lebanon and the Falklands War, Thompson could wonder at the 'slender' 'cultural and political defences against the surge of nationalism'.[242]

Perry Anderson also raised questions about Thompson's interpretation of the Cold War. Like Thompson, Anderson rejected the idea of co-responsibility for the Cold War, arguing that an aggressive anti-socialist American foreign policy was at the origin of international enmity. However, unlike Thompson, Anderson believed that origins mattered. Thompson was wont to consider origins, *in the context of stopping the Cold War*, beside the point. Anderson disagreed.[243] He disagreed because he believed that explication of the Cold War's origins revealed 'a conflict founded on the ceaseless determination of major capitalist states to stifle every attempt to build socialism ... and the deformities the resistance to it has wrought within them'.[244] As at its genesis, so in its present, the Cold War, according to Anderson, was a form of global class-struggle. When viewed through this Marxist lens, he contested, superpower rivalry was no less explicable than any other historical process, and required no reliance on the 'isomorphism' of equivalence. Anderson also differed from Thompson in his interpretation of the Soviet Union.[245] A commitment to the October Revolution as a historic break with international capital remained, at least at this time, a feature of Anderson's socialism, no less than his explanation of the Cold War.

If there was disagreement among New Left thinkers about the Cold War's nature, there was no less contest surrounding its end. The peace-movement,

---

241. E.P. Thompson 1982, p. 41.
242. See E.P. Thompson 1982.
243. See Anderson 1982, pp. vii–xii.
244. Anderson 1982, pp. 95–6.
245. Anderson 1983.

according to Thompson, had played an important role in breaking down the ideological barricades that sustained the Cold War. 'I have argued', Thompson wrote, 'that it was the non-aligned peace movement in the West entering into dialogue and certain common actions with the human-rights movement in the East which gave rise to the "ideological moment" when the Cold War lock was broken'.[246] Anderson rejected Thompson's interpretation. He highlighted military and economic imbalance between the two superpowers (something Thompson hardly denied), and explained the Cold War's termination in terms of the Soviet Union's economic and ideological exhaustion. Where Thompson believed the end of the Cold War opened up the potential for a third force in European politics, Anderson believed that its termination represented the unambiguous victory of capital.

Thompson stuck to his guns – about the meaning of the Cold War, about the peace movement's role in bringing it to an end, and about the importance of new social movements to the reinvigoration of Left politics, a point on which Williams agreed, but Anderson remained unrepentant. No doubt, much of the dispute hinged on Thompson's understanding of ideas, and Anderson's new found political realism. Thompson believed that a conclusion like that of Anderson's encouraged 'immobilism'.[247] He believed that *New Left Review* had been consistently struck dumb by ' "two-camps" thinking'.[248] Suffering no illusions about the kind of politics filling the political vacuum in Eastern Europe, Thompson argued that the Left should be offering an 'alternative internationalist script or affirmative values' to that of Milton Friedman and Francis Fukuyama.[249] Between the pessimism of Anderson and the trumpets of capital, Thompson argued, there was little to choose.

In the end, the difference between Thompson and Anderson's interpretation of the Cold War can be abbreviated in terms of theory and practice. Thompson believed that rationality and internationalism were not just theories and traditions, but also practices. 'In my view', he wrote in 1989, 'the movements and the practices may now well be ahead of the theorists'.[250] Anderson, characteristically, reverted to the tradition of 'scientific socialism' to establish not only the origins of the Cold War, but also the 'particular agencies and strategies' which offered the promise of a 'transition beyond a world haunted by nuclear fear as well as divided by social misery and injustice'.[251] Thompson might have considered this position utopianism writ large. No doubt Anderson believed that

---

246. E.P. Thompson 1982, p. 143.
247. E.P. Thompson 1982, p. 144.
248. E.P. Thompson 1982.
249. E.P. Thompson 1989, p. 145.
250. E.P. Thompson 1989, p. 144.
251. Anderson 2005, p. 186.

Thompson's too close involvement with the politics of peace precluded the kind of cool analysis the termination of the Cold War deserved. 'Between the ideals of END and the realities of Soviet breakdown', Anderson concluded, 'is a large gap'.[252] With an eye to the Left's political reinvigoration, Thompson saw it very differently. 'We cannot know what spaces the third way might inherit', Thompson wrote, 'unless we press in practice beyond the old "two camps" thinking and find out'.[253]

VII

E.P. Thompson thought from 'in the provinces'. This was an identity he discovered first, perhaps, through Frank Thompson's wartime letters, and which he had confirmed by his own war experience, and his post-war involvement as a volunteer on a railway-building project in Yugoslavia. It was reconfirmed during 1956, within the early New Left and later within Europe-wide campaigns against nuclear weapons. Thompson was a socialist internationalist, too, evidenced in a life-long hatred of imperialism in general, and the British Empire in particular. But this socialist internationalism had nothing to do with elite conceptions of cosmopolitanism, much less with high table discussions of theory at Oxford or the Sorbonne. For Thompson, the best theory would be found in any number of places, in the labourer's field, in the seditious letter, or in poetry and the novel. Socialist-internationalism, the 'spirit of Europe', the tradition of the 'freeborn Englishman' – each makes some sense of Thompson. But only if it is remembered that he approached all three awkwardly.

That awkwardness encouraged a stubborn disregard for the centre, whether defined in terms of power, thought or value. If there is a thread that runs throughout Thompson's intellectual work, then it is contempt for the British state, for modes of thought isolated from political experience, and for aspiration removed from actuality. Thompson's opposition to the centre's condescension toward the provinces was consistent, evident equally in his historical work and in his political interventions. Thompson once wrote that the historian could not be without values, since this would be to imagine an historian who was not in some way a product of history. The question of values, of choice and of political commitment consistently informed and unified his manifold writings. They were the tracer beam of his polemic, his historical argument and his immediate political interventions. They were fired from the provinces.

---

252. Ibid.
253. E.P. Thompson 1989, p. 146.

Chapter Four
Raymond Williams's Love of Country

I

Raymond Williams's writing was located at the intersection between the conceptual and the immediate, his
writing signalled by the always punctual, sometimes pun-
gent, intervention into contemporary socialist politics.
This location could be a source of strain. In Williams's
case, the strain was registered in oscillating tones – his
writing capable of unusual warmth, 'Culture is Ordinary'
comes to mind, but also of the chill of abstraction
reminiscent of sections of *The Long Revolution*. These
tensions, however, were the surface effect of a deeper
movement that survived and informed the diversity of
his writing – an ongoing dialogue between his early, but
enduringly evoked, 'lived experience' of working-class
community and later dislocations of class, culture and
nation that took him beyond the warmth of social relations associated with rural Welsh village-life to 'centres
of settled and often magnificent achievement'.[1]

Related to other keywords in his writing, such as
culture and communications, place and community
formed the genetics of Williams's work.[2] Indeed, revaluation of these terms, and his argument for their intimate association with socialism, was the animating
intent of Williams's contribution to New Left political
thought in the late 1950s and early 1960s. The revaluation did not go unchallenged, however. Following a brief

---

1. Williams 1973, p. 5.
2. See Hall 1991d, p. 56, for the centrality of 'community' to Williams's work.

biographical interim, Williams's revaluation, and the contest it generated, will constitute the object of this chapter's first substantive section. The subsequent section will track the under-considered argument of *May Day Manifesto* (hereafter *Manifesto*), and will relate that argument to issues of national identity and nationhood. A third section will investigate Williams's relationship to Wales and Welsh nationalism. Alongside this assessment of Wales and Welsh nationalism in Williams's work, this section of the chapter will also probe his co-incident immersion in a cosmopolitan milieu of (Marxist) theory and practice. The chapter's final section will review Williams's warnings about the dangers associated with a socialism, and indeed a critical theory, that ignored what he called 'lived and worked and placeable social identities'.[3] In sum, the chapter will illuminate the tensions, indeed the frequent ambivalence, that marked Williams's encounter with the national question; and, by situating that encounter within larger New Left debates, bring to those tensions a clarity his work sometimes obscured.

II

Where was the 'somewhere' from which Raymond Williams wrote? Perry Anderson, an early champion of Williams's work, placed him within the tradition of 'English socialist thought'.[4] Echoing this interpretation, Raphael Samuel, writing soon after Williams's death in 1988, claimed that cultural studies' founding father wrote as an 'English socialist'.[5] In the view of his first biographer, a combination of 'Britishness' and 'internationalism' characterised Williams's social being.[6] The national appellation, has, of course, been much contested. 'That Williams was Welsh', Dai Smith has concluded, 'was clear'.[7] For Smith, his latest biographer, it was the 'Welsh experience which [stood] out as the abiding preoccupation of [Williams's] life'.[8] Endorsing this conclusion, but offering an

---

3. Williams 1983a, p. 197.

4. Anderson 1965b, p. 283. In this essay, Anderson also refers to Williams as an 'Englishman' (see p. 222). 'English Marxist' was a description offered by Martin Jay in Jay 1984, p. 9.

5. Samuel 1989, p. 145. Samuel, however, goes on to note other aspects of Williams's identity that contradict this view.

6. Inglis 1995, p. 2. Williams's 'Britishness' has constituted the basis of a critique of his socialism in Gilroy 1987, pp. 49–50.

7. Smith 1989, p. 34.

8. Ibid. In his new biography of Williams, Smith focuses on the identity 'Welsh European', Williams's own self-description in the late 1970s, to explain Williams. See Smith 2008, p. 1.

alternative, perhaps minatory, view of his politics, Jan Gorak has suggested that Williams was a 'Welsh nationalist'.[9]

Commentators have also zeroed in on Williams's birthplace to explain the 'somewhere' from which he wrote – not Wales, but Pandy, a 'rural working-class community' on the Welsh border.[10] It was the values associated with 'community' that determined the rhythm of his life's work according to this assessment, despite the fact that he lived the majority of his adult life in other centres, such as Cambridge.[11] A variation on this theme has also been popular in elucidations of Williams's social being. According to Terry Eagleton, Williams 'lived in border country the whole of his life', the border country between the 'knowable community' he had been born into and 'the life of educated intelligence' he later inhabited.[12] Not surprisingly, some, like E.P. Thompson, have described Williams as a 'revolutionary socialist',[13] implying that social transformation, rather than any particular place, was his homeland. Internationalist and nationalist, English/British and Welsh, rooted and rootless – when it comes to placing Williams, comrades and commentators alike have waxed contradictory.

The subject now of two biographies, Raymond Williams's life-story does not require detailed elaboration.[14] He was born in August 1921, the only son of a railway-worker and his wife, and grew up in Pandy, a rural community on the Welsh side of the Wales-England border. 'I was born under the Black Mountains', he recalled with characteristic warmth and feeling, 'on the Welsh border, where the meadows are bright green against the red earth of the ploughland, and the first trees, beyond the window, are oak and holly'.[15] So important was the border country to his imagined formation that Williams later claimed that the Black Mountain region alone landscaped his dreams.[16] The border country was equally important in conscious recollection and reflection on his sense of self. 'When I go back to [the border country]', Williams remarked, 'I feel a recovery of a particular kind of life, which appears, at times, as an inescapable identity, a more positive connection than I have known elsewhere'.[17]

---

9. Gorak 1988, p. 1.

10. Eagleton 1989, p. 1.

11. O'Connor 1989, p. 6.

12. Eagleton 1989, p. 4. For a similar use of the 'border' metaphor in placing Williams see Di Michele 1993, p. 27.

13. E.P. Thompson 1994, p. 243.

14. The most recent biography tracks Williams's development up until 1961. Smith 2008.

15. Williams 1973, p. 84. See also Williams's comment where he suggests that the border country was considered neither England nor Wales (Williams 1979, p. 26).

16. Williams 1973, p. 84.

17. Williams 1973, p. 3.

It should go without saying, however, that the border country's importance to Williams's political formation was a product of memory. Over time, the rural Welsh village where he was born did not just take on varied meaning, but also divergent description. Williams first explored the border country in class terms, a sense that would survive in later recollections.[18] His memory of Pandy, supposedly disguised under general comment about working-class community, was elaborated in the concluding sections of *Culture and Society*, where the Welsh village represented the unique proletarian values of mutuality and solidarity. In *Border Country*, his first novel, Williams's birthplace was approached through the trope of the 'return of the native'.[19] Exploring issues of migration and displacement central to modern life, and the processes that give rise to conflicting senses of identity, class, nonetheless, predominated in *Border Country* through recollection of the General Strike of 1926. This was a central event of Williams's father's life and, moreover, an event that Williams would return to 'again and again as living proof of the self-realising capacities of the working-class, and also of its limits, when confronted with the world of power'.[20]

If class remained central to Williams's recollection of the border country, then it did not remain the only, or indeed the dominant, affective inflection he would attribute to his homeland. In *The Country and the City*, published in the early 1970s, Pandy, its rural dimensions brought to the fore, is described as home to a 'customary way of life'.[21] If customs, for Perry Anderson, 'conjured up only the local caitiffs of seedy clericalism, peering at books on the quay-side to see if they were on a blacklist based on the Papal index',[22] for Williams they were associated with the rural needs and values of a 'settled active community': 'I have had the luck to thin a wood and watch the cowslips and the bluebells come back; to repair and rebuild old drystone walls; to hedge and ditch, after long neglect, and to see from skilled men how the jobs should be done'.[23] At the same time, the border country of Williams's childhood would also become increasingly representative of a characteristic Welsh experience. Indeed, Williams's recollection of his early years became increasingly portrayed through the 'Welsh-not', English oppression, the loss of the Welsh language, and with his felt sense of Welsh 'cultural' identity.[24] Finally, returning to themes evident as early as

---

18. See Williams 1989, pp. 3–14, for Williams's encounter with Cambridge.

19. See Yeo 1989, p. 277, for insightful comment on this.

20. Samuel 1989, p. 149. See Brenkman 1995, pp. 239–44, for more on Williams's connection to the 1926 General Strike.

21. Williams 1973, p. 2. See also Williams 1989, p. 113.

22. Anderson 2005, p. 345.

23. Williams 1989, p. 85. On Williams's suggestion that 'the land' played an important role in his life's work, consider Williams 2003, p. 92.

24. As an example, see his response to questions about his childhood in Williams 1979a, pp. 25–8.

Border Country, Williams's imagined homeland emerged more and more through the prism of capitalist transformation. Notions of a 'precarious and threatened identity', Williams believed, were associated with dynamics of mobility characteristic of a 'modern international capitalist market' at work in the world of rural Wales just as much as they were in metropolitan centres.[25] This potentially gave rise to a species of identity, he maintained, signified more by ambivalence and contingency than settlement.

Williams saw the place of his early years in all these ways, though his affection for place remained constant. But if Williams saw the border country as a place to live and to return to, he also saw it as a place to leave. In *Fight for Manod*, the third volume of Williams's Welsh trilogy, Matthew Price remarks that the history of rural Wales 'is that the young go away'.[26] Williams left early, first through politics, later through education. Williams's life-long (socialist) internationalism was nurtured through youthful participation in labour politics and the Left Book Club's campaigns of solidarity with China and Spain. In *Politics and Letters*, he recalled drawing inspiration from Edgar Snow's *Red Star over China* and being moved by the internationalism of Konni Zilliacus, later a contributor to Thompson and Saville's *New Reasoner*.[27] He also recalled a trip to Geneva for a League of Nations youth-conference – surely not a typical experience for a young man from rural Wales – and his first encounter with Marx and Engels at the Soviet pavilion in Paris's International Exhibition on his return journey home.[28] Internationalism, it might be said, was there at the beginning.[29]

Hannah Arendt once remarked that individual freedom involves 'getting away from home, going out into the world and meeting other people in deed and word'.[30] In Williams's case, freedom was first glimpsed through a scholarship to Cambridge, beginning an association with that university that would endure, with breaks, until the early 1980s: he initially went to Trinity College for two years before the War, completed his degree there following War's end, and returned as fellow of Jesus College in 1961,[31] finally retiring as professor of Drama in 1983. His chosen subject was English literature, though study, as it did for many communist students during these years, mostly took a backseat to politics.[32] Already in a sense alienated from Welsh culture – a limiting and limited culture of castles, battles and heroes that had come down to him through grammar-school history

25. Williams 2003, p. 29; Williams 1983, p. 189.
26. Williams 1979b, p. 27.
27. Williams 1979a, pp. 37–8.
28. Ibid. For second-hand accounts of this period in Williams's life, see Inglis 1995, pp. 43–69; Smith 2008, pp. 72–3.
29. Consider Blackburn 1998, p. 16.
30. Arendt 1968, p. 148.
31. Eagleton 1989, p. 2.
32. O'Connor 1989, pp. 6–9.

in Abergavenny,[33] – Williams's Cambridge 'exile' involved him in an international milieu of theory and politics, in a 'culture' that has been described as 'combative, cosmopolitan, experimental, eclectic, modernist and avant-garde'.[34] In his first years at Cambridge, Williams interest in modernism developed through his involvement with the Cambridge University Socialist Club (CUSC). Film predominated. 'Eisenstein and Pudovkin, but also Vigo and Flaherty', Williams later recalled.[35] A member of the 'Aesthetes' group within the CUSC, this son of a Welsh railway-man was exposed to the full range of avant-garde culture,[36] a culture which would reverberate through some of his earliest writing, including *Preface to Film*, up to his last works, many of which were collected in *Politics of Modernism*.[37]

Connections with the past were nonetheless kept. Cambridge involved him in communist politics, his membership in the Communist Party of Great Britain (CPGB) an extension of the Popular Front politics he had briefly lived in Wales. A pamphlet written with Eric Hobsbawm in 1941, justifying the Soviet invasion of Finland, took its place alongside more typical communist student-activities, such as debates in the Cambridge Union and editorship of Cambridge's student-journal. Support for Spain and anti-fascism were natural extensions of earlier internationalist impulses, even for someone whose socialism was more a matter of filial inheritance than the mode of production.[38] Williams would effectively resign from the CPGB in 1941, though resignation involved 'absolutely no change in [his] political positions'.[39] Thus (communist) politics and (modernist) letters – both manifestly metropolitan – certainly internationalist, were two connecting practices that claimed Williams during his initial spell of dislocation from the border country. Not oaks and holly, but Engels and expressionism.

Like many of his student generation, including many student communists, Williams's Cambridge education was interrupted by Hitler's invasion of Poland. A tank commander who landed on Juno Beach in late June 1944, and whose battalion fought battles across western Europe, Williams's experience of the War was recorded in a diary and in letters sent home to his parents and future wife, Joy Williams; they received public expression in regimental newspapers, all of which form the basis for the detailed description of his experience of the War in Dai Smith's *Raymond Williams: A Warrior's Tale*. After early demobilisation, Williams returned to Cambridge to finish his degree. Cambridge now felt like a

---

33. See Williams 1979a, pp. 42–3.
34. Pinkey 1989, p. 18. See also Eagleton 1981, pp. 64–8.
35. Williams 1989, p. 6.
36. Williams 1979a, pp. 41–54.
37. See Williams 1989.
38. Williams 1989, p. 4.
39. Williams 1979a, p. 53.

'totally different world',[40] something registered in a critique of his earlier self's unproblematic trust in Marxism's ability to grasp all realms of human experience. 'Eventually', he later recorded, 'I found the new alternative sub-culture, which in English, but also in Anthropology, was the group around F.R. Leavis'.[41] Concerned now as much with Eliot as with Marx, Williams undertook an in-depth study of the themes of Ibsen's drama, exploring issues which he believed foreign to Marxism. The upshot of this intense period of revaluation was *Drama from Ibsen to Eliot*, published in 1951.[42]

Graduating from Cambridge in 1946, Williams, like E.P. Thompson, Richard Hoggart and a host of other socialist intellectuals, chose a career in Adult Education over further study or a prospective career in the academy.[43] A future as a writer, of fiction and some combination of cultural analysis and literary criticism, was not in doubt. Appointed by the Workers' Education Association (WEA) to work in East Sussex, Williams spent the next fifteen years making what he believed was the common human inheritance of culture available to trade unionists, white-collar workers and unpaid housewives in southern England.[44] It was during these years, within the vibrant intellectual milieu of Adult Education, that Williams developed the set of ideas – relations between culture, politics and economics within a conception of social totality – that would find expression in *Culture and Society, The Long Revolution*, and *Border Country*.[45] Indeed, the immediate post-war years, for Williams, were ones of extraordinary activity and energy. That energy was evident in a number of creative endeavours, including the establishment of the literary-cultural journal *Politics and Letters*.[46] Conceived in the afterglow of Labour's triumph in 1945, Williams established the journal with two Cambridge friends, Wolf Mankowitz, who had provided Williams with an introduction to Leavis's work, and Clifford Collins. *Politics and Letters*, which published work by Christopher Hill, Sartre and Orwell among others, sought to 'unite radical left politics with Leavisite literary criticism' – a somewhat schizophrenic ambition that perhaps explains the journal's rapid demise in 1948.[47] The journal's denouement, interpreted by Williams as a political and personal failure,

---

40. Williams 1979a, p. 61. See also Inglis 1995, pp. 107–9.
41. Williams 1989, p. 12. See Smith 2008, pp. 218–19, for Williams's relationship with Leavis through these immediate post-war years.
42. Williams 1952.
43. Fieldhouse 1985, p. 22.
44. See McIlroy 1993, pp. 269–323; Steele 1997, pp. 176–99, for reflections on Williams's experience of adult education.
45. Smith 2008, pp. 301–17.
46. See Smith 2008, pp. 362–72, for this involvement in various film-projects with Michael Orrom from this period.
47. Williams 1979a, p. 65. See Woodhams 2002, pp. 75–83, for more on Williams's involvement in the journal *Politics and Letters*.

enacted Williams's alienation from politics for the next decade or so – that is, until the birth of a New Left.

The years between the demise of *Politics and Letters* and the genesis of the New Left can seem like a blank wall in Williams's biography. He was now mostly a watcher in politics, and perhaps with good reason. These years were characterised by a generalised rout for the intellectual Left – ' "progress", "liberalism", "humanism" and (unless in the ritual armoury of cold war) "democracy" became suspect terms: and all those old banners which the Thirties had too easily assumed to be stowed away in ancestral trunks were raised in the wind again'.[48] But it would be wrong, however, to pass over these years in Williams's biography as though an infertile interregnum between two eras of growth. Williams rejected the trends of the time – whether 'mere apathy', 'erudite specialisms', 'the defensive rhetoric of Communist dogma', or 'academic careerism'.[49] But alienation from the 'broken vocabulary of socialism',[50] – his repudiation of both the CPGB and the Labour Party – provided Williams with the necessary distance to re-imagine 'new' socialist values. It was during these years that Williams developed those projects that would become *Culture and Society* and *The Long Revolution*, books which would provide a grammar and semantics for a new Left. As E.P. Thompson suggests, 'Raymond Williams [was] one of the very few intellectuals in this country who was not broken in some degree during that decade; and who maintained his independence from the attractive poles of cold war ideology'.[51] That independence, what we might call, to misuse a concept synonymous with Williams's oeuvre, a structure of feeling, provided a facsimile for the explosion of socialist ideas after 1956.

Indeed, Williams was an active presence at many moments in the making and remaking of the New Left in Britain, although his role before 1958 should not be overstated. *Culture and Society* and *The Long Revolution* were, of course, important moments in the socialist formation's intellectual generation.[52] He contributed to early numbers of *Universities and Left Review* (his first contribution appeared as a review of Richard Hoggart's *Uses of Literacy*), and he spoke at the journal's club alongside E.P. Thompson, Isaac Deutscher and others.[53] He played a role as broker in the merger between the two journals that led to the formation of *New Left Review*, and he became a member of the journal's first, soon to be

---

48. E.P. Thompson 1961a, p. 27.
49. Ibid.
50. Ibid.
51. Ibid.
52. Both texts also played an important role in the birth of cultural studies – see Mulhern 1996, pp. 27–37; Jones 1994, pp. 394–416.
53. See Williams 1957, pp. 29–32, for the review of Hoggart. See also Collini 1999, pp. 210–30.

fractured, board. He was an enthusiastic supporter of Campaign for Nuclear Disarmament (CND), finding in the peace-movement not only an authentic expression of his long-held pacifism but also intimations of the self-determination he saw as vital to a new socialism. Williams was also an important bridge between the 'first' and 'second' New Left formations, providing guarded support for the editorial team of Anderson and Nairn that replaced Hall.[54] Almost alone among the original founders of *New Left Review*, he continued to write for the journal after 1964, nonetheless joining with other original New Left figures to establish *May Day Manifesto* movement in 1967.[55] The movement broke on the shoals of electoral politics in the early 1970s. A similar project – the Socialist Society – would be briefly imagined in the early 1980s, with Williams once again pushed to the forefront.

Identities, Eric Hobsbawm has remarked, are not like hats.[56] In practice, if not always in theory, identity can be constituted by seemingly incompatible attachments and loyalties. Unlike hats, people can wear more than one identity. Indeed, we should neither assume that people have only one 'country', nor that we always know what that 'country' is.[57] This is certainly true in the case of Williams. Britain and Wales, even England, internationalism and 'localism', rooted and rootless, socialism and nationalism – all make sense of Williams, at least within specific contexts. The different 'countries' that claimed Williams, and which Williams claimed, was the site of what his fictional self in *Border Country* characterised as 'feeling it several ways at once'.[58] How these tensions worked and were worked out in Williams's negotiation of the nexus between socialism and the national question will constitute the focus of what follows.

III

Raymond Williams consistently championed concrete relations attached to place and community as essential socialist resources, rather than figuring them as the detritus of capitalist development as Marx and Engels, for instance, sometimes did. Drawing on his memories of growing up amid the bracken and heather-filled fields at the foot of the Black Mountains, Williams argued that among 'the deepest emotions human beings can have are emotions about ... place, which in a way has been their community, their society'.[59] Alienated from territorially

---

54. Williams 1979a, pp. 367–97.
55. Williams 1979a, pp. 373–5.
56. Hobsbawm 1992, p. 123.
57. An idea borrowed from Hobsbawm 1984, p. 49.
58. Williams 1960, p. 37.
59. Williams 1989, p. 22.

embedded identities, socialism, Williams maintained, was a 'mode of thought which really has made relations between men into relations between things or relations between concepts'.[60] Indeed, an emphasis on the importance of community and place to socialist values was central to Raymond Williams's theoretical and political interventions, no more so than in *Culture and Society, The Long Revolution* and his other early New Left work. Taken together, these writings – and critiques of them advanced by E.P. Thompson, Stuart Hall and Perry Anderson, among others – offer a unique window on debates within the New Left around national identity and nationhood, and their relation to socialism.

The general argument of *Culture and Society* is well known. The book was essentially divided into two sections – the first, the majority of the book, was a stadial account of transformations in the meaning of particular terms (industry, democracy, culture, art and class) from Burke to Orwell, a narrative of 'a general pattern of change' that devolved into a fairly conventional history of ideas;[61] and the second, the book's conclusion, illuminated Williams's unique, if sometimes less than clear, judgment on this pattern of change, and his hope that it would be extended 'in the direction of certain meanings and values'.[62] For our purposes, it is the concluding argument, the source of the book's contemporary influence, which is vital. It was here that Williams's now-famous definition of culture as 'a whole way of life' appeared.[63] Indeed, *Culture and Society*'s conclusion elaborated a conception of culture as 'a general social process' which could not be associated with the selective tradition of elites or with certain compartmentalised areas of experience, such as art.[64] This idea of culture as a human inheritance provided the touchstone for Williams's vision of alternative social relations based on the values of community.

Community was clearly central to the argument of *Culture and Society*, but Williams never made it clear what he meant by the term, a lack of clarity that invited cheap acceptance (who is not for 'community'?) without political gain.[65] In one sense 'community' was contrasted with bourgeois values of individualism and equated with an 'organic society'.[66] In another, although again opposed to the acquisitive ethos, it was allied with something that Williams called 'working class culture',[67] a way of life based on the 'collective democratic institution' (trade-unions, the cooperative-movement, working-class parties). And, in a yet

---

60. Williams 1989, p. 117.
61. Williams 1983a, pp. xiii, xvii.
62. Williams 1983a, p. xix.
63. Williams 1983a, p. 325.
64. Williams 1983a, p. 337.
65. This is the point that Williams basically made in Williams 1979a, p. 119.
66. Williams 1983a, p. 296.
67. Williams 1983a, p. 327.

further sense, and here closely associated with the last, it was equated with 'mutual responsibility', 'common betterment', and 'solidarity',[68] where the latter was understood as the 'positive practice of neighbourhood',[69] and was oriented towards the future.[70] The concept was also sometimes prefixed with the caveat 'actual',[71] suggesting that a community could be in some sense false, as Williams claimed when 'community' was limited to 'national' and 'imperialist' lines.[72] In whichever sense it was meant, it was closely associated with communication.[73] Mass communication – a 'dominative' understanding of community where a minority exploited a majority – was the signal of 'uncommunity', while real communication – an equalitarian conception of communication – implied an 'effective community of experience'.[74]

Some guide through this thicket of confusion was provided by a series of companion articles to *Culture and Society* that appeared in *Universities and Left Review* and elsewhere. The promise inherent in culture, Williams argued in one of those articles, was a vision of community established on the basis of the extension of kinship relations. 'The primary affections run all the way through', Williams wrote, 'for the working class sees no reason, in experience, why these primary values should not be made the values of society as a whole'.[75] An 'actual' community would be characterised by the extirpation of the barriers between art and work, between consciousness and existence, between communication and experience, and between public and private – divisions which Williams believed were crucial to capitalism. Indeed, for Williams, socialist democracy alone would realise culture's potential – the 'working-class way of life', with its 'emphases of neighbourhood, mutual obligation, and common betterment' projected onto the totality of social relations.[76] As *Culture and Society* concluded, 'The human fund is regarded as in all respects common, and freedom of access to it as a right constituted by one's humanity; yet such access, in whatever kind, is common or it is nothing'.[77]

Culture and Society, however, stopped short of championing revolutionary socialism. Williams had rejected communism, in both theory and practice, and made no direct reference to social democracy as a superior alternative. In place of these dominant senses of socialism, *Culture and Society* pledged allegiance

68. Williams 1983a, pp. 329–32.
69. Williams 1983a, p. 334.
70. Ibid.
71. Williams 1983a, p. 312.
72. Williams 1983a, p. 326.
73. Williams 1983a, p. 313.
74. Williams 1983a, pp. 314, 316, 319, 330.
75. Williams 1957, p. 31.
76. Williams 1983a, p. 8.
77. Williams 1983a, p. 326.

to the working class's 'democratic collective institution', to trade-unions and political parties and an incipient, if opaque, conception of socialist democracy. The book, however, made no mention of *which* trade-unions and *what* political party, nor how socialist democracy – an 'actual' community – differed from other socialisms equally claiming the appellation democratic. Indeed, the crisis of the international socialist movement, the book's immediate context, though left as hazy shadow, may explain the unrelenting abstraction and the vacuity of the political formulas that constitute the book's conclusion. The immediate context of *Culture and Society*'s composition was not only the suppression of socialist dissent in East Germany and Poland, but also the growing popularity of socialist revisionism within the Labour Party. The icy climate of Cold War offered seemingly frost-hoared ground for any renaissance of socialist values. This might also explain Williams's felt need to uncover resources for a socialist future in a tradition of thinking that could encompass Morris *and* Burke, Tawney *and* Carlyle.

Victor Kiernan had another explanation for Williams's hesitation before socialist revolution. Kiernan, writing in *New Reasoner*, wondered why 'neither nationalism nor imperialism is not in his [Williams's] list of key new words' and suspected that it might have something to do with Williams's neglect of class-conflict and his evasion of culture's foundation on barbarism.[78] 'Mr. Williams's Interregnum is oftener and better called the Age of Imperialism', Kiernan thundered, 'and the renovated common consciousness of modern nations has been made up as to nine parts in ten by envy, fear and hatred of their neighbours'.[79] A 'common culture', for Kiernan, signified the false-consciousness of nationalism, an ersatz community rather than the instantiation of socialist democracy. Kiernan also rebuked Williams for his naïve suggestion – it would become definitive in cultural studies – that 'There are in fact no masses; there are only ways of seeing people as masses'.[80] 'One authentic feature of all traditional societies was the Tory Mob', Kiernan reminded Williams, 'drilled in our improving age into an S.S. Division'.[81] In sum, Kiernan spotted the absence of socialist politics in *Culture and Society*, evidenced not just in the easy assimilation of Williams's conception of culture to nationalism and his neglect of imperialism, but also in his evasion of class-struggle and his romancing the stone of 'working-class culture'.

Reflecting on *Culture and Society* twenty years after its publication, Williams claimed that the books purpose was 'oppositional' – 'to counter the appropriation of a long line of thinking about culture to what were by now decisively

78. Kiernan 1959, p. 82.
79. Ibid.
80. Williams 1983a, p. 300.
81. Kiernan 1959, p. 83.

reactionary positions'.[82] *Culture and Society* thus provided what philosophers call an 'internal criticism'.[83] Williams took an established tradition of English social thought, argued within its terms, and concluded that the socialisation of production was that tradition's telos. This was *Culture and Society*'s professed audacity: it offered a genealogy of 'radical England' that included Burke, Carlyle, and Arnold, thinkers who were seen to barrack against radicalism. 'I had', as Williams remembered with pride, 'discovered themes profoundly related to my sense of the social crisis of my time and the socialist way out of it, not in the approved list of progressive thinkers, but in these paradoxical figures'.[84] In other words, *Culture and Society* fought reactionary Englishness from the perspective of an 'oppositional Englishness' – boxed it to a stand still, as Thompson put it.[85] The book, however, had another opponent, 'orthodox' Marxist cultural criticism. *Culture and Society*'s main adversaries in this corner were Christopher Caudwell and Alick West (and perhaps Williams's earlier self).[86] However, if instead of reaching back to the 1930s to find exemplary Marxist theories of culture, Williams had sparred with British communism's contemporary cultural policy, he may have found homologies between his own manoeuvre and the CPGB's attempt to claim 'Englishness' for socialist revolution. These homologies were only surface deep, however. Williams distanced himself from contemporary communism through an insistence on 'socialism from below', and his view that Marxist cultural criticism replicated the conservative bifurcation between elites and masses.[87]

The great advantage of 'internal criticism' is that it offers a challenge to a dominant position on that positions' own terms, opening up the possibility of transforming hegemony.[88] However, internal criticism also runs the risk of replicating not just your opponent's terms, but also the meaning of those terms. In some sense this was the burden of E.P. Thompson's critique of *Culture and Society*. In 'Andersonian mode', Thompson taxed Williams with an undue parochialism. 'The Tradition (if there is one) is a very English phenomena ... If Williams had allowed himself to look beyond this island, he might have found a very different eleven of players fielding against him, from Vico through Marx to Weber and Mannheim, beside whom his own team might look, on occasion, like gentleman amateurs'.[89] This parochialism, Thompson believed, was reflected in *Culture and Society*'s dominant tone, in its tendency to 'depersonalise' social forces, and in

---

82. Williams 1979a, p. 97.
83. See Geuss 2005, p. 166, for a description of internal criticism.
84. Williams 1979a, p. 106.
85. E.P. Thompson 1961a, p. 27.
86. Williams 1983a, pp. 269–80.
87. See, in particular, Williams's critique of Lenin, in Williams 1983a, pp. 283–4.
88. Geuss 2005, pp. 166, 177.
89. E.P. Thompson 1961a, p. 30.

what Thompson believed was the book's correlated avoidance of class-struggle and the question of class-power.

In *New Left Review* in the 1970s, Terry Eagleton also advanced a reading of *Culture and Society* along these lines. *Culture and Society* was too close to Leavis and *Scrutiny*, Eagleton believed, miming their conception of 'organic society' (community) and their conservative – for Eagleton the Salford-born Irishman there was no other – interpretation of Englishness.[90] A 'systematic inattention to the reactionary character of the tradition with which it [*Culture and Society*] dealt',[91] claimed Eagleton, rehearsed a 'romantic populism' and reconfirmed working-class labourism.[92] As Thompson had put it, without the obloquy of populism, 'the function of bourgeois culture is not questioned in its entirety, and the surreptitious lines of class interest and power have never been crossed'.[93] Socialism was supposed to turn the world upside down, not find consolation in the world as it was, no matter how intelligently interpreted.

The charge of 'Englishness' seems off-centre given its object was a Welshman, and one who would come more and more to be a self-confessed, even self-confessional, Welshman. Williams later claimed that he had 'deliberately kept [*Culture and Society*] English'.[94] The book's 'Englishness' is perhaps easy enough understood: England was where Williams lived ('We begin to think where we live',[95] Williams later wrote). England's cultural and intellectual tradition had made-up his education and the influence of Leavis, no matter how mediated, left its national mark. In addition, Williams later claimed that it was during this time that he was most removed from Wales. However, he also noted that his discussion of 'cooperative community and solidarity' in *Culture and Society*'s conclusion was really about 'Welsh social relations'.[96] 'I was drawing very heavily on my experience of Wales, and in one way correctly locating it as a certain characteristic of working-class institutions'.[97] This, perhaps, speaks better to Williams's concerns in the 1970s (when the comment was made) than it does to the issues of *Culture and Society*. But even so, it is hard to make sense of what Williams meant by 'Welsh social relations'. After all, were not the values evoked in Williams's discussion of working-class community equally distinctive of social relations in Scottish mining villages or in steel communities in England's northeast?[98] Williams's

---

90. Eagleton 1976, pp. 3–23. Eagleton, of course, would later revise much of this criticism of Williams.

91. Eagleton 1976, p. 10.

92. Eagleton 1976, p. 12.

93. E.P. Thompson 1961a, p. 37.

94. Williams 1979a, p. 113.

95. Williams 1989, p. 33.

96. Williams 1979a, p. 113.

97. Ibid.

98. See Macintyre 1980a, for a discussion of such communities.

suggestion that 'working-class institutions' could be reduced to characteristically *Welsh* social relations is absurd. Equally absurd is the supposed subterranean influence of Wales on the conclusions of *Culture and Society*. If Williams's use of community had a national inflection – arguably the class-inflection jostled for priority – then it was English, perhaps even English in that (then dominant) sense where England included – perhaps better occluded – Scotland and Wales. It was left to Victor Kiernan to remind the author of *Culture and Society* of the Celtic fringe.[99]

The question of the nation was also a concern for Williams's *New Left Review* interlocutors (among whom were Perry Anderson, Francis Mulhern and Robin Blackburn) in the late 1970s, although for slightly different reasons. Echoing Kiernan's point, they noted the 'silence of the book [*Culture and Society*] on the theme and problem of the nation as such'.[100] They pointed to the dominant association of 'community' with 'nation', and the problematic political intentions and interests of 'community' in Europe between the wars. Indeed, ethnicity – implicit in *New Left Review*'s hesitations over the meaning of 'community' – might be considered the outstanding omission of Williams's discussion of culture, at least in terms of our own context where culture is so often equated with ethnicity. But in a sense, nationality and ethnicity were arguably present, if unconscious, props of Williams's conception of community and culture. For sure, Williams's model of the characteristic social relations of a future socialist society was the familial relation augmented to encompass society. 'The primary affections and allegiances, first to family, then to neighbourhood', Williams wrote, 'can in fact be directly extended into social relationships as a whole'.[101] This sentence was absent from *Culture and Society*, but the sentiment was not. 'The tending of natural growth' is Williams's less remembered definition of culture in the book.[102] Both 'tending' and 'natural growth' have more characteristic inflections of 'organic community', than of a socialist society. Thus, ethnicity – what else could familial relations mean? – was evident in Williams's conception of culture even if the word itself did not appear. Indeed, *Culture and Society* could easily be associated with an 'ethnic socialism', a conclusion which, as we shall see below, both Stuart Hall and Perry Anderson warned against.

Culture and community were keywords not just of Williams's work, but also of the early New Left. Most New Left thinkers considered culture an important location of socialist dissent and most connected 'community' with a reinvigoration of

---

99. Kiernan 1959, p. 79.
100. Williams 1979a, p. 117.
101. Williams 1959, p. 31.
102. Williams 1983a, pp. 335, 336.

socialist values.[103] Many questioned, however, Williams's rehearsal of both terms in *Culture and Society* and his other early New Left writings. For a start, Stuart Hall, in an article that probed the uneven effects of capitalist modernisation and transformations in a 'working class way of life', pointed out that though the 'old working class communities' had given rise to values of solidarity, they were also often 'defensive or aggressive towards other communities, other national and racial groups, towards the "queer" fellow and the "odd man out", towards the "scholarship boy" or even, sometimes, the militant'.[104] As Williams later suggested, it was only when he was composing *Keywords* in the late 1960s that he realised that 'community' always contained positive meanings, and for that reason was inherently dangerous.[105] Hall made another point. If 'community' was to be the basis of a new socialism, as Williams and others within the New Left believed, and if changes in capitalism were rendering 'community' obsolete, then on what basis could socialism be argued for? Alert to so many of the transformations within capitalist property-relations, especially within the region of communications, it was strange, Hall seemed to suggest, that Williams's socialist vision was reliant on 'ways of life' that capitalism having once made had now either appropriated – the values of 'neighbourhood' transmogrified into 'status distinction' – or in fact obliterated.[106]

E.P. Thompson and Raphael Samuel countered that Hall's conclusion was too hasty, although neither addressed Hall's point about the 'racial' nature of community. Samuel reminded Hall that capitalism had changed before, and that 'working class communities were formed against just those hostile pressures' in the past that Hall claimed were breaking them up today.[107] Capitalism, for Samuel, was no less class-ridden in the 1950s than it had been in Marx's time, and was arguably now considerably less open and considerably less mobile, although its sense of closure and stasis better hidden. The working class, Samuel claimed, far from the status-enslaved, second-car-desiring people of Hall's painting, constituted the only contemporary agent of potential social change. Thompson's objections followed a slightly different track. Like Samuel, he offered a perspective informed by a 'sense of history' as a corrective to Hall's presentism. Like Williams, Thompson recalled 'the creative potential – not in the remote future, but here and now – of working people' against Hall's supposedly mechanical conception of the relationship between capitalism and class.[108] But against Hall's and Williams's differently sided evasions, Thompson recalled the 'context of

103. Besides Williams's own work, see also C. Taylor 1958, pp. 11–18.
104. Hall 1958a, p. 27.
105. Williams 1979a, p. 119.
106. Hall 1958a, pp. 28–9.
107. Samuel 1958b, p. 45.
108. E.P. Thompson 1958b, p. 50.

class power' and 'that impolite historical concept – the class struggle'.[109] Specifically, against Williams, he countered that a 'working class way of life' was 'a way of struggle, between competing moralities' – between 'the acquisitive ethic' and the 'communal ethic'.[110] The torchbearers of the latter, Thompson claimed in a residual vanguardist temper, had been a 'political minority'.[111] 'It is in the socialist movement itself', Thompson reminded Williams, 'that the aspiration towards community should find its most conscious expression'.[112]

Perry Anderson's response to the complex of ideas outlined in *Culture and Society* echoed Hall's concerns about the 'ethnic' basis of Williams's conception of community. In a two-part study of Sweden – 'Mr. Crosland's Dreamland' – Anderson opposed 'working-class community' to a 'national collectivity', which only took shape within the presence of 'the common solidarity of danger'.[113] However, against Williams's argument for the extension of affective relations to the whole of society, he suggested that 'what is surely striking about working-class values is that they are so often not transposed from the private realm to the public one: there is a typical hiatus between personal values of solidarity and humanity and public attitudes of indifference or intolerance (chauvinism, sexual bigotry, callousness and even relish in social punishment)'.[114] He added that Williams's conception of class was 'too formal and neatly simple', and, against the common sense of New Left political thought, that the negative aspects of working-class culture could be explained by the absence of the 'arts and intellectual enquiry' within the 'working-class context'.[115] Incipient here was the later *New Left Review's* belief that socialist transformation would be dependent on the development of socialist theory by intellectuals – a view which Williams, to say nothing of Thompson, would reject.

The charge of ethnic socialism, however, is an inadequate *final* assessment of *Culture and Society*, as Anderson and Hall would no doubt agree, if not Paul Gilroy. Ethnicity was certainly an allochthonous presence in Williams's definition of culture and community, and this because it ran against the grain of so much else that is in *Culture and Society* and because, in a larger political context, Williams regularly dismissed imperialism and ethnic nationalism. *Culture and Society*, despite some ambiguity, made the argument that no real community, no proper establishment of common culture, could survive class-difference. 'The inequalities of many kinds which still divide our community', Williams wrote,

109. E.P. Thompson 1958b, p. 51.
110. E.P. Thompson 1958b, p. 52.
111. E.P. Thompson 1958b, p. 53.
112. Ibid.
113. Anderson 1961b, p. 12.
114. Anderson 1961a, p. 36.
115. Anderson 1961a, pp. 36–7.

'make effective communication difficult or impossible'.[116] The book's vision of a clash between alternative forms of social relationship was an attempt, though weak, to instantiate the reality of class-conflict. Williams's reach for 'affective relations', associated with family, neighbourhood and community as the basis for a future socialist society, spoke to his respect for place and to his belief that socialism must constitute an extension of affective social relations. To put this in other words, Williams believed that a (socialist) political community based on the appeal to abstract ways of being would provide insufficient bonds to hold society together. As dangerous as the appeal to 'affective relations' was in the context of nationalism's purchase on felt senses of identity, Williams would have argued that they were nonetheless necessary resources of any future socialist society.

The Long Revolution might be read as Williams's response to the concerns of his New Left comrades, though it was much more an extension and summation of the argument to be found in *Culture and Society*, now focused on 'ideas of society' and institutions – drama, language, the press. The book's conclusion – 'Britain in the Sixties', which would later be reprinted as part of *Towards 2000* – contained a closer argument for the establishment of what Williams called a 'participatory democracy'.[117] A self-governing society, Williams wrote in explanation of participatory democracy, would promote a 'real feeling of community' which was currently 'cancelled by the plain fact that most of us do not own or control the means and product of our work'.[118] But the 'human energy' contained in the long revolution, he argued, 'springs from the conviction that men can direct their own lives, by breaking through the pressures and restrictions of older forms of society, and by discovering new common institutions',[119] something *The Long Revolution* deemed necessary in the wake of 'the visible moral decline of the labour movement'.[120] The guide for socialist policy, whether in communications or industry, should be the belief, or so Williams argued, that people can collectively control the circumstances and product of their own labour.[121] As *New Left Review*'s editors later admitted, 'Britain in the Sixties' constituted 'the first extended case made within the New Left for a socialism of production, focused on work relations'.[122]

---

116. Williams 1983a, p. 325.
117. Williams 1961, pp. 319–83.
118. Williams 1961, p. 363.
119. Williams 1961, p. 375.
120. Williams 1961, p. 328.
121. Williams 1962 provides some concrete recommendations for participatory democracy in communications.
122. Williams 1979a, p. 148.

Perhaps in response to the perceived limitations of *Culture and Society*, certainly in a pre-emption of Williams's later concerns and arguments, *The Long Revolution* also claimed that the nation-state was an 'abstracted social order',[123] now outmoded. For Williams, 'Britain' or 'England' were not 'real places but particular interpretations which include definitions of duty, function and character',[124] definitions which were largely residues from antediluvian images of society. Here Williams foreshadowed the Anderson-Nairn position that the British state was a historical relic, an aging rusted hulk long overdue for reconstruction. 'The fact that "Britain" and "England" have been, successively, very different places', he went on, 'subject to constant change, is obscured by a mode of description which ... suggests something absolute and permanent rather than something relative and changing'.[125] Indeed, the nation-state, in Williams's view, extended a 'way of thinking about society which started from an existing order and subordinated to this [the] needs of actual persons'.[126] If the definition made sense in some contexts – for example, security – 'they have never necessarily done so, any more than the needs of the serf necessarily included the maintenance of his lord'.[127] To the 'abstraction' of the nation-state, Williams contrasted what he called 'the brotherhood of man' or socialism, a social order which 'starts from the needs of all men, on a basis of practical equality'.[128]

As a definition and discussion of the nation-state, this was weak and, as we shall see, probably misguided. Indeed, if the nation was an imagined community, though undoubtedly a false one, which forced upon people an interpretation of their society abstracted from the way they really live, who was this imagining for? This was the temper of Thompson's objection to *The Long Revolution*'s tone, which, he argued, favoured 'impersonal social forces' over a telling which told who rode whom and why. Protesting against Williams's almost Aesop-like obscurantism ('system of maintenance' rather than 'capitalism'), Thompson noted that 'a sense of extreme fastidiousness enters whenever logic prompts us to identify these "patterns", "systems" and "forms" with precise social forces and particular thinkers'.[129] Beyond Williams's sometimes-abstracted prose, it might be asked in what sense the nation-state could be described as outmoded ... in 1961. It was definitely not outmoded for Algerians, Kenyans, or any number of other peoples fighting imperialism. For them, no matter the partial error of the view – errors

---

123. Williams 1961, p. 123.
124. Williams 1961, p. 122. Here we can see, in embryo, the view of the British nation-state that would be found in the Anderson-Nairn theses. For a latter statement of this view, see Nairn 1977, pp. 3–61.
125. Williams 1961, p. 123.
126. Ibid.
127. Ibid.
128. Williams 1961, p. 128.
129. E.P. Thompson 1961a, p. 25.

that Williams did well to explain – the independent nation-state was the agent of the rights of man, democracy and liberty. Entry into the 'brotherhood of man', as Tom Nairn would later point out, is nearly always gained through a doorway marked 'the nation', the invitation – more often a self-invitation – nearly always scripted in the native tongue of 'the people'.[130] Absent in *The Long Revolution*, this insight would nonetheless partially inform Williams's assessment of Welsh nationalism in the 1970s.

If these were shortcomings associated with Williams's discussion of the nation, *The Long Revolution* did contain a salutary, oft-neglected, emphasis on the artificiality of the nation-state. This was a view that would persist throughout Williams's work. Rather than permanent and natural political forms, nation-states, Williams explained, were always wrapped-up with questions of interest, power and class, though, as we have already seen, *The Long Revolution* was less than forthcoming about which interests, powers and classes the nation-state served. He was clear, however, that the nation-state did not serve the interests of socialism and did not reflect the 'true interests' of people in place. 'The moral decline of socialism', according to Williams, was 'in exact relation to its series of compromises with older images of society and to its failure to sustain and clarify the sense of an alternative human order'.[131] Uniquely perhaps, *The Long Revolution* opposed socialism to the nation-state. Thus Williams's critique of the nation-state – the 'national interest' is an interest designed to deny working-class interests – raised a number of important questions about the relationship not only between community and the nation-state, but also about socialism's social location. In short, if the nation-state was an inadequate framework for the construction of a socialist society – participatory democracy, workers' control, public ownership – then what type of political form might socialism imagine?

The opportunity to discuss these questions was missed in *The Long Revolution*, though Williams would increasingly attend to them over the next two decades. Effectively, *The Long Revolution* seemed to imagine a 'socialist Britain' which had somehow sloughed off the nation-state as an image of society, but which remained recognisably intact as 'Britain', as though the state was an empty signifier open to transformation by any political means. This conclusion is encouraged by much of the discussion of 'Britain in the Sixties'. Here, in addition to conflating 'nation' and 'community', the complaint of *New Left Review*, Williams advocated the control of the 'British economy' by 'society', argued for the reform of 'British democracy' and proposed a new 'national framework' of 'public ownership' in the sphere of communications.[132] The nation-state thus remained the

---

130. See Nairn 1975, pp. 3–27.
131. Williams 1961, p. 133.
132. Williams 1961, pp. 341–2.

horizon of *The Long Revolution*'s socialist vision, despite Williams's rejection of the nation-state as an 'abstraction' and an 'outmoded image of society'. 'Democratic planning', Williams wrote at one point in *The Long Revolution*, 'is an easy phrase, but nobody really knows how it will work'.[133] The same could be said of 'participating democracy' and 'an alternative human order', particularly when it comes to imagining the framework of political community they might require.

In a (1968) retrospect on that set of ideas which constituted *Culture and Society, The Long Revolution* and his other early New Left writings, Williams reflected that 'In talking of a common culture ... one was saying first that culture was the way of life of a people ... and one was using the idea of the common element of the culture – its community – as a way of criticising that divided and fragmented culture we actually have'.[134] Here is manifest much of the tension and ambiguity that characterised Williams's contribution to early New Left political thought. First, in the description of culture as 'the way of life of *a* people' Williams provided no barrier to the conclusion that his conception of culture was, even if unconsciously, based on a number of inclusions and exclusions. At the very least, it ignored the possible lines of difference that might disrupt community. Second, and related to this, Williams never provided a definition of what community was. If community is equal to 'the common element of culture' and culture is 'the way of life of a people', then, potentially, community was coterminous with the 'national community'. *The Long Revolution* provided a partial response to this argument when it suggested that the nation-state constituted an 'abstracted social order' opposed to socialism. However, the logic that deemed the nation-state a 'false' imagined community could easily have been applied to community itself, arguably no less abstract, despite its supposed instantiation in concrete social relations. Finally, Williams offered community as a critique of private property and declared socialist democracy the self-realisation of a common culture. Unintentionally perhaps, this formulation pointed up the homologies between socialism and nationalism. Nationalism, no less than socialism, has often been opposed to private property, based its appeal on the ethic of solidarity and recognised the intrinsic value of community over the individual. The difference, as, variously, Hall, Anderson and Thompson put it: socialism rejected community as ideology and favoured the language of class over talk of peoples.

Williams would have disagreed. He maintained that affective relations – relations that he argued were as fully constitutive of culture as were the great works of art – were precisely the kind of bonds necessary to hold a socialist society together. Familial affections, love of place and warmth of community – these basic human sensibilities he considered necessary and crucial to socialism's

---

133. Williams 1961, p. 321.
134. Williams 1989, p. 35.

potential hegemony. Should they be simply given up to socialism's opponents? Williams's suggestion was that they could not, and that the values they represented were in line with socialism's objectives of care, love and welfare. If socialism could not be made with kinship relations, warmth of community and love of place – those meanings and values which finally made sense of things – because these were forces that undermined its appeal to a general interest beyond particular interests, then perhaps socialism could not be made at all. Again, Williams would have disagreed. But he was honest enough to contemplate the chance that, in the terms of *Culture and Society* or indeed Thompson's *The Syakos Papers*, we would not survive after all.

IV

In 1964, Williams cautiously welcomed Labour's general election victory – a victory, Williams wrote, 'which, in a resigned but yet eager realism, we have worked for and now support'.[135] The chance of social democracy realising the potential inherent in a 'working-class way of life', was, for Williams, that – a chance, and, given the drift of his analysis in *The Long Revolution*, an outside one at that. Still hopes were raised, including the hopes, now somewhat improbably, of the new team at *New Left Review* (Perry Anderson, Robin Blackburn and Tom Nairn), in whose book collection Williams's ambivalent welcome appeared. By 1966, Williams's hopes had been dashed by Wilson's support for American imperialism in Vietnam and by Labour's attack on the trade union movement. However, if Williams withdrew his hesitant support for Labour, he did not withdraw from politics as he had done in 1948. Instead, he bent his arm to a socialist critique of the Labour government and to a revival of the New Left 'beyond the fragments'.[136] The result was *May Day Manifesto* – a self-printed text written by Williams, with help from Thompson and Hall, in 1967, then a 1968 Penguin special that Williams edited, and finally an incipient, though quickly fractured, socialist movement against labourism.[137]

May Day Manifesto began from the premise that the 'origin of the present (British) crisis' was international and could only be solved by a 'different whole society'.[138] *Manifesto* argued that sometime during the twentieth-century the capitalist mode of production had undergone a transition from 'free

---

135. Williams 1965a, p. 368.

136. Williams 1979a, p. 373.

137. Williams later recorded that he 'wrote all of the '67 issue myself'. He then went on to suggest that, although he was made editor of the Penguin version and was charged with the final re-write, 'Edward [Thompson] and Stuart [Hall] contributed more to the second *Manifesto*'. See Williams 1979a, p. 373.

138. Williams 1967, p. 3; Williams ed. 1968, p. 16.

market capitalism' to an 'organized capitalism', the latter characterised by state-intervention in the economy, an extensive welfare-state and the incorporation of trade-unions and social democracy into what *Manifesto* increasingly called, in a sign of the times, 'the system'.[139] For *Manifesto*, the political intent of this (British and international) transformation of capitalism was clear: 'to muffle real conflict, to dissolve it into a false political consensus; to build, not a genuine and radical community of life and interest, but a bogus conviviality between every social group'.[140] Indeed, *contra* the semantics of capitalist 'theology', transformations in private property and commodity production produced increasing inequality and a diminution of people's quality of life, understood in its widest terms, rather than in terms common to the *Economic History Review* or a Royal Commission.[141] The transmogrification of capitalism's basic dynamics was not unique to Britain, however. According to *Manifesto*'s analysis, it was a feature of 'global development', and could only be appropriated in 'international terms',[142] as part of what *Manifesto* called the 'new imperialism'.[143] 'Our allegiances can be given no longer to any partial description of international crisis', *Manifesto* concluded, 'but only to a total description, in which both movements of resistance are seen – and are to converge – so that a socialism which is both democratic and revolutionary can be realized once more as international aspiration and actuality'.[144]

Themes common to *Culture and Society* and *The Long Revolution* were evident in *Manifesto*, including Williams's characteristic emphasis on the importance of culture and communications to capitalism's reproduction.[145] However, *Manifesto* also marked a number of ruptures in Williams's politics, not least his move toward the unambiguous view that socialist revolution was the only solution to capitalism's inherent economic, political and cultural deficiencies. But, above all, *Manifesto* marked Williams's recognition that the British state and its complicity with imperialism were among the primary obstacles to social transformation in Britain. Imperialism and the state had been a concern of Williams's politics since the 1930s, but they had received little attention in his published work. But from *Manifesto* onwards, Williams's hostility toward imperialism and the British state became customary emphases in his work.

---

139. 'The system'? This very sixties term referred to 'a world system, of a new international capitalism and a new kind of imperialism'. See Williams ed. 1968, p. 18.

140. Williams 1967, p. 7; Williams ed. 1968, p. 143.

141. See Williams 1967, pp. 9–15; Williams ed. 1968, pp. 20–30, for the analysis of 'poverty' and 'inequality'.

142. Williams 1967, p. 19.

143. See Williams 1967, pp. 20–7; and the much expanded analysis in Williams ed. 1968, pp. 66–100, for the analysis of the 'new imperialism'.

144. Williams 1967, p. 31; Williams ed. 1968, p. 142.

145. Williams ed. 1968, pp. 39–44.

Manifesto identified a number of antagonists, not least the Labour Party and bureaucratic elements within the trade-union movement. But, perhaps above all, *Manifesto* figured the British state as *the* enemy. This was primarily because the state was beholden, indeed willingly subordinate, to the imperatives of capital accumulation. Because the state operated in the interests of 'foreign capital', including the 'international firm', rather than the interests of the British people. Because it was compliant and complicit in the new imperialism and opposed the anti-colonial rebellion in the Third World.[146] Because it suffered 'still gross and intolerable areas of traditional poverty and inequality'.[147] Because it put the profit motive before national sovereignty, whether that profit was British or not. Because it favoured 'a technocratic model of society',[148] rather than a society where human needs were put first. And, because, the state had captured, disciplined and subordinated the socialist dissent initially constitutive of the labour-movement.[149] The author of that sham concept 'political consensus', the state, according to *Manifesto*, was a pivot that connected the 'new capitalism' to the 'new imperialism', and whose very existence was an obstacle to social change.

But according to the analysis of *Manifesto*, the state was not some all-powerful Leviathan. Quite the reverse. The British state, *Manifesto* argued, had been reduced '[to] creating a climate of goodwill and co-operation in the business community'.[150] Indeed, a favourite trope of *Manifesto* was to represent the British state as subordinate to other interests – international firms, 'foreign capital', the City, American foreign policy. Even the state's increased role in the economy was an indication of its subordination, since that role was in the interests of capital, sometimes 'foreign capital'. In fact, part of the problem, as *Manifesto* conceived it, was that there was too little state or the state was not powerful enough. 'We have not yet adequate planning arrangements', *Manifesto* remarked, 'for dealing with these [issues of distribution], nor does the evidence suggest that either the methodology of current planning or the instruments at governments' disposal for implementing such plans are in anyway adequate'.[151] The state lacked both the power and the will to challenge capital. Even worse: 'It is also that in the financial difficulties over sterling, and in the increasing penetration of the British economy by United States capital, pressure to support particular policies can be put on us, directly, in ways not unlike those of the new colonialism and

---

146. Williams 1967, p. 23.
147. Williams ed. 1968, p. 20.
148. Williams ed. 1968, p. 45.
149. Williams 1967, p. 5.
150. Williams ed. 1968, p. 52.
151. Williams ed. 1968, p. 53.

imperialism in the most backward parts of the world'.[152] In short, the British state was a 'client apparatus',[153] and for that reason was 'difficult to recognise because his accents and appearance are English, though his decisive agency runs back to the corporate power of the United States'.[154]

From this perspective, it is not surprising that *Manifesto* called for a transformation of the British state. Calls for workers' control in industry and communications, for participatory democracy, and the enlargement of self-government in all aspects of life underwrote *Manifesto*'s conclusion that the state and socialism were antithetical. Yet at the level of immediate reform, or indeed that of long-term transformation, *Manifesto*'s politics most often assumed the existence and continuing necessity of the state, the very institutions it imagined barriers to socialist advance. Not just 'a socialist national plan' and the 'public ownership of the means of cultural production',[155] but the appropriation of 'British overseas private holdings of foreign shares and securities' implied the structures of the (existing) British state.[156] For *Manifesto*, somewhat confusingly, socialism meant both the end of the state and the state as the end of socialism.

The source of some of this confusion derived from *Manifesto*'s contention that national economies had been undermined by the rise of the 'international firm'.[157] 'The large international companies', the 1967 *Manifesto* argued, 'are now the central institutions of the world economy'.[158] Alongside GATT American-inspired European economic co-operation, the IMF and the World Bank, the 'giant international firm' was one, perhaps the dominant, signal of the 'internationalization of the bourgeoisie'.[159] As the 1968 *Manifesto* explained, 'For their [international firms] very size, both absolutely and in relation to the size of the economies in which they participate, coupled with their economic and technological advantages, gives them an often decisive power to impose their logic on whole economies'.[160] The power of the international firm, *Manifesto* argued, was an effect of post-war American economic domination, evident not just in the (economic, cultural and ideological) penetration of Britain and Europe by American capital, but also in the degree to which British and other European states were complicit in the extension of the new (American) imperialism.[161] A decisive effect of capitalism's transformation into an 'international system' was

---

152. Williams ed. 1968, p. 100.
153. Williams ed. 1968, p. 138.
154. Ibid.
155. Williams 1967, p. 18.
156. Williams 1967, p. 20.
157. Williams ed. 1968, p. 55.
158. Williams 1967, p. 21; Williams ed. 1968, p. 47.
159. Williams ed. 1968, pp. 83–4.
160. Williams ed. 1968, p. 58.
161. Williams (ed.) 1968, p. 66.

thus the enervation of 'national economics' and 'national sovereignty', no less in advanced capitalist countries like Britain than in newly-independent states in the 'Third World'.[162]

However, *Manifesto* hardly argued that an intensified international division of labour had obliterated the nation-state, despite its anxiety about the deleterious 'national' effects – economic, political and cultural – of the 'new capitalism' and the 'new imperialism'. No matter how deleterious these effects, *Manifesto* recognised the continuing reality of 'national economics' and the national economy, regardless of how strenuously state managers or a putatively 'national' bourgeoisie might operate against its interests. Indeed, there was much confusion around 'the state' in each version of Williams's *Manifesto*. On the one hand, *Manifesto* pointed to the enhanced role of the state in the economy, perhaps the key characteristic of 'organized capitalism'. On the other hand, *Manifesto* argued that in order to 'save' British capitalism and maintain Britain's imperial role, the state had to allow 'the increasing penetration of the British economy by United States capital' and to collude in the rise and rise of 'the giant international companies'.[163] The state in this view had been reduced to creating conditions for the successful accumulation of (American) capital, although *Manifesto* stopped short of describing the state as the executive arm of the (American?) bourgeoisie. Whatever it was, the state, according to *Manifesto*, no longer represented the interests of 'the (British) people'.

From this perspective, *Manifesto* could represent socialism as the defender of the 'true national interest' – independence from American foreign and global economic policy – and situate the nation as the object of socialist practice.[164] *Manifesto* contrasted 'the true national interest' with a false 'national interest', coterminous with the interests of the City and bankers,[165] while the needs of 'the British national economy'[166] were opposed to the purpose of the international firm, and the British state's rapprochement with international capital was figured antithetical to the needs of the British people. Socialism could be finally described as 'the true future of Britain'.[167] But *Manifesto*, perhaps more in line with the sense of the radically 'international' determination of capital, also suggested that 'we are committing ourselves...to an international political struggle which includes the important political struggle within the United States'.[168] The problem was that this sense of 'international' struggle remained

---

162. Williams (ed.) 1968, p. 56.
163. Williams ed. 1968, pp. 105–6.
164. Williams 1967, p. 20.
165. Williams 1967, p. 8.
166. Williams 1967, p. 21.
167. Williams ed. 1968, p. 131.
168. Williams 1967, p. 32.

at the level of rhetoric and support, and found no representation in terms of political institutions or an alternative political community. Hence *Manifesto*'s reliance on the traditional appurtenances of a nationalised socialism, the creation of what it called a 'socialist Britain'.[169]

Manifesto, however, stopped short of endorsing nationalism, although the logic of its argument approached this precipice. *Manifesto* understood national identity as a powerful potential and actual antonym of capitalism, especially in the context of what it called Britain's 'practical dependence on the United States, expressed in political and military alliances, locked in financial arrangements and the penetration of our economy by United States capital, and supported, as a planned operation, by many kinds of cultural and educational colonization'.[170] Although *Manifesto* warned against 'English Gaullism',[171] it nonetheless rejected European integration and bemoaned 'the increasing cultural and ideological penetrations of Europe by the U.S.' – red herrings of all sorts of British nationalisms, as Tom Nairn would shortly point out. The 1967 *Manifesto* argued that '[to] be a socialist, now, is to be at the point where a firm is taken over, by foreign capital'.[172] 'Foreign capital'? Was not capital's homeland profit rather than any particular nation? That capital's first love was the balance sheet was certainly the logic behind *Manifesto*'s claim that 'companies will invest not according to a national interest, but where profit opportunities are brightest on the international market'.[173] *Manifesto* considered the view that 'the British people must go on being in need so as to make Britain strong' an 'evident lie', yet maintained nonetheless that '[it] is certainly necessary to make Britain strong'.[174] This sounded much like the 'crude nationalism' that *Manifesto* warned against.[175] While noting the dangers of the growth of British nationalism as a response to perceived American domination, *Manifesto* suggested that 'the potential emergence of this cultural contradiction has, even so, a value, indicating that we are caught, not within a sealed and inevitable system of increasing U.S. dominance, but between a series of different options, which can be taken or neglected'.[176] *Manifesto* decided that the socialist response to such nationalism would be 'ambivalent'.[177] In circumstances where Powell was mobilising the British people for a nationalism directly opposed to socialism, such hesitation was arguably a luxury that could not be afforded.

---

169. Williams 1967, p. 33.
170. Williams 1967, p. 32.
171. Williams 1967, p. 22.
172. Williams 1967, p. 42.
173. Williams ed. 1968, p. 64.
174. Williams ed. 1968, p. 133.
175. Williams ed. 1968, p. 140.
176. Williams ed. 1968, p. 66.
177. Ibid.

Manifesto's ambivalence, however, might have another source, one tied to the ambiguities of the desire for self-determination. After all, *Manifesto* was composed in an era when movements marrying social and national liberation appeared the outstanding medium of self-determination. Indeed, *Manifesto*, somewhat insensitively, and surely misguidedly, imagined Britain to be similarly located in relation to American hegemony as nations in the 'newly awakening continents'.[178] If there was an 'area of major conflict between the logic of the international firm and that of the host economy', the 'host economy' could be represented as either Britain or Zambia. In both cases foreign – American – capital ruled. Yet, *Manifesto* also characterised Britain as an 'imperialist' country. Britain's 'attempted continuation of a "world role"', *Manifesto* argued, 'of a global military system, in company with other western powers, and especially the United States, is... a fact of history'.[179] In addition, *Manifesto* held no illusions about decolonisation. Having won political independence, formerly colonial countries, *Manifesto* suggested, quickly came to appreciate their continuing subordination when they attempted to take control of their own economies. From this perspective, nationalism was a poor educator of socialism's desire, a foreshortened form of self-determination.

In its caustic view of labourism, its abhorrence of the British state, and its solidarity with 'the leaders of popular revolution in Asia, Africa and Latin America',[180] *Manifesto* could sound a lot like the Nairn-Anderson theses and the contemporaneous 'Third Worldist' politics of *New Left Review*. But *Manifesto* clearly distanced itself from *New Left Review*, and not just in its attempt to situate socialism within the 'British scene'. In internationalist terms, *Manifesto* advocated solidarity with those movements fighting against imperialism, but reserved 'the right to criticize, in the most fundamental way, their particular features'.[181] Consequently, it repudiated forms of international solidarity like that of *New Left Review* – where 'imitative forms and an imitative ideology are imported into the British movement' – which *Manifesto* described as 'damaging' and 'ridiculous'.[182] More widely, *Manifesto* argued, many socialists in Britain – whether Trotskyist, Maoist or otherwise – had become a 'client Left' responsive only to developments elsewhere. 'The many kinds of effective alienation, and of rationalization of our own predicaments', *Manifesto* argued, 'are only likely to be overcome by direct political organization and struggle in our own society'.[183] Against *New Left Review*'s tendency to primarily define socialism in 'terms of events elsewhere', *Manifesto*

178. Williams ed. 1968, p. 90.
179. Williams ed. 1968, p. 67.
180. Williams 1967, p. 32.
181. Williams ed. 1968, p. 141.
182. Ibid.
183. Williams ed. 1968, p. 171.

called for 'primary definitions of a serious, immediate and involving strategy where we live'.[184]

The national question assumed an importance in *Manifesto* that would be characteristic of Williams's work for the next twenty years. But *Manifesto* points up sharply some of the contradictions within Williams's analysis of nationhood and national identity. These contradictions, however, were less the effect of *Manifesto*'s 'Britishness', and cannot be simply considered an effect of inadequate political theory. More concretely, they were ambiguities of the social reality that the New Left reflected and reflected upon. The 'national economy' did exist alongside a capitalist world system, increasingly constituted by transnational firms whose homeland was profit rather than any particular nation. If capitalism's homeland was ultimately profit, capitalists, nonetheless, sometimes produced surplus value in national, even nationalist, terms. American hegemony, whether in terms of culture or economics, was an undeniable reality, and national identity, or something of its kind, was a natural, perhaps even necessary, response to what we would now call globalisation. Furthermore, if *Manifesto* remained caught in a national matrix, this was because this was the matrix within which most British people were caught. To be sure, the British working class, when faced with the increasing international division of labour, had a welfare-state, trade-union rights and labour-legislation to lose in addition to its chains. Calls for participatory democracy and workers' control in *Manifesto* were earnest, and a reflection of a groundswell of alienation from processes of centralisation, but the transposition of self-government to practical policy was always likely to be convoluted, if not utopian, given the 'national' nature of society. In short, *Manifesto* wrestled with a social reality constituted by a bewildering mix of national and international impulses, whose domestication eluded Williams, and continues to elude, not just socialism but political theory more generally.

Manifesto is nonetheless a remarkable document. Without justification, *Manifesto* is often overlooked in accounts of Williams's work. 'May I express to you my unreserved admiration for the way in which you have pulled us round and given us a new opportunity?' Thompson wrote at the time in relation to Williams's involvement in *Manifesto*. 'You must have sensed you alone could have performed this role, uncongenial as it may be'.[185] *Manifesto* is remarkable in pointing up the centrality of national issues to New Left political thought in general, and in Williams's thought in particular. It is, above all, a salutary reminder to those who believe that Williams always neglected imperialism and was always insensitive to the Empire's role in the production of British identities. The relationship between the nation-state and the world-market, between

---

184. Ibid.
185. E.P. Thompson, cited in Smith 2008, p. 9.

national and social liberation, and between national identity and class were central to *Manifesto*, as they would be to Williams's writings in the 1970s and 1980s.

V

In concert with its radical critique of the British state, *Manifesto* also offered support for Britain's peripheral nationalisms, at least to the extent that these anti-British nationalisms heralded a potential challenge to the state, the profit motive and the routines of capitalist politics.[186] The combination, however, contained a different potential, to say nothing of a different politics: not a challenge to the British state because it was capitalist but because it was British, not support for peripheral nations because they were potentially anti-capitalist but because they were Scottish or Welsh. Here socialism's emphasis on people's self-determination could be transformed into the self-determination of peoples, a very different thing; and socialism's *telos* could become less a classless society than a society that was anything but British.[187] The slippage from a concern with the self-determination of people to a concern with the self-determination of peoples because they were Welsh or Scottish was arguably evident in Williams's engagement with Wales.[188] But, if witness to Williams's increasing concern with Welsh national liberation, *Manifesto* also documented Williams's increasing radicalisation, his unambiguous allegiance to revolutionary socialism. From the mid-1960s, alongside an increasingly confessed sense of Welsh identity, Williams pledged allegiance to revolutionary socialist politics and, eventually, to an international milieu of Marxist theory and practice. Beside the tension their juxtaposition caused, how these issues fit together in Williams's writings in the 1970s and 1980s will be the concern of what follows.

Williams belief that British socialism was doomed – doomed not because socialism was ruined but because 'Britishness' and the British state were antithetical to socialism[189] – was, no doubt, an important factor in his increasing engagement with Welsh nationalism from the late 1960s onwards (he joined the Welsh nationalist party Plaid Cymru in 1969).[190] However, he mostly chose other, more positive, terms to account for the engagement. 'When people', Williams said, 'started saying that there are specific experiences of democratic communities,

---

186. Williams ed. 1968, p. 163.
187. See Hobsbawm 1977, pp. 3–23.
188. The general slippage is elucidated in Eagelton 1999, pp. 41–66.
189. See Williams 2003, p. 65.
190. Smith 2008, p. 478. See Davies 1983; McAllister 2001, for histories of Plaid Cymru.

specific moral concerns within the religious tradition, specific attachments through language and the literature to values which are under pressure nearer the centre; and that out of this there are the materials for an alternative direction...when these feelings came together to identify themselves with Wales, I began to feel I could relate, and not just to my own area but to an entity one was then calling Wales'.[191] It was never as easy as this, as his writings on Wales testify. Connection with Wales was always a struggle; most of all against what others might consider Wales, especially other Welsh.

Initially, Williams figured Welsh nationalism a function of those energies that were propelling the 'new socialism'. According to him, 'through [Welsh nationalism's] radical emphasis on identity and community, and in its turn to popular campaigning, to demonstrations and to direct action, this new Welsh movement...has come through as part of the new socialism and the new thinking which in many parts of the world has been called the New Left'.[192] Indeed, highlighting Welsh nationalism's openness to the world, Williams compared – somewhat cavalierly and surely misguidedly – Wales's nationalist movement to Black Power in the US and to the Civil Rights campaign in Ulster, even to the student movement and women's liberation.[193] Increasingly, however, Williams saw Welsh nationalist politics as a replacement for socialism. *Contra* the contemporary doldrums of British socialism, nationalist politics, according to Williams, offered a 'sense of what any of this liberation is for, the sense of what the struggle would be able to attain, the sense of what that human life would be, other than merely Utopian rhetoric, which is the object of all the preoccupied conflict and struggle and argument'.[194] For Williams, the negations of socialism, its critique of capitalism and bourgeois politics, was never enough. 'You've got to have some sense of what genuinely would be a different way to live',[195] and this Williams suggested was precisely what British socialism had lost.[196] It is then surprising to remember that the New Left itself offered this critique of socialism, but that figures like Thompson believed that the meaning of what it was all for was still to be found in socialism's past and present.

The rejection of socialism, as we will see, was far from complete in Williams's encounter with Welsh nationalism. That encounter was triangulated by three distinctions: between a political and a cultural sense of nationhood, between a progressive and a reactionary nationalism and between a genuine and a false nationalist passion. Responding to his *New Left Review* interlocutors, Williams

191. Williams 2003, p. 88.
192. Williams 2003, p. 4.
193. Ibid.
194. Williams 2003, p. 185.
195. Williams 2003, p. 90.
196. Williams 1979a, p. 255.

remarked that 'Wales had never been a nation: it had always had a cultural rather than a national existence'.[197] For Williams, people's 'real identity' would be found in 'culture' rather than the 'state', a seemingly curious reversal of the common-sense view that a 'good' national identity is associated with 'politics' and a 'bad' national identity with 'culture' (or ethnicity). But by 'culture' Williams did not mean 'race' or 'ethnicity'. As he explained, he referred to language, literature and distinctive social relations, a complex history of ruptures and continuities in the life of the Welsh people.[198] 'All the real processes have been cultural and histori-cal', he believed, 'and all the artificial processes have been political in one after another dominative proclamation of a state and an identity'.[199] The national revival in Wales, he reckoned, was 'the working through of a history, among now radically dislocated as well as subordinated people, rather than the fortunate re-emergence of a subdued essence'.[200]

The contention that Wales's nationalist movement projected an identity based on history rather than 'race' or 'ethnicity' was further elaborated in Williams's distinction between a 'progressive' and a 'reactionary' nationalism.[201] Wales's nationalism, according to Williams, was an example of a 'progressive' nation-alism – that is to say, a nationalism 'which questions the whole basis of the unitary British state',[202] and was based on a 'marginal or absorbed or oppressed nationality'.[203] A reactionary nationalism, on the other hand, '[reinforced] the idea of the traditional nation-state', was based on an assumed stable essence, whether biological or cultural, and was associated with 'some particular domi-nant large nation-state or...empire'.[204] Finally, Williams drew a distinction between a 'false' nationalist passion based on 'fancy dress', an invented, in the sense of unreal, national identity, and a 'genuine' nationalist passion that was grounded in the popular desire for self-determination.

Thus, an outstanding feature of Williams's re-engagement with Wales was his repudiation of what he considered an inauthentic – political, reactionary, false – Welsh nationalism. Indeed, Williams consistently repudiated versions of Welsh nationalism based on 'bardism and druidism'.[205] Not for Williams that 'tourist version of a wholly distinct people, with bits and pieces of local colour'.[206] Con-sistent with a long-held abhorrence of racism (something perhaps confirmed in

197. Williams 1979, p. 26. See also Williams 2003, pp. 23, 34.
198. See Williams 2003, p. 5.
199. Williams 1983b, p. 196.
200. Williams 2003, p. 22.
201. This distinction was adumbrated in Williams 2003, p. 86.
202. Williams 2003, p. 204.
203. Ibid.
204. Ibid.
205. Williams 2003, p. 10.
206. Williams 2003, p. 188.

a tank fighting Nazism), Williams repudiated any sort of nationalism based on 'race' or 'nation'. But Williams, like Tom Nairn, was always careful to pay due respect to popular forms of Welsh nationalism, rather than simply dismiss them as reactionary archetypes, as he argued many internationalists did. Williams understood that it was precisely this type of nationalism that gained recognition from the Other (England), that it was in some sense an inevitable and determined response to being 'oppressed' as Welsh.[207]

Against what he dubbed 'romantic nationalism',[208] Williams drew a picture of an emergent, historically-aware, self-reflective Welsh culture and a 'genuine and significant nationalist movement'[209] – a movement which worked for an 'effective modern community' and which encouraged people 'to take control of [their] own energies and resources'.[210] The overwhelming advantage of Welsh nationalism, for Williams, was in this sense twofold: on the one hand, it offered new meanings of 'community' and, on the other hand, it constituted a unique political process 'by which people can really govern themselves'.[211] Both of these concepts – community and participatory democracy – will be recognisable from Williams's earlier work, although here transformed from something distinctively working-class to something distinctively Welsh. According to Williams, 'the most valuable emphasis in Welsh culture is that everybody should speak and have the right to speak: an idea of an equal-standing and participating democracy which was there in experience before it became theory',[212] while 'community' was coterminous with the Welsh nationalist project of 'trying to find terms which represent an emphasis on certain kinds of direct and directly responsible relationships, as against a centre of power and display'.[213] Indeed, according to Williams, the attempt 'to extend new meanings of community towards a whole movement', that process of 'extending obligations of neighbourhood, very much attached to place',[214] to the whole of society, was emblematic of the Welsh nationalist movement at its best.

Williams, then, offered an attractive vision of a Welsh nationalism that sought to repudiate all that was bad about nationalism (race, mythic past, fancy dress) and recover all that was positive about place, community and belonging. It was a Welsh nationalism that stressed diversity and the 'complexity' of history,[215] and that was associated with good sounding phrases like 'new perspectives' and 'new

207. Williams 2003, p. 11.
208. Williams 2003, pp. 23–4.
209. Williams 2003, p. 189.
210. Ibid.
211. Williams 2003, p. 188.
212. Williams 2003, p. 26.
213. Williams 2003, p. 178.
214. Williams 2003, p. 185.
215. Williams 2003, p. 16.

affirmatives'.[216] However, it might be argued, and indeed Stuart Hall would later suggest as much, that such an emergent 'anti-nationalist nationalism'[217] overlooked the political necessity of 'strategic essentialism'.[218] Hand-wringing about identity and 'the real complications of history' was not a feature of successful national-liberation struggles in the so-called Third World.[219] Arguably, the (partial) successes of decolonisation relied on a relatively clear bifurcation – us ('the people') versus them ('the foreign imperialists'). This is the strategic essentialism that Hall considered vital to political and cultural hegemony, indeed to politics itself – the necessary illusion that a people is articulated by a coherent essence. Initially a division created by 'the imperialists', since it is 'the imperialists' who exploit, oppress and condemn groups of human beings as *a* people, these metaphysical categories have been crucial to struggles against oppression. As Tom Nairn put the argument, nationalism 'meant the conscious formation of a militant, inter-class community rendered strongly (if mythically) aware of its own separate identity vis-à-vis the outside forces of domination'.[220] And that separate (mythical) identity required the appeal to 'ethnos, speech, folklore, skin colour, and so on'.[221] No matter how disquieting the results, a settled, part-fantastical, identity has been the wretched of the earth's entry ticket into modernity, and arguably the basis of any successful (nationalist) politics.

Williams was aware of the dilemma, and of that dilemma, faced by all nationalist movements, of steering a course between highlighting subordination and projecting an identity capable of resistance.[222] Indeed, Williams could sometimes lurch toward projecting an essential Welshness. He could make claims that a 'communal feeling' was stronger in Wales than in England.[223] He could speak of 'Welsh social relations', a 'Welsh structure of feeling',[224] and wax rhapsodically about his relationship to Wales's landscape.[225] Nationalists often think of their nation as the best, capable of leading the world to liberation, and Williams sometimes fell into this trap when describing the Welsh as 'a cultured and radical people',[226] better placed than any other to realise self-determination. And his hard-won sense of culture as a 'common human inheritance' was sometimes lost in his subjective wrangling with the complexities of 'Welsh culture'. But Williams

216. William 2003, p. 103.
217. Williams 2003, p. 24.
218. See Hall 1991a, p. 51, for an explication of 'strategic essentialism'.
219. Williams 2003, p. 16.
220. Nairn 1977, p. 340.
221. Ibid.
222. Williams 2003, p. 9.
223. Williams 2003, pp. 20–1.
224. Williams 2003, p. 103.
225. Williams 2003, p. 88.
226. Williams 2003, p. 26.

mostly remembered that a nationalist politics could not stop at nationalism if it was to fulfil the project incipient in its emphasis and appeal.[227] 'Radical and communal Wales', Williams commented, 'will be real to the extent that it develops, in plan and practice, new forms of co-operative and communal socialism, new kinds of educational and cultural collectives'.[228] Nationalist politics, Williams believed, had to be gone through, but he also believed it had to come out the other side on 'effective new common ground'.[229]

However, there were other problems with Williams's assessment of Welsh nationalism, problems that began with the divisions on which that assessment was based. Williams's argument that a 'political' nationalism always gives rise to a false national identity will come as a surprise to numerous nationalism scholars. More in the train of Williams's own thought, it might be pointed out that culture is always political whether it represents a state or not. Indeed, it is strange for someone who considered trade-unions a distinctive and valuable aspect of culture to make such a distinction, unless by the difference Williams was simply stating the banal truth that Wales had never been a nation-state. The distinction between 'good' and 'bad' nationalisms is also false, the argument that 'small' nations are more kindly and internationalist than 'big' nations dubious. The distinction between a 'false' and 'actual' – favourite words of Williams's discourse – nationalist passion is also highly debatable for many of the same reasons. A nationalist desire defined in terms of liberation and democracy is a fact of history. But so is its possible transmogrification into a nationalism of empire, the denial of liberty and democracy to others.

At its best, Williams's version of Welsh nationalism represented what Henri Lefebvre termed 'the great collective project'. As Fredric Jameson explains Lefebvre's meaning, the great collective project is 'the attempt to construct a nation' which will always involve mobilisation of 'the people'.[230] The sense of 'the people' creating the nation for their own needs and in their own interests was crucial to Williams's illumination of Welsh nationalism. So was the sense that Welsh nationalism would speak to those primary emotional bonds of place and belonging that capitalism and big states such as Britain overrode in the interests of profit and power. But from another perspective it might appear irresponsible, especially to socialists. British socialism was not complete nonsense, even that limited form associated with labourism, as Thompson would remind New Left comrades again and again. If the British (or English) state had oppressed the Welsh, it also had been forced to concede elements of democracy and a

---

227. Williams 2003, p. 178.
228. Williams 2003, p. 26.
229. Williams 2003, p. 72.
230. Lefebvre cited in Jameson 2008, n. 11, p. 469.

welfare-state – much of which had been fought for and won by a British working class. If Britain had exploited Welsh natural resources for its own (capitalist and self-serving centrist) ends, it had also been the most effective framework of the British working class's struggle against capitalism. By the early 1980s, socialists – including Williams – would be fighting a rearguard action to save much of this state. In its assessment of peripheral nationalisms, *Manifesto* had claimed 'There will be Scots and Welsh to oppose, as well as 'the English'; and there will be English to ally with'.[231] And this, in *Manifesto*'s logic, because the British state was bad for everyone – not because it was British, but because it was capitalist and complicit in all sorts of old and new imperialisms.

Adjacent to Williams's engagement with Welsh nationalism, much of his thinking throughout the 1970s was concerned with issues of revolution, class-struggle, Marxist theory and a really existing sense of socialist internationalism. Shortly after Williams's death, Terry Eagleton remarked that in 'a welcome reversal of the usual clichéd trek from youthful radical to middle-aged reaction', Williams's 'career [moved] steadily further to the left'.[232] The political road less travelled began from *Modern Tragedy*, published just prior to Williams's involvement in the *May Day Manifesto* project. *Modern Tragedy* contained an appeal for revolution and an awareness of the 'terror' that would inhabit such a transformation – an awareness that this was tragic, but nonetheless necessary and inevitable in the creation of what the book called 'an acceptable human order'.[233] As Williams nuanced this argument in *Politics and Letters*: 'there is…a very problematic relation between a liberating humane movement and the necessity of attacking repression, of defending the revolution against counter-revolution and external intervention, of sustaining discipline and democracy inside the revolution'.[234] This argument has an air of 'unreality' about it, and not because it pointed to the complex relationship between terror and revolution, something which has returned to discussions of revolution in our own time, but because it appeared just five years after Williams's elucidation of a very different sort of revolution.

Williams's political pathway was also reflected in *The Country and the City*, published in the early 1970s. A book that tracked interpretations of the relationship between 'the country' and 'the city' and related these to transformations in social, economic and political history, *The Country and the City* contained a powerful critique of 'socialist progressivism'.[235] Beside insightful assessments of 'retrospective radicalism' and elucidations of the ways in which 'community' in

231. Williams ed. 1968, p. 163.
232. Eagleton 1988, p. 7.
233. Williams 1966, pp. 76–7.
234. Williams 1979a, p. 398.
235. Williams 1973, pp. 36–7.

rural Britain had been transformed, and not in necessarily bad ways, by techno-logical development, the book also included an idiosyncratic defence of peas-ant socialisms in Vietnam, Cuba and other 'Third World' countries. 'In a whole epoch of national and social liberation struggle', Williams argued, 'the exploited rural and colonial populations became the main sources of continued revolt'.[236] Williams experienced this epoch in a very personal way. 'This change of basic ideas and questions [about the relation between humans and nature], especially in the socialist and revolutionary movements, has been for me the connection which I have been seeking for so long, through the local forms of a particular and personal crisis, and through the extended inquiry which has taken many forms but which has come through in this inquiry into the country and city'.[237] On an international scale, Williams believed, 'the country' was reminding 'the city' of the values that made a fully human order.

The Country and the City contained much else beside an appeal to the human values of socialist revolution in the Third World. Most of all it wrestled with the problem of the relationship 'between customary and educated feeling and thought', and how this tension might be worked out in a socialist politics that while aware of the impossibility of going back to some pre-industrial age none-theless imagined a different society based on values lost in the past.[238] All the characteristic and productive tensions that have become associated with Williams's writing were present in *The Country and the City*, not so much the 'border country' between custom and knowledge, but the ways in which a con-temporary social theory and socialist strategy might bridge the gap between the two. Something of the bridging process was captured in the book's concluding pages. 'For we really have to look', Williams wrote, 'in country and city alike, at the real social processes of alienation, separation, externality, abstraction. And we have to do this not only critically, in the necessary history of rural and urban capitalism, but substantially, by affirming the experiences which in many mil-lions of lives are discovered and rediscovered, very often under pressure: expe-riences of directness, connection, mutuality, sharing, which alone can define, in the end, what the real deformations may be'.[239] That Williams saw this pro-cess at work in Third World revolutionary socialisms and their struggle against imperialism spoke to some of his deepest-felt convictions. 'When I look at the history of the Chinese, Cuban and the Vietnamese revolutions', Williams wrote,

---

236. Williams 1973, p. 304.
237. Williams 1973, p. 305.
238. Williams 1973, p. 37.
239. Williams 1973, p. 298.

'I feel a basic solidarity not merely with their aims but with their methods and with the ways in which they came to power'.[240]

Williams's defence of revolutionary socialisms in the Third World was bound to please the editors of New Left Review, although it might have raised the hackles of some old New Left comrades, such as Thompson, who perhaps might have pointed out that some of these peasant socialisms were Stalinist and as such no friend of the countryside. Indeed, Williams expanded on that defence in the series of interviews with New Left Review that became Politics and Letters. As a document of the time, the interviews reflect a sustained vindication of revolutionary socialism, something revealed not just in Williams's assessment of contemporary communist movements in China or Vietnam, but also in an eclectic rationalisation of the Russian Revolution.[241] Still, for all his enthusiasm for China and Cuba, Williams took his distance from the politics that he associated with some tendencies within New Left Review. When probed about the differences between Stalin and Trotsky in Politics and Letters, Williams responded to his New Left Review interlocutors that '[there] is a certain contrast between the banality and frustration of contemporary British politics and the enormous élan of the Russian Revolution and its successors, which can lead to a kind of perpetual miming of these past historical situations'.[242] 'A particular kind of political alienation', he went on, 'can occur when people opt for revolutionary processes which have happened elsewhere, coming alive more when they are relating to those than when they are engaging with the drabness of their own situation'.[243] In other words, the association with Third World socialist revolution, or indeed with socialist revolution's past, could be a way of avoiding the problems of the present, and missing the socialist 'signs in the street'.

The process by which Williams grew more dangerous as he aged was also manifest in his increasing engagement with continental Marxist theory. Thompson, writing in the early 1970s, maintained that Williams stood apart from that 'fashionable and sometimes scholastic Marxism that derives...from Paris or Milan'.[244] In actual fact, from the mid-1960s onwards Parisian and Milanese Marxism played a big part in his thinking, even if it did not result in a rapid or fashionable assimilation to their modes. Coming upon the work of Lucien Goldmann – the other thinker he mentioned in this connection was Lukács – Williams found many of the concerns with totality that had motivated The Long Revolution, and noted the connections between Goldmann's 'genetic structures'

---

240. Williams 1989, p. 73.
241. Williams 1979a, p. 405.
242. Williams 1979a, p. 403.
243. Ibid.
244. E.P. Thompson 1994, p. 243.

and his own 'structures of feeling'.[245] After reading Marcuse, he experienced 'a sense of meeting, after a long separation',[246] while Gramsci became an important influence on his journey through Marxist theory. Williams's dialogue with these different traditions of Marxism placed him within 'an international context in which', as he suggested, 'for the first time in [his] life' he felt he belonged 'to a sphere and dimension of work in which [he] could feel at home'.[247] The mature product of Williams's engagement with continental Marxism was *Marxism and Literature*, a credo for 'cultural materialism' that has had an influence far outside Britain and far outside literary studies. No-one could now charge Williams with parochialism.

An important practical effect of Williams's encounter with continental Marxism, at least in terms of his thinking about literature and society, was his rejection of 'Englishness' and the project of 'English studies', although he did not give-up the need to challenge and engage these modes of thinking, he did so now less on their own terms. Indeed, his engagement with 'theory', for this engagement was not just with Marxism but also with structuralism and semiotics, was a way of repudiating that dominant sense of 'Literature' as a canon of received imaginative works and which, in England at least, had become associated with a national identity under contemporary threat.[248] Against this conception of literature, Williams moved to a position 'which instead of privileging a generalised Literature as an independent source of values insists on relating the actual variety of literature to historical processes in which fundamental *conflicts* had necessarily occurred and were still occurring'.[249] Melding Thompson with Althusser might be one way of describing this stance. Thus, Williams's long revolution in theory resulted in a definition of culture 'as a (social and material) productive process and of specific practices, of "arts", as social uses of material means of production (from language as material "practical consciousness" to the specific technologies of writing and forms of writing, through to mechanical and electronic communications systems)'.[250] This was a long way from Leavis.

The rejection of 'Englishness' as an ideology in literary criticism was reflected in Williams's increasing sense of himself as European, and the strengthening political and cultural hope he placed in the process of European integration.[251] *Manifesto* had been circumspect to say the least about Britain's proposed entry

---

245. Williams 1980b, pp. 11–30.
246. Williams 1970b, pp. 164–5.
247. Williams 1977, pp. 4–5.
248. Williams 1985, p. 195.
249. Williams 1985, p. 211.
250. Williams 1980b, p. 243.
251. Williams 1979a, p. 296.

into Europe, describing the common market, with some justification, as little more than a capitalist symphony conducted by the United States. However by the mid-1970s Williams saw 'Europe' in more hopeful terms, belying the expectation of Tom Nairn.[252] Indeed, it was at this time that Williams felt able to connect his sense of Welshness, his interest in continental Marxist theory and his perception of Europe as offering an alternative to the dominations and redundancies of the British state. Europe, he suggested, was a means by which people, especially people in regions like Wales and the Basque country, could determine 'the conditions of their own social being' – a need that he believed was at the basis of both 'Marxism' and 'nationalism' (in the best sense of that term).[253] Europe, Williams believed, 'was a perspective that can be shared by all those who in loyalty to their own actual people refuse to assimilate to singular and romantic national traditions'.[254]

Wales, Europe and international socialism – Williams imagined these as connected and connecting 'identities' all pulling in the same direction. Was this the case? Williams would have replied that it had to be the case if socialism, on an international scale, was to be anything more than a quixotic fancy. The obverse argument, that emotional bonds connected with family are more often the basis of ethnic nationalism than socialism, that community most often disabled rather than enabled working-class politics, that the nation, even the 'marginal' nation, was an imagined community which imagined away divisions of class, that Europe was a way of making the nation-state stronger and democracy weaker, is obvious enough, a feature, as we will see of a variety of New Left thinkers' engagement with the national question. But it would be silly to suggest that Williams was not aware of them. As we shall review at greater depth in the final section, Williams nonetheless believed that reason would never be enough to establish a socialist society because, unlike less 'rational' bonds associated with kinship, place, and community, reason alone could not establish identities that would hold.

VI

The fortunes of Welsh nationalism, to say nothing of his interest in the deep past of Wales, remained a preoccupation of Williams's work up until his death in 1988. But the rebirth of socialism was no less a concern of Williams's late theoretical and political interventions, and this very much due to the hegemony of a reinvigorated New Right and the prospect that industrial societies like Britain were

---

252. Nairn 1972, pp. 106–8.
253. Williams 2003, p. 86.
254. Williams 2003, p. 68.

in the process, as he put it, of smashing themselves up.[255] The two – Wales and socialism – were always connected in Williams's mind. However it is undeniable that Williams returned in significant ways in his final decade to reconsider the question of socialism separate from Welsh nationalism – both the question of the types of social identity that were crucial to its future and the question of its social location in the terms of a salient political framework. This is perhaps unremarkable given the specific nature of the social and political crisis which constituted Williams's final years, not just crises of social inequality generated by de-industrialisation and bitter class-conflict, but also global crises of environment, technology (nuclear weapons) and international relations (the Second Cold War).

In an interview shortly before his death, Williams argued that any 'new theory of socialism must centrally involve place'.[256] For Williams, 'full social identities' attached to place had always been crucial to the strength and success of proletarian politics. He believed the General Strike of 1926, and the miners' strike of the mid-1980s, had clearly shown how imperative communal social relations were to proletarian organisation. In both cases, he argued, place had been integral to the formation and unusual strength of workers' class-consciousness. 'During the General Strike itself, and in the long months after it, when the miners held out', he suggested, 'it mattered, in our village, that we had a physical and communal and not an abstract connection'.[257] For Williams, 'the real and powerful feelings of a native place and a native formation' were crucial to the strength of working-class consciousness,[258] and just as significant to a vision of an alternative social order – an organisation of society that was not just an extension of, but also liberation from, the capitalist enterprise.

Indeed, Williams made the idiosyncratic argument – at least for someone who described himself as a 'revolutionary socialist' – that 'country' rather than 'class' was the more basic, determining, hard-held social bond and the more hopeful location for the production of socialist identities. This was partly a concession to the empirical record. The class-bond, Williams supposed, had not trumped 'the more local bonds of region or nation'.[259] But, in his mind, the empirical fact had a more constructive potential. Class solidarity, Williams argued, 'begins in very local, even physical ways'.[260] 'It is the ethic of a group', he went on, 'which has already been decisively established, often it is true by the initial action of

255. Williams 2003, p. 190.
256. Williams 2003, p. 208.
257. Williams 2003, p. 43.
258. Williams 1983b, p. 181.
259. Williams 2003, p. 216.
260. Williams 2003, p. 40.

others... but then, in shared immediate working experience, in the developing experience of a local community, in growing ties of family and kinship, a group which has the potential of solidarity already physically within it'.[261] His examples, as always, were working-class communities in south Wales. According to Williams, class-consciousness, at least in the case of the working-class, was always parasitic on other types of bonding. 'For, historically, it seems to be more and more true that where centres of proletarian consciousness developed, their strength really drew from the fact that all the bonds were holding in the same direction'.[262] Socialism was akin to love for Williams, as it was for Thompson, but in the case of Williams this was meant in a very literal sense. For Williams, class-solidarity began at home and not only in objective economic positions.

Williams's emphasis on territorial social identities can be seen as a reflection of workers' historical embeddedness in specific places. As Williams once remarked, it is the bourgeoisie not workers who have lived capitalist globalisation.[263] But there is another perspective, very much neglected in Williams's late reflections on socialism and place. It is not just that it was precisely those 'places' which Williams's considered the locus for a 'reviving socialism' that had been ruthlessly abandoned by intensified, increasingly transnational, modes of capital accumulation. Williams would have retorted that 'place' became even more important the more footloose capital became, and that his point was very much about the *construction*, not just through kinship and neighbourhood, but also the political struggle of communal relations. Rather, what Williams's late reflections on socialism neglected was Perry Anderson's insight that confined to place – whether community, region, even the nation-state – working-class-militancy has constituted an easy target for capital. Thus it is not so much that place was crucial to the success of proletarian politics, but rather that the failure of socialist politics has been an effect of the centrality of place to the working-class's lived experience. Put another way, 'territorially based popular mobilization' has been one way in which the proletariat has been constrained from an awareness of its universal class-interest. Even the nation-state – the basis of so much working-class struggle – has proved an inadequate framework for working-class solidarity, as the history of twentieth century socialism proves.

Williams would have agreed that the nation-state was part of the problem. But he also believed that the politics of place had nothing to do with 'the nation', at least not in the sense that the nation was a 'political and administrative

---

261. Ibid.
262. Williams 2003, p. 208.
263. Williams 1989, p. 252.

organisation.[264] Nations like Britain might well recall 'real and powerful feelings of a native place and a native formation',[265] but they were a betrayal of those emotions rather than their fulfilment. States, and the nations which were joined to them, were a product of ruling-class triumph, not popular sovereignty Williams argued. The nation was associated with exploitation, oppression and war not love, nurture and welfare. Indeed, according to Williams, the nation-state was a function of capitalism, a mode of production 'which has disrupted and overridden natural communities, and imposed artificial orders'.[266] It was, then, not just ironic but an outrage that 'capitalist states have again and again succeeded in mobilising patriotic feelings in their own forms and interests'.[267] No doubt, Thatcher's Britain, on the verge of war in the south Atlantic, was foremost in Williams's mind. 'It is human nature', Williams wrote, 'to belong to a society, and to find value in belonging to it'.[268] Patriotism or nationalism (Williams most often elided the two) spoke to this deep human need, but in a language bound to occlude its realisation. The modern Judas rather than the modern Janus – this was the better description of nationalism, according to Williams.

From this perspective, socialism's proper object was to rescue the 'real' social identities attached to place from the grip of nationalist casuistries. Socialism needed to oppose capitalism and undermine its nationalist supports in the cause of human nature. But it could not oppose them with abstractions, such as 'the international proletariat' or 'humanity'. It must, Williams went on, mobilise 'deeply grounded and active social identities',[269] those bonds associated with belonging and place that potentially worked against both 'mobile privatized relations of capitalism' and the false identities of nationalism. 'A socialist position on social identity certainly rejects, absolutely, the divisive ideologies of "race" and "nation", as a ruling class functionally employs them. But it rejects them in favour of lived and formed identities either of a settled kind, if available, or of a possible kind, where dislocation and relocation require new formation.'[270] Politics and law – what we might term 'instrumental reason' – was not enough. This was the source of Williams's rejection of appeals to purely contractual definitions of citizenship as a response to racism and nationalism, both significant features of the British political landscape in the early 1980s. 'It is by working and living together, with some real place and common interest to identify with, and as free as may be from external ideological definitions, whether divisive or universalist, that

---

264. Williams 1983b, p. 181.
265. Ibid.
266. Williams 1983b, p. 184.
267. Ibid.
268. Williams 1983b, p. 179.
269. Williams 1983b, p. 195.
270. Williams 1983b, p. 196.

real social identities are formed'.[271] For Williams, socialism would constitute the realisation of those values of sharing found in a 'knowable community', shaped as much by consciousness as face-to-face relations. Such a constitution of social relations, he argued, was the best safeguard against racism.

Williams's mature reflections on socialism and identity, and on the nation-state and nationalism, recall many of his arguments from the early 1960s. Like those arguments, his late assessment of nationhood, nationalism and the relationship between socialism and identity can sometimes appear thin, if not misguided. For example, Williams could be surprisingly deaf to the genuine hold that nationality had on people's sense of self, even in places like Britain. Far from merely a capitalist ruse, or a misplaced appropriation of people's need for nurture, belonging and welfare, nation-states constitute the locus of collective identities that have proven remarkably resilient, emerging unscathed from the wars and revolutions of modernity and the 'para-national' trends associated with postmodernity. Their functionality for capital accumulation – 'flags of convenience' in Williams's phrase – is not explanation enough for this resilience.[272] No matter how inadequately, nations have been sources of welfare, nurture and care, and even of genuine affection. As Perry Anderson has suggested, Williams had overlooked 'the overpowering dimension of collective meaning that modern nationalism has always involved: that is, not its functionality for industry, but its fulfillment of identity'.[273] This oversight is particularly striking in a thinker otherwise attuned to the sensibilities of place and the psychical value of belonging, and the role they play in the construction of social identity. Williams arguably had a point when he suggested that old nation-states like Britain were both too big and too small to operate in a world increasingly constituted by trans-national economic flows and the particularisms associated with ethnicity, but he was wrong to suggest that this would imply any lessening of their hold over identity.[274] Tom Nairn would have added that he was also wrong to designate Britain as either normal or a nation-state.

Williams's appeal to 'full social identities' beyond the legalisms of political citizenship, particularly as a response to communal oppression and racism, was also misguided. The problem was not his rejection of the instrumental reasons of state and the law. If Williams did reject this type of reason, it was in the cause of a substantive human reason, one manifest in the clearing of a field, the composition of a poem or the establishment of local ties and affections out of economic exploitation and metropolitan neglect. Williams's formulation of the

---

271. Ibid.
272. Williams 1989, p. 253.
273. Anderson 1992b.
274. See Williams 2003, p. 204, for the 'end of the nation-state' argument.

problem, however, overlooked the place of such legalisms in any response to communal oppression, a necessary if not sufficient solution for racism as Stuart Hall has often pointed out. Hall would have agreed with Williams that place and territorially – embedded identities become more important as a response to capitalist globalisation, and that attachments based on 'class' and 'nation' were outdated and shop-soiled, but he would have repudiated Williams's solution to racism arguing instead that blacks in Britain must proclaim both their blackness and their Britishness.[275] Nairn, however, would have agreed with Williams, suggesting that the propagation of Britishness, no matter in what cause, was simply a way of denying other sorts of identity.

In the spirit of his rejection of the nation-state, and in concert with his support for the European Union, indeed with his own sense of himself as a Welsh European, Williams evoked 'self-governing societies' as socialism's proper social location. 'We've all noticed', he remarked to his *New Left Review* interlocutors, 'the general vagueness of the social location of socialism: at one stage it was the world, or perhaps a continent; or it can be half a continent, or one of the old nation-states, or a new federation of them, some nation or region breaking away'.[276] In *Towards 2000*, Williams decided that a prospective socialism would be located in 'effective self-governing societies' below the level of the nation-state, a reflection both of his belief that the nation-state was hopelessly outdated and of his long-held belief in the value of 'participatory democracy'.[277] The emphasis was on 'variable socialisms', on the fact of pluralism, and on a recognition, indeed, celebration of diversity: *'since there are many peoples and cultures'*, Williams concluded, *'there will be many socialisms'*.[278] Open to pluralism, Williams also looked toward the new social movements – the ecology-movement, the women's movement and the peace-movement – as 'our major positive resources'.[279] The new social movements, Williams believed, offered a useful reminder to socialism of 'those ultimately deeper attachments and purposes, which capitalism tries to push into a lower importance, or where necessary to cancel'.[280]

Strangely in a thinker who, as Thompson suggested, had been so resistant to fashion, Williams's late reflections on socialism could be astonishingly modish. It was not just the appeal to pluralism and diversity, concepts that were about to effect the take-off, and eventual hegemony, of identity politics. And it was not just that Williams seemed to have finally succumbed to the dominant meanings

275. Hall 1996a, p. 472.
276. Williams 1979a, p. 433.
277. Williams 1983b, pp. 197–8, 259.
278. Williams 1989, p. 297 (original emphasis).
279. Williams 1983b, p. 173.
280. Williams 1983b, p. 171.

of 'peoples and cultures' as commensurate with ethnicities. It was, above all, that Williams saw socialism's most precious resource in the gathering power of the new social movements. This is a striking judgment in a socialist thinker who had always seen socialism's greatest cultural resource in trade-unions, the co-operative movement and working-class parties, and who just a few years before had exclaimed that 'one cannot look realistically anywhere else but to the industrial working class for a socialist transformation of our societies today'.[281] More often than not, 'the new social movements' have been defined against socialism, precisely viewing the organised labour-movement as an obstacle rather than a solution to their cause. The history is more complex than this. But Anderson and others within the New Left tradition would have argued that Williams gave too much away to a politics opposed to collective labour. In addition to an overestimation of the anti-capitalist potential of feminism, ecology politics and the peace movement, Williams overlooked the failure of the new social movements to offer anything like an alternative social order.

Whether early or late, Raymond Williams's contributions to socialist thought were built on a repudiation of universalism, of socialism's necessary break with more local affections of family, community and place. Universalism, according to him, was not just a form of abstraction from the realities of 'lived and formed identities' but also a means of overriding and diminishing more concrete human ties and affections. 'It is ineffective and even trivial', he argued in *Towards 2000*, 'to come back from a demonstration of the universality of the human species and expect people, from that fact alone, to recognise their lives by treating all their immediate and actual groupings as secondary'.[282] However, it would only be half-true to describe Williams as an enemy of universalism. To be sure, he consistently repudiated 'bloodless' appeals to humanity and class, concluding, for example, that class has 'nowhere come near to realizing [its] own apparent logic, by which the offered universalities would prevail over more local forms'.[283] In this sense, Williams imagined socialism to be much more like nationalism than say Christianity, dependent on kinship relations, local affections and cultural identity rather than universal love, justice and equality. But this does not tell the whole story. For a start, Williams's rejection of 'abstraction' and his privileging of 'experience' sounds odd coming from a social theorist whose ultimate goal remained the representation of social totality, something hardly comprehensible through experience, no matter how it is defined. Indeed, it would be wrong to suggest that Williams rejected the role of love, justice and equality – no

---

281. Williams 1979a, p. 322.
282. Williams 1983b, p. 180.
283. Ibid.

more abstract or bloodless than nation or family, although Williams was likely to overlook the fact – in any effective socialist politics. Williams did believe in 'universal principles' and did imagine 'universal principles' as part of any actually existing socialism. It is just that he believed that to be binding justice and equality must be rooted in concrete relations and ties.[284]

Thus, Williams did recognise that socialism was commensurate with a general or common interest that transcended particular and particularising relationships, no matter how crucial the latter to the creation of socialist values. Williams did believe that we necessarily feel more for those around us than for abstractions like 'humanity' that, he maintained, would always lack the required psychological force to inspire either socialist dissent or socialist hegemony. But he never imagined that these feelings would operate in contradiction to a more general interest. Hence his involvement in the politics of nuclear disarmament at the height of the Second Cold War – a politics that he believed, alongside E.P. Thompson, would have to take at least a European dimension and was ultimately rooted in 'general human grounds'.[285] Hence his increasing concern with environmental degradation and the world's ecology, a concern steeped in his respect for the countryside and his concern with human care.[286] Hence his growing repudiation of 'protectionism' and Keynesian economics in the context of what he believed was a world crisis of economics and society in the 1980s.[287] And, hence his continuing definition of culture as a human inheritance that must be protected against limiting and limited definitions, whether social or biological. 'The basic campaigns for peace and for socialism', he wrote, 'will only converge if a clear socialist view of the global political economy comes through in forms that will allow the negotiation not only of general disarmament, but also of a new international economic order, and with that a new information order, which those who should be our comrades in the poorest and most exploited countries now demand'.[288] In this sense, neighbourhood, for Williams, was a practice of international socialism not someplace on the border between England and Wales.

Raymond Williams would have agreed with E.P. Thompson's suggestion that 'Socialism is the expression of man's need for his fellow men, his undivided social being, and hence it must find expression in love, even when attained only through the throes of class-hatred and conflict'.[289] Thompson's elucidation of

---

284. Ibid.
285. See Williams 1983b, p. 240; Williams 1980a, pp. 189–209.
286. See, in particular, Williams 1989, pp. 210–26. But also consider Williams 1989, pp. 67–85.
287. See Williams 1989, p. 182.
288. See Williams 1989, p. 293.
289. E.P. Thompson 1957a, p. 128.

a practical humanism more than hints at a dilemma that haunts Williams's socialist writings: how could a practice of hate (class-conflict) produce a society of love (socialism)? Williams resolved the contradiction by suggesting that socialism would move outwards from affective relations in family, neighbourhood and community. But it would be wrong to see Williams as some sort of dewy-eyed romantic. He could be remarkably hardheaded about socialism's prospects. If socialism was in some sense, and perhaps ultimately, aesthetic, a matter of feeling and emotion as much as economics, this was not because Williams imagined socialism as some sort of version of a hippie love-in. The structures of capitalist society, Williams believed, are 'maintained also and inevitably by a lived culture: that saturation of habit, of experience, of outlook, from a very early age and continually renewed at so many stages of life, under definite pressures and within definite limits, so that what people came to think and feel is in large measure a reproduction of the deeply based social order which they may even in some respects think they oppose'.[290] This is a more chilling vision than anything Althusser wrote. But it points to where Williams believed socialism would have to be made.

VII

In *The Long Revolution*, Raymond Williams distinguished a number of possible relationships between an individual and his society – member, servant, subject, rebel, exile, and vagrant.[291] Rebel perhaps most adequately captures Williams's own relations with society, an appellation even more apt when we remember that Williams divided 'rebel' into two – the reformer and the revolutionary. Contrasting the two senses, the revolutionary, Williams argued, 'lacks that sense of membership of a particular society which makes it possible for the reformer or critic to suppose that their own ends can in fact be achieved within the society's existing forms'.[292] The revolutionary's relationship to his society, Williams went on, 'is one of declared opposition and struggle for a different society'.[293] But the description hardly fits all the facts, and this because it fails to register the importance of the border-country, and Williams's memory of the warmth of community associated with it, to his sense of self and his sense of socialism. From one perspective, Williams's contributions to New Left thought offered 'a new way of life'. But the vision of that alternative was largely commensurate with the

---

290. Williams 1989, p. 74.
291. Williams 1961, pp. 104–11.
292. Williams 1961, p. 107.
293. Ibid.

recovery of a mode of living he had experienced growing up in a community on the border between Wales and England. Here, Williams found a connection that rendered him more member than rebel.

If the concept of 'individual' is fraught enough in our postmodern times – who, any longer, believes in a continuous, centred sense of the subject? – then 'society' is no less so. To get any sense of who Williams was and what his relationship to society was we would have to attach a settled meaning to society. Such settlement is elusive. Williams's first 'society' was Pandy, and this in some sense remained the most important. Cambridge was another, though here exile seems to make most sense. 'It was not my Cambridge', Williams later remembered. The New Left offered a society much more attuned to Williams's sense of self. Here member again makes most sense, but only if the meaning of membership includes difference, sometimes sharp difference. Following the dissolution of the *May Day Manifesto* movement, Williams increasingly felt Wales to be his society, not just the Wales of the border-country and the mining valleys, appropriate enough given his socialist politics, but also north Wales and a historical and cultural Wales represented by a past of rupture and continuity. At times, Williams imagined Wales as a synthesis of border-country and the New Left – home to a socialist politics warmed by the fires of community, energies of self-determination and love of place. But there were other societies too that Williams had relations with, some, like the 'European republic of Marxist letters' out of which grew *Marxism and Literature*, suggest much more cosmopolitan connections.

Williams's relationship to all these societies was complex and subtle, involving tension and pressure, words familiar from his own discourse. Perhaps unsurprisingly, much of the complexity and the pressure was characteristic of Williams's encounter with the national question. There can be few figures in the New Left, perhaps only Anderson overtops him, who displayed a more evident outrage against nationalism and a hatred of the nation-state. Yet this outrage and hate derived from a sense of the way that nations overrode actual communities and that nationalism betrayed genuine feelings of attachment to place. In this sense, he was as close to Nairn or Hall as he was to Anderson. He retained a connection with working-class politics in common with E.P. Thompson, but this connection had as much to do with a sense of kinship as class-struggle. He had international contacts equal to Anderson, but, like Thompson, he eschewed metropolitan elitism, retaining a faith in the creativity of ordinary people. Like Nairn, he placed much faith in nationalist movements on Britain's periphery but, unlike Nairn, never believed that nationalism was enough. If there was a constant course through the stream of William's political interventions, it was his ambition to reintegrate personal and social values into a movement which he believed would have to be built as much from aesthetics as from economics, as much from local affections and ties of kinship as from the solidarities created out of economic exploitation.[294] To the end he believed that socialism could not be made against those basic human emotions generated by place and community, and that any socialism that was made without them was not worth having.

---

294. Williams 1989, p. 76.

Chapter Five
Stuart Hall's Identities

I

Stuart Hall is not a cultural theorist, although he has
been among theory's most consistent, and convincing, champions. When pushed to describe his work,
Hall has always prefaced the conjunctural location
between the conceptual and the concrete.[1] Like the
overwhelming majority of contributions to New Left
thought, Hall's writings have been deliberately strategic, political interventions, whether the object is the
'glossies' or photography.[2] That many of those interventions engaged popular culture was less because
of Hall's regard for the subject and more because he
believed, like Raymond Williams, that popular culture was one of the sites where socialism might be
developed.[3] Also, like Williams's work, Hall's work
cannot be separated from a series of physical and psychical displacements that have crucially shaped his
analysis of capitalist modernity's characteristic, though
ever-changing, social and cultural relations.[4] Indeed,
it might be argued that given his colonial formation,
Hall was well prepared to tackle a series of problems
that were crucial to the nexus between socialism and
national sentiment in the twentieth century.

---

1. See Hall 2003, pp. 113–49, for a methodological elucidation of this location.
2. Hall 2009, p. 663.
3. Hall 1981, p. 239.
4. See Turner 1990, pp. 58–61, for Hall's influence on the development of cultural studies in Britain.

This chapter begins with a cursory overview of those processes of identification that have inflected Hall's thinking about the national question. Following sections of the chapter will focus on his political interventions within the context of New Left thought. The first of these sections will investigate Hall's early New Left writings. The next section will explore his writings on race and racism in the 1970s. It was during this period that Hall was interpellated as a 'black intellectual', and began to perceive 'identity' as vital to the re-invention of (new) Left politics.[5] The penultimate section of the chapter will consider Hall's part in establishing the politics of the new-look *Marxism Today* and his analysis of Thatcherism, taking his conception of national identity and nation as its touchstone. Beginning with his contribution to 'New Times', the final section of the chapter will interrogate the place of ethnicity in Hall's recent contributions to an analysis of the national question. The chapter will end with a cursory examination of the peculiar contribution that Hall has made to an understanding of the nexus between national identity and social transformation.

II

If Hall believes that identity is a matter of culture rather than nature, and that it works through difference rather than sameness, then he also believes that in order to say or write anything at all we must be placed somewhere.[6] 'What we say', Hall wrote, 'is always "in context", positioned'.[7] Where is the somewhere from which Hall has spoken? Most recently, Hall has favoured 'out of place' as the location from where he writes.[8] Escaping Jamaica, and colonialism, in the early 1950s, he arrived in Britain only to discover that he was West-Indian. Ironically, after he decided to stay, he realised that he was not West-Indian after all. 'Black Britain' was his chosen, if not exclusive, homeland from the late 1950s onwards, but this was a homeland constituted by ambiguity and contingency. Being 'out of place' has arguably inflected all Hall's political interventions. This position, however, has always been defined against somewhere else. Not just against essentialised conceptions of settlement, but also most obviously, and most recurrently, against the 'old' Left – a Left, whether communist or social-democratic, supposedly hamstrung by a shop-worn understanding of the relationship between class, identity and political interest.

---

5. For this discovery consult Hall 1991a, pp. 54–5. See Freedman 1983, p. 143, for exploration of Hall as a 'black intellectual'.

6. See Hall 1989a, pp. 9–20.

7. Hall 1996a, p. 492. In this connection, Hall much admired Edward Said's memoir *Out of Place*.

8. Hall 2009, p. 669.

Hall was born in 1932 in Jamaica – a country then enfolded in an advanced, if petrified, imperial system. His mother came from a 'lighter-skinned English-orientated faction' of Caribbean society, while his father, 'manifestly dark-skinned', came from a lower-middle class background.[9] Hall, the 'blackest' of his family, repudiated his parents' negotiation of the complex stratifications of class, colour and status characteristic of the Caribbean,[10] later recalling with disgust their attitude to everyday imperialism.[11] Hall came to see himself in the mirror of an aspiring postcolonial society, the upside-down image of his parents' relation to the culturally-inflected hierarchies typical of the Caribbean.[12] His experience of growing up in Jamaica, however, appears to have been almost wholly negative. 'I felt I couldn't fulfil my potential there [Jamaica]', he later said, 'and I couldn't work out my relationship to Jamaican culture'.[13]

'When individuals go to a new society', it has been argued, 'they experience a major gap between the alien culture and the self (in)formed elsewhere: collective and individual subjects no longer coincide'.[14] For Hall, this was only partly true. 'Having been prepared by colonial education', he later remarked, 'I knew England from the inside'.[15] He arrived in England – to study at Oxford on a Rhodes schol-arship – in 1951, just prior to the major period of West-Indian immigration to the United Kingdom in the late 1950s and 1960s.[16] Constructed as the 'familiar stranger' by his West-Indian past, England, for Hall, never felt, and would never feel, like home.[17] Displacement there, did, however, induce an intensified awareness of the place he had just escaped. In England, he became immersed in West-Indian expatriate-politics. Thus, like many migrants, Hall initially found relief from iso-lation and alienation in a 'collectivity of landsmen'.[18] Inspired by the hope of a 'united, socialist West Indian federation', he planned to return to Jamaica, along with many of his comrades, following the completion of his studies. But as hopes

---

9. Hall 1996a, p. 485.
10. Jaggi 2000, p. 8.
11. Hall 1996a, pp. 484–90; Rojeck 2003, p. 7.
12. Hall 1996a, p. 486. Later, Hall admitted that one of the reasons he left Jamaica was because of his parents: 'I hate the way my mother lords it over the servants; I hate the way my father wants to be seen as the person going out with the Americans'. See Hall cited in Segal 2003, p. 19.
13. Hall 2009, p. 662.
14. JanMohamed 1992, p. 107.
15. Hall 1996a, p. 490.
16. See Eagleton 2003a, p. 209. See Hall 1988, for an overview of West-Indian migra-tion to Britain after 1945.
17. See Hall 1993, pp. 349–50. Despite this, Chris Rojeck has suggested that 'English-ness' played a large role in the determination of Hall's political thought. Indeed, that his thought, in important senses, was constructed by his attachment to Englishness. See Rojeck 1998, pp. 45–65, for this thesis. See Schwarz 2005, pp. 196–9, for a critique.
18. The phrase is taken from Suvin 2005, p. 117. See also Hall 1996a p. 492; MacCabe 2008, p. 13.

for the establishment of a West-Indian federation discomposed, Hall realised that his future would not include a return to his roots. By 1957, he was sure he could not return home, that, indeed, there was no 'home' to return to.[19]

Assimilation or marginality, according to Darko Suvin, has constituted the idiomatic migrant response to the questions 'where to belong'? and 'how to belong'?[20] Despite his preference for 'the margins' in his later writings, Hall accepted neither reflex. Instead, he attempted to negotiate a passage between assimilation and marginality, the refusal of both considered one signpost of modernity. Indeed, feeling at home in neither Jamaica nor England, Hall initially found shelter from the physical and psychical problems of displacement under the roof of socialist internationalism, in small radical groupings, such as the Oxford Socialist Society, and in collective publishing ventures, such as *Universities and Left Review*, each important forerunners of the New Left in Britain.[21] As he later reflected: 'if you're out of place the Left becomes a kind of home'.[22] With like-minded 'outsiders' Charles Taylor, Raphael Samuel, Allan Hall and Gabriel Pearson, Hall probed the boundaries of a socialist 'third way' between 'actual existing communism' and 'actual existing social democracy'.

From 1956 onwards, Hall was a central figure in the making of the New Left. In the wake of 'Hungary' and 'Suez', he left Oxford – and his postgraduate research on Henry James – for London and co-editorship of *Universities and Left Review*. The journal published seven editions between 1957 and 1959, and was home to some of the New Left's defining debates. Following the merger of *Universities and Left Review* and *New Reasoner*, he became the inaugural editor of *New Left Review*, though he resigned after a torturous, if productive, two-year tenure in 1961.[23] He was central to the establishment of the New Left clubs, particularly the original London club, and became an important link between the New Left

---

19. Hall 1996a, p. 490.

20. Suvin 2005, p. 117. For a somewhat heavy-handed account of the intellectual politics of migration see Ahmad 1992, p. 86; compare Eagleton 2003b, pp. 21–2.

21. See Hall 1989b, pp. 11–38, for Hall's account of his activities in the early New Left. In addition, see Dworkin 1997, pp. 45–78, particularly pp. 67–8, for reference to Hall and the early New Left.

22. Hall 2009, pp. 673–4.

23. See Williams 1979, p. 365, on Hall's editorship of *NLR*. For an insight into some of the criticisms of Hall as editor of the *NLR*, consider the correspondence between Thompson and Hall. This correspondence reveals the pressures that Hall operated under as editor of *NLR*. In a letter written to Thompson following the acrimonious Stockport Conference of the New Left, Hall argued that Thompson would have been the natural choice for the journal's first editor. Much of Hall's difficulties as editor derived from this feeling. While it is often suggested that Saville operated as a useful mediator between Thompson and Hall in the early days of the journal, what is less often mentioned is the significant disagreements between Hall and Saville over the direction of the journal. I have found no great need to quote directly from these personal letters in the construction of this chapter.

and the Campaign for Nuclear Disarmament (CND). In the late 1960s Hall contributed to *May Day Manifesto* alongside Raymond Williams and E.P. Thompson,
and to the political movement it briefly spawned. His central contribution to the
New Left, however, was undoubtedly intellectual.[24] Hall played a vital role in
the revision of socialist theory, including the relation between base and superstructure and the nexus between objective economic interests and political and
social identity. Hall's association with the New Left did not end in 1962 or 1968.
As late as 1992, he suggested that 'I remain identified with the project of the *first*
New Left',[25] an emphasis which distinguished him from the 'second' New Left
of Anderson and Nairn, and, most particularly perhaps, from the 'second' New
Left's rapprochement with Leninism.

Hall's perspective on socialism, as Terry Eagleton has suggested, was always
informed by his experience of colonialism and his migration 'from the Caribbean
to the Cowley Road'.[26] Yet there were less mediated affiliations between Hall's
politics and his Caribbean formation than his emphasis on the importance of
culture to an understanding of imperialism and the construction of socialism.
Connecting rather than prefiguring his later interest in ethnicity and diaspora,
Hall was active in the defence of the West-Indian community following the Notting Hill riots in 1958.[27] Thus a 'disaporic' idiom shaped Hall's socialism from the
beginning. Well before Powellism, moral panics around black crime in the 1970s
and the emergence of ethnicity as a key concept of social theory in the 1980s,
Hall's socialism already engaged difference, even if not in quite the way that
would become characteristic of his later writings.

Following his resignation from *New Left Review*, Hall was invited by Richard
Hoggart to assist in the establishment of the Centre for Contemporary Cultural
Studies (CCCS) at the University of Birmingham.[28] Four years later, in 1968, he
became the Centre's director.[29] Hall's role in the CCCS's establishment constituted not just an extension, but also an intensification, of his New Left intellectual agenda.[30] Undeniably, Hall's decade and a half long involvement with the

---

24. This is true, but only if it is remembered that Hall was also seriously concerned
with establishing a political movement based around the New Left clubs. This view
comes through in his correspondence with Thompson.
25. Hall 1996a, p. 493.
26. Eagleton 2003a, pp. 208–9.
27. Hall cited in Segal 2003, p. 21. See Hall 1978, pp. 27–8, for a consideration of these
events in his own work. See also Hall 1996a, p. 497; Hall 2009, p. 671.
28. For Hall's reflections on Hoggart see Hall 2009, pp. 39–49.
29. See Hall 1980a pp. 15–47; Hall 1980b, pp. 277–94, for his account of his time at
the Centre. See Dworkin 1997, pp. 141–81, for an overview of the CCCS during Hall's
directorship.
30. According to Frederic Jameson, 'Cultural Studies [in Britain] . . . was essentially a
political project and indeed a Marxist project at that'. See Jameson 1993, p. 28. This is
true, but more so in 1978 than in 1964.

Centre coincided with his deepest encounter with Marxist theory – first with traditional 'English' Marxian critiques of orthodox Marxism, and later with the heavyweights of Western Marxism.[31] The effect on Hall's thinking, and on cultural studies, was revolutionary. Out of a process of theoretical distillation, culture (and Marxism!) emerged all but unrecognisable to an earlier generation of dissident Marxists – transformed from a whole way of life and struggle to a field of signification, interpellation displacing experience as the crucial mediation between subjectivity and politics.[32] However, the Centre's relentless ideological velocity, which Hall had done so much to nurture, and which had made the CCCS synonymous with cutting-edge developments in cultural studies, partly prompted his resignation from the Centre in 1979.[33]

Hall's Birmingham period saw not just his deepest encounter with Marxist theory, but also his first systematic engagement with race and nation.[34] It was during this period that ' "black" was coined as a way of referencing the common experience of racism and marginalisation in Britain and came to provide the organising category of a new politics of resistance, among groups and communities with . . . very different histories, traditions and ethnic identities'.[35] This new discourse, as Hall later admitted, increasingly 'spoke' his work from the 1970s onwards. Despite the Centre's theoretical dynamism and its openness to new points of enquiry, cultural studies was initially resistant to putting critical questions of race and racism on its immediate agenda – that is, exploring the genesis of cultural studies in what Hall later called 'a profoundly English or British moment'.[36] Hall changed all that. Once again, there was no necessary divorce between Hall's lived experience and Marxist theory and socialist politics. Rather, his investigation of the conditions of intellectual production in cultural studies involved the revaluation of Marxism in the light of the historical experience of colonisation, an experience that had reached full circle with the creation of a lack diaspora in Britain. Hall did not seek to explain race and ethnicity through Marxism. He brought his lived experience to Marxism in an attempt to transform its understanding of the relationship between the state, hegemony, and race.

However, an uncritical acceptance of Marxism was hardly characteristic of Hall's intellectual thought, not even during that period when he was most intensely engaged in working through the nexus between historical materialism

---

31. See Hall et al. 1978.

32. In a moment of profound understatement Richard Hoggart later recalled that under Hall's tutelage the CCCS became both more 'theoretical' and more 'political'. See Gibson and Hartley 1998, p. 19.

33. Hall 1996a, pp. 499–501, where he explains his reasons for leaving the Centre in 1979. See also Brunsdon 1996, pp. 276–86.

34. See Hall 1972, for an early example.

35. Hall 1996a, p. 441.

36. Hall 1980b, p. 270. In addition, see Hall 1992, pp. 10–18.

and popular culture. Hall felt a continuous, conscious ambivalence toward Marxist theory, 'orthodox' or Althusserian, whether understood as a 'science of society' or a 'politics of revolution'. Hall worked 'within shouting distance of Marxism, working on Marxism, working against Marxism, working with it, working to try to develop Marxism'.[37] Hence, it would be wrong to suggest that Hall was at any time fully reconciled to Marxism (making Hall's 'road from Marx' unlikely),[38] and it would be wrong to suggest that Hall ever found a homeland in Marxism. It would, however, be equally misjudged to argue that those formative experiences of colonialism, migrancy, and metropolitan racism were automatically irreconcilable with a commitment to the Marxist tradition.[39] Hall did not just work with, at the side and against historical materialism, Marxist theory constituted the primary touchstone for his thinking about culture and society.[40] As late as the early 1990s, he would declare 'I am still a Marxist'![41]

On leaving Birmingham (he became Professor of sociology at the Open University in 1980, and retired from this position in 1997), Hall became involved with the theoretical journal of the Communist Party, *Marxism Today*, which had been reinvigorated under the editorship of Martin Jacques in 1978. *Marxism Today* provided the primary vehicle for Hall's political interventions during the 1980s, including his influential, Gramsci-inspired, interpretation of Thatcherism. The Communist Party journal was an unlikely publishing success, becoming, according to some, the most widely read political magazine in Britain in the 1980s. It provided a perfect, if ironic, place for Hall to re-imagine socialism beyond its traditional concern with class and production – a project, it might be argued, that constituted a continuation of the original project of *New Left Review*. *Marxism Today* was also home to the 'New Times' thesis. This thesis – that socialism should be 'committed to, rather than dismissive of, diversity and difference'[42] as Hall put it – had important implications for Hall's analysis of nationhood and national identity, and his conception of their relationship to a project of social transformation. New Times looked beyond the 'old Left' at the same time that it defined itself against it. It is odd, then, that *Marxism Today* wound-up at precisely

---

37. Hall 1996a, p. 265. The complexity of Hall's relationship to Marxism from the early 1990s is now much diminished, at least for some. As Terry Eagleton has remarked, Hall has 'moved decisively into the non-Marxist camp'. See Eagleton 2003a. However, Hall is still often mistaken for a Marxist. For an example, see Denning 2003, p. 174.
38. See Sparks 1996, pp. 71–101, for this thesis.
39. This argument can be found in Farred 1996, p. 24.
40. See Mulhern 2000a, p. 124, for this point. Until at least 1986, Hall claimed that 'I still operate somewhere within what I understand to be the discursive limits of a Marxist position'. See Grossberg 1996, p. 148.
41. See Hall 1991b, p. 68.
42. Hall 1996a, p. 234.

the moment that communism came to grief in the Soviet Union, an oddity that was not lost on Hall.[43]

From the 1990s onwards, Hall became more fully engaged with black cultural politics, specifically with the Institute of International Visual Arts and the Association of Black Photographers.[44] During this period, his politics were, perhaps, best defined by his involvement with the Campaign Against Racism in the Media and the Runnymede Trust's Commission on the Future of Multi-Ethnic Britain.[45] At the same time, he became less interested in changing Marxism or in transforming socialist politics. There was no direct correspondence, since Hall had been interested in black politics since at least the late 1950s. But there is little question that Hall's belief in an alternative to capitalism ended along with the Soviet Union, even though he had always defined his socialism against 'actual existing socialism'.[46] This constituted no simple act of apostasy, as many intellectual comrades bemoaned, and certainly did not imply any repudiation of New Left traditions of thought. Hall had always approached socialism at a tangent, an angle informed by his experience of the Caribbean and of being a migrant in Britain. Formed there and in that way, and living at the intersection of class and colour, it was no surprise that ethnicity would become an increasing preoccupation of his thought, particularly at a time when, at least according to some, ethnicity seemed one of the final bulwarks against capitalist globalisation.[47] Perhaps, however, the increasing appearance of ethnicity in Hall's work had less to do with an inherent interest in cultural identity than it did with the fact that he always sought to turn his face violently toward the present.[48]

What, then, has been, and is, Hall's country? Black Britain has certainly constituted Hall's homeland since the late 1950s, both in terms of 'belonging' and 'otherness', both in the accepted and imposed sense of identity. It remains to be said just what Black Britain means, especially what it means to Hall. But with someone so attuned to the making of identities, it would be wrong to overlook Hall's own sense of identification, and that sense has been consistently defined

43. Hall 2007, p. 36.

44. See, in particular, Hall 2009, for a reflection on these activities.

45. The analysis and recommendations of this commission where collected in Runnymede Trust 2000.

46. See Hall 1997, p. 37, for his repudiation of the anti-capitalist tradition of social democracy. But also consider Hall's lament for the end of the Soviet Union in McCabe 2007, p. 36, where he says that 'Even for people who didn't believe it [the Soviet Union] was a place where everything was going to be new, it was a kind of place in the mind, it was a kind of symbolic place'.

47. Any number of students of nationalism could be mentioned, here. For a recent example, consider Calhoun 2007, p. 171.

48. This is a paraphrase of a Gramsci quote that Hall has frequently cited. See also Hall 1995, p. 4, where he suggests that 'the question of cultural identity' is 'at the very centre of the contemporary political agenda'.

in terms of a country called Black Britain. Hall, however, has not positioned himself in just one country. If Black Britain has constituted one of Hall's imagined communities, it has not constituted the only one. The New Left was another, and one that has arguably been just as important. His connections with other countries, such as the universe of Marxist discourse, were more fraught with tension. But, nonetheless, these remain important in any explanation of Hall's political interventions, especially those concerned with the relationship between socialism and national identity.

III

Part of the intellectual dynamic that generated the New Left between 1956 and 1967 was the widespread belief that politics, even socialist politics, no longer reflected people's everyday experience. Stuart Hall was crucial to the definition and exploration of this gulf between 'politics' and 'experience', and to the New Left's ambition to create a 'movement of ideas' more attuned to people in the 'here and now'.[49] As Hall later put it, 'this struggle to ground socialism in a new analysis of "our times" was primary and originating – where the whole New Left project began'.[50] A characteristic aspect of Hall's New Left writings in this sense was his belief that socialists needed to take identity seriously. Indeed, if there is a warm current that runs through Hall's early New Left writings, then it was the view that socialists could no longer expect the working class to be socialist just because they were workers. Put in other terms, Hall understood that the working class had many countries, some which co-existed easily enough and some that did not, but none of which were natural.

Hall's early New Left writings were defined not just against the 'old' Left, and socialism's 'traditional' reduction of political interest to class, but also against conservative constructions of identity. Indeed, the repudiation of imperialism, and the national identity that Britain's Empire encouraged, constituted a key feature of Hall's early New Left writing.[51] Assessing conservatism's post-war transformation in the first issue of *Universities and Left Review*, Hall suggested that there was much that was recognisable about the 'new conservatism', particularly its ongoing commitment to the imperial idea and to a vision of British national identity based on race, social hierarchy and counter-revolution.[52] For all its purported 'newness' – reconciliation with the welfare-state, modest social redistribution and class-compromise – conservatism was still home to

49. *New Left Review* 1960, p. 1.
50. Hall 2010, p. 185.
51. In this sense, Hall was typical of the New Left.
52. Hall 1957, p. 21.

the most egregious versions of British 'prestige' and 'imperial heritage'.[53] The 'end of empire', or what Hall called 'Britain's declining prestige abroad',[54] had produced a particularly virulent anti-socialist conception of national identity, and not just in the Conservative Party. The deformations built by the Cold War played a role, here, as well. 'It is clear', Hall remarked, 'that Britain has identified herself everywhere with policies calculated to thwart the colonial and national revolutions'.[55] Disorientated by the rapids that sustained post-war social and economic change, contemporary conservatism, Hall argued, had 'hoisted' the flag of 'Britain's prestige abroad' as its 'unifying factor',[56] at once connecting the 'Free World' to British Empire.[57]

Indeed, an important task of *Universities and Left Review* was to bear witness to the brutalities of capitalist imperialism, and to remind socialists that the British Empire was alive and well, not least in Britain. But Hall also edged toward a conception of imperialism's new character – the systematic impoverishment of colonial and recently liberated countries by the United States and its allies. It was not just that Britain sought to disrupt the process of political decolonisation, most evident in Suez and Cyprus. 'For the economic consequences of colonial exploitation', 'The Insiders' author's, among whom was Hall, remarked, 'are to deprive the primary producing regions of the profits which should be used to finance their development, and to restrict their role to that of raw material suppliers. Its political consequences are to obstruct their progress once it is gained...'.[58] Against the grain of British foreign policy, Hall argued for 'the strengthening of a sense of responsibility to international organizations'.[59] While 'The Insiders' recommended not just political independence but economic self-determination for lands formerly strangled by Britain's, or other imperial nations', 'prestige'. As an answer to imperialism's economic distortions, Hall called for 'the industrialization of the backward two-thirds of the world',[60] an early argument for vernacular modernity that was common to the New Left. This was to advocate the extension of socialist humanism – what Hall described as 'the restoration of the belief in the power of the human individual over life' – to the four corners of the Earth.[61]

If Hall rejected nationalism, he didn't reject what Perry Anderson and Tom Nairn would soon castigate as the 'first' New Left's populism. But this is true only if we ignore Anderson and Nairn's assumption that populism and nationalism

53. Hall 1957, p. 22.
54. Ibid.
55. Hall 1957, p. 23.
56. Ibid.
57. Hall et al. 1958, p. 4.
58. Hall et al. 1958, p. 37.
59. Hall 1957, p. 24.
60. Hall 1960a, p. 3.
61. Hall 1958, p. 87.

was the same thing. Hall championed populism in its 'narodnik', rather than its 'nationalist', sense.[62] From this 'narodnik' perspective, Hall understood populism as the strategic endeavour to construct a constituency for socialism from the lived experience of 'the people'. Populism, Hall believed, implied the recognition that the 'humanist strength of socialism ... must be developed in cultural and social terms, as well as in economic and political'.[63] 'What we need', Hall went on in *New Left Review*'s inaugural editorial, 'is a language sufficiently close to life – all aspects of it – to declare our discontent with' capitalism.[64] This was why, he explained, the New Left was interested in popular culture. Not because it was inherently important, but because it was 'directly relevant to the imaginative resistances of people who have to live with capitalism – the growing points of social discontent, the projections of deeply-felt needs ...'.[65] This implied a specific understanding of the New Left's task: 'to meet people where they *are*, where they are touched, bitten, moved, frustrated, nauseated – to develop discontent and, at the same time, to give the socialist movement some direct sense of the times and the way we live'.[66]

Populism, though antithetical to socialism, was nonetheless a matter for rebuke in Hall's most recognisable contribution to early New Left thought. 'A Sense of Classlessness' was structured by the question: '*why* [do] people accept their own exploitation?'[67] In opposition to the 'old Left', Hall sought to take the post-war transformation of British capitalism seriously, but without colluding in the revisionist assertion that it had fundamentally changed its nature. Hall's point was that transformations within the capitalist mode of production – rising wages, increasing working-class consumption and redistribution of profits through welfare – had potential, negative, consequences for socialist consciousness. Capitalism, Hall lamented, could unmake socialists. Side by side with an industrial capitalism recognisable to Marx, were transformations in economic, social and cultural relations that the author of *Capital* barely imagined. As a result, the 'pattern of social life' had been turned upside down, no more so than in what Hall called 'working-class culture'.[68] People's capitalism was producing class confusion, indeed 'a false consciousness in working class people'.[69] The result was workers' self-enslavement: 'Both in consumption and production',

---

62. This is a point that Hall himself makes in Hall 1989b, pp. 194–5.
63. *New Left Review* 1960, p. 1.
64. Ibid.
65. Ibid.
66. Ibid.
67. *Universities and Left Review* 1958, p. 3.
68. Hall 1958a, p. 28.
69. Hall 1958a, p. 30.

Hall wrote, 'the working class is gradually becoming factors in its own permanent alienation'.[70]

Hall's analysis was mostly tentative and exploratory, but showed little caution in arguing that 'consumption...has become the most significant relationship between the working class and the employing class',[71] and even less in claiming that 'the whole nature of private property has been revolutionized'.[72] These were infelicities in Hall's argument that Raphael Samuel and E.P. Thompson dispatched all too easily.[73] However, there were also limitations to their response to Hall's thesis. Neither Thompson nor Samuel denied capitalism's various transformations after 1945. But, they both missed Hall's argument about the qualitative nature of economic and social change, and what the implications for socialist politics might be. They missed Hall's stress on capitalism's dynamism – that it constantly revolutionised social relations, that it melted all that was solid into air, including the solidities of working-class consciousness. Thompson and Samuel might have been good on history, as Hall admitted, but there was an argument to suggest that they were stuck there in unhelpful ways too. Just as importantly, 'A Sense of Classlessness' illuminated the way that 'images of the self' were increasingly formed outside the sphere of production,[74] and in ways antagonistic to socialist consciousness. However, the analytic and political centre of the article was the idea of incorporation – the way that the working-class had become increasingly domesticated to the routines of capitalist consumption, and this despite, and in some sense because of, decades of socialist theory and practice. The forward march of labour halted . . . in 1958.

Perhaps the source of Hall's sensitivity to 'incorporation' can be found less in his familiarity with British class-relations, and more in his colonial formation. After all, 'incorporation' would have constituted an apt description of Hall's understanding of his parent's relation to imperialism.[75] In this sense, the class that Hall was born into – the Caribbean 'black middle class' – was precisely part-author of their own oppression. Hall was all too aware of people's ability to find enjoyment, meaning and virtue in deference to their superiors. He was no doubt wrong to attribute this wholly to false-consciousness, since there were significant material benefits to blacks' collusion with imperialism in Jamaica, just as there was to the working class's new-found faith in the market. But it is not hard to

---

70. Hall 1958a, p. 29.
71. Hall 1958a, p. 28.
72. Hall 1958a, p. 27.
73. See Samuel 1959, pp. 44–9; E.P. Thompson 1959, pp. 50–5. Hall's response to critics appeared in Hall 1959, pp. 50–1.
74. Hall 1958a, p. 31.
75. See, in particular, Hall 1959 pp. 484–91; Hall 1998a, p. 190, for Hall's reflections on his parents.

empathise with the feeling that produced its use in an analysis of class relations in Britain (or the Caribbean). Working-class consumerism, just like black deference, could no doubt make a socialist or an anti-imperialist mad with rage, blind for the moment, with some justice, to Gramsci's notion of contradictory consciousness and the insights gained from a 'Benjaminian' reading against the grain. And there might, after all, be some point to false consciousness as a partial explanation for why the subaltern accepts the power that rests on their subordination – a value that Hall recognised in his analysis of social relations in Britain in the 1950s but would soon lose sight of.

There were, however, other pitfalls associated with Hall's analysis of post-war British social relations. Much of Hall's analysis of the 'new capitalism' and of 'prosperity Britain' focused on the figure of the 'consumer', the supposed new subject produced by 'people's capitalism'.[76] Against capitalist conceptions of subjectivity, Hall, along with the majority voice of the New Left, recalled a vision of human nature structured by labour, moral imagination and creativity. As an editorial in *Universities and Left Review* put it, 'His imagination, his moral sense, his capacity for communion, as well as his labour, his skill and his technology represent – *together* – the powers with which he can remake his life and give it value'.[77] Writing of the need for public ownership, 'The Insiders' argued that socialisation was required 'because capitalist society could find no place for the exercise by the worker of responsibility and initiative, or for the development of his creative potentialities, in short for his development as a human being'.[78] Likewise, 'A Sense of Classlessness' was structured by this 'socialist-humanist' conception of human nature – the idea that only socialism could produce 'a freedom within which man could develop a true individuality and a true consciousness of himself and his possibilities'.[79] However, this vision of humanity's species-being sat awkwardly beside Hall's argument about incorporation. Either capitalism had reduced human nature beyond redemption, making socialism impossible or, socialism had nothing to do with humanity's inherent 'creative potentialities'. Whatever Hall imagined in 1958, he believed that making socialists would be no easy thing.

If evidence of human nature's potential was hard to find in 1950s Britain, it was perhaps more easily discerned in Third World struggles against capitalist imperialism. No more so, perhaps, than in Cuba. Though the dangers of the Cuban Revolution's 'totalitarian' degeneration were great, socialism in Cuba, Hall reported in 1961, was being taken at full stretch, and was still open to the

---

76. Hall 1958a, p. 28.
77. *Universities and Left Review* 1958, p. 1 (original emphasis).
78. Hall et al. 1958, p. 24.
79. Hall 1958a, p. 31.

'third way' between social democracy and communism.[80] Indeed, Hall's unbending support for national liberation movements in Africa, Asia and the Americas, was a characteristic feature of his New Left writings. Both *Universities and Left Review*, and the Hall-led *New Left Review*, engaged with decolonisation and national liberation movements in the Third World, with Hall making personal contributions to the analysis of events in Algeria and Cuba (Hall would visit Cuba in 1961). But, Hall's peculiar take on colonialism was above all revealed through his encounter with West Indians in Britain. 'The Habit of Violence', a contribution to *Universities and Left Review*'s special section on the Notting Hill riots, advanced the argument that racism in Britain was a direct affect of the brutalities associated with Britain's Empire.[81] In fact, the way imperialism on the periphery of Britain's Empire shaped racism in the centre would be an enduring theme of Hall's analysis of the national question in Britain. It was first discovered through his personal experience of the Notting Hill riots in 1958.[82]

In a recent interview, Hall suggested that E.P. Thompson, Raymond Williams, John Rex and Peter Worsley were among his formative influences.[83] The cases of Thompson and Williams are obvious, and have been explored elsewhere, not least in Hall's work. But the influence of Rex and Worsley on Hall's thinking is less well known. It is not hard to see why Rex and Worsley exerted such an influence on the young Hall, however. It is not just that Hall shared an interest in decolonisation and Third World liberation with Rex and Worsley.[84] A more important influence was the character of Rex and Worsley's thinking on colonialism's affects in Britain. 'Small wonder', Worsley argued in *Out of Apathy*, 'that racial prejudice is deeply entrenched in Britain, where tens of thousands of men have brought the infection home with them [from the Empire] to their families.... Small wonder when we get Suez lunacies at the top, we get Notting Hill riots at the bottom. For imperialism pervades every sphere of our social life'.[85] These remarks might have stood as a masthead over Hall's writings in the 1970s and beyond. Rex and Worsley also argued for a conception of political and social identity that refused 'class-reductionism', another leitmotiv of Hall's intellectual product. There are 'other facts besides [class]', Rex suggested, 'which have a profound affect on people's lives and which are no less essential for the understanding of their political motivation'.[86] Chief among these facts, according to Rex and Worsley, were national and ethnic identity. Indeed, for Worsley,

---

80. Hall and Fruchter 1961, pp. 2–12.
81. Hall et al. 1958b, pp. 4–5.
82. For this personal experience, see Hall 2009, p. 671.
83. Hall 2009, p. 675.
84. See McCabe 2007, p. 15.
85. Worsley 1960, p. 119.
86. Rex 1957, p. 60.

the politics of subjectivity, at least in Africa, was the primary means of defining a way of life outside the 'social identity of the Organization Man'.[87]

The influence of these arguments can be seen in *The Young Englanders*, Hall's 1967 report to the National Committee for Commonwealth Immigrants, an independent body convened to advise the Labour government on problems of integration among migrant communities. *The Young Englanders* argued that 'Migrants are highly conscious of themselves as a group – a group which is constantly being watched and tested and which is aware that what they do as individuals is accredited to the group as a whole'.[88] In other words, migrants were constituted as a 'race' by the eyes and value concerns of the 'English'. 'They carry their social identities around with them', Hall reported, 'like packs on their backs'.[89] Hall described the dilemma of the migrant in terms that would not be out of place in his later writings on identity. Migrants, he suggested, 'can't go home again. The route back is closed. But so too is the route forward'.[90] It was this existential, and structural, dilemma that led to Hall's recommendations. In a clear repudiation of the Committee's presumptions, Hall concluded that young migrants are 'closing-in their lines of contact, re-discovering their own racial and national identities and stereotyping their white counterparts. In itself this is not a bad thing – if integration means the enforced loss and rejection of their own identity, then it is too high a price to pay'.[91]

The Young Englanders is a remarkable document, not least because it pre-empted so many of Hall's future concerns. However, it is of interest for other reasons too. Hall's report is clear: it is 'the oppressors' who construct categories of 'race'. This reduction of people to a 'racial identity' constituted a universal loss, even if the loss was unevenly dispersed. It is in this context – the establishment of migrants as a 'race' by the British – that the re-discovery of racial or national identity by young migrants' was in no way a bad thing, according to Hall. Integration, he believed, would not lead to reconciliation or a 'race-less' society, but to the institutionalisation of social hierarchy based on race. If integration was the goal, Hall argued, then better that young migrants fought back, even if in their oppressors' terms. This, he suggested, allowed a measure of 'pride and independence' that integration on the oppressors' terms did not.[92] *The Young Englanders* also elucidated the dilemmas facing any sort of black politics, not

---

87. Worsley 1961, p. 21.
88. Hall 1967.
89. Ibid.
90. Ibid.
91. Ibid.
92. Ibid.

least the way that a politics based on ethnicity, though necessary, could harden lines of difference if it did not transcend its presumptions.

If identity in part comes from 'the outside', then it is clear that Hall was importantly formed by his colonial experience and the dilemma of being a West Indian in the imperial metropolis. This is obvious enough and explains, at least in part, not only his involvement with the West-Indian community in London, and his role in the Commission on second generation migrants, but also his sensitivity to social and political location in the construction of identity. In the same way it partly explains his attention to national liberation movements in Cuba and elsewhere, and his understanding of the way that 'racial' and 'national' identities could not just disrupt the development of socialism, but force a reconsideration of socialism's basic terms. All these pressures informed Hall's early New Left writings. Just as important, however, was another sort of difference, one that came from the 'inside' – namely, the identification he constructed against the 'old Left', whether communist or social-democratic. Here, to some degree, 'outside' and 'inside' potentially pulled in the same direction, since the 'old Left', Hall believed, was precisely rendered 'old' because of its inability to accord the 'here and now' of people's lived experience, including the 'here and now' of their national and ethnic identities, a role in the construction of socialism.

IV

Raymond Williams's initial *May Day Manifesto* document, published in 1967, had made no mention of race and the social and economic problems facing migrant communities. However, the revised edition published in 1968 did, and it is hard to imagine that, alongside Powellism, it was not Hall's influence on this version that accounts for the change. The 1968 *May Day Manifesto* (hereafter *Manifesto*), edited by Williams with help from Thompson and Hall, suggested that racism was a form of false consciousness and that migrant communities in Britain '[live] out, more sharply than any other identifiable group, the whole range of a general social deprivation'.[93] But *Manifesto* did not recommend 'racial consciousness' as an antidote to racism. Rather the New Left document sought a solution to racism through socialist politics, a politics, that is, opposed to capitalism and racism. Undoubtedly, *Manifesto* afforded priority to class and class-conflict, even though it recognised, if somewhat inchoately, that class was inflected by race. It is unclear whether Hall agreed with this stance in 1968, though in light of *The Young Englanders* it seems improbable. Whatever his feelings about *Manifesto*,

---

93. Williams ed. 1968, p. 167.

it is clear that throughout the 1970s the question of relations between class and race would constitute the most important theme of his political interventions.

During his directorship of the CCCS, Hall wrote a great deal, and on a varied number of topics. The media was perhaps the primary subject of his writings in the 1970s, alongside, and in relation to, subcultures, deviancy and crime.[94] On a more theoretical plane, Hall's writings broached questions of ideology and method, the base-superstructure relationship and the theory of class.[95] In terms of other thinkers, these years marked his deepest engagement with the intellectual giants of Western Marxism, from Luckács to Althusser. Little that Hall wrote during his Birmingham period came from his head alone, however. This was antithetical to the purpose of the CCCS, which prised collaboration above all. It was true of *Resistance through Rituals: Youth Subcultures in Postwar Britain*, which was not only an example of the CCCS's commitment to intellectual co-operation, but also to interdisciplinarity.[96] It was also true of *Policing the Crisis: 'Mugging', the State, and Law and Order*, co-authored by Hall and four other members of the CCCS, a book which combined Hall's interest in the media, ideology, Marxist theory and, perhaps most indicative of his political concerns in this period, race.[97]

Manifesto certainly did not make race or racism central to its analysis of the 'new capitalism', nor had any New Left writer made race and racism in Britain central to their thinking, despite the characteristic New Left concern with imperialism. Hall later provided reasons for this. 'The black cause, the politics that arises from race', he said, 'is not an autonomous political arena to which you could relate, until I would say the mid-60s'.[98] It was not that he did not think about race, he said. It was that race and racism was considered a part, and a subordinate one at that, of class-politics.[99] *Policing the Crisis* was an attempt to correct this reductionism, and to investigate the question of race and class in the context of the break-up of Britain and the formation of a black-diaspora. For Hall and his co-authors, it was no longer possible to conceptualise race in Britain solely in terms of the mode of production.[100] As *Policing the Crisis* argued, racial structuration reproduced a ' "racial division of labour" within, and as a structural feature of, the general division of labour'.[101] The book also provided insight into

---

94. See, for example, Hall 1973a; Hall 1980a.
95. See, in particular, Hall 1977; Hall et al. 1978.
96. Hall and Jefferson (eds.) 1976.
97. Hall et al. 1978. See Solomos et al. 1982, for an overview of the context of the book's production, and a critical account of its argument. *Policing the Crisis* had an earlier incarnation. See Hall and Jefferson 1973.
98. Hall 2009, p. 674.
99. Ibid.
100. Hall et al. 1978, pp. 337, 339.
101. Hall et al. 1978, pp. 345-7.

the co-determination of black labour in Britain – by a Caribbean social formation entangled within global modes of capitalist exploitation, and by a 'domestic' capitalism and a cultural hierarchy steeped in racism.[102] It also investigated
means of 'black resistance' to blacks' subordination in both economic and cultural terms and the 'growth of black consciousness'.[103] Indeed, the authors understood race as a 'structural feature of the position and reproduction of [the] black
labour force – as well as an experiential category of the consciousness of class'.[104]
Thus, *Policing the Crisis* represented a critique of the New Left conception of the
relationship between race and class, a rebuke to the almost systematic neglect
of race's relative autonomy among New Left thinkers.

This critique reached a theoretical pitch in Hall's Althusserian-inflected essay
'Race, Articulation, and Societies Structured in Dominance'.[105] In this 1980 essay,
Hall repudiated the idea that 'those social divisions which assume a distinctively
racial or ethnic character can be attributed or explained principally with reference to economic structures and processes'.[106] However, if Hall believed that
race could not be reduced to the capitalist mode of production, nor was the
position of black labour in Britain, he argued, explicable without attention to
the economic exploitation characteristic of class-society. To ignore blacks' position in objective class relations, Hall argued, would constitute an obfuscation as
disabling as that produced by economism, one likely, moreover, to reproduce
social relations of racism rather than overcome them. Thus racism, according
to Hall, was not simply a matter of what contemporary neo-Hegelian theory has
termed 'misrecognition'.[107] Summarising the argument of *Policing the Crisis*, Hall
suggested that 'the structures through which black labour is reproduced...are
not simply coloured by race. The relations of capitalism can be thought of as
articulating classes in distinct ways at each of the levels or instances of the social
formation – economic, political, ideological'.[108]

The theoretical purpose of Hall's work on race was to hold economic reductionism at bay while giving due weight to economic structures in the construction of racial hierarchies. Theory, particularly the Althusserian brand, was the

---

102. Hall et al. 1978, p. 381.
103. Hall et al. 1978, p. 351.
104. Hall et al. 1978, p. 345.
105. Hall 1980c, pp. 305–45. Hall would later call this essay a 'text of the break' – that
is, a break, with deliberate Althusserian inflection, 'with the conventional way in which
race and racism had been analyzed [in both Marxist and pluralist works]'. See Hall 2002,
p. 449.
106. Hall 1980c, p. 305.
107. See C. Taylor 1994, for an example of contemporary neo-Hegelian social
thought.
108. Hall 1980c, p. 340.

preeminent touchstone of this manoeuvre. Hall did not share E.P. Thompson's profound repudiation of structuralism, and nor did Hall consent to *The Poverty of Theory*'s dismissal of Althusser. Hall maintained that Althusser, despite the many weaknesses characteristic of his form of structuralist Marxism, had marked a theoretical line in the sand.[109] After Althusser, taking 'relative autonomy' seriously, according to Hall, was no longer a theoretical option but the starting point of conjunctural analysis. Hall also felt that Althusser had finally dispatched the notion of the 'integral, authorial individual subject'[110] to a humanist coffin.[111] Hall's work, shaped by the rise of the new social movements, advanced an argument for the 'relative autonomy' of race in political terms too that was steeped in Althusser's attempt 'to think determinacy in a non-reductionist way'.[112] No longer could race be reduced to or elided with class or a necessary solution to racism wait for the establishment of Marx's 'realm of freedom'. Indeed, an emphasis on the role of black politics, among other new social movements, in socialism's reinvigoration would become a leitmotiv of Hall's strategic recommendations into the 1980s. As Hall later admitted, Althusser had taught him how to think and to live in and with difference.[113]

Still, Hall's work in the 1970s was not simply about race.[114] The crisis of *Policing the Crisis* was a crisis of national identity which had its origins in the breakdown of state and economy, the 'end of Empire', and Empire's return in the form of a black diaspora. *Policing the Crisis* was an account of the 'break-up of Britain' from the angle of 'race relations', fractured through the 'moral panic' surrounding black crime and not, as Tom Nairn had imagined it, from the perspective of the rise of peripheral nationalisms. The argument of the book was that race in Britain had become a lightning rod for arguments about the wider crisis in British society, a crisis whose meaning was increasingly shaped by the New Right.[115] As a response to this crisis, *Policing the Crisis* explained, Thatcherism's shock troops had marshalled the discourse of law and order and resurrected the spectre of traditional values, including traditional, imperial-inflected, conceptions of national identity. In a remarkably prescient analysis, *Policing the Crisis* suggested that coercion rather than consent had become the default mode of political hegemony in Britain; an 'authoritarian populism' welded to a form of national identity defined against blacks among other 'internal enemies'.[116]

---

109. Hall 1981, p. 379.
110. Hall 1988, p. 48.
111. See Hall 1981, p. 380.
112. Hall 1981, p. 381.
113. Hall 1985a, p. 92.
114. McCabe 2007, p. 25.
115. Hall et al. 1978, p. 333.
116. Hall 1980d, pp. 157–85.

The dominant response to Hall's writings on race from within the New Left was silence – at least according to Hall. In a recent interview, Hall explained this silence by suggesting that New Left figures like Thompson and Williams, although 'committed to the anti-imperialist struggle as part of left politics', 'didn't understand that the black presence within Britain would be a transformatory social and political presence, that it was going to expand, that it was part of the first tip of a wave which was going to follow in much expanded numbers after'.[117] According to Hall, the New Left had recycled the Left's traditional reduction of race to class. In other words, when it came to race there was little that was new about the New Left. Hall picked out Thompson for particular opprobrium. Hall suggested that following the publication of *Policing the Crisis*, Thompson had argued that race was a distraction from socialism, and that only socialism would cure the iniquities characteristic of racism.[118]

There is a half-truth buried away in this remembrance, but it is far from the whole truth. Thompson had been writing about many of the issues that animated *Policing the Crisis* for much of the 1970s. Like Hall, Thompson had spotted the rise of 'authoritarianism' and the emergence of what he called the 'secret state'.[119] Thompson had been interested in crime and law and order too, and had been active in alerting his fellow citizens to what Hall called the 'authoritarian drift' in British politics, evident above all, Thompson believed, in attacks on the jury system.[120] 'The national crisis', he suggested in 1976, 'the State of Emergency – the deployment of armed forces – the attempts to induce panic on the national media – the identification of some out-group as a "threat to security" – all these are becoming part of the normal repertoire of power'.[121] Thompson also showed himself no less aware than Hall about the relation between colonialism and racism. 'The rapid erosion of Empire', Thompson wrote, 'had perforce retracted the imperial ideology, has brought it back home, into the security services, the army, and the police, where experience gained in Ireland, India, or Rhodesia, looks restively for new fields of application – these services are the last refuges of imperialism, within which a ghostly imperial ideology survives its former host'.[122]

However, Thompson, like many other New Left thinkers, did not pay enough attention to race as a *relatively autonomous* factor in British politics, and he failed to incorporate race successfully into any aspect of his historical and political writing, and this despite a long-life hatred of and concern with British

117. Hall 2009, p. 675.
118. Ibid.
119. See E.P. Thompson 1980a, pp. 149–80.
120. See E.P. Thompson 1994, pp. 141–66.
121. E.P. Thompson 1980a, p. 163.
122. E.P. Thompson 1980a, p. 157.

imperialism.[123] It was also true that Thompson was sometimes, in terms of political strategy, too quick to move to solidarity beyond difference, but there was arguably some need for this under the threat of nuclear war. In any case, Thompson's defence of solidarity against difference was always pitched as a reminder that a common humanity would be found in collective praxis, something that Hall, in one mind at least, had believed in *Policing the Crisis*. And Thompson could hardly have been accused of 'economic reductionism' or of explaining politics simply in terms of class. Certainly not in view of his analysis of the Cold War, and certainly not in view of his involvement with successive anti-war movements. In fact, like Hall, Thompson understood the dangers of economic reductionism – indeed Thompson had arguably first taught Hall what those dangers were – and he was as open as Hall to the ways in which socialism might be constructed in places other than at the point of production.

There were, however, multiple, though connected, sources of Hall's discontent with Thompson in the late 1970s and beyond. It was not just that Hall and Thompson clashed over the relationship between 'theory' and 'history' and the value of Althusser's insights on the question of ideology.[124] What was more to the point in explaining Hall's breach with Thompson, perhaps, was Thompson's oblique, though for that reason no less felt, critique of Hall's work on race and crime. In 'The Secret State', for example, Thompson rebuked those on the Left who, employing the language of 'crisis of hegemony' and 'conjuncture', went in for the 'wholesale dismissal of *all* law and *all* police' and who coupled this blanket dismissal 'with a soppy notion that all crime is some kind of displaced revolutionary activity'.[125] Hall must have seen himself in the mirror of this polemic. But it was bad polemic, since it made a travesty of Hall's actual writings. Even more to the point, as an explanation of Hall's discontent, was Thompson's suggestion that 'Libertarians, some of whom suppose themselves revolutionary, are some of the last to defend our traditions, to care about who we are and how we have done things in the past, to search our precedents and to fight to uphold our constitution'.[126] In this sentence perhaps lies the seed of Hall's suggestion that Thompson was too English. For Hall, 'our traditions', 'our precedents', and 'our constitution' was a load of rubbish. There was no 'our' about it.

---

123. With fairness, it should be pointed out that it was during the 1980s that Thompson was most alienated from intellectual work and consumed by the anti-war movement. There were also indications that Thompson was moving toward a consideration of some of these issues in the context of a study of Native-American history shortly before his death.

124. The relevant contributions to this debate are collected in Samuel ed. 1981, pp. 378–408.

125. E.P. Thompson 1980a, p. 166.

126. E.P. Thompson 1980a, p. 211.

In retrospect, Hall imagined himself to have been far ahead of other New Left thinkers on questions of race in the late 1970s, and in one sense this was obviously true. *Policing the Crisis*, drawing connections between Britain, America and the Caribbean, prefigured the idea of the Black Atlantic, which would become influential in the 1980s and beyond. However, *Policing the Crisis*, and Hall's other work on race, while innovatory, was hardly free from contradiction or ambiguity. In truth, Hall was never sure how best to approach the complexities of the relationship between race and capitalism, nor was he absolutely clear about what sort of politics would effectively counter racism. If all sorts of Althusserian concepts such as 'relative autonomy', 'social formation', and 'ideological class struggle' marred Hall's theoretical approach to race (they would soon be tossed overboard for concepts derived from Gramsci's *Prison Notebooks*, and later still for Derrida), his view of an effective anti-racist politics was caught adrift the opposing strategic shores of 'solidarity' and 'difference'.[127] On the one hand, he argued that racism 'contains and disables the representative class organizations by confining them, in part, to strategies and struggles which are race specific... Through race, it continues to defeat the attempts to construct, at the political level, organizations which do in fact adequately represent the class as a whole – that is, which represent it against capitalism, against racism'.[128] This was an argument for class-solidarity familiar to *Manifesto*. On the other hand, he suggested that 'racist interpellations' could become a site of ideological struggle and 'the elementary forms of an oppositional formation – as where "white racism" is vigorously contested through the symbolic inversions of "black power" '.[129] The first view advised an anti-racist politics that went beyond, though incorporated, difference, the latter counselled difference as a sufficient response to racism.

Arguably, the contradiction was not a product of muddled thinking, however. Hall, no doubt, would have claimed that both difference and solidarity were necessary components of any anti-racist politics – an argument that perhaps only made sense in the peculiar circumstances of Britain in the 1970s. *Policing the Crisis* dealt almost exclusively with 'black labour' in Britain – the black working class, Hall and his co-authors wrote, constituted 'the *permanent basis of the modern industrial reserve army of labour*' – and made no mention of a black bourgeoisie, for obvious reasons.[130] As Tom Nairn wrote in 1970, Black Britain was 'almost entirely proletarian in character, and unlikely to be anything else

127. Hall 1986, pp. 5–27.
128. Hall 1980c, p. 341. This sentence originally appeared in Hall et al. 1978, p. 395.
129. Hall 1980c, p. 342. Also see Hall 1985, pp. 108–13.
130. Hall et al. 1978, p. 381 (original emphasis). The concept of the 'reserve army of labour' is still used in contemporary explanations of racism. For an example, see Wallerstein and Balibar 1991, pp. 83–92.

for some time to come'.[131] In this context, it was possible to argue for the establishment of race-blind working-class institutions *and* to argue that the discovery of a Black identity was a non-anomalous aspect of class-struggle. The presence of a Black bourgeoisie would have complicated this solution, since 'black' was potentially an identity that crossed class-boundaries. At least in the late 1970s, the absence of a black bourgeoisie allowed Hall to avoid the potential problem of melding difference and solidarity.

In truth, though, Hall was not the only one considering questions of race and national identity in the 1970s. Well before the publication of *Policing the Crisis*, Tom Nairn had considered the phenomenon of 'Powellism', and the implications of Powellism for English nationalism. He agreed with Hall that Blacks in Britain constituted 'a new bottom layer of the old class-structure',[132] but he was not optimistic, at least in the early 1970s, about the progressive potential of Black politics, claiming that 'black militancy' had been successfully assimilated to 'the traditions of English social conservatism'.[133] However, while Nairn had noted the rise of English authoritarianism and the crisis of 'consensus politics', and this at much the same time as Hall, he could not foresee the way that Powellism would itself become assimilated to conventional conservatism. Nairn's suggestion that English national identity is 'the least *popular* nationalism of any major country' seems outlandishly wrong given that Thatcherism was just around the corner.[134] The source of this weird judgment could be found in Nairn's particular definition of nationalism – Britain had nationalism, just not the right kind – rather than in any peculiar blindness to nationalist realities. What Nairn missed, however, and what Hall had been so adept at describing, was the emergence of a genuinely populist conservatism rooted in race.

Indeed, a further consequence of Hall's writings on race was his repudiation of a 'populist discourse' structured by an idea of 'the people', a continuing feature, for example, of Thompson's writings on the state in the 1970s. The reasons for this might be obvious, particularly given the way in which the New Right had constructed an image of 'the people' defined against trade-unions and social change. In terms that would have been almost impossible to imagine in 1960, 'the people', Hall concluded, 'is highly problematic'.[135] The consequence of this, he claimed, was that it could no longer be assumed that any sort of politics could be automatically attached to 'the people'. ' "The people" ', Hall went on, 'are not always back there, where they have always been, their culture untouched, their

---

131. Nairn 1977, p. 276.
132. Ibid.
133. Nairn 1977, p. 278.
134. Nairn 1977, p. 270.
135. Hall 1981, p. 238.

liberties and their instincts intact, still struggling on against the Norman yoke or whatever: as if, if only we can "discover" them and bring them back on stage, they will always stand up in the right, appointed place and be counted'.[136] This was clearly a direct rebuke to Thompson's socialism of 'freeborn Englishmen', and, what Hall considered, his unthinking endorsement of 'the people'.

Hall was no doubt right to counsel caution about this rhetoric, and not just because it was central to the ideological discourse of conservatism. Anderson and Nairn had argued for a similar caution in the very different context of the early 1960s. They had argued that 'the people' had no place in a properly socialist politics, castigating Thompson, in particular, for his vulnerability to an unhappy and unhelpful populism – a charge Thompson would vigorously deny. Hall's point, however, was somewhat different. He argued there was no seamless correspondence between 'the people' and socialism. Yet, according to Hall, 'the people' was a crucial, if not the crucial, feature of 'ideological struggle', and a political concept, *pace* Anderson and Nairn, which could not simply be dismissed. His argument was that the meaning of such terms would be decided by politics and could not be an assumed reflection of objective conditions. However, Thompson had made much the same point in the early 1960s. In the context of building a New Left political movement, Thompson had suggested that the job of 'ideological struggle' was to 'fix' the consciousness of 'the people' in ways conducive to a socialist transition.[137] 'Political consciousness', he concluded, 'is not a spontaneous generation, it is the product of political action and skill'.[138] Thus, Hall was arguably repudiating an argument of Thompson's that Thompson had in fact never held – and using arguments borrowed from Thompson to do it.

Policing the Crisis appeared before Thatcher's victory in the 1979 General Election, though the book had outlined the principal means by which resurgent conservatism laid the ideological groundwork for its future hegemony. 'The Great Moving Right Show', also published before the election, argued that Thatcherism's aim was not simply electoral victory but the construction of a 'national consensus'.[139] Into a 'populist discourse of market values', Hall claimed, Thatcherism had adroitly condensed the traditional conservative values of 'nation, family, duty, authority, standards, self-reliance'.[140] Thatcherism, he went on, had captured 'populist common sense' as a preparation for its ambition to turn the world upside down – that is, to obliterate the social-democratic consensus established after 1945. Part of that common sense was a conception of national identity

---

136. Hall 1981, p. 239.
137. E.P. Thompson 1960b, pp. 3–9; E.P. Thompson 1960b, pp. 18–31.
138. E.P. Thompson 1960a, p. 28.
139. Hall 1979, p. 16.
140. Hall 1979, p. 17.

defined against blacks, the labour-movement and popular democracy – what Powell, and then Thatcher, considered the 'enemy within'. It was on the side of this enemy that Hall intervened in the 1970s and 1980s. Increasingly, Hall would position himself as not just the pathologist of Thatcherism's rise, but as the surgeon attempting to salvage from Thatcherism's hegemony a future for socialism.[141] That future, as Hall outlined it in a series of contributions to *Marxism Today*, would be based on the Left establishing an alternative version of the 'national-popular'.

V

Hall never really saw his reflection in the mirror of British socialism. By the 1980s this was not so much because of British socialism's collusion with imperialism and the Cold War, as it had perhaps been in the 1950s. Hall failed to see his reflection in the mirror of British socialism after 1979 mostly because of the paucity of its political ambition and because of its failure to take Thatcherism seriously, and seriously on its own terms. This was also, and as a signpost of this failure, because British socialism, at least as Hall saw it, failed to engage culture and identity with proper forethought or sober consideration. Not just in terms relevant to Black Britain, but also in terms relevant to other new social movements. In Hall's view, British socialism lacked a 'philosophy of life'.[142] Indeed, content in its tired old labourist ways, British socialism, Hall reckoned, failed to take men and women at full stretch and, because of this, was 'increasingly out of touch with where real people are at'.[143]

Hall abhorred Thatcherism. The New Right's programme of 'regressive modernization', as Hall termed it, combined, if contradictorily, free-market zealotry with an 'archaic' social ideology based on conservatism's traditional values of nation, empire and family.[144] But, if Hall shared in the general New Left antipathy for the New Right's economic and social thinking, he distinguished himself from other New Left thinkers in his view that socialism had much to learn from Thatcherism. Not from Thatcherite ideology of course, as some of Hall's more crude critics claimed he meant, but from Thatcherism's ambitions and political strategy. Hall argued that to approach Thatcherism as merely a political programme whose project was to capture state power would constitute a categorical mistake. Thatcherism's aim, Hall believed, was not 'government' but hegemony, 'that process', as Terry Eagleton explains, 'whereby the particular subject so

141. These essays were collected in Hall 1988d.
142. Hall 1984a, p. 35.
143. Hall 1984b, p. 20.
144. Hall 1987, p. 17.

introjects a universal law as to consent to its imperatives in the form of consent-ing to his own deepest beliefs'.[145] Hall, then, believed that the New Right's bud-ding ascendancy was grounded in its ability to constitute itself as the ideological framework through which people defined and lived their social existence.[146] As such, its project had been long in the making, and was as much ideological as economic or political.

It was Thatcherism's intention to rule not just the state, but civil society too: 'They [the New Right] mean', Hall wrote, 'to reconstruct the terrain of what is taken for granted in social and political thought – and so to form a new com-mon sense'.[147] Misunderstanding this ambition, the Left had missed Gramsci's point that power was concentrated neither in any 'Winter Palace' nor in any 'economic base'. In other words, Thatcherism, unlike the Left, understood that political interests were constructed, not given; that the correspondence between class and politics was contingent not automatic; and that dominating civil soci-ety constituted a triumph more momentous than the capture of state-power. According to Hall, labourism, in an argument formerly owned by Anderson and Nairn in the 1960s, 'is not a culture which has ever seemed capable of assuming a national-popular leadership or of refashioning bourgeois culture in its own image'.[148] Thatcherism, Hall believed, sought a more lasting, and more deeply entrenched, form of authority, an authority which enabled the establishment of a new 'national-popular culture'.[149]

Central to the establishment of that authority, Hall believed, was Thatcherism's appropriation of national identity.[150] Hegemony, in Hall's view, was dependent on the success of any particular political ideology to imagine the nation in its own image, and its concomitant success in rendering its ideological enemies as the 'alien' Other.[151] Thatcherism had not just created 'an active popular consent',[152] Hall suggested, but had made 'Englishness' consonant with a certain understanding of the relationship between capital and labour, and with a par-ticular attitude toward difference. To be English was to be against trade-unions, state-intervention and cultural diversity, and in favour of private enterprise, free markets and an essentialised conception of national identity.[153] Thatcherism, Hall wrote, 'is addressed to our collective fantasies, to Britain as an imagined

145. Eagleton 1990, p. 32.
146. Hall 1996a, p. 39.
147. Hall 1985d, p. 119.
148. Hall 1982, p. 20.
149. See Hall 1980d, pp. 236–7, for Hall's most extensive account of 'national-popular culture'. See Hall 1988c, p. 55, for this idea in relation to Thatcherism.
150. Hall 1988a, p. 29.
151. Hall 1988d, pp. 15–6.
152. Hall 1979, p. 15.
153. Hall 1979.

community, to the social imaginary'.[154] In brief, Thatcherism was able 'to speak to and for "the nation" '.[155]

Indeed, Hall supposed that Thatcherism appreciated 'the irreversible way in which British politics and society has become imprinted by the ethnic factor',[156] even if in ways that he found wrongheaded. Again, this knowledge, he believed, demonstrated the strategic divide between the New Right and British socialism. Thatcherism addressed 'the fears, the anxieties, the lost identities, of a people',[157] while the Left had failed to engage the discourse of identity at all. Thatcherism understood that 'the identities which people carry in their heads ... have become massively *politicised*',[158] while the Left either maintained that identity was made by objective economic interest or that subjectivity was irrelevant to politics. In this sense, the Left failed to realise that Thatcherism was 'formulating new subjectivities for the positions they are constructing, working through interpellation'.[159] The Left, Hall believed, had not grasped that 'everybody comes from someplace – even if only an "imagined community" – and needs some sort of identification'.[160]

Thatcherism's appropriation of 'the people' was not a consequence of false-consciousness according to Hall, but a result of its ability 'to address real problems, real and lived experiences, real contradictions'.[161] Indeed, crucial to Hall's interpretation of Thatcherism was his belief that 'economic relations' provided no automatic guarantee of political or ideological location, although he was careful to reject the extreme discursive interpretation that implied the 'total free floatingness of all ideological elements and discourses'.[162] Hall certainly spurned Thatcherite nationalism, even though he recognised the importance of national belonging to its political dominance, that national identity was 'as central to Thatcherism's hegemonic project as the privatization programme or the assault on local democracy'.[163] He matched Raymond Williams in his outrage at Thatcherism's appropriation of real feelings toward place for its 'de-nationalizing' project.[164] But, like Williams, he believed that the Left could not simply give up the space that Thatcherism's nationalism occupied in the political terrain,

154. Hall 1987, p. 19.
155. Hall 1984b, p. 22. See also Hall 1988d, p. 188. This understanding of the articulation of nationhood with a hegemonic ideology can be found in Laclau 1979. Hall repeatedly acknowledged his debt to this work.
156. Hall 1985b, p. 14.
157. Hall 1987, p. 19.
158. Hall 1987, p. 21.
159. Hall 1988c, p. 49.
160. Hall 1988a, p. 29.
161. Hall 1979, p. 20; Hall, 1988d, p. 13.
162. Hall 1996a, p. 40.
163. Hall 1988d, p. 8.
164. Williams 1983, p. 184.

as though the Left could simply shut its eyes to people's need for identity and thereby wish that need, and Thatcherism, away.

Hall's interpretation of Thatcherism was a strikingly original analysis of the rise of the New Right. Nonetheless, it drew considerable fire from the Left, including from the New Left. Some pressed Hall on his definition of ideology, claiming he had too readily dismissed a critical interpretation of the concept, smoothing away its productive ambiguities in his effort to pin it down to a settled, neutral, meaning.[165] Umbrage was taken at Hall's suggestion that ideologies produced subjects, which seemed to run against the grain of socialism's traditional stress on 'class experience'. Others claimed Hall went too far with his arguments about the centrality of 'ideological struggle' to Thatcherism's hegemony, arguing that he had underestimated the economic foundations of the New Right's political dominance.[166] Again, discontent grouped around his supposed 'discursive reductionism'. Hall refused both charges, with some justice, particularly the charge of 'ideologism'.[167] In any case, for Hall most of the critiques were beside the point because they did not engage the central proposition of his interpretation of Thatcherism.[168]

The Anderson-led *New Left Review* was perhaps the most intransigent critic of Hall's interpretation of Thatcherism.[169] Indeed, a pre-eminent purpose of *New Left Review* throughout the 1980s was to defend the socialist belief that the organised working class was 'the principal (not the only) "gravedigger" of capitalism'.[170] In opposition to Thatcherism, *New Left Review* offered a resolute socialism, sometimes allying itself with Bennism (a prime example of what Hall considered the 'old Left'),[171] sometimes charging that Bennism suffered from traditional labourist illusions.[172] In an alliance of the 'first' and 'second' New Left, Ralph Miliband led the charge against Hall's so-called 'new revisionism', where revisionism was defined as the belief that socialism could only be made outside, and perhaps against, the traditional institutions of labour. Miliband did not deny the importance of the 'new social movements' in the struggle for socialism, but he did reiterate that the working class was 'the necessary, indispensable "agency

---

165. The most composed of these critiques was Larrain 1991, pp. 1–28. But also see Eagleton 1992.

166. This is the tenor of the criticisms found in Bonnett, Bromley, Jessop, and Ling 1984, pp. 32–60.

167. Hall 1985d, pp. 120–2.

168. Hall 1985d, p. 123.

169. Although Robin Blackburn was the editor from 1983, Anderson still had a large role in setting the tone of the journal, particularly in relation to the journal's interpretation of Thatcherism. See Elliott 1998, p. 165; D. Thompson 2007, p. 123.

170. Miliband 1985, p. 13.

171. Hall 1985c, pp. 15, 19.

172. For example, see Ali and Hoare 1982, pp. 59–81; Coates 1982, pp. 49–63; Arblaster 1985, pp. 45–60. Consider also Benn 1982.

of social change" '.[173] More specifically, he charged Hall with a misconceived notion of the state and the 'dominant class' and with an underestimation of the revolutionary past of the British working class. With reference to psephology, Miliband also claimed that there had been no 'great ideological and political shift to "Thatcherism" '.[174]

Hall did not believe that Thatcherism had achieved hegemony, as many of his critics, including Miliband, claimed. Nor did he maintain the revisionist assertion that the working class was irrelevant to social transformation. True, he did believe that the working class 'was remorselessly divided and fragmented' and that there was 'no single class there waiting to take the political stage'.[175] And, true, he had disavowed any faith in the belief that there was automatically a working-class agent of socialism.[176] But he never abandoned, at least during the 1980s, the belief that such a class could be made, no matter how pessimistic he became about the Left's prospects. He simply maintained that the traditional Left was not capable of producing 'a genuinely popular democratic social force'.[177] Miliband, Anderson and others were right that, 'in economic terms, [Thatcherism] has been a dismal, dreadful failure',[178] but Hall was also right to suggest that Thatcherite ideas had come to constitute the common sense of the age, a point Anderson would later concede. If there was any justice to Miliband's critique, it could be found in his impression that Hall's socialism was based on the assumption that 'the "traditional" Left was "backward-looking", "fundamentalist", unwilling to face hard reality, authoritarian, statist, and of course sexist'.[179] Hall saw no inherent value in 'working-class culture', and, post-Foucault, he certainly had no faith in the 'creative potentialities' of the working class, a faith he now believed a 'humanist fantasy'.[180] Thirty years later, there was perhaps some justice to E.P. Thompson's suggestion that Hall's thinking contained an 'ambiguity as to the place of the working class in the struggle to create a socialist society: a tendency to view working people as the *subjects* of history, as the pliant *recipients* of the imprint of the mass media, as *victims* of alienation, as *data* for sociological enquiry: a tendency to underestimate the tensions and conflicts of working-class life, and the creative potential . . . of working people'.[181] But this

173. Miliband 1985, p. 13.
174. Miliband 1985, p. 18.
175. Hall 1980d, p. 28.
176. Hall 1996a, pp. 2–3.
177. Hall 1980d, p. 28.
178. Also see Leys 1985, pp. 115–24.
179. Miliband 1985, p. 20. This is a claim that Hall made again and again. What was problematic with the claim, at least according to Hall's critics, was that this was not all that the working class was.
180. Hall 2009, p. 275.
181. E.P. Thompson 1958b, p. 51.

ambiguity had its origins in more than Hall's understanding of socialism. The ambiguity, Hall would have argued, was embedded in the history of the working-class movement itself.

Tom Nairn approached Hall's interpretation of Thatcherism from another angle. Like Hall, he recognised that Thatcherism was a form of modernisation that promised, on paper at least, to effect a 'bourgeois revolution'.[182] And, again like Hall, he suggested that this 'modernisation' took place within a fundamentally 'regressive' attachment to the old signifiers of 'Britishness' – Monarchy, Westminster, United Kingdom. But for other aspects of Hall's interpretation, Nairn had much less time. Nairn argued that the Thatcher revolution, and particularly its regressive aspect, actually broke 'the back of British identity'.[183] Thatcherism unintentionally reinvigorated separatist nationalism, 'brought the effective end of the monarchy', and provided England's 'centre' with a much stronger sense of difference from the backward 'north' (Wales, Scotland, northern England, and Northern Ireland).[184] Thatcherism, Nairn claimed, was a last-ditch attempt to rescue Britishness against all sorts of centrifugal forces, and one that was bound to fail.

Hall cast Thatcherism's demise in remarkably similar terms, though he was wont to emphasise the unsustainable tension between Thatcherism's nationalism and its embrace of the world market.[185] Before that, he believed if socialism was to grow again, then it would have to attend to what he called 'the root values, the root concepts, the root images and ideas in popular consciousness, without which no popular socialism can be constructed'.[186] The Left, Hall judged, had to engage the semantic battle 'over what the nation means'. It was in this context that he could celebrate George Orwell's effort 'to ground the prospects for a genuinely indigenous British socialism in a reading of the tensions within British national-popular culture'.[187] According to Hall, the nation was an 'existing symbol or slogan' which could nonetheless be detached 'from the connotative chains of association [it had] acquired'.[188] National identity could be won away from the New Right, and the Left could construct 'new possible subject positions' conducive to the making of socialism, even if that would require a politics of the long haul. 'There is a popular content to English identity', Hall

---

182. Nairn 1994, p. xx.
183. Nairn 1994, p. xxiii.
184. Nairn 1994, pp. xxii and xxvi.
185. See Hall 1993, p. 354; Hall 1990a, p. 21.
186. Hall 1996a, p. 18.
187. Hall 1982, p. 18.
188. Hall 1988c, p. 58; Hall 1980d, p. 139.

argued, 'the content of the struggle to make the nation into a popular nation rather than a nation of elites and kings'.[189]

At first sight, it is not clear how Hall's strategic vision differed from Thompson's 'socialism of the freeborn Englishman', with its own attempt to redefine 'the nation' in terms of dissent, opposition and class-struggle. In *The Defence of Britain*, a pamphlet he wrote during the 1983 General Election campaign, Thompson called forth an 'alternative Britain of citizens not subjects which, summoned up all the strengths of its long democratic past and cut through the world's nuclear knot'.[190] Be that as it may, Hall differentiated his version of 'popular Britain' from other versions in two ways. The first was his emphasis on ideological struggle, and his suggestion that the nation was a political symbol that constituted something like a 'meta-discourse' governing associations of identity and belonging. The second was his claim that politics could be understood as a form of theatre – in his own words, 'as a production'.[191] Thus 'national identity' was the supposed product of subjective imagining and had neither an intrinsic meaning nor an immutable sociology.

Yet Hall also wondered whether socialism could ever possibly disentangle national identity from the weight of its past meanings. It was not just his belief that the Left would have to undertake a hard road to renewal through a contest over associations of national identity. It was that he worried that in Britain, 'national identity' was so 'intimately bound up with imperial supremacy, tinged with racist connotations, and underpinned by a four-century-long history of colonisation, world-market supremacy, imperial expansion and global destiny over native peoples'.[192] In these circumstances, the sheer weight of the past was not just a nightmare on the living, but an eternal present. This, of course, was the position of Tom Nairn, who could imagine no progressive future with Britain, a position that E.P. Thompson, who was always ready to see some good in Britain's past, strongly denied.[193]

Whatever the doubts and hesitations that surrounded Hall's analysis of national belonging, it nonetheless illuminated nationalism's power to fulfil people's emotional need for identity. In addition to this, there was his illumination of the centrality of national identity to the establishment of political hegemony.[194] However, Hall's sensitivity to these aspects of national identity came at the cost of an inverse insensitivity to other aspects of national belonging, not least national belonging's seeming perpetual reliance on a 'particularistic

189. Hall 1988c p. 66.
190. E.P. Thompson 1985, p. 104.
191. Hall 1987, p. 169.
192. Hall 1996a, p. 43.
193. E.P. Thompson 1985, p. 103.
194. See Freeden 1998, pp. 748–65.

mystique' – not love of country but hatred of others – which has been so central to the political purchase,[195] the sociological opaqueness and the deep emotional appeal of the nation. Of course, Hall, more than most, was cognisant of the terrors associated with national belonging, whether in terms of riots in Notting Hill or colonialism in the Caribbean. The problem was that nations were not only imagined communities, but were most often imagined in anti-socialist ways. If national identity is crucial to socialist hegemony, as Hall supposed, and if socialism is incompatible with national identity, as Hall sometimes argued, then perhaps socialism had no future after all.

This was certainly a strain in Hall's 'New Times' argument. A product of debates within *Marxism Today*, New Times was one way that Hall sought to grasp the nature of Thatcherism.[196] In one sense, it constituted a recognition of the international dimensions of neo-liberalism; in another sense, New Times was an attempt to explain why the old (one-nation) socialism could no longer work. According to Hall, 'New Times' constituted a new epoch of capitalist civilisation 'characterized by diversity, differentiation and fragmentation, rather than homogeneity, standardization and the economies and organizations of a scale that characterized modern mass society'.[197] New Times was an explanation for transformations in every region of social existence, from economics to culture, and from politics to epistemology. It also explained 'new ethnicities', cultural hybridity and diaspora as emergent, if not yet dominant, features of modern society. In the New Times mirror, Hall would increasingly see his own reflection – but no future for socialism, however conceived.

VI

Hall was writing about New Times as early as 1985, though the 'project', as it would come to be described, did not take off or receive coherent form until 1988 or thereabouts.[198] New Times was an intellectual and political intervention – an attempt to interpret the world in order to change it, providing a series of arguments about economics, culture and politics, and reasons for why socialism, at least as it had been hitherto understood, had become increasingly irrelevant. In terms of economics, it acknowledged what would soon be called 'globalisation'. Importantly, however, New Times argued that globalisation involved the proliferation of difference rather than its disappearance, as Marx, and many liberals,

---

195. See Balakrishnan 1995.
196. For a brief history of the project, consider Mulhern 2000a, p. 114.
197. See Hall and Jacques 1989, p. 11.
198. See Hall 1985b, pp. 12–17; Hall 1988a, pp. 24–9. See McRobbie 1996, pp. 238–61, for a review of the New Times project.

had sometimes supposed. The world-market did not, Hall explained, 'translate everything in the world into a kind of replica of itself, everywhere'.[199] In terms of politics, the most salient aspect of New Times was the suggestion that the world's increasing economic interdependence, plus forced and unforced mass migration, had trumped the nation-state. But it also acknowledged the 'return of the subjective dimension' to politics.[200] Culturally, according to Hall, New Times were indicated in the rise of 'new ethnicities', where 'ethnicity' was understood as 'positioning' rather than 'essence', and the related emergence of multi-cultural society as the modern world's fate.[201]

Although a grand narrative, New Times was supposed to mark the end of grand narratives, much like the postmodernism to which it was ambiguously related. New Times was about the shift, if uneven, from Fordist to Post-Fordist modes of accumulation and production. About the shift from a highly centralised labour market to one based on flexibility and decentralisation; about new forms of consumption; and about a new international division of labour. And it was about the de-stabilisation of social identities, especially those identities based on nation, class and race.[202] 'The individual subject', Hall wrote in an early exposition of New Times, 'has become more important'.[203] New Times produced the end of the 'innocent' notion of the subject, revealing behind the façade of a unitary sense of self the nakedness of contradiction, fragmentation and difference that (discursively) constituted actual (multiple) selves. If New Times could be boiled down to a formula, it would be this: There is no such thing as identity/experience/politics outside of representation. Signifiers, much less the identities they produced, no longer had moorings in anything solid, at least not in ways commonly imagined. They had been set free from material referents.

This is partly to caricature something that was much more serious, although New Times did produce much nonsense, and almost as much nonsense in response from critics.[204] For the most part Hall stayed clear of the postmodern celebration of New Times. He was sensitive to the uneven development of New Times, and to those who were caught up in its maelstrom. Because, for Hall, New Times was not just about fragmentation, the celebration of difference and the expansion of choice, it was also about forced mass migration, the break-down of the state and the destruction of everyday forms of life. Increasingly, Hall wrote

---

199. Hall 1991b, p. 29. See also, Hall 1993, p. 353.
200. Hall 1988a, p. 25.
201. See Hall 1991a, p. 54.
202. See Hall 1996a, pp. 223–6.
203. Hall 1988a, p. 24.
204. As an example of nonsense, consider Martin Jacques's suggestion that 'Mass production, the mass consumer, the big city, big-brother state, the sprawling housing estate, and the nation-state are in decline: flexibility, diversity, differentiation and internationalisation are in the ascendant'. See Jacques 1988, p. 1.

from the perspective of those 'millions of displaced peoples and dislocated cultures and fractured communities of the "South", who have been moved from their "settled communities", their "actual lived relations", their "placeable feelings", their "whole ways of life" ',[205] in spirit if not substance, something to be expected from someone who knew the ambiguities involved in the pleasures of exile. He was alert to the 'difference that didn't make a difference' and the ruthless economic deprivation characteristic of New Times – that, following Frederic Jameson, New Times were connected 'with the revolutionary energy of modern capital'.[206] New Times, for Hall, 'clearly belong to a time-zone marked by the march of capital simultaneously across the globe and through the Maginot Lines of our subjectivities'.[207] There was nothing to celebrate about that.

The 'other' of New Times was not just the neoliberalism characteristic of Thatcherism, but much more importantly 'classical Marxism'. Reinventing the New Left wheel, politics, Hall argued, was about culture rather than just economics in the way Marxists had once supposed. Indeed Hall argued that 'questions of culture and ideology, and the scenarios of representation', that is 'subjectivity, identity, politics', now had 'a formative, not merely an expressive, place in the constitution of social and political life'.[208] Culture now predominated over nature,[209] and this fact, Hall argued, 'distances us from invoking the simple, transparent ground of "material interests" as a way of settling any argument'.[210] In this context, Hall believed that Marxism, no less than labourism, was no response to New Times. Classical Marxism's failure, according to Hall, was not only theoretical. It was also empirical. This was no more apparent, he believed, than in 'its lack of adequate explanatory power about the concrete empirical development of consciousness and practice in the working classes of the advanced capitalist world'.[211]

New Times was submitted to stinging rebuke by sections of the Left, particularly the New Left. John Saville, original co-editor of *New Reasoner*, argued that New Times overlooked both economic reality and history, and was an inadequate

---

205. Hall 1993, p. 361. See also Hall 1996b, p. 249.
206. Hall 1996a, p. 228.
207. Ibid.
208. Hall 1996a, p. 165. Sometimes, in statements like these, Hall's work could border on the absurd. Was he really suggesting that 'politics' had a formative place in the 'constitution' of 'political life'?
209. Hall 1996a, p. 235. For a critique of this view, consider Eagleton 2004, pp. 162–4.
210. Ibid.
211. Hall 1988e, p. 43. This is not true. Indeed Marxists have been at the forefront of explaining 'the concrete empirical development of consciousness and practice in the working classes of the advanced capitalist world'. Harry Braverman, Frederic Jameson, David Harvey, Perry Anderson, to mention just a few, have been adept at accounting for these developments. What might be called – after Alvin Gouldner – 'nightmare Marxism'.

tool for analysing 'the ownership of wealth, the distribution of income, or the relationship between economic power and political control'.[212] Arguments about class, poverty and exploitation, Saville suggested, were ignored by New Times because it could not 'get away from the consumer society' and because its 'horizons are bounded by words like choice, individualism, increased individual responsibility, flexibility, and the like'.[213] Saville's was not the most sophisticated response, mostly because it preferred a New Times caricature to the realities it sought to illuminate. However this did not greatly diminish the force of his rebuke. Similar reproofs appeared in *New Left Review* and *Socialist Register*. In the first, Mike Rustin countered that New Times neglected 'the primacy of the actions and strategies of class in the exploration of changes in the political economy of capitalism',[214] and involved a 'tacit accommodation to the values of resurgent capitalism'.[215] In *Socialist Register*, Christopher Norris took umbrage at the way that New Times implied the suspension, if not the obliteration, of socialist hope.[216] New Times, Norris concluded, represented more 'a symptom of the present malaise than a cure for modernity and its manifest discontents'.[217]

New Times eventually disappeared from Hall's discourse (mostly without comment),[218] but its central contentions did not, especially not what he called 'the revolution of the subject', an aspect of Hall's analysis which his critics mostly failed to engage. There is no doubt that identity, and the manifest problems with identity, have constituted the richest seam in Hall's writings since New Times. For Hall, capitalist globalisation, far from destroying attachments to locality and culture, had given 'cultural identity' a new lease of life, promoting a proliferation of identities based on ethnicity. There was a normative as well as an empirical aspect to this assertion. Hall presented cultural diversity as a simple fact of globalisation giving rise to what he called the 'multi-cultural drift' in societies like Britain. But it was also Hall's intent to suggest that this was a good thing, and mostly because it put an end to those forms of ethnicity based on a spurious closure and a fixed essence. It wasn't that ethnicity had disappeared. It was that a cultural struggle – the 'new politics of representation'[219] – was taking place

---

212. Saville 1990, p. 56.
213. Ibid.
214. Rustin 1989a, p. 61.
215. Rustin 1989a, p. 68.
216. The question of the relationship between New Times and New Labour is complex. Hall has strenuously denied that he ever became assimilated to Blair's project. However, he did refer repeatedly to Blair's 'courage' in Hall 1995, pp. 24, 26, though this was only in the context of the 'modernisation' of the Labour Party. For a later, less complimentary, view, see Hall 1998b, pp. 9–14.
217. Norris 1993, p. 75.
218. Though consider Hall 1995, pp. 27–30.
219. Hall 1996a, p. 165.

around what ethnicity meant.[220] The 'new ethnicities', Hall argued, eschewed coercions associated with nationalism, imperialism, racism and the state. A 'positive view of ethnicity' was more diverse, and involved the recognition 'that we all speak from a particular place, out of a particular history, a particular culture, without being contained by that position'.[221]

Broadly, Hall believed that there had been two dominant responses to the 'radically new historical moment' produced by capitalist globalisation.[222] On the one hand, cultural diversity had produced 'new ethnicities' and the 'end of the innocent notion of the subject'.[223] On the other hand, globalisation had been refused through a return to the old sense of ethnicity, not least in the invention after tradition associated with ethnic nationalism. By the late 1990s, Hall wondered whether the second response was perhaps trumping the first, despite the promise of his original interpretation.[224] 'There is more closure of an ethnic, religious, national, quasi-national or regional kind going on around the world, as a kind of defensive movement against openness and diversity, than we would ever have imagined'.[225] Hall did not believe this was inevitable. 'Ethnicity can be a constitutive element', he wrote, 'in the most viciously regressive kind of nationalism or national identity. But in our times, as an imaginary community, it is also beginning to carry some other meanings, and to define a new space for identity. It insists on difference – on the fact that every identity is placed, positioned, in a culture, a language, a history'.[226]

This interpretation of the re-emergence of ethnicity would be contested by both Tom Nairn and Perry Anderson, though for different reasons. Nairn would have agreed with Hall that 'everybody has an ethnicity because everybody comes from a cultural tradition, a cultural context, an historical context'.[227] And Nairn would have assented to Hall's contention that 'nationalism is not only *not* a spent force; it is not necessarily either a reactionary or a progressive force, politically'.[228] But he would have disagreed with Hall's distinction between 'old ethnicities' and 'new ethnicities', seeing the bifurcation as a reinvention for new times of that hoary old division between Eastern nationalism (bad) and Western nationalism (good). Even if the fit was not quite as snug as this, since Hall was an unlikely champion of Eurocentrism, there remained the fact that 'new ethnicities' were more likely to be found in London than Kiev or Zagreb. Nairn would also have

220. Hall 1996a, p. 168.
221. Hall 1996a, p. 169.
222. Hall 2007, p. 281.
223. Hall 1996a, p. 165. See also Hall 1993, p. 353; Hall 2007, p. 282.
224. Hall 1993, p. 354.
225. Hall 1991b, p. 43.
226. Hall 1988e, p. 119. See also Hall 1991c, p. 19.
227. Hall 1999, p. 228. See also Hall 2000, p. 233.
228. Hall 1993, p. 355.

disagreed with Hall's suggestion that capitalist globalisation had subverted the nation-state. It's not that Nairn would have necessarily disagreed with Hall's contention that the nation-state had lost some of its power.[229] But he would not have seen this as a positive thing, as Hall sometimes did. And he would have absolutely rejected Hall's suggestion that 'diaspora now is obliterating...the moment of the nation-state'.[230] If that was the case, Nairn would have suggested, then there was little or no hope for self-determination or democracy.

But this is to draw the differences between Nairn and Hall too starkly. Of course Hall had no time for ethnic nationalism, that 're-invention' of being associated as much with the Balkans as with Britain. However, at least in the context of Eastern Europe and the formerly colonial world, he recognised ethnic nationalism as 'a bid for modernity'.[231] Indeed, according to Hall, peoples on the 'periphery have no other cultural resources with which to defend themselves against the homogenising "indifference" of globalisation, no other languages in which to define a different, more vernacular, set of modernities'.[232] If he could agree with Nairn on these matters, Hall could also admit that political action was always based on an invented sense of identity. But this had nothing to do with ethnic nationalism and could only be confused with it, Hall suggested, 'if we mistake this "cut of identity" – this positioning, which makes meaning possible – as a natural and permanent, rather than an arbitrary and contingent "ending"'.[233] Hall, like Nairn, understood that postmodernism's celebration of fragmentation was a poor substitute for the 'strategic essentialism' that had given rise to the bid for national self-determination in the period of de-colonisation.[234]

It is not exactly clear how Anderson would have responded to Hall's interpretation of identity and politics, though he would have surely resented the suggestion that class was a wholly inadequate tool for the investigation of late capitalist societies. And he would have considered Hall's conception of 'classical Marxism' a falsification and a travesty of the actual record, something, Anderson would have reflected, not to be expected from a thinker, like Hall, so immersed in the Marxist tradition. However, some of Anderson's differences with Hall would have been a matter of emphasis rather than fundamental disagreement. Anderson preferred to stress globalisation's homogenising tendencies, the inevitable result of a conjuncture in which neo-liberalism had become 'the dominant idiom of

---

229. Hall 2007, p. 282.
230. Hall 2007, p. 289.
231. Hall 1991a, p. 18.
232. Hall 1991a, p. 19.
233. Hall 1990a, p. 230.
234. Hall 1988e, p. 117.

the period',[235] rather than its role in the facilitation of cultural diversity. For him, cultural homogeneity was a more convincing, and more dominant, sign of the times than the hybridity celebrated by Hall.[236] Nor would Anderson have disagreed with Hall's belief that the 'nationalist passion' was a continuing feature of modern societies,[237] though he might have found in this a cause for regret. Anderson would have found even less to disagree with in Hall's thesis that the nation-state, rather than national cultures, had been eviscerated by global economic, political and social trends.[238] However, Anderson would not have been afraid to denounce ethnic nationalism *tout court*, and he would not have been afraid to consider votes for Le Pen a matter of false-consciousness, the 'socialism of fools'. And, finally, he would have considered the difference between 'new ethnicity' and 'old ethnicity' a false and unconvincing one. Just as all 'citizen nationalism' necessarily contained a good deal of the racism supposedly common to ethnic nationalism, so too the 'new ethnicity' contained much of the essentialism associated with the old.

Reflections on 'the emergence of a black British identity' were a guiding thread of Hall's work in the final decades of the twentieth century.[239] The basis of those reflections was Hall's belief that 'black cultural politics' was undergoing a shift 'from a struggle over the relations of representation to a politics of representation itself' – a shift driven by 'the recognition that "black" is essentially a politically and culturally *constructed* category, which cannot be grounded in a set of fixed transcultural or transcendental racial categories and which therefore has no guarantees in Nature'.[240] No longer, Hall believed, could 'black' operate as a cultural identity blind to difference, and no longer did 'black' constitute an unproblematic identity, as it had perhaps done in the 1970s. 'The moment the signifier "black" is torn from its historical, cultural, and political embedding and lodged in a biologically constituted racial category', Hall wrote, 'we valorize by inversion, the very ground of racism we are trying to deconstruct'.[241] As a warning to those who would base their politics on identity, Hall suggested that the ultimate destination of a 'pure assertion of difference' is *'apartheid'*.[242]

And no longer, Hall believed, could 'black' imply a repudiation of Britishness. 'Fifteen years ago', he wrote in the late 1980s with reference to Paul Gilroy's influential book, 'I didn't care, whether there was any black in the Union Jack.

---

235. Anderson 2005, pp. 310, 316. Though, also consider Anderson 2009, p. 187 where he waxes lyrical about the need for diversity.
236. Anderson 2005, p. 319.
237. Hall 1993, p. 353.
238. See Hall 2000, pp. 214–5.
239. Hall 1998c, p. 38.
240. Hall 1996a, p. 166.
241. See also Hall 2006, p. 20. In addition, see Hall 1988e, p. 116.
242. Hall 2000, p. 233.

Now not only do we care, we *must*.[243] Hall's point was that an alternative sense of Britishness was necessary to undo the harm associated with dominant conservative visions of national identity. 'There have always been very different ways of "being British"'.[244]

Britishness, Hall claimed, was an 'empty signifier'[245] whose meaning was up 'for extensive renovation and renegotiation',[246] as easily articulated with diversity and democracy as it had been with intolerance and privilege. Reinvention, Hall believed, would constitute an 'act of imaginative rediscovery' in Benedict Anderson's sense, and such a rediscovery would belong more to the future than the past.[247] This is why Hall devoted so much attention to 'black cultural politics', because it was here that Britain was being imagined in terms far removed from 'the old, the imperializing, the hegemonizing, form of "ethnicity"'.[248]

It was in the context of this urgent need to redefine Britishness that Hall mounted a critique of the late work of Raymond Williams, in particular his affirmation of 'rooted settlements' and 'lived, worked and placeable social identities' in *Towards 2000*.[249] Williams's stress on 'actual and sustained social relationships', Hall suggested, overlooked the cultural diversity associated with multicultural societies, and paid no attention to the increasingly universal experience of the migrant. 'It is true', Hall wrote, 'that social identity cannot be reduced to formal legal definitions'.[250] But the legalities associated with citizenship, Hall argued, 'cannot be made conditional on cultural assimilation'.[251] Hall, indeed, endorsed Paul Gilroy's reading of *Towards 2000* which suggested that Williams had offered 'a racially exclusive form of social identity',[252] and that Williams's work '[remained] both blind to questions of race and framed by certain unexamined "national" cultural assumptions'.[253]

Hall seemed to want to have it both ways here: on the one hand, he wanted to argue that culture was constitutive of politics; and on the other hand he argued that 'far from collapsing the complex questions of cultural identity and issues of social and political rights, what we need now is *greater distance between them*'.[254] Moreover, Hall seemed to offer a deliberately unsympathetic

---

243. Hall 1996a, p. 170. See also Hall 1996b, p. 473.
244. Hall 2000, p. 229.
245. Hall 2001, p. 9.
246. Hall 2000, p. 237.
247. Hall 1996a, pp. 224–5. See also Hall 1995, p. 14.
248. Hall 1996a, p. 235.
249. Hall 1993, p. 359.
250. Hall 1993, p. 360.
251. Ibid.
252. Ibid.
253. Ibid.
254. Ibid. (original emphasis).

reading of Williams's reflections on social identities, a reading that overlooked much of Williams' text, like his assertion that it is necessary to '[assert] the need for equality and protection within the laws'.[255] More ironically, the argument of *Towards 2000* actually mirrored Hall's view. Williams argued that socialists should reject 'the divisive ideologies of "race" and "nation" ',[256] reject them 'in favour of lived and formed identities either of a settled kind, if possible, *or of a possible kind, where dislocation and relocation require new formation*'.[257] Turning to his own 'homeland', the Welsh mining valleys, Williams argued for the 'practical formation of social identity' – a formation that was necessitated by 'massive and diverse immigration'.[258] His 'ground of hope' was that peoples with diverse histories could create a loyalty to community around common need – what he understood as the necessary basis for socialism. Williams offered no comfort to 'a racially exclusive form of social identity'.

Nairn, like Williams, would have repudiated Hall's attempt to re-imagine Britishness. Nairn did not believe that Britain could be re-defined, at least not without excluding other forms of identity, such as his own sense of Scottishness. 'The British realm', he wrote, 'needs replacing, not "transforming" '.[259] Nairn would have agreed with Hall that there is not only one way of being English (though he believed there was only one way of being British), and he would have agreed with Hall that democracy demanded a more inclusive sense of identity. However, it was precisely because Britain implied the denial of ethnicity that Nairn saw the need to get rid of Britain. 'A genuine community of citizens is the only real safeguard for incomers and minorities – and this is exactly what Old Britain in its pickle-preserved state is not'.[260] Nairn placed his hope in Europe – the European Union, for him, providing 'the best example of nationalities combining to escape their past – and enshrining their new formula in written-constitutional terms'.[261] Hall harboured few illusions about Europe, however. For him, 'Europe' was as much about keeping others out, as embracing them.

It is not too difficult to spot the source of Hall's interest in diaspora, ethnicity and cultural identity.[262] What prevented Hall's writings on these subjects from descending into banal navel-gazing or narcissism was the intelligence with which he was able to link these concerns to larger social forces. His engagement with identity was a political intervention, and was based on his belief

---

255. Williams 1983b, p. 195.
256. Williams 1983b, p. 196.
257. Ibid. (emphasis added).
258. Ibid.
259. Nairn 2002, p. 167.
260. Ibid.
261. Nairn 2002, p. 169.
262. See Hall 2007, p. 284.

that displacement and diaspora were becoming typical conditions of 'global modernity'.[263] However, if there were limitations associated with Hall's writings in the wake of New Times, it was that he was not always willing to admit the potential problems associated with his primary concerns or the politics they funded. That diaspora was crucial to long-distance nationalism, that ethnicity was often a cover for the 'return of barbarism', that cultural identity was a means of occluding class difference, and that difference, no matter how it was defined, was an unlikely basis for the establishment of a politics of equality. Hall, of course, was well aware of all this. It was a question of emphasis. Too much Derrida, perhaps, and not enough 'spirit of Marx'.

VII

E.P. Thompson once suggested that C. Wright Mills offered a '*style* rather than a comprehensive theory of social process; and it is the style of the responsible and catholic eclectic, playing by ear because the issues were so momentous, the time so short – drawing now upon one, now upon another, of the concepts available in the work of previous sociologists, testing them in practice by their adequacy for the work in hand'.[264] Much of this can be said about Hall too. He also offered a style, a way of thinking, rather than any overarching theory of society. Like Mills's, Hall's thinking was also responsible, whether it was put to work for the reinvigoration of socialism or in defence of the 'enemy within'. Hall, too, searched the work of others and tested the concepts he found there in concrete conjunctures, their adequacy determined not by their theoretical sophistication but by how well they helped him understand the 'history of the present', and whether that understanding could aid in changing the world. At once modest and effective, Hall's style has constituted a major contribution to New Left thought.

That contribution was unique. Hall was always alert to the signs in the street, particularly those signs that pointed toward the politics of the future. Like Anderson, Hall was mostly without a country. But he wrote from where he lived, and was always passionately engaged in the politics of where he was. In this way, he resembled Nairn. But unlike Nairn he was much less likely to place great hopes in nationalism, nor reduce democracy to national self-determination. But, like Nairn, he was aware of the communitarian limits of liberalism and socialism.[265] Hall obviously took much from the work of Williams, who had always highlighted people's attachment to place and a lived culture. However, with whatever justice, he feared the reduction of community to ethnicity associated with

---

263. Hall 1999a, p. 212.
264. E.P. Thompson 1985, p. 264.
265. Hall 2000, pp. 228–9.

Williams's advocacy of lived and worked and placed identities. His elective affinities with Thompson were less obvious. They crossed often, but both believed that political identities were constructed by political action and skill, and that socialism was about more than just economics. Like Thompson and Williams, Hall always eschewed elitism and anti-intellectualism. Hall mostly wrote with others in mind, and always for a politics against racism, imperialism and ethnic nationalism.

Indeed, Hall consistently repudiated nationalism, especially the imperialist-inflected sort that was dominant in Britain in the 1950s and 1980s. This perhaps goes without saying. But he did not reject national identity or the need to position yourself somewhere. Not only did he make a distinction between nationalism and national identity, Hall urged socialists to enter discussion about what national identity is, and how it might be reconciled to socialism. This was especially the case during the Thatcher years. More recently, he has suggested that a 'nationalist' sense of national identity no longer has cultural and political purchase in a world that increasingly reflects the phenomenology of migrancy, diaspora and cultural hybridity.[266] But even in such circumstances, he still maintains that national identity has potentially progressive identifications, and that the national-popular is still important to the construction of political and cultural hegemony. A national identity defined with rather than against ethnicity and difference, and one eschewing any form of essentialism.

Hall never felt completely at home in any of the countries that he acknowledged or that acknowledged him. This was not just the case in the Caribbean of his youth or the Britain of his early manhood. It was also the case in relation to the New Left and to Black Britain; the two imagined communities that exerted the most enduring claims on his loyalty. As far as the New Left was concerned, Hall approached the socialist formation with both passion and caution. His caution was a product of the New Left's sometime unthinking conception of working-class community, and later with its 'narodnik' populism. Black Britain was no less problematic for Hall, however. If his allegiance could easily be given when black labour was considered an internal enemy of dominant representations of British national identity, it was not so easily extracted when Black Britain came to mime the essentialising features of Britishness. Black Britain could sometimes make him uncomfortable. It was this discomfort, whether with the New Left or Black Britain, that spurred his most enduring insights on the relationship between national identity and socialism.

---

266. Hall 1997, p. 34.

Chapter Six
Perry Anderson against the National Culture

I

Perry Anderson's work traverses not only historical epochs and academic disciplines, but, like his own biography, national borders, languages and ideational cultures. A cosmopolitan intellectual, more at home in the realm of universal ideas than any particular national culture, Anderson has been central to the history of the New Left in Britain, not just as long-time editor of *New Left Review*, but, above all, as chief interlocutor in a number of the New Left's definitive debates.[1] Perhaps consequent to an extra-territorial and anti-national, certainly anti-populist, social-being, and one that had its origins in the Anglo-Irish Ascendancy, Anderson's contributions to New Left thought have mostly assumed the 'top down view'.[2] This aspect has been reflected in a style and tone that others have described as 'Olympian'.[3] Not without predicament, and not free of certain interests, Anderson's cosmopolitanism has provided New Left thought with a unique and illuminating perspective on the nexus between socialism and national identity. But this perspective has entailed

---

1. See D. Thompson 2007, on Anderson's long-standing association with *NLR*. He was editor of *NLR* between 1962 and 1983, although he stood down for one issue in 1968. After 1983, he remained closely involved with the journal, and eventually became editor again in 2000. Recently, he has handed editorship over to Susan Watkins, but he remains on the journal's editorial board.

2. Anderson's most pregnant description of the 'somewhere' from which he writes appears in Anderson 1974b, p. 8.

3. This characterisation recurs throughout secondary discussions of Anderson's work. It began with Sedgwick 1976, p. 148. More recently, see Elliott 1998, p. xi; Collini 2008, pp. 187–95.

costs, encouraged ambiguity, and at times resulted in myopia. In Anderson's case, the telescopic vision from above has produced both illumination and evasion.

This chapter will explore Anderson's engagement with national identity from the angle of his association with New Left political thought; it will pay particular attention to debates with other figures of the New Left, particularly E.P. Thompson, and 'missed' debates with Nairn and Hall. It will proceed in the following manner. After a brief biographical intermission, the chapter will consider Anderson's encounter with the national culture in the 1960s, beginning with an analysis of his contributions to the anti-nationalist project of *New Left Review* after 1962, which will close with an assessment of the ambiguities in his support for revolutionary nationalism in the 'Third World'. Following on this discussion, the chapter will consider Anderson's conception of the historicity of nationhood through a brief survey of his historical sociology. This survey will be juxtaposed with an enquiry into the nature of Anderson's post-1968 socialist internationalism informed as it was by the 'classical Marxist tradition'. Third, it will investigate Anderson's most recent contributions to the national question, an assessment of his conception of the relationship between nationhood and capitalism, and the fortunes of socialism in relation to both. The chapter will conclude with a brief review of the place and value of Anderson's (socialist) cosmopolitanism in our nationalist world.

II

Anderson's biography constitutes the antithesis of the nineteenth century nationalist project.[4] He was born in London (although conceived in China – this odd biographical detail revealed in a recent essay on his father) in September 1938,[5] the same month that Neville Chamberlain consigned the Sudetenland to Nazi dictate and Britain to the brief illusion that war with Germany could be avoided. The instance of Anderson's birth proves the truth of what his brother, the scholar of nationalism Benedict Anderson, has called the 'counterfeit quality' of the birth certificate.[6] He spent his earliest years in China, where his brother was born, and where his father was employed in the Imperial Customs Union, subject now of an affecting and illuminating study in Anderson's collection of essays, *Spectrum*.[7] At the outbreak of war in 1939, Anderson went with his aunt to America and

---

4. Perry Anderson, as Skidelsky has suggested, 'is notoriously elusive': see Skidelsky 1999, p. 18.
5. Anderson 2005, p. 345.
6. B. Anderson 1998, p. 70.
7. Anderson 2005, pp. 343–88.

then, after 1945, to Ireland, his father's birthplace, where Anderson would spend the remaining years of his childhood before boarding school in England.

Anderson's 'cosmopolitan' childhood was followed by education at parochial Oxford,[8] where he arrived at Worcester College in 1956, on the verge of the New Left's political take-off. 'It was', he later remembered, 'virtually impossible for any lively young person not to be very quickly and deeply politicized by [the] experience' of that year.[9] New Left politics and the Marxist intellectual tradition rapidly filled the vacuum encouraged by Anderson's 'background of *depaysements*'.[10] Noticeably influenced by two thinkers – Raymond Williams and Isaac Deutscher – Anderson was part of a 'third generation'[11] of New Left thinkers that coalesced around the Oxford student journal *New University*.[12] Through the auspices of Stuart Hall and others, Anderson wrote for *New Left Review* in 1961, a study of Sweden and a co-authored piece on European integration were among his earliest contributions.[13] In 1962, having been invited by the editorial board to take direction of the review, he brought with him a new theoretical architecture to reconstruct the New Left; his orientation borrowed from other places and other traditions. No heart-felt sentiment of home, no feeling of love attending reflection on roots, guided this reconstruction, a theoretical and political overhaul that signalled perhaps the defining crisis of the early New Left. Consequent to a series of 'cultural estrangements' (China, America, Ireland and England),[14] Anderson sought to rebuild New Left socialism on the basis of a radical separatism from the politics of native (English) radicalism.[15]

III

In 1951, Britain hosted a festival celebrating itself in what was contemporaneously described as an 'act of national autobiography'.[16] Two years later, the nation crowned a new national monarch amid pomp, ceremony and recollections of Britain's imperial splendour. The nation of Empire was still supremely important, and not just in the speeches of Winston Churchill, prime minister (for

---

8. See Anderson 1999, p. 1.

9. Anderson 1999, p. 1.

10. Elliott 1998, p. 1.

11. Anderson has written of the three generations of the New Left in Anderson 1992b, pp. 195–6.

12. See Blackledge 2004, pp. 2–5.

13. See Anderson 1961a, pp. 4–12; Anderson 1961b, pp. 34–45; Anderson and Hall 1961, pp. 1–14.

14. B. Anderson 1990, pp. 1–2.

15. See Blackburn 1992, pp. v–xi, for a somewhat anodyne overview of this history. See Rustin 1985, pp. 46–75, for an acute overview from a former editor.

16. Herbert Morrison cited (without direct attribution) in Mandler 2006, p. 208.

the second time) from 1951. The deliberate traditionalism of monarchical regeneration and parliamentary routine was reflected in a structural conservatism that framed politics and social relations as much as it did sport and culture. 'In literary and cultural terms', explains Stefan Collini, 'the period after 1945 ... saw a self-conscious return to values and forms of expression identified as essentially English'.[17] English culture, for T.S. Eliot writing at the time, was a matter of 'nineteenth-century Gothic churches and the music of Elgar',[18] while, for others, it was associated with the domestic and with gentlemanly civility.[19] Eulogies to the nation could be heard from the cinema to the pulpit, from *The Story of England* to *The British Road to Socialism*.[20] Ideas, like West Indians, were suspect in such a conformist intellectual milieu. The facts, in England if not in other countries, still spoke for themselves. As Peter Hennessy, a leading historian of the period, has recently concluded, Britain in the 1950s was 'the most settled, deferential, smug, un-dynamic society in the advanced world'.[21]

There was, of course, another 1950s. But, from the perspective of Oxford, rather than say Halifax, it is not surprising that the overwhelming conservatism and nationalism of Britain shaded everything else. Anderson and other members of the 'second' New Left came to political maturity amid this renaissance of conservative nationalism, a revival conducted through the ventriloquism of a new monarch's coronation, through attachment to US hegemony and through imperial adventure abroad, all counterfeit conceptions of Britain as leading actor in international relations. It was a bad time for socialism. National sentiment, recently enlarged through the experience of the War and social reform, appeared to shrivel up and turn in on itself, defined against rather than with T.H. Marshall's contemporaneous conception of social citizenship. By the 1950s, people's peace had morphed into the patriotism of Church and King mobs in Notting Hill and Nottingham.

Attending to the generational divide between the two New Lefts in *Arguments within English Marxism*, Anderson believed the 1950s were distinguished by 'reactionary consolidation'.[22] 'In Britain', Anderson recalled in characteristic prose and anti-nationalist invective, 'its major idiom was glutinously chauvinist – reverent worship of Westminster, ubiquitous cult of constitutional moderation and common sense, ritualized exaltation of tradition and precedent'.[23] British intellectual life, he claimed, was complicit in this anti-modernist condensation,

---

17. Collini 2006, p. 138.
18. Eliot 1948, p. 41.
19. See Stapleton 1994, pp. 154–76.
20. See Stapleton 2006, pp. 221–32.
21. Hennessy 1999, pp. 435–6.
22. Anderson 1980, p. 148.
23. Ibid.

mimicking the 'wizened provincialism'[24] the political and social establishment declaimed.[25] Replaying terms employed in the 1960s, the English idiom, according to Anderson, was 'parochial and quietest'.[26] Whether viewed from above or below, at no matter what point on Britain's political topography, traditionalism and empiricism structured the order of discourse, ensuring maintenance of social hierarchy, economic inefficiency and ideational nullity. 'British culture', as he put it in 1968, was 'a deeply damaging and stifling force, operating against the growth of any revolutionary theory'.[27] It was in this felt context that Anderson, helmsman of *New Left Review* from 1962, organised a conceptual assault on the national culture.

Anderson's revolt against Englishness was manifest in two complementary forms: on the one hand, dismissal of Britain's national culture and, on the other, deliberate and polemical embrace of internationalism, in politics and theory. Both – his 'fierce hatred of the reigning cultural conformism in Britain' and his commitment to the internationalisation of the intellectual culture – were the provocation of the Nairn-Anderson theses,[28] a series of interventions published in *New Left Review* between 1962 and 1968.[29] It was the burden of the theses to account for the present crisis of society and economy in Britain, manifest in an antiquated ruling elite, a declining manufacturing sector and an outdated orientation to finance rather than industry. Anderson believed that a coherent account of generalised British entropy across economy, society and culture – one capable of providing a guide to future socialist strategy – would require a conceptual anatomy of Britain's history as a 'structural totality'. Deploying the recently assimilated universe of Western Marxism,[30] Anderson set out to provide a global map of the English experience that would enable comprehension of the contemporary crisis of society and economy and illuminate the ruinous shortcomings of the intellectual inheritance. Above all, the Nairn-Anderson theses had an intended polemical motive – root and branch repudiation of the national culture associated equally with conservatism and (New Left) socialism. In this

---

24. Anderson 1968, p. 8.
25. See also the comments of Mulhern 1981, p. xix, cited in Anderson 1992b, p. 194.
26. Anderson 1980, p. 148.
27. Anderson 1968, p. 57.
28. Anderson 1980, p. 149.
29. Conventionally included among the essays which make up the Nairn-Anderson theses are the following (in order of publication) – Nairn 1964a, pp. 19–25; Anderson 1964, pp. 26–53; Nairn 1964b, pp. 43–57; Nairn 1965, pp. 38–65; Nairn 1965, pp. 33–62. A defence of the theses (against attack from E.P. Thompson) was offered in Anderson 1966, pp. 2–42. The theses were continued in Anderson 1968.
30. See Forgacs 1989a, pp. 74–7, for the theoretical inspiration behind the Anderson-Nairn thesis. Anderson recalls the debt his particular contribution to the theses owed to Lukács and Sartre in his 'Foreword' to Anderson 1992b, pp. 3–4.

resolve, the Nairn-Anderson theses induced open confrontation with (early) New Left thought.

The general contours of the Nairn-Anderson theses have been repeated numerous times.[31] What has been less often rehearsed is the impulsion driving their composition in relation to the early New Left's assimilation of aspects of the national tradition. Anderson's contribution to *New Left Review*'s jacquiere against Englishness was framed and characterised by a series of national laments – 'we' lack a 'structural study of our society';[32] England had an 'impure' bourgeois revolution, was minus a genuine capitalist ruling stratum and suffered a 'pre-mature' and corporate working class;[33] while English universities had spawned no 'coherent and militant student movement' – a series of temporal and cultural abnormalities (as compared variously with France and Italy) which, according to Anderson, helped actuate the nation's present crisis.[34] The historical and contemporary deficiencies were overdetermined, and the present malaise rendered incomprehensible, by England's peculiar national culture and the willed absence of an English intelligentsia on the European model.[35] England's ideological inheritance – and Anderson understood that inheritance in Arnoldian (and Western Marxist) terms as the best that had been thought and written – was distinguished by traditionalism and empiricism: 'traditionalism sanctions the present by deriving it from the past, empiricism shackles the future by riveting it to the present'.[36] Telescoping the acerbic loathing which he felt toward England's intellectual culture, Anderson concluded that 'A comprehensive, coagulated conservatism is the result, covering the whole of society with a thick pall of simultaneous philistinism (towards ideas) and mystagogy (toward institutions), for which England has justly won an international reputation'.[37]

It was no doubt easy, especially for a socialist and a cosmopolitan, to make this face in England in the early 1960s. Anderson had no doubt learnt some of the anti-nationalist gestures in the mirror of the early New Left, in *New Reasoner*'s frustrations with the chauvinism, parochialism and racism of the dominant culture, even at times the parochialism of the English working class, and in *Universities and Left Review*'s discontent with socialist revisionism, advertising and the ideologies of classlessness. But Anderson's anti-nationalist animus was meant not just as a reproof to the hegemonic national culture. It was also intended as a

---

31. See Nield 1980, pp. 479–507; Johnson 1980, pp. 48–70, for elucidation of those general contours.
32. Anderson 1965b, p. 12.
33. Anderson 1965b, pp. 13, 17–21.
34. Anderson 1968, p. 3.
35. The conception of 'the intellectual' to be found in the Anderson-Nairn theses has been examined in Collini 2006, pp. 175–83.
36. Anderson 1965b, p. 32.
37. Anderson 1968, p. 5.

rebuke to British socialism in general, and the New Left in particular. The British Left, Anderson believed, had consistently recapitulated the conservative dimensions of England's ideological inheritance constituting a 'deluded accomplice' in the national culture's homage to traditionalism and empiricism.[38] Indeed Britain's Left, he judged, 'has never truly questioned [the] national inheritance which is one of the enduring bonds of its subordination'.[39] There was no radical past, certainly no socialist past, worth recovering in Britain, according to him, and to actively rescue what was there was to surrender before a heritage toughened against social transformation. It was the absence of socialism – as a hegemonic force with a total vision of society – that marked out Britain from other advanced European capitalist countries, something typically burked by English socialists.[40] 'Marxism', Anderson suggested in a terse summation of the labour-movement's ideological defects, 'had missed it'.[41] This was not just a consequence of early industrialisation or the historical timidity of Albion's bourgeoisie. 'In England, everything was against [Marxism]: the wounds of the past, the diffidence of the present, the national culture of past and present'.[42] The effect of this failed rendezvous was immanent in the 'immovable' corporatism of the contemporary working class and socialism's procumbence before England's intellectual heritage.[43]

In short, the weight of England's ideological past sat like a nightmare on the mind of English socialists. Here lay the immediate political purpose of the Nairn-Anderson theses: the historical illumination of the absence of an authentic English socialist culture. This absence was present even in those centres where it might have been expected to emerge, above all within the New Left. The New Left, according to Anderson, lacked a totalising perspective,[44] which Marxism alone could have provided, and was thus rendered 'populist' and 'pre-socialist', prone to speak in the vacuous sociology of 'the people' and 'the monopolies' rather than in the rigorous language of labour and capital.[45] 'Theoretical and intellectual work', Anderson suggested, 'were sacrificed for a mobilizing role

---

38. Ibid.
39. Anderson 1968, p. 4.
40. Anderson 1965b, p. 25.
41. Ibid.
42. Anderson 1965b, pp. 25–6. This view was hardly new among British Marxists. In the 1920s, as Stuart Macintyre has argued, British Marxists 'lamented 'the backward state of British socialism' which they believed 'corresponded to the backwardness and insularity of the national culture, and could only be overcome by challenging the whole of that culture'. See Macintyre 1980, pp. 233–4. Thus, without acknowledging the fact, Anderson was continuing a venerable tradition of 'cultural cringe' within British Marxism.
43. Anderson 1965b, p. 6.
44. Anderson 1965a, p. 17.
45. Anderson 1965c, p. 259.

which perpetually escaped it [the New Left]'.[46] Assimilation to the national culture was one half product of the New Left's immersion in the English radical past, the other half consequence of England's failure to produce 'an autonomous, antagonistic intelligentsia'.[47] Such was the origin of the New Left's tendency to 'give pious reverence to our forebears',[48] rather than open up British socialism to outside intellectual influence. Indifferent to theory, like the national culture in general, the New Left failed to provide the labour-movement with either a 'rudimentary diagram' of British social relations or the horizon of an 'ideal society'.[49] According to Anderson, 'the basis of [Left] politics was a *moral* critique of society, dissociated from the complex historical process in which values can alone ultimately find incarnation'.[50] Like British socialism at large, the New Left, Anderson concluded, was a pallid reflection of an already waxen national culture.

There was something about the tone of the Nairn-Anderson theses that was also meant as a reproof to actually existing British socialism. Anderson revealed an intention in the way he wrote. His essays were deliberately shorn of warmth and local reference. His sentences, complete with archaic words unsympathetic to the acoustics of the 'common reader', deliberately grate against what E.P. Thompson called the English idiom. It was not just the nature of the authority appealed to – say, to Althusser and the Sartre of *Critique of Dialectical Reason* rather than to Morris or Blake's 'Milton' – or the repeatedly conveyed sense that the English past was worthless from the perspective of the renovation of socialist theory. Rather, it was the degree of affected alienation established by the assumption of a deliberate viewpoint outside the subject under judgment. English thought was dismissed with summary commination, as though by a stranger to its shore. The social thought of the Webb's was reduced to 'bovine admiration for bureaucracy' and 'bottomless philistinism'.[51] English Marxists in the 1930s had been gripped by a 'collective fever', and produced 'no serious intellectual dimension' only 'bad art and false science'.[52]

Anderson dispatched whole political and ideological movements in this tone. Puritanism was a 'useless passion', liberalism lacked 'courage', chartist struggle was a 'pure loss', Fabianism inherited the 'poisoned legacy' of utilitarianism.[53] Even contemporary socialist protest was discarded in this manner. The peace-movement 'lacked a theory of the cold war'; the New Left 'lacked a systematic

---

46. Anderson 1965a, p. 17.
47. Anderson 1965c, p. 269.
48. Anderson 1966, p. 33.
49. Anderson 1965b, p. 39.
50. Anderson 1965c, p. 221.
51. Anderson 1965b, p. 37.
52. Anderson 1968, p. 11.
53. Anderson 1965b, pp. 17, 33, 35.

sociology of British capitalism'.[54] These judgments were made with an acerbic axe, sharpened on a rationalist stone, which could only have been a product of a deeply felt depatriation. 'The incursion of rationalism into the hermetic world of the English working class is a necessary stage in its emancipation', Anderson characteristically explained. 'It is the foundation of a genuinely ideological collectivism – founded on ideas, and not merely on instinct'.[55] Rationalism versus hermeticism, ideology versus instinct – these were the founding antagonisms of Anderson's repudiation of New Left socialism.

The major response to the Nairn-Anderson theses came from E.P. Thompson in a long essay published in *Socialist Register* in 1965. It was the purpose of Thompson's response to remind the New Left of 'certain strengths and humane traditions in British life',[56] including the past and present of working-class culture and politics, and the respect for experience, and corresponding suspicion toward universals, found in the 'English intellectual tradition'.[57] Thompson's point was not that the tradition of dissent or the thought of Darwin and Bacon were worth something in themselves, although he certainly believed this to be the case. It was that he believed a successful restoration of socialism would only take place in the 'intellectual idiom' provided by the national culture. 'England', Thompson reminded his New Left interlocutors, 'was unlikely to capitulate before a Marxism which cannot at least engage in a dialogue in the English idiom'.[58] Socialism, according to him, must be felt and thought with rather than against national habits of thinking. 'There is a stridency in the way our authors [Anderson and Nairn] hammer at class and tidy up cultural phenomena into class categories', Thompson noted, 'as well as a ruthlessness in their dismissal of the English experience'.[59] 'The Peculiarities of the English' contained more than a hint of what Anderson later called 'gestures of Englishry',[60] mobilised for calculated ironic effect rather then earnestly endorsed. But there was something more than mischief about Thompson's Englishness.

Indeed, the chief political intention of 'The Peculiarities of the English' was to argue that there was initiatives of resilience within the national culture that could speak back to what Thompson conceded was a culture predominantly hostile to socialism. From this perspective, he vindicated the empirical mode. He recalled the radical resonance of English dissent. He emphasised the protestant, less religious than oppositional, character of English cultural traditions. He defended

---

54. Anderson 1965a, p. 12.
55. Anderson 1965c, p. 265.
56. E.P. Thompson 1978, p. 266.
57. E.P. Thompson 1978, pp. 266–7, 271.
58. E.P. Thompson 1978, p. 274.
59. E.P. Thompson 1978, p. 297.
60. Anderson 2005, p. 185.

the obdurate reformism of the working-class movement, seeing in its character-istic tenacity less cause for regret than a historical basis for a growing socialism. And he illuminated and revalued the valences of Marxism's English past, from Morris through working-class education to the CPGB. 'If our authors will leave their Parisian journals for a moment', Thompson characteristically retaliated, 'and encounter the actual personnel of the labour movement they will find very many of them to be a good deal more sophisticated than the conservative *semplici* of their imagination'.[61] *New Left Review's* current active disengagement from the real movement of things, its self-conscious hibernation in the long night of theory, was a constant refrain of Thompson's sometimes-homiletic rhetoric. 'A politics which ignores immediate solidarities will become peculiarly theoretic, ruthless, and self-defeating'.[62] And, as the commination 'ruthless' was meant to portend, this 'politics', 'heard in *that* tone',[63] had uncomfortable memories for those socialists who had fought on the side of humanism in 1956.

The central obfuscation of Thompson's response was in a sense obvious, at least in retrospect. He confused Anderson's *New Left Review*, in fact and tone, with the Marxism of the CPGB. No matter his fears, and even allowing for the liberal rules of polemic, Anderson and Nairn were not Gollan and Matthews, and Thompson was wrong to impute the association. Anderson waited until after Thompson's death to give his final accounting of the debate in a respectful, often illumi-nating, eulogy. As in *Arguments within English Marxism*, if with less abrasion, Anderson was unrepentant about the tone and purpose of the Nairn-Anderson theses. Alluding to Thompson's evasion of Edward Gibbon in his Blake-study *Witness against the Beast*, and what Anderson believed was the book's sometimes too-sympathetic appraisal of Blake's mysticism and political quietism, Anderson remarked that 'The intellectual emancipation wrought by [Gibbon's] *The Decline and Fall* lay in what might well be described as its "enormous condescension" – what else is the inimitable tone of those six famous volumes? – to the Christian, even Classical past'.[64] Anderson understood *New Left Review* as undertaking a similar operation in relation to the English (radical) past, an operation designed to raze the national culture, perhaps over-enthusiastic, perhaps bending too far the other way, but nonetheless necessary. The task of the 'second' New Left as Anderson conceived it was to bring the Enlightenment to English socialist thought, no matter the cost, and to emancipate the New Left of its association with the particularisms of England's past. There was something to be said for this as decolonisation and the rapacious border-crossing of capitalist globalisation

---

61. E.P. Thompson 1978, p. 286.
62. E.P. Thompson 1978, p. 278.
63. E.P. Thompson 1978, p. 297.
64. Anderson 2005, p. 184.

transformed the frames of internationalism. Where Anderson arguably erred was in imagining, given the intellectual and political cosmopolitanism of Locke or Paine, that the 'second' New Left was cultivating virgin land.[65]

In fact, from one angle, Anderson's contributions to *New Left Review*'s anti-English revolt were more hesitant than Thompson supposed and Anderson later represented. 'Origins of the Present Crisis', opened with the suggestion that *Culture and Society* and *The Long Revolution* undoubtedly represent the major contribution to socialist thought in England since the War,[66] although Anderson criticised both, as Thompson had done, for their lack of historical perspective. Anderson also drew on the argument of Hoggart's *Uses of Literacy*, and used the work of Cole, Tawney and even Crossman as a prop for his argument about the working class's corporatism and labourism's subordination to the 'host culture'.[67] He even paid due respect to the economics of Keynes. Feasibly, his handling of Gramsci, Sartre and Lukács was continuing a venerable internationalist tradition emblematic of *New Reasoner*, although Anderson himself was unlikely to represent it this way. If Marx's thought, as Thompson supposed, had been domesticated to English structures of feeling through the work of Morris, the national labour colleges and the CPGB, his ideas had once been considered 'foreign', as 'foreign' as Thompson now considered 'existentialism' or the *Prison Notebooks*. Thompson was on better ground when he claimed that the 'national culture' had received neural pathways from the continent for hundreds of years, than when he was castigating Anderson for a politically damaging association with the abstractions of French thought. In other places – for example when expounding the universal values of socialist humanism – Thompson saw no issue with ethical or political abstractions such as justice and liberty, or spied damaging 'French' tendencies in 'universal socialist values'.

If these seem slight arguments against the charge of 'national nihilism',[68] there was still 'Problems of Socialist Strategy', Anderson's recommended passageway to socialism. Having established that cultural supremacy was axiomatic to social transformation, Anderson argued that 'socialist culture must be the heir of all the most advanced and critical traditions of the nation'.[69] The deep, corporate class-consciousness of working-class reformism, the 'long and important legacy

---

65. Whether under the sign of Thompson's response or for other political reasons, the Anderson-Nairn theses have often been unwarrantably dismissed. This dismissal is wrong-headed. More accurate is Colin Leys's suggestion that they 'set the agenda for much of the whole contemporary debate about the nature and causes of the British crisis'. See Leys 1989, p. 14, a judgment that does not preclude sharp critique – like Thompson's – or imply agreement.
66. Anderson 1965a, p. 11.
67. Anderson 1965b, pp. 39–41.
68. See Anderson 1992, p. 5, a direct judgment of Deutscher.
69. Anderson 1965c, p. 243.

of classical English liberalism', and 'the complex lineage of moral and aesthetic criticism, which descends from the Romantics to Arnold and Morris, and Lawrence and Leavis in the twentieth century' – a socialist party whose objective was hegemony, Anderson claimed, would have to liberate and build from all these aspects of the national cultural tradition.[70] 'Any socialist ideology in Britain', Anderson concluded, 'which does not incorporate these traditions as constituent elements will necessarily fail; it will remain abstract and external, unable to affect popular sensibility or imagination'.[71] Anderson's conclusion sounded a lot like the counsel of 'radical England', less Gibbon than Blake, Paine than Cobbett, familiar reflections to *New Reasoner* or the early *New Left Review*.

Thus, in effect, Anderson's work in that transition period between 1962 and 1968, replicated the vacillations common to the New Left's encounter with the national culture. The hesitations were multiple. Anderson argued that nationalism was an instance of false consciousness that 'deflected [the proletariat] *from* undistracted confrontation with the class exploiting it',[72] *and* that socialists must annex aspects of national identity if socialism was to achieve cultural hegemony. Anderson bemoaned the 'lack' of a genuine Marxist culture in Britain, calling for the endogenous growth of a 'national Marxism',[73] *and* countered Thompson and the first New Left with the view that socialism must be the antithesis of the national culture. Anderson claimed that English working-class consciousness was overdetermined by the ruling class's chauvinism and spoiled by imperial privilege, *and* that the working class existed in its own world, separated off from English society by an immovable, corporate class-consciousness. And the 'national economics' that underpinned the analysis and tacit modernising instruction of 'Origins of the Present Crisis', sat alongside the view, common to the early New Left, that 'the gigantic international corporation is increasingly emerging as [capitalism's] basic unit'.[74] Like the early New Left, the Nairn-Anderson theses offered directed national production and nationalisation of national resources as the solution to capitalism's inherent limitation, while at the same time characterising socialism as 'the promulgation of human freedom across the entire existential space of the world'.[75] Anderson also replicated some of the evasions associated with the early New Left's encounter with national identity, neither registering awareness of the British state's own national dilemmas (particularly

---

70. Ibid.
71. Ibid.
72. Anderson 1965b, p. 24 (original emphasis).
73. Anderson 1968, p. 11.
74. Anderson 1965b, p. 49.
75. Anderson 1965c, p. 289.

odd for someone who had grown up in Ireland?), nor clearly elucidating relations between imperialism, nationalism and national identity.

IV

Categorical dismissal of the English ideology was one element of Anderson's professed internationalism in the 1960s. A further aspect of that internationalist desire was *New Left Review*'s self-conscious association with national liberation movements in Asia, Africa and Latin America.[76] Here, unlike in the English past or present, 'the masses', Anderson believed, had met with Marxism. Anderson's metropolitan anticipation of the 'Third World's' regeneration of socialism began with the Cuban Revolution – to which all sections of the New Left, including Thompson, had looked with hope – welcomed by *New Left Review* as an event of 'universal significance' and judged 'the decisive phenomena of our time'.[77] Socialism might constitute an absent agenda in the birthplace of the industrial revolution, Anderson supposed, reduced to the technics of welfare-reform, abbreviated national plans and Keynesian fiddling with national debt levels and interest rates. But on the periphery of capitalism's world-system, socialism's emancipatory potential appeared undiminished, regenerated in the Sierra Maestra and Vietnam's paddy fields. Cuba, Algeria, Angola and Vietnam – national-liberation movements in these centres had picked-up socialism's banner laid down by a European working class seemingly satisfied with improved access to consumer goods, promising at once to overthrow imperialism and 'liberate the dialectic in the oppressor'.[78]

Under the impetus of the real movement of things in Asia, Africa and, especially, Latin America, from 1967 Anderson increasingly turned away from the Fabian-inspired 'left social democracy' that he later claimed informed 'Problems of Socialist Strategy',[79] and recalibrated the New Left as a movement for revolutionary socialism guided by 'Marxism-Leninism'. The new note was sounded in 'The Marxism of Régis Debray', Anderson's co-authored introduction to *New Left Review*'s presentation of the French Marxist's writings on revolutionary strategy

76. See Anderson 1980, pp. 151–3.
77. Blackburn 1963, p. 52. Anderson has maintained a long-standing association with Cuba. See Anderson 2004b, pp. 48–9, for the latest manifestation of this interest.
78. See Therborn 1968, p. 11. Reflecting on this mood among Western socialists, Victor Kiernan likened it to 'a new stirring of the old European dream of the noble savage: humanity uncorrupted by the fleshpots of Egypt was to arise from the Andes or the Mountains of the Moon (even, it appeared at times, from Harlem) to accomplish what a degenerate Western working class no longer cared to attempt'. Kiernan 1970, p. 9.
79. See Anderson 1976–7, p. 27, n. 48 for this terse auto-critique.

in Latin America.[80] This shift was far from abrupt, and had been prepared since the early 1960s. Support for or sympathy with Third World national-liberation movements, particularly those influenced by revolutionary socialism, had been a proclaimed purpose of *New Left Review* since 1963. In an editorial manifesto – 'On Internationalism' – of that year, Anderson had argued that the British Left was 'parochial' and 'for too long simply affirmed its internationalism, while showing little knowledge or understanding of the world [particularly the Third World] which is now affecting its destiny'.[81] (This, of course, was a willed misreading of *New Reasoner* and *Universities and Left Review*). Anderson called for the 'internationalization of British socialist thought' and mapped out a passage for *New Left Review* defined by closer attention to events and movements in the Third World.[82] This began with Keith Buchanan's essay 'The Third World – Its Emergence and Contours' (which was published in the edition the manifesto headed).[83] Inspired by Fanon's *The Wretched of the Earth*, and endorsing Sartre's 'Preface' to the book, Buchanan condemned the British Left's 'euro-centrism' and 'narcissism', celebrated 'peasant-based socialisms' in Cuba and China and argued, for good measure, that the Western proletariat had 'contributed more to the deterioration of the position of the underdeveloped countries than has the profit motive of industrial or commercial leaders'.[84] Buchanan's riposte to the British Left was preceded by Anderson's study of the demise of Portuguese imperialism in Angola, and the rise of an Angolan national-liberation movement.[85] Between 1965 and 1967, *New Left Review* published articles by Lucien Rey (Peter Wollen) on Zanzibar, Indonesia and Iran, by Roger Murray on Algeria and Ghana, and other articles on Brazil, Ethiopia, and the Dominican Republic, while carrying Debray's 'Latin America – The Long March' and Che Guevara's call-to-arms 'Vietnam must not Stand Alone'.[86] This honourable openness to national liberation in the Third World, and critique of the exigencies of imperialism in Asia, Africa and Latin America, led up to Anderson's (and Robin Blackburn's) approbation for the 'Marxist-Leninist' writings of Régis Debray with their 'focus on *making the revolution*, as a political, technical and military problem'.[87] Later that year,

---

80. *New Left Review* 1967, pp. 8–11. Anderson travelled to Bolivia as part of an international delegation to secure the release of Debray from prison. See Ali 1988, pp. 209–10, for an account of this 'departure-lounge internationalism'.

81. *New Left Review* 1963, pp. 3–4.

82. *New Left Review* 1963, p. 4.

83. Buchanan 1963, pp. 5–23.

84. Buchanan 1963, p. 22.

85. Anderson 1962a, pp. 83–102; Anderson 1962b, pp. 88–123; Anderson 1962c, pp. 85–114.

86. Debray 1965, pp. 17–58; Guevara 1967, pp. 79–91.

87. *New Left Review* 1967, p. 8.

following the Argentinean revolutionary's death in the Congo, *New Left Review* held up Che Guevara as an 'unparalleled example of internationalism'.[88]

Anderson's 'Marxist-Leninism', and his support for revolutionary nationalist movements in the Third World, constituted a paradigmatic rupture in the political discourse of the New Left. Anderson published little between 1968 and 1974, making exact elucidation of his politics during this period difficult to establish.[89] That he had embraced 'revolutionary socialism' by 1967 is clear. Others have spoken of flirtations with Maoism in 1968 to 1969,[90] before a shift to Trotskyism (informed by Isaac Deutscher and Ernest Mandel) in the early 1970s under the impact of international worker and student radicalism.[91] Undoubtedly, Anderson trumpeted the cause of student radicalism through the aborted Revolutionary Socialist Students Federation (RSSF), and the cause of Vietnamese communism through the Vietnam Solidarity Committee (VSC), with its call for socialist triumph in Southeast Asia. Anderson welcomed the events in France in May 1968, drawing consequences from them for a restoration of revolutionary socialism in Britain.[92] With a now well-practiced emphasis on the importance of revolutionary culture and socialist theory to social transformation, Anderson argued that the 'May events highlighted the potential of small revolutionary groups in helping to unleash a class storm that shook society to its foundations'.[93] Recalling the

---

88. *New Left Review* 1967, p. 16. This eulogy included the somewhat astounding remark, from the perspective of Anderson's critique of the original New Left, that Guevara 'was never more materialist than in his insistence on the primacy of moral incentives in the building of socialism'.

89. There are two unpublished texts from this period – 'The Founding Moment' (1969) and 'State and Revolution in the West' (1970). The former dealt with communist movements in Europe; the latter was an assessment of Antonio Gramsci. A summation of the former – partly used by Anderson in Anderson 1981, pp. 145–56 – is offered in Elliott 1998, pp. 72–7. Elliott was denied access to the second text, although speculates that it formed the basis for Anderson's published essay, 'The Antinomies of Antonio Gramsci'.

90. See Elliott 1998, pp. 56–61 for Anderson's association with Maoism. Elliott's view rests on both unpublished ('A Decennial Report [of *New Left Review*]', unpublished document, [1975], pp. 30–2) and published sources, which includes *New Left Review*'s publication of Mao 1969, pp. 83–96. On published sources, consider also *New Left Review* 1969, pp. 74–89 which includes favourable comment on Mao's revolutionary strategy. This article appeared without attribution, though Elliott in Elliott 1998, n. 54 on p. 260 attributes authorship to Anderson based on the 'Decennial Report'. The 'Decennial Report', p. 44 also makes mention of Anderson's dissension from the 'red bases' strategy. Note of this is made in Elliott 1998, n. 15 on p. 256. Maoist tendencies within the review are also noted by Blackburn 1992, p. vii. They were abandoned by 1971. For criticism of China within *New Left Review*, see *New Left Review* 1971, p. 1.

91. See Elliott 1998, pp. 61–71 and Blackledge 2002, pp. 47–51 and 56–60. See D.Thompson 2004, pp. 43–72, for the politics of *New Left Review* more generally.

92. *New Left Review* published the manifesto of RSSF, and a collection of essays on the student movement – RSSF 1969, pp. 21–2 and Cockburn and Blackburn (eds.) 1969. For a discussion of both RSSF and VSC, see Ali 1998, pp. 233–56.

93. *New Left Review* 1968, p. 7.

Bolshevik spirit of October 1917, a familiar Andersonian refrain over the following decade or so, VSC and RSSF, Anderson argued, joined the revolutionary struggle against imperialism in the periphery with the metropolitan struggle against capitalist imperialism. In *Arguments within English Marxism*, he singled out Swedish Marxist Göran Therborn's 'From Petrograd to Saigon' as an authentic representation of 'second' New Left politics in these years,[94] an analysis which banished the 'left liberalism' of the first New Left to the gnawing criticism of revolutionary guerrillas, and counted the 'movements of liberation in Asia, Africa, and Latin America' as 'an immediate ideological inspiration'.[95]

New Left Review's intention to internationalise British socialism was sounded not just by attention to the harmonics of high (mostly Marxist) theory (Glucksmann, Althusser, Lacan, and Colletti),[96] but also by the strains of a new rhetorical tone attuned to Third World revolutionary struggle. This tone deliberately mimicked the voluntarism of guerrilla-struggle and the propaganda-idiom of Latin American revolutionary machismo, a characteristic new signature song captured in articles by *New Left Review*'s editors. '[T]he revolutionary party', according to Anderson, 'strives to increase the magnitude of the revolutionary forces and to exacerbate the contradictions and vacillations of the enemy';[97] capitalist power, according to James Wilcox (aka Robin Blackburn), 'must be smashed and broken up by the hard blows of popular force'.[98] This was a rhetoric unsuited to Anderson's long-distance internationalism (something of the strain is registered in the gap between 'vacillations' and 'the enemy' in the quotation above), but, nonetheless, marked an authentic engagement with the political issues of the day. There was no need for revolutionary socialists to look to the English past, this rhetoric supposed, when they could look to the Latin American (or Chinese) present to find an example of revolutionary socialism at work. It would be easy, in retrospect, to mock these associations given that Cultural Revolution in China would descend into brutal chaos, and that other peasant socialisms would debouch through Pol Pot's killing fields. Such mockery, however, would involve a willed forgetting of much else about those years, including the struggles against racism in the United States and South Africa, American napalm-bombing in Vietnam and state-terrorism in Latin America. Which is not to say that Anderson's support for what has been termed 'nationalisms under the Red Star' is beyond criticism.[99] Apart from a failure to ever revisit the cost of this politics, particularly to socialism, and *New Left Review*'s seeming lack of political

94. Anderson 1980, p. 152.
95. Therborn 1968, p. 6.
96. One product of *NLR*'s attention to Western Marxism was *NLR* 1977.
97. *New Left Review* 1968, p. 3.
98. Wilcox (Robin Blackburn) 1969, p. 24.
99. Ascherson 2009, p. 15.

responsibility to any social movement revealed in the supermarket-quality of its socialist allegiance – Castro then Guevara then Mao then Trotsky – Anderson's internationalisation of British socialism was characterised by calculated detachment from other sorts of politics in Britain. Indeed, detachment can be signalled by activist rhetoric misplaced just as easily by the abstractions of theory.

This had been E.P. Thompson's concern as early as 1963. Responding to *New Left Review*'s manifesto 'On Internationalism', and Keith Buchanan's article which was attached to it, Thompson wrote that 'I hope we are not to exchange the Workers' State for the Third World'.[100] Internationalism, he reminded *New Left Review*'s editors, involved a dialogue, a relationship between fraternal socialist voices, and not 'intellectual abasement' before 'the example of other peoples'.[101] Transfixed by the Third World, Thompson worried, the New Left would deteriorate into 'pharisaical self-isolation'.[102] He was particularly concerned with *New Left Review*'s uncritical assimilation of Fanon's *The Wretched of the Earth*. 'It is one thing', Thompson wrote, 'to respond with deep sympathy to the writings of Fanon, Toure, Senghor or Che Guevara. More: we have a clear duty to publish these views, and to measure our preoccupations against their force. It is another thing to ape these views, or to propagate them uncritically because they are moving and authentic in their own context'.[103] Theory's unmediated travel from the Third World to the metropolis was not Thompson's only apprehension. Nationalist consciousness might well lead to socialism, Thompson reasoned, but it was just as likely 'to distract attention from intractable problems',[104] devolving into ideology. 'We have at the same time', Thompson concluded, 'to see (and interpret) the great liberating impulses of the Soviet and Chinese revolutions, and of the emergent nationalisms of Asia and Africa; and to adopt a critical and at times uncompromising stand as to certain socialist principles and humanist values'.[105] This was a dialectic he had seen at work in the original New Left, critical of Stalinism, but maintaining links with a libertarian communism, that spoke across national borders, neither giving way before the claims of socialism's universalism nor reducing socialism to a set of local concerns.

Thompson detected a '*deracinee*' impulse behind the 'second' New Left's credulous orientation to the Third World, 'analogous', he supposed, 'to the ouvrierism current in some left intellectual circles in the Thirties'.[106] According to Thompson,

---

100. E.P. Thompson, 'Where Are We Now?', Unpublished Memo, 1962, DJS/109, University of Hull Archives.
101. Ibid.
102. Ibid.
103. Ibid.
104. Ibid.
105. Ibid.
106. Ibid. (original emphasis).

'it seems the fashion now will be to attach ourselves to peasant-revolutionary movements: adopt their dismissal of "the west": tolerate a mystique of violence, virility and simplicity, in which men can only find their humanity with a rifle in their hands aimed at a white face'.[107] The other side of *New Left Review*'s deracinate coin, according to Thompson, was 'a lack of real knowledge and concern with British problems, a lack of any real sense of the possibilities and growing points within the British scene'.[108] The ground of internationalism, Thompson claimed, had been evacuated from both sides.

The only (published) record we have of Anderson's response to these criticisms is 'Socialism and Pseudo-Empiricism', an article, largely given over to a defence of the Nairn-Anderson theses, which left Thompson's objection to indiscriminate 'Third Worldism' untouched. However, in this article Anderson did claim that Thompson's general opposition to *New Left Review*, and his 'invincible provincialism',[109] initiated 'against any real internationalism, which can only be founded on a close, familiar, unjealous knowledge of the culture and politics of other nations other than one's own' – a conception of internationalism central to Anderson's oeuvre, but one that Thompson would not have questioned.[110] To be fair, whether under the impetus of Thompson's obloquy (or, indeed, that of Ralph Miliband and John Saville) or not,[111] *New Left Review* published a response by Michael Barratt Brown to Buchanan's article, which protested and repudiated many of Buchanan's arguments, but not *New Left Review*'s concern with the Third World.[112] If not in a manner congruent with Thompson's own inclinations, *New Left Review* would pay attention to 'the British scene', whether in the Nairn-Anderson theses or through its coverage of British working-class politics between the ascension of Harold Wilson and the May events in Paris. Anderson and the 'second' New Left made connections with the British labour-movement where they could too, particularly with prominent left-wing figures in trade-unions, which led to the publication of *The Incompatibles*, with VSC and the student-movement and with smaller socialist groupings. Solidarity with anti-imperialist movements, whether in Cuba or Vietnam, was arguably consistent with what *New Reasoner* called the duties of socialist internationalism. Indeed, the *May Day Manifesto* movement, which Anderson and *New Left Review* studiously avoided, itself noted the socialist juncture between the defeat of American

---

107. Ibid.
108. Ibid.
109. Anderson 1966, p. 12.
110. Anderson 1966, p. 36.
111. Ralph Miliband wrote to Anderson expressing his discontent with Buchanan's article. The letter is quoted in Kozak 1995.
112. Barratt Brown 1963, pp. 32–6. Buchanan responded in Buchanan 1963, pp. 21–9.

imperialism in Vietnam and working-class advance in Britain.[113] Nor was there anything contrary to the duties of socialist internationalism in *New Left Review*'s publication of the work of Althusser, Lukács, Della Volpe and Colletti. This aspect of Anderson's 'internationalisation' of British intellectual culture was undoubtedly salutary, as Raymond Williams would later appreciate.[114] Where Thompson was more acute was in his view that such internationalist duties could become alternately romantic and abstract if they were not self-consciously embedded in argument and dialogue from *somewhere*.

Thompson had also implicitly objected that the anti-imperialism commensurate with Anderson's internationalism involved a regression from socialist humanism's ideal of the unity of humankind.[115] Along with the loss of this animating purpose went the postulate, equally central to one register of New Left thought, that it is classes rather than nations or peoples that constitute the basic units of history. This had certainly been the effect of Keith Buchanan's intervention, according to Thompson and Barratt Brown. Castigating Thompson for his subordination to 'populism' in 'Socialism and Pseudo-Empiricism', Anderson had argued that 'Where "the people" rather than concrete determinant social groups are continually invoked as the victims of injustice and the agents of social change, it becomes natural to speak of "the people" as a nation with a pre-eminent destiny among other peoples'.[116] This was Anderson's critique of Thompson's sometime militant 'Englishness'. However, it is arguable that *New Left Review*'s embrace of what were called 'national Marxisms' – Cuba, Vietnam, China – had the same effect.[117] As George Lichtheim explained, 'nationalism is identified with socialism, the peasantry with the proletariat, anti-imperialism with anti-capitalism, until all the distinctions painfully elaborated in Marxist literature for a century are cast overboard in favour of a simple dichotomy: Western imperialism versus the starving masses of the Third World'.[118]

If it is unclear to what degree this criticism might be applied to Anderson's politics in the late 1960s, it can certainly be applied to some strains in the 'second' New Left and *New Left Review*. What is clear is the homology between Thompson's and Anderson's encounter with the national question. Both supposed that there were 'good' and 'bad' nationalisms, that nationalism could be both an ideology prone to deflect awareness of fundamental social conflict *and* that nationalism could act as socialism's ally in projects of social transformation. Thus when Eden

---

113. Williams (ed.) 1968, p. 140.
114. Williams 1979, pp. 349–50.
115. E.P. Thompson, 'Where Are We Now?', Unpublished Memo, 1962, DJS/109, University of Hull Archives.
116. Anderson 1966, p. 36.
117. Buchanan 1963, p. 18.
118. Lichtheim 1974, p. 139.

or Johnson mobilised the nation in the service of imperialism, nationalism was repudiated. But when marshalled against empire by insurrectionary Budapest or Havana, national impulses were endorsed. Mostly such endorsement was not without condition, limit and ambiguity – Thompson's by the universal socialist values inherent in socialist humanism, Anderson's by a corresponding sense of socialism's 'cosmopolitan' commitment to universal emancipation. However, like Marx and Engels, neither was immune from the seductions of an instrumental nationalism. This instrumental nationalism, arguably, was far less useful when Mao's China opposed Khrushchev's Russia, when open conflict erupted between socialist Vietnam and ostensibly socialist Cambodia, or when 'the people' were mobilised by Enoch Powell rather than by socialist dissent.

V

During the 1970s, in complementary endeavours, – a history of the genesis of the capitalist state and an elaboration of Marxist thought through an account of Western Marxism's and English Marxism's history – Anderson married a perspective on world history with a conception of socialist practice – endeavours designed to illuminate socialism's failure to account, much less successfully oppose, the modern capitalist state. Building on the 'East-West' dichotomy elucidated in 'Problems of Socialist Strategy', *Passages from Antiquity to Feudalism* and *Lineages of the Absolutist State* explored the mystery of why a fully developed system of private property and market-directed commodity-production first emerged in Western Europe.[119] Thus, Anderson's history-project hunted the historical preconditions of the asymmetric trajectories tracked by eastern and western Europe in the wake of antiquity's dissolution, a seemingly intransigent riddle for both modern historiography and contemporary history, to say nothing of modern socialist theory. Anderson found answers to both problems in the divergent nature of the transition to feudalism in each half of Europe, divergences which produced contrasting forms of absolutism east and west of the Elbe.[120] Essentially, 'what rendered the unique passage to capitalism in Europe (in contrast to Asia)', Anderson claimed, 'was the *concatenation of antiquity and feudalism*'.[121] But the Romano-Germanic synthesis characteristic of Western Europe was attenuated in eastern Europe. Here neither an urban bourgeoisie emerged to mediate class-struggle between landed nobles and landless peasants, nor did the preconditions of commodity-production or civil society develop within the interstices

---

119. For responses to Anderson's history-project, consult Heller 1977, pp. 202–10; Fulbrook and Skocpol 1984, pp. 170–210; Hirst 1985, pp. 91–125.
120. Anderson 1974a, p. 213.
121. Anderson 1974b, p. 420 (original emphasis).

of Eastern Europe's medieval social formations.[122] Consequently, it was only in Europe's Western half that a mature capitalism developed endogenously.

Described later in *English Questions* as a detour through the prehistory of European bourgeois revolutions,[123] Anderson's history-project did not just seek to explain the genesis of an international mode of production. It also sought to explicate the state structures that facilitated or obstructed its emergence, in the process providing some illumination for why socialism emerged first in relatively backward Russia, rather than relatively advanced England or France. Anderson found this instrument of capitalist mediation in the absolutist state, the 'transitional' form between pre-capitalist social formations defined by the organic unity of polity and economy, and the modern capitalist state characterised by the formal separation of economics and politics.

The genesis of the European absolutist state in the sixteenth century, according to Anderson, marked the final political outcome of the long crisis of economy and society that Europe suffered in the fourteenth and fifteenth centuries. It was to the emergence of this political power that Anderson devoted the longer volume of his two-volume genealogy. Tracking the class-determinations of political forms in Europe prior to the October revolution, *Lineages of the Absolutist State* provided a typology of absolutism that separated it off from the modern mode of capitalist power – the nation-state, typical political dome of industrial capitalism. Well before Gellner's seminal contribution to the historical sociology of the transition from agriculture to industry,[124] and pre-empting ground covered in Nairn's account of nationalism's constitutive role in the production of modernity,[125] Anderson provided an account of transformations within and between modes of production, one that rejected traditional conceptions of historical temporality, and that built on, and argued against, traditions of Marxist thinking in Britain after 1945.[126]

The absolutist state, Anderson argued, could be distinguished by a number of institutional features whose coexistence sealed it off from medieval social formations – 'standing armies, a permanent bureaucracy, national taxation, a codified law, and the beginnings of a unified market'.[127] This typology of the absolutist state might be mistaken for an ideal-typical description of the national state. Not so, according to Anderson. Wary of militarising the peasantry, absolutism

---

122. Anderson 1974b, p. 195.
123. Anderson 1992a pp. 7–8.
124. Gellner 1983.
125. Nairn 1975.
126. See Anderson 1974b, pp. 7–8. Anderson's book should also be read in relation to the classic 'transition debate' among British (and other) Marxists from the 1940s and 1950s collected by New Left Books in Rodney Hilton et al. 1976.
127. Anderson 1974b, p. 17. See Marx 2003, pp. 33–72, for an account of the relationship between absolutism and nationalism that directly critiques Anderson's.

established military forces dominated by 'foreign' mercenaries rather than national conscripts, an essential feature of the modern nation-state.[128] War, in the epoch of absolutism, remained, as it had been in medieval times, a zero-sum game whereby states expanded at the direct expense of competitors, rather than a medium of inter-economic competition where increased capital-accumulation might accrue to each antagonist.[129]

Scarcely more national was the absolutist state's bureaucracy, system of law, taxation or its dominant mode of production and exchange. Object of financial trade between private individuals, the bureaucracy characteristic of the absolutist state provided a contrast to the bureaucratic networks staffed by interchangeable subjects on the basis of meritocracy described by Gellner as typical of the modern nation-state.[130] If a meritocratic bureaucracy was foreign to the absolutist state, so were notions of the 'juridical "citizen" subject to fiscality by the very fact of belonging to the nation' – an entity crucial,[131] liberal nationalists have argued, to the later dominance of national sentiment.[132] Under absolutism's rule, the poor overwhelmingly shouldered the burden of taxation: the seigniorial class remaining free from the exactions of direct fiscal levies.[133] Finally, while the ruling economic doctrine of the epoch extinguished particularistic impediments to exchange within territorial borders, and sought to create an integrated 'national' market for commodity-production, it still subordinated profit to power – the separation of economics and politics characteristic of the modern capitalist state constituted the antipode of the absolutist state dominated by mercantilism.[134] In the epoch of absolutism, Anderson concluded, a state's legitimacy rested on dynasty not territory, language or ethnicity.[135]

Anderson's comparative history of pre-capitalist state-formations prefigured two common assumptions of later nationalism studies: on the one hand, the view that nationalism, even the nation-state, was definitively modern[136] and, on the other hand, the claim that states create nations, not nation-states.[137] *Lineages of*

128. Anderson 1974b, pp. 29–30. See Tilly 1995, p. 196; Mann 1992, p. 143, on the centrality of a 'national conscript' army to the 'nationalization of the masses'.
129. Anderson 1974b, p. 31.
130. Anderson 1974b, pp. 33–4. See Gellner 1983, for his conception of the relationship between nationalism and a meritocratic bureaucracy.
131. Anderson 1974b, p. 35.
132. See C. Taylor 1998, pp. 191–228; Tilly 1996, pp. 1–18.
133. Anderson 1974b, p. 35.
134. Anderson 1974b, pp. 35–6.
135. Anderson 1974b, p. 39.
136. A consensus has developed around the modernity of nationalism, but no consensus surrounds the necessarily modern nature of the nation, with many claiming an antiquity for it. See Hastings 1997, for an example.
137. Taken together the two positions constitute what is called the 'modernist' theory of nations and nationalism. See Ernest Gellner 1996, for an influential expression of

the Absolutist State was unambiguous on the first point: 'The ideological conceptions of "nationalism" as such were foreign to the inmost nature of absolutism'.[138] Not only was the modern state an effect of those various ruptures that assaulted the European *anciens régimes*, beginning with the English revolution in the seventeenth century and ending with the dissolution of the majority of surviving monarchies after 1918. The modern nation-state, according to Anderson, was also the preeminent response to certain developments within the capitalist mode of production. In this sense, nationhood was a function of international (and national) capital at a particular stage of its evolution. Thus, the absolutist state 'accomplished certain partial functions in the primitive accumulation necessary for the eventual triumph of the capitalist mode of production' and prepared the preconditions for the emergence of the industrial-capitalist nation-state, precisely the vehicle of private property's global triumph.[139] It followed from this, Anderson concluded, that it was the state rather than pre-existing ethnicities that laid the basis for the genesis of nationalism and nationhood. The full history of this process – states making national citizens – would have to wait for the later part of the nineteenth century.[140] After all, neither the warfare-state nor the welfare-state, highly efficient instruments of national integration, would have made any sense to those social formations 'whose permanent political function was the repression of the peasant and plebian masses at the foot of the social hierarchy'.[141]

In a review of Anderson's prehistory of the capitalist state, one that described it as 'an outstanding contribution to historical writing in the historical materialist mode',[142] Ralph Miliband protested Anderson's tendency to reduce classes to abstract social groups. Anderson may well have retorted that his was a 'history from above' and that from such a height classes necessarily assume a 'bloc-like quality'.[143] He may also have added that classes, even sometimes ruling classes, are mostly unaware of the 'historical totality' that went on behind their backs, and over whose direction they were powerless. However, this 'top-down view' arguably obscured not only the agency of class, but also Anderson's engagement with key aspects of the national question.

The body of *Lineages of the Absolutist State* was divided into a number of separate chapters corresponding to definite social formations – England, France,

---

this theory, which provides a review and revision of Gellner's now seminal *Nations and Nationalism*. See Hobsbawm 1997, for another influential account.

138. Anderson 1974b, p. 39.
139. Anderson 1974b, p. 40.
140. See Hobsbawm 1997, pp. 101–30, for such an account.
141. Anderson 1974b, p. 19.
142. Miliband 1975, p. 309.
143. Miliband 1975, p. 313.

Sweden, Russia and so on. These social formations may not have been properly constituted nation-states, but what was it about them that allowed Anderson to talk of 'England' or 'France'? Anderson was less than circumspect about these social formations' status as 'primordial' ethnic communities, ethnic communities not just unprocessed but completely obviated by his long-distance conceptual telescope. *Lineages of the Absolutist State* spoke of 'patriotic sentiment',[144] but only to dismiss it as ruling-class stupefaction rather than as authentic cultural identity.[145] The idea of 'nations before nationalism' was as foreign to Anderson's 'top-down view' of modernity's genesis as the conception of class-agency.[146]

A coda to Anderson's *Lineages of the Absolutist State*, composed in the mid-1970s, threw some light on these issues. Not published until it appeared in *English Questions* in 1992, 'The Notion of Bourgeois Revolution' constituted an abbreviated synopsis of what the third volume of a proposed tetralogy of the history of state-formations would have looked like.[147] The essay's ostensible ambition was 'to establish the formal structures and limits of any possible "bourgeois revolution" that would allow anomalous versions of the actual phenomenon to be seen as intelligible variations within a common field'.[148] Anderson argued that there were essentially two phases of bourgeois revolution. The first – stretching from the sixteenth to the eighteenth century – was consonant with the dominance of agrarian and mercantile capital (Holland, England, France and America), while the second – principally restricted to the nineteenth century – was coeval with the industrial revolution of factories and proletariats (Germany, Italy and Japan).[149] In the earlier cycle, bourgeois revolution was undertaken from below and gave rise to nation-states consonant with the 'rights of man'; while, in the later cycle, bourgeois revolution was undertaken from above and gave rise to nation-states based on language and ethnicity.[150] In the second cycle of bourgeois revolution, Anderson argued 'the banners of Liberty, Equality and Fraternity' were exchanged for 'the signs of Nationality and Industry'.[151]

---

144. Anderson 1974b, p. 39.
145. Ibid.
146. J.A. Anderson 1982.
147. See Anderson 1974b, p. 11 where Anderson outlines forthcoming volumes (which never appeared).
148. Anderson 1992a, p. 109.
149. Ibid.
150. Anderson 1992a, p. 110.
151. Anderson 1992a, p. 118. Anderson here seems to be drawing on the well-known distinction between 'Western' and 'Eastern' forms of national state. See Kedourie 1993; Kohn 1968, for classic expressions of this distinction.

'The Notion of Bourgeois Revolution' was a highly compressed and suggestive illumination of relations among class, class-struggle and nationalism as ideology. Historical varieties of nationalism, according to the essay, were overdetermined by capitalism's vitality and the nature of class-society.[152] The distinction Anderson drew was between two types of nationalism, coloured by the nature of the relationship between labour and capital. In the first period of bourgeois revolution nationalism appeared as a (revolutionary) function of the expansion of capital-accumulation; in the second period, nationalism constituted a means of capital-aggrandisement, but now as an ideology which obscured the antagonism between exploiters and exploited. Prior to the industrial revolution, when capitalism was relatively weak, nationalism – in the form of bourgeois revolution from below – acted to emancipate fettered relations of production, subsequent to the industrial revolution, when capitalism was in a position of relative strength, nationalism acted as a brake on the political ambition of the proletariat. Nationalism functioned to expand capital accumulation, the essay concluded, while different cycles of bourgeois revolution gave rise to varied forms of nationalism and distinguishable types of national state.

Thus, Anderson's conception of nationalism and nationalism's history diverged radically from the contemporaneous argument of Tom Nairn, whose theory of nationalism explained it as a distinctive, though paradoxical, response of subjected (in some sense already 'national') peoples to the process of uneven development.[153] No full confrontation between Anderson and Nairn over the national question has ever reached print, but Anderson's class-explication of modernity, and his conception of nationalism as ruling-class perfidy, might be interpreted as a significant reproof to Nairn's revision (perhaps better repudiation) of historical materialism in 'The Modern Janus'.[154] Nairn, if incompletely, rejected the equation nationalism equals false consciousness, upheld the importance of the 'subjective' side of national identity ('inherited *ethnos*, speech, folklore, skin-colour, and so on'),[155] and rejected class-struggle as the key determinant of world-history. The distinction might be reduced to a sense of different turning points as explanations for contemporary politics and history: for Nairn, it was August 1914 (when proletarian internationalism was smashed by nationalism),

152. See Brubaker 1992; Breuilly 1993, pp. 88–93 and 96–114, for a broad overview of the nation-building process in these two temporalities.
153. Nairn 1975.
154. Though there was some divergence among the editorial board about this article, Anderson's exact views remain unknown. Perhaps the fact that it was published is an indication of at least Anderson's awareness that a debate had to happen on nationalism – particularly in view of his comments in Anderson 1976.
155. Nairn 1975, p. 11. According to Duncan Thompson, Nairn's text caused substantial dissension within the *NLR* collective, with Robin Blackburn and Quinten Hoare particularly critical. See D. Thompson 2004, pp. 71–2.

for Anderson, it was October 1917 (when the first post-capitalist society was inaugurated).[156] Inveterate cosmopolitan, Anderson believed that nationalism, given its close association with the obfuscation of class-conflict and the legitimation of capitalist power, constituted the antithesis of social revolution, an ideology for labour-movements to oppose and transcend, rather than embrace and surrender before as a 'world norm'.[157] No assessment of the national question, 'The Notion of Bourgeois Revolution' implied, could either bracket-off nationalism from imperialism or understand either without consideration of the class-project represented by capitalist modernity.

VI

Like the Nairn-Anderson theses out of which it grew, Anderson's two-volume history was a diachronic project informed by 'the enterprise of understanding the present and mastering the future',[158] typical ambition of scientific socialism. In this sense, *Passages from Antiquity to Feudalism* and *Lineages of the Absolutist State* were a product of Anderson's political reorientation in the early 1970s, his shift from the practical quietism of Western Marxism, and the voluntarisms associated with revolutionary anti-imperialist Marxisms, to the classical revolutionary socialism of Marx, Lenin and Trotsky. Indeed, the shift had been forecast in his illumination of the practical deficit of Western Marxism in 'Socialism and Pseudo-Empiricism', and his belief that a reinvigoration of Marxist theory would result from mass revolutionary struggle.[159] A note of future direction was also sounded in his assessment of 'France 1968', where he maintained that events on the continent had 'vindicated the fundamental socialist belief that the industrial proletariat is the revolutionary class of advanced capitalism, whose collective social power – once liberated – could transform our societies beyond imagination'.[160] Events in Europe during the early 1970s, waves of industrial militancy and a hoped-for Portuguese revolution[161] seemed to confirm this assessment.

Considerations on Western Marxism summed up and provided an instantiation of these passages in Anderson's socialist politics. The book was not just a mirror of Anderson's new-found disappointment with the political consequences of continental Marxism, but also with the negative international implications of

---

156. See Anderson 1992a, p. 7.
157. Nairn 1975, p. 14.
158. Anderson 1980, p. 84.
159. Anderson 1966, p. 41.
160. *New Left Review* 1968, p. 7.
161. For this broad context, consult Sassoon 1996, pp. 357–88.

revolutionary Marxist nationalism in the Third World, particularly as these were manifest in the trajectory of Maoism. In Andersonian terms, whereas socialist strategy was the 'absent centre' of Western Marxism, revolutionary socialisms in the 'east' provided an inadequate strategic compass to socialists in the 'west'. In *Considerations of Western Marxism*, Anderson lamented west European Marxism's distance from the mass politics of revolutionary socialism, bemoaned its undue preoccupation with philosophy and aesthetics and questioned its 'specialized and inaccessible idiom'.[162] Despite the 'Thompsonian' timbre of this argument, Anderson's recommended antidote for such demerits was the revolutionary socialist tradition associated with Trotsky, expanded, revised and illuminated by Deutscher, Mandel and Rosdolsky – a tradition in the West which, he suggested, had remained sensitive to both socialist praxis and political economy and aloof from the university.[163] Tersely: 'It concentrated on politics and economics. It was resolutely internationalist'.[164] Thus, *Considerations on Western Marxism*, protesting the divorce between theory and practice, and the cultural and political pessimism effected by west European Marxist theorising after 1917, concluded that revolutionary socialist theory, once considered by Anderson the necessary pre-condition of social revolution, would only advance alongside revolutionary socialist practice and not at all without it.

Anderson was not alone in foregrounding the practical shortcomings of (Western) Marxist theorising in these years. In 1980, Raymond Williams extended a 'welcome to an observable if still small current tendency to move beyond the theoretical loud-hailing, the fiercely excluding and damning spirit of the late sixties and most of the seventies, into a more open and more actually rigorous reexamination and practical construction'.[165] With Anderson and *New Left Review* in mind, perhaps, Williams claimed that 'legitimating (Marxist) theory, at its best, leads to clearer orientations within an inescapably international political process, it can lead, at its worst, to a series of self-alienating options, in which our real political presence is as bystanders, historians or critics of the immense conflicts of other generations and other places, with only marginal or rhetorical connections to the confused and frustrating politics of our own time and place'.[166] E.P. Thompson had come to similar judgments somewhat earlier. With less reserve than Williams, Thompson taxed Anderson and the 'second' New Left with an over-hasty and elitist rejection of the 'ordinary language' of the English

---

162. Anderson 1976, p. 53.
163. Anderson 1976, p. 100.
164. Ibid. See Mandel 1995, pp. 13–31, for a different, though complimentary, account of Trotsky's internationalism.
165. Williams 1980, p. 251. This was not included in the original essay published in *New Left Review* in 1976, perhaps for obvious reasons.
166. Williams 1976, p. 85.

idiom, an insufficient engagement with Stalinism and the promotion of Marxism 'as a self-sufficient body of doctrine'.[167] The result, Thompson claimed, was not just politically damaging, but also 'a caricature of rational thought'.[168] Extending the assault in 'The Poverty of Theory', Thompson, echoing Williams, alleged that the New Left had become a sect disengaged 'from the actual political and intellectual contests of our time'.[169] Anderson, and the 'second' New Left, Thompson raged, were modern-day Godwinians summoning Enlightenment gods to strike down lightning bolts of reason against supposedly theory-deprived, recalcitrant earth-bound natives. Voices of the 'old' New Left, themselves often enough at odds, united here, in widely varied tones, to condemn the theoretical elitism, religious exhortation and practical nullity of their New Left successors.

Where Anderson was alone was in his Trotskyist prescription, and his confidence in the immanent restoration of revolutionary socialist practice in the West. *Considerations on Western Marxism* looked forward to Marxism's re-engagement with the struggle of the revolutionary masses, a position which Trotskyism, according to Anderson, was well placed to fill. Thompson dismissed *Considerations on Western Marxism*'s practical formulations as nonsense, its reference to 'masses' redolent of 'anti-intellectual magic'.[170] There was certainly something 'magical' about Anderson's emphasis on 'revolutionary practice' and the 'revolutionary masses' in *Considerations on Western Marxism*, arguably an emphasis no less abstract than earlier practical formulations about 'revolutionary theory' and the need for a 'socialist intelligentsia'. To borrow a more general conclusion from Raymond Williams, *Considerations on Western Marxism* marked Anderson's 'lurch from an abstract over-confidence in various kinds of theoretical enquiry to an equally abstract setting aside of theory in the (in fact dispersed) urgency of immediate struggles'.[171] But these were very definitely the struggles of other peoples in other places, and had little to do with Britain or, perhaps, anywhere in particular. As others have noted, Anderson's rendition of the revolutionary inheritance descended from Trotsky was largely an 'invented tradition' which paid scant regard for past or existing Trotskyist organisations and parties.[172]

Indeed, few agreed with Anderson's political conclusions. Even within *New Left Review* there was much dissension, particularly from Nairn, which prompted an 'Afterword' to *Considerations on Western Marxism* that significantly emended

---

167. E.P. Thompson 1978, pp. 320, 315.
168. E.P. Thompson 1978, p. 332.
169. E.P. Thompson 1978, p. 181.
170. E.P. Thompson 1976, p. 7.
171. Williams 1980, p. 250.
172. I borrow this term from Hobsbawm, but the idea to which it is applied from Elliott who charges that Anderson's was an 'imaginary Trotskyism'. See Elliott 1998, p. 104.

conclusions in the main body of the text, including its confidence in the tradition of 'classical Marxism'.[173] In the 'Afterword', Marx and the classical Marxist tradition were castigated for a range of theoretical and practical deficits, including a failure to come to terms with the capitalist state and nationalism. This rubbed rough with a good deal of the argument of the main text, especially Anderson's confident espousal of the tradition of socialist internationalism associated with Trotsky and the Trotskyist heritage. Anderson now criticised the book's 'apocalyptic tone', which he measured a 'suspect sign, of difficulties evaded or ignored'.[174] 'What is the constitutive nature of bourgeois democracy? What is the function and future of the nation-state? ... How can internationalism be made a genuine practice?' – these according to Anderson were among 'the great unanswered problems that form the most urgent agenda for Marxist theory today'.[175]

Anderson's attempt to assay these problems began in the book-length essay 'The Antinomies of Antonio Gramsci'. The essay contested Anderson's earlier interpretation of hegemony as 'cultural supremacy'. Overturning that assessment, Anderson now argued that

> the general form of the representative State – bourgeois democracy – is itself the principal ideological lynchpin of Western capitalism, whose very existence deprives the working class of the idea of socialism as a different type of State, and the means of communication and other mechanisms of cultural control thereafter clinch this central ideological 'effect' ... The bourgeois State ... 'represents' the totality of the population, abstracted from its divisions into social classes, as individual and equal citizens ... The economic divisions within the 'citizenry' are masked by the juridical parity between exploiters and exploited ... This separation is then ... represented to the masses as the ultimate incarnation of liberty: 'democracy' as the terminal point of history....[176]

Anderson concluded that the power of the capitalist state was based as much on coercion as consent. But, in the absence of emergency – the point where coercion revealed itself as capitalism's final defence – its 'normal structure' rested on cultural domination in the shape of bourgeois democracy.[177] If this constituted an advance over other Gramscian interventions, it nonetheless replayed some of the evasions of Anderson's earlier texts. Above all, Anderson's assessment of Gramsci's conception of hegemony evaded the issue of ethnicity, no less real for

---

173. Anderson 1976, p. viii. See Elliott 1998, pp. 104–5, for Nairn's criticisms, which draws on the unpublished document 'Comments on "Western Marxism: An Introduction"', (September 1974), pp. 2–10.

174. Anderson 1976, p. 109.

175. Anderson 1976, p. 121.

176. Anderson 1976, p. 28.

177. Anderson 1976, p. 42.

being imagined, and its cultural function in securing capitalist power, an issue arguably confronted, if incompletely, by Gramsci through his conception of the 'national-popular'.[178] Gramsci's insights aside, Anderson's evasion of ethnicity involved neglect of nationalism's role in establishing, and then reinforcing, the sense of community necessary for bourgeois democracy, something to which Nairn had pointed in 'The Modern Janus'.[179]

Anderson's assessment of the national question, and some of its evasions, was brought into sharper relief in *Arguments within English Marxism*. This book marked Anderson's re-engagement with the 'old' New Left through an assessment of E.P. Thompson's oeuvre, impelled by the publication of *The Poverty of Theory and Other Essays*. *Arguments within English Marxism* took in the full-sweep of Thompson's work, from historical studies like *The Making of the English Working Class* and *Whigs and Hunters* to political interventions published in *New Reasoner*, early *New Left Review* and elsewhere. Claiming Thompson as the most important contemporary socialist writer in Europe,[180] Anderson's tone was far more respectful than in 'Socialism and Pseudo-Empiricism', many of whose judgments *Arguments within English Marxism* capsized. But, if more appreciative, Anderson was no less combative, taking issue with much of Thompson's interpretation of Althusser, with his conception of the relationship between structure and subject in historical process, with his assessment of the New Left and with the 'poverty' of his conception of socialist strategy. Much had changed since 1965 though, not least Anderson's own understanding of the value of Western Marxism, of the historical limits of revolutionary nationalism in the Third World and the valences of the national culture.[181]

Arguments within English Marxism took issue with the conception of agency and class-consciousness in *The Making of the English Working Class* – the idea that the working class made itself as much as it was made – and argued that Thompson overlooked keys aspects of class-formation, including industrialisation and the determinate process of the real subjection of labour to capital.[182] Indeed,

---

178. This idea of Gramsci's would be central to that other appropriation of Gramsci in the work of Stuart Hall in the 1980s. In this appropriation, the 'national-popular' would be central to Hall's socialist revisionism. See Forgacs 1993, pp. 177–90, for more on Gramsci's conception of the 'national-popular'.

179. Nairn 1975.

180. Anderson 1980, p. 1.

181. It was noted in the introduction to Williams 1979b, *NLR*'s interviews with Raymond Williams, that 'In the past decade, for the first time since the war, active socialist culture in England has come to be predominantly Marxist' (p. 7). The interviews were conducted by Anderson, Barnett, and Mulhern. The view was extended later when he claimed that 'Marxist culture for the moment prov[ed] more productive and original than that of any mainland (European) state'. See Anderson 1983a, p. 25.

182. Anderson 1980, pp. 16–58. An alternative reading of Thompson's understanding of class in that book is offered in Palmer 1981.

Anderson claimed that it was Thompson's 'subjectivist' notation of class – the equation that class equals class-consciousness – that had led to the chief defects of *The Making of the English Working Class* – its inability to account for the persuasive chauvinism within the English working class from the Napoleonic wars onwards.[183] Pre-empting the argument of Linda Colley in her influential *Britons*,[184] and repeating an earlier criticism of Geoffrey Best,[185] Thompson's conception of the English working class, Anderson claimed, missed the chief source of the proletariat's subordination, thus circumventing the problem of class without class-consciousness. 'The prime weapon in [the English *ancien régime*'s] arsenal, after twenty years of victorious fighting against the French Revolution and its successor regimes', Anderson argued, 'was a counter-revolutionary nationalism'.[186] A similar shortcoming inhered in Thompson's conception of 'the rule of law', central to *Whigs and Hunters*, and his contemporary polemics against the increasing authoritarianism of what Thompson called the secret state, later published in *Writing by Candlelight*. In this case, however, the reverse applied. Sensitive to resources within the national culture that could be pushed in socialist directions, Thompson's defence of the 'rule of law', Anderson suggested, was insufficiently alert to the ways in which invocation of liberties against the state could be given liberal inflections.[187]

In a 'Foreword' to *The Poverty of Theory and Other Essays*, Thompson argued that internationalism 'ought not to consist in lying prostrate before the ("Western Marxist") theorist of our choice, or in seeking to imitate their modes of discourse'.[188] Anderson agreed with this judgment, suggesting in *Arguments within English Marxism* that the 'second' New Left's internationalism was primarily 'theoretic' and without anchorage in any practical movement for socialism – an acknowledgement of Thompson's view that 'theoretical internationalism' 'can very often mean no more than the evacuation of the real places of conflict within our own intellectual culture, as well as the loss of real political relations with our people'.[189] But Anderson argued that contextual vicissitudes explained this. Underlining temporalities, which separated the 'second' New Left from Thompson's generation of the New Left, Anderson maintained that his internationalism was based on a 'frontal rejection of national mystification, at the most immediate

183. Anderson 1980.
184. Colley 1992. See the review of *Britons* in E.P. Thompson 1994, pp. 319–29.
185. See Best 1965, p. 278 cited in 'Postscript' to E.P. Thompson 1968, p. 916. See Philip 1995, pp. 91, 99, for a later elucidation of this critique.
186. Anderson 1980, p. 35. See the contributions to Dickinson 1989, for more on the question of proletarian nationalism during the French revolutionary wars.
187. Anderson 1980, pp. 204–5.
188. E.P. Thompson 1978, p. iv.
189. Ibid.

level'.[190] Whereas the context of Thompson's political formation – Popular Front and people's war – encouraged the co-existence of national and international impulses without obvious strain, the context of his own formation, Anderson explained, was 'much colder',[191] preventing instructive dialogue between nationalism and internationalism. Repudiation of all aspects of the national culture, Anderson suggested, was its unambiguous result (though this would make the argument of 'Problems of Socialist Strategy' difficult to explain).

Anderson, however, remained unrepentant, re-affirming in *Arguments within English Marxism* the international impulses of his own socialism, defending a version of socialist internationalism, as we might expect in the wake of *Considerations on Western Marxism*, associated with the Trotskyist tradition. Anderson maintained that the significance of Trotsky's legacy was revealed 'in the standard and mode of internationalism it embodied'.[192] Highlighting Thompson's refusal to engage with this tradition (Thompson did engage with it, whether at meetings of socialist forum or New Left clubs – he rejected it), *Arguments within English Marxism* held up Trotsky's assessment of the national question as an example that deserved socialists' praise and emulation. 'No other revolutionary', according to Anderson, 'ever practiced so long and so consistently proletarian internationalism, in his own politics'.[193] Trotsky's exemplary internationalism, Anderson argued, could be measured not just by his aversion to 'every form of social patriotism or great-power chauvinism',[194] but also by his distance from 'socialism in one country' and 'intransigent refusal to compromise with national sentiments within the ranks of the labour movement in the developed world'– the latter meant as a shot across Thompson's New Left bow.[195]

Arguments within English Marxism thus defended Anderson's version of socialist internationalism, measuring it against the confluence of nationalism and internationalism which defined Thompson's. However, the book contained a misreading of both Thompson's socialist internationalism and the differences that separated it off from Anderson's own. Where Thompson's socialist internationalism was steeped in internationalist traditions within the English radical past – Morris, Mann, British communism in the 1930s and 1940s – and connected with socialist humanisms (Hungary and Poland) and various anti-imperialisms (India and Kenya) abroad, Anderson's socialist internationalism involved a repudiation of British socialism at home and the support of anti-colonial Marxist nationalisms (Vietnamese, Chinese and Cuban) abroad, (these associations were

---

190. Anderson 1980, p. 148.
191. Ibid.
192. Anderson 1980, p. 155.
193. Ibid.
194. Ibid.
195. Anderson 1980, p. 156.

mostly passed over in *Arguments within English Marxism*) and subsequently transposed to Trotsky's internationalist standards. In other words, Thompson's was a 'rooted' internationalism that understood internationalism as a space of complex negotiation between national traditions; Anderson's internationalism was primarily long-distance and imagined, and always imagined to be in better shape somewhere else – or, in the case of Anderson's Trotskyism, nowhere in particular. What separated Thompson's internationalism from Anderson's was not its assessment of nationalism, as Anderson implied – both Thompson and Anderson rejected reactionary nationalisms – but their specific valuation of the internationalist tradition in England. Thompson believed that this tradition was worth something, Anderson did not.

In addition to illuminating Anderson's standard of internationalism, *Arguments within English Marxism* constituted his most sustained reflections on socialist transition since 'Problems of Socialist Strategy' in the mid-1960s. In Anderson's Morris-inspired reading of social transformation, the left-social democracy of the 1965 article was overturned in favour of Lenin and Trotsky's revolutionary realism. Pointing to the homology between Thompson's early New Left writings and the CPGB's 'British Road to Socialism', Anderson charged both with reformism, drawing attention to their distance from Morris's repudiation of the parliamentary route to socialism.[196] For the 'second' New Left, according to Anderson, 'a socialist revolution [meant] something harder and more precise'.[197]

> For us, a socialist revolution means ... the dissolution of the existing capitalist state, the expropriation of the possessing classes from the means of production, and the construction of a new type of state and economic order, in which the associated producers can for the first time exercise direct control over their working lives and direct power over their political government.[198]

Recalling institutions – 'communes, soviets, or councils' – associated with the revolutionary heritage of Marx, Lenin and Trotsky,[199] Anderson argued that socialist revolution would not be effected without either a fundamental displacement of bourgeois hegemony or the creation of alternative centres of proletarian power – strictures, he claimed, foreign to the socialist strategy of the original New Left.

Thompson would have rubbished Anderson's claim that his socialist politics were reformist. As recently as the 'Postscript: 1976' to his revised edition of *William Morris: Romantic to Revolutionary*, Thompson had written that 'Mor-

---

196. Anderson 1980, p. 194.
197. Ibid.
198. Ibid.
199. Anderson 1980, p. 193.

ris saw it as a task of Socialists (his own first task) to help people to find out their wants, to encourage them to want more, to challenge them to want differently, and to envisage a society of the future in which people, freed at last of necessity, might choose between different wants'.[200] This had been Thompson's task too, relatively faithfully fulfilled in his own terms, since 1956. Anderson took issue with Thompson's 'unwitting assimilation' (Thompson had not read *Anti-Oedipus*) of desire in a context in which desire had been appropriated by Parisian irrationalism.[201] Thompson would have responded that Paris could go to hell, and that Morris's conception of desire was crucial to understanding not only socialism's past but also its present doldrums. Thompson, however, would have agreed with Anderson that Morris was an instrumental aide in contemporary socialist interventions against reformism, but he would have added that he and the New Left had been saying as much since the mid-1950s. Thompson would have maintained Morris's distance from what Anderson called 'revolutionary Marxism after Lenin',[202] – a tradition Thompson had consistently belied for its 'lack of moral self-consciousness or even a vocabulary of desire [and] its inability to project any images of the future'.[203] By 1980, Thompson was more interested in Morris than Marxism precisely because of this. Anderson meanwhile maintained allegiance, in terms of strategy, 'to the greater cogency and realism of the tradition of Lenin and Trotsky' on the basis of an 'examination of a known past'.[204] Thompson might have retorted that it was precisely this tradition's 'known past' which separated him from the 'second' New Left, and Morris from Marxism.

Anderson's socialist strategy might be questioned from the perspective of his own rejection of 'Marxism in one country'.[205] Arguably, Thompson's and Anderson's socialist internationalism equally lacked 'a clear conception of how, nationally and internationally, there could actually be a political order which permits human beings, in the wildly unequal situations in which history has left them, to cooperate together in rational mutual trust for a genuinely shared good and in an economy which is not based upon private ownership'.[206] Both Thompson and Anderson had primarily practiced socialist internationalism in the style of support for socialist movements in other countries, or for movements of national liberation against imperialism. At times, indeed, each had bent both their back and their pen to these struggles in conversation or dialogue with those

---

200. E.P. Thompson 1976, p. 806. This postscript was also published in *NLR* in 1976.
201. Anderson 1980, p. 161.
202. Anderson 1980, p. 178.
203. E.P. Thompson 1976, p. 792.
204. Anderson 1980, p. 197.
205. Anderson 1980, pp. 148–9.
206. Dunn 1985, p. 117.

other movements. How such socialist internationalism might be transformed into a different society beyond capitalism, and what that society would like look, neither had spent time contemplating.

Examples of what such contemplation would have involved can be rendered through a series of questions put to *Arguments within English Marxism*. The book associated itself with a revolutionary tradition defined by its antagonism to 'socialism in one country'. However, Anderson made no mention of the social-ist problematic raised by the apparent contradiction between an inter-national state system and a transnational economic order. He referred to a post-capitalist future, where the 'associated producers can for the first time exercise direct con-trol over their working lives and direct power over their government',[207] but made no mention of the cultural, national or territorial composition of 'their' government. In other places, Anderson spoke of 'the structural unity of the capi-talist order',[208] and 'capitalist relations of power' implying that capitalism dis-played an extra-national nature.[209] But, whether this meant that both socialist revolution and a post-revolutionary order would be likewise extra-national we are not told. What set of cultural commonalities would prevent a post-capitalist social order from falling apart into either interminable difference or intolerable bureaucracy? What would a socialist society do with existing structures of senti-ment tied to nationality and ethnicity? In short, the problem of socialism and the nation-state, socialism and national identity – in this sense – was bypassed.

Arguments within English Marxism ended with a call to leave New Left squab-bles behind, and to explore issues together in the future. This gesture was almost immediately fulfilled when *New Left Review* published Thompson's 'Exterminism and the Cold War', clarion-call to a new European peace-movement. If collec-tive debate ensued, however, agreement between Anderson and Thompson did not. Anderson disagreed with Thompson about the genesis of the Cold War – Anderson believed the United States was overwhelmingly culpable, Thompson argued that a distinctive exterminist logic common to both propelled confron-tation – while Anderson advocated anti-anti-communism and defence of the Soviet Union as the appropriate socialist response to the current disorder of international relations. For Anderson, the planetary contest between socialism and capitalism was 'a deformed and displaced' expression of international class-struggle.[210] The 'scientific socialism' Anderson had defended against the utopian strains of Thompson's socialist humanism marked out socialist transformation in

---

207. Anderson 1980, p. 194.
208. Anderson 1980, p. 178.
209. Anderson 1980, p. 194.
210. *New Left Review* 1982, p. ix. The 'foreword' was written by Anderson. See Elliott 1998, p. 145. See also Anderson 1983a, pp. 95–6.

the Soviet Union as the prime hope for socialist advance in the West. In a talk in
Montreal in 1978, Anderson had argued that no socialist could be unaware

> of the profound historical vices and defects of the societies and states that
> have been constructed in the USSR...and Eastern Europe. But it will be vital
> for the future course of the West European Left that it be able to reject the
> fashionable equation...between the USSR and USA as two 'super powers',
> from which a socialist Europe should be equidistant... [T]his language is thor-
> oughly unreal and unscientific... [T]he myth of the two 'super powers' and of
> the ultimate similarity between them is a notion that has been most... fero-
> ciously propagated by the leadership of the Chinese Communist Party. The
> political logic of it has been very clear. It rapidly leads...to a rapprochement
> with the United States...Any turn within the mass communist movement of
> Western Europe towards a similar ideological position would be very likely to
> have a similar diplomatic outcome...Any attempt to foreclose the possibility
> of constructing a more positive dialectic with these societies...will lead only
> to regression and defeat.[211]

Anderson would maintain this position throughout the 'second Cold War',
advancing an interpretation of Cold War as 'the awful, but intelligible product
of, global class struggle',[212] and proclaiming an internationalist politics based on
opposition to Stalinism, but a qualified defence of the Soviet Union as a post-
capitalist state.[213]

The defeat of socialist internationalism in August 1914 haunts this imagined
internationalism, as it does so much else of Anderson's approach to the national
question. In a contribution to the 'problems of communist history', Eric Hobsbawm argued that there was 'something heroic about the British and French
CPs in September 1939'.[214] 'Nationalism, political calculation, even common
sense', he continued, 'pulled one way, yet they unhesitatingly chose to put the
interests of the international movement first'.[215] 'They were', Hobsbawm concluded, 'tragically and absurdly wrong'.[216] Communist internationalism, in 1939,
was a result of the association of socialist internationalism with the interests of
a particular state. The deformity of this transposition arguably resided in the
misassociation. Was deformity operative in Anderson's case? Anderson might
have judged it such at any moment from 1960 to 1976. But, at any one of those
moments, he supposed revolutionary socialist advance in the West at least an

---

211. Anderson 1978, pp. 27–8.
212. Anderson 1983a, p. 95.
213. Anderson 1983a, pp. 124–6.
214. Hobsbawm 1999, p. 6.
215. Ibid.
216. Ibid.

open possibility. This was much harder to entertain from 1980 to 1984. Other options, whether the socialist nationalism (invocation of Gramsci's 'national-popular' in the work of Stuart Hall) associated with *Marxism Today*, or the shriller version associated with a modernising Labour party, were tastes foreign to Anderson's palate. Likely, Anderson believed his imagined internationalism the only socialist option on the table. But, if so, it was distanced from the peace politics associated with European Nuclear Disarmament (END). In the conclusion to his 'Foreword' to *Exterminism and Cold War*, a collection of New Left essays on the peace-movement, Anderson suggested that 'peace must acquire a tangible social shape capable of inspiring the positive dreams and loyalties of millions. For all the tragedies that have befallen the ideal in this century, what could that shape be if not socialist'?[217] For all that, Anderson's long-distance internationalism was likely to miss the 'signs in the street'.[218]

VII

In the mid-1980s, following his resignation as editor of *New Left Review*, and his move to the United States, where he was now employed as a professor of history at the University of California, Los Angeles, Anderson resumed interrogating issues first broached two decades earlier in 'Origins of the Present Crisis' and 'Components of the National Culture'. However, a transformed political optic – disillusionment with prospects for revolutionary socialism in the East and the West – now governed Anderson's engagement with economic, social and cultural realities in Britain. The final surrender of social democracy to the free market, the exhaustion of revolutionary energies in the Third World and the historic economic and moral decline of communism gave to this resumption of earlier concerns a political hesitancy that was far removed from the hint of socialist triumphalism which informed the earlier essays. In comparison with the Anderson-Nairn theses, the tone of 'Figures of Descent' and 'A Culture in Contraflow' was much chastened, much more academic, the belligerent correctors of revolutionary theory, and a revolutionary socialist culture, thrown overboard. If much differed about Anderson's updated assessment of British economic decline and the state of the national culture, they nonetheless shared their predecessor's 'offshore' approach, with Britain once again engaged as a foreign country through the lens of the long-distance telescope.

Returning to the principal problematics of his analysis of English history in 'Origins of the Present Crisis', Anderson affirmed in 'Figures of Descent' the basic

217. *New Left Review* 1982, p. xii.
218. Taken from Berman 1999, pp. 153–70.

contours of his earlier intervention, now stiffened, he claimed, by decades-long developments in historiography, from Corelli Barnett's *The Audit of War* to Arno Mayer's *The Persistence of the Old Regime*. Anderson's renovated account of British decline, and the debate it sparked in *New Left Review* from the likes of Michael Barratt Brown and Alex Callinicos is not in need of review, given attention paid to it elsewhere.[219] What might be noted is Anderson's claim that in the interlude between 'Origins of the Present Crisis' and 'Figures of Descent' a major development in international capitalism had occurred which demanded revision of the prescriptions tacitly implied in the Nairn-Anderson theses. The crisis of British capitalism, 'Figures of Descent' noted, was no longer peculiar to Britain, a prospective revival no longer susceptible to a manipulation of the national economy or a modernisation of the British state and social structure, let alone the excelled economic performance promised by socialist transformation. In the two decades between 'Origins of the Present Crisis' and 'Figures of Descent', a 'radical internationalization of the forces of production',[220] barely perceptible in 1964, had supervened to explode his earlier assessment of British economic and societal crisis. Capitalist globalisation, and a prospective restoration of private property in the societies of actually-existing socialism, portended a potential universalisation of the crisis of British capitalism, disabling any suggested national solution to economic stagnation. Liberalisation of exchange rates, the increased mobility of capital and the deterritorialisation of finance – these trends among others had rendered national economics antique.[221] No one was a Keynesian now. The rapid internationalisation of production, exchange and circulation, in short, had made 'all national correctors, whatever their efficacy to date, increasingly tenuous in the future'.[222]

'A Culture in Contraflow', Anderson's up-dated account of the national culture, echoed the conclusions, to say nothing of the chastened tone and politics, of 'Figures of Descent'. Just as capitalist globalisation had enervated national economics, so analogously, and interconnected, transnational cultural forces had made autarkic national cultures vulnerable to dissolution. Whereas Anderson's earlier panorama of the national culture was situated within the contours of an unproblematically national state, 'A Culture in Contraflow' was forced to question the very object of its optic.[223] Ideas tracked economic developments. 'In this epoch', Anderson concluded, 'no culture could remain national in the

---

219. See Barratt Brown 1988, pp. 21–51; Callinicos 1988, 97–106; Ingram 1988, pp. 45–65, for the debate.
220. Anderson 1992a, p. 192.
221. Anderson 1992a, p. 181. See Anderson 1994, pp. 17–18, for a slightly later analysis along the same lines.
222. Anderson 1992a, p. 192.
223. Anderson 1992a, p. 201.

pristiner senses of the past'.[224] The consequences, however, were not unambiguous for a radical culture. In one sense, the denationalisation of the national culture was undeniably positive: 'The ferruginous philistinism and parochialism of long national tradition', Anderson supposed, 'were discomposed'.[225] No superstructural tariffs existed to hold up the traffic of cultural exchange; no culture could erect Chinese walls high enough to prevent the transnational exchange of ideas. 'British culture', Anderson argued, 'became looser and more hybrid'.[226] In another sense, however, the metamorphosis of the national culture had not redounded to the benefit of a 'radical intellectual culture': hegemony, in the new vicissitude, remained with the ideological forces of capital.

The outstanding source of capital's hegemony in the region of intellectual culture, argued Anderson, 'was the absence of any significant political movement as a pole of attraction for intellectual opposition'.[227] Labourism's denouement during the Thatcher era, the 'retirement of Communism' and the abbreviated biography of the Alliance, according to him, had 'created a vacuum that set certain unmistakable limits to the cultural turnover of those years'.[228] 'The one bold attempt to break the political log-jam... Charter 88', with which Anderson himself was associated alongside former *New Left Review* editor Anthony Barnett, 'was a bold initiative of socialist and liberal forces within the intellectual world, aiming at constitutional reform'.[229] It too, however, proved no match for the 'ideological vision of the Right'.[230] An indication of the foreshortened nature of Anderson's socialist ambition, reform of Britain's parliament and polity here replaced revolutionary socialism as a solution to the shortcomings of the national culture. Indeed, just a decade earlier *Arguments within English Marxism* had suggested that the deficit of Marxist theory in Britain could be explained by 'the absence of a truly mass and truly revolutionary movement in England, as elsewhere in the West'.[231] By the beginning of the last century's *fin de siècle*, according to Anderson, such hopes had been reduced to nothing by capital's unchallenged supremacy.

The argument that the nation-state and national cultures have been enervated by capitalist globalisation has constituted one of the primary leitmotivs of Anderson's work in the last two decades.[232] In the contemporary debate over the future of the nation-state and nationalism, Anderson has found himself in

---

224. Ibid.
225. Anderson 1992a, p. 204.
226. Ibid.
227. Anderson 1992a, p. 300.
228. Ibid. See Anderson 1998, p. 91, for this view, expressed slightly later.
229. Anderson 1992a, p. 300.
230. Anderson 1992a, p. 301.
231. Anderson 1980, p. 207.
232. See Anderson 1998, p. 92.

agreement with those, like the Marxist historian Eric Hobsbawm, who maintain that both have exhausted their world-historical force.[233] Following the end of what Robert Brenner has phrased 'the long-upturn in the fortunes of the world economy',[234] capitalist productive forces, according to Anderson, entered a new transnational phase, signalled by the OPEC oil-crisis and the downfall of the Bretton Woods system.[235] The reconstruction of capital on a truly global plane, he argued, impacted most severely on the nation-state and its post-war champion, social democracy. The welfare-state, tightly restricted labour-markets and the achievement of full employment had constituted the historical triumphs of social democracy in advanced capitalist countries. But, Anderson judged, in the wake of capitalist reconstruction after 1973 the instruments through which these achievements had been secured were no longer operable. 'The internationalization of capital flows released by the deregulation of financial markets', he argued, 'has made it increasingly difficult either to devalue to restore trade balances, or lower interest rates to stimulate demand'.[236] International monetary markets, minutely sensitive to inflationary pressures, and the prospect of capital flight, had disabled traditional instruments of (national) social-democratic government.

This argument has much force, but it has been challenged. Few dispute globalisation – its depth or novelty, however, is contested – but many dispute that globalisation involves diminishment in the force and influence of nationalism or national identity. After all, national identity does not require a nation-state to flourish, and nationalism and the nation-state should not be confused. Indeed, while it might be agreed that nation-states are nominal, there is a large literature now that suggests as much, the same could not be said about national identity or the politics of national sentiment, an equally large literature attests to this too.[237] However, the explosion of ethnic antagonism generated in the wake of communism's denouement, the growth of nationalist conflict on the periphery of capitalism's world-system, and the surge in xenophobia and separatism in centres of advanced capitalism – none of these trends, Anderson suggested, disproved the contention that nationalism was likely to constitute a residual force in the future development of world-history.[238] European integration, the spread

---

233. Hobsbawm 1990, p. 163.

234. Brenner 2003.

235. See Anderson 2002, pp. 18–9. See also Anderson 2003, p. 56. See Panitch and Gindin 2005, for the argument that the Bretton Woods system was established on just those principles which are regularly characterised as typical of the 'neo-liberal' phase of globalisation.

236. Anderson 1994, p. 14.

237. See Calhoun 2007, particularly, pp. 1–10, for a recent example of the argument that both the nation-state and nationalism are in rude health.

238. See Anderson 2002, p. 23.

of global capitalism and a globalised American culture were far better guides to the present state of things than conflicts between Serbs and Croats in Bosnia, Tamil insurgency in Sri Lanka or votes for Le Pen or the SNP, no matter how important in their local context.[239]

Liberal democracy – elections, parliament and prosperity – had progressively displaced national identity, in Anderson's version of the end of nationalism argument, as the primary mechanism of integration in advanced capitalist societies. It was expanding income, demotic access to consumer durables, and the ideological association of free markets with freedom and democracy, not the nation-state or primordial ethnicity, which consistently reconciled labour to capitalism. Recalling an argument of 'The Antinomies of Antonio Gramsci', parliamentary democracy, for Anderson, had displaced ethnicity 'as the dominant means of discursive integration in the West'.[240] Following the end of the Cold War, he explained, nationalism had been tamed by consumerism, national sentiment undermined by cultural homogenisation and national sovereignty subverted by the discourse of human rights.[241] 'The object-world of all the rich capitalist countries has been relentlessly hybridised, as the circuits of multi-national production and exchange grow more pervasive. The old signifiers of difference', Anderson concluded, 'have progressively waned'.[242]

However, Anderson's conclusion rendered opaque at least one question that has exercised the minds of recent nationalism scholars – why does nationalism still 'command such profound emotional legitimacy',[243] and why does the nation remain the preeminent 'taken-for-granted frame of reference' for human identity?[244] In a respectful valuation of Ernest Gellner's historical sociology, Anderson argued that the sociologist from Prague had 'theorized nationalism without detecting its spell'.[245] Gellner, Anderson suggested, had neglected 'the overpowering dimension of collective meaning that modern nationalism has always involved: that is, not its functionality for industry, but its fulfillment of identity'.[246] There is more than a sense here of the Marxist kettle calling the liberal pot black. After all, this is precisely the aspect of nationalism that Anderson's work has consistently overlooked. One signal of this evasion can be found in Anderson's deliberately delimited definition of 'national culture', as a matter more of books and words than ethnicity or national sensibility. Francis Mulhern's

---

239. Anderson 1992b, p. 337.
240. Anderson 2002, p. 19. Consider also Anderson 2005, p. 309.
241. Anderson 1992b, p. 270.
242. Anderson 1992, p. 266.
243. B. Anderson 1996, p. 4.
244. B. Anderson 1996, p. 12.
245. Anderson 1992b, p. 205.
246. Ibid.

suggestion that culture's 'main substance . . . is ethnicity' has been systematically neglected in Anderson's encounter with 'his' national culture and the national culture of others,[247] even at those moments, like his endorsement of Charter 88, when such evasion seemed impossible. Ethnicity, privileged container of contemporary instantiations of custom and preeminent, if paradoxical, defence against modernity, is the shortest answer we have for why nationalism is not only the pre-eminent source of self but also of political society.

Indeed, according to a persuasive set of arguments, 'old signifiers of difference' have not waned but expanded, that 'nationality, read under the sign of "identity", is on the rapid rise as people everywhere are on the move'.[248] Like a process of nuclear fission, uneven capitalist development, according to this view, has proliferated difference from the Arctic Circle to the Horn of Africa. In the opinion of both Tom Nairn and Stuart Hall, for example, the internationalisation of productive forces has not melted the solidities of ethnicity into air but refigured, transformed and strengthened them. Capitalist globalisation, and the various cultural and social processes that have followed in its train, from the emergence of global communications-systems to mass migration, has encouraged and necessitated the amplification of ethnicities – both in terms of number and depth.[249] Balkanisation *and* globalisation, according to Nairn, has characterised the post-Soviet era. 'Even before 1989 it was clear that medieval particuralism still had a future. Only after that year could it be more convincingly argued that it had *the* future too'.[250] Nationality, not class, in Nairn's view, provided 'the general political climate of world development',[251] ethnicity offering the only experiential framework for democracy and political community.

Anderson has addressed this argument, perhaps somewhat obliquely, by reminding national identity's enthusiasts of the other side of nationalism's Janus-like nature.[252] In his most recent work, he has maintained that it is states and political elites (not 'the people') who make nations, and that national identity most often hides inherent material divisions within all nation-states, to say nothing of differentials between nation-states. He has highlighted the paradox of the extension of democracy and democracy's increasing depthlessness, following the 'global triumph of neo-liberalism' as a challenge to the view that national self-determination is an enabling structure of democracy. Not the will of national peoples, but 'the steady loss of substance of parliamentary and electoral systems'

---

247. Mulhern 2009, p. 39.
248. B. Anderson 1996, p. 9.
249. Nairn 1996, p. 269.
250. Ibid.
251. Nairn 1996, p. 270.
252. See Anderson 1992b, p. 274.

constitutes one of 'the hallmarks of the age'.[253] Massive, constitutive and determining disparities between social groups within nation-states have constituted a more formidable and defining characteristic of the post-communist world, according to him, than the hyper-separatist calculation which equates more nation-states with greater extents of human liberation.[254] For Anderson, nationalism is precisely designed to obscure both the shallowness of contemporary democracy and the depth of class-difference.

Anderson's obdurate anti-nationalism has been effected with brio,[255] a consequence of an intellect which has consistently refused popular intellectual trends, to say nothing of a specious populism that rides a lowest-common-denominator political demotic falsely associated with 'the people'. Indeed, with the fear of 'Asiatic hordes' reanimating the politics of an 'extreme new right' across Europe, with the continuing explosions of ethnic-based conflict in the post-colonial world, and with a belligerent chauvinism filling the void at the center of formerly socialist countries, from China to Yugoslavia, Anderson's stubborn association with a politics self-discursively descended from enlightenment rationalism offers an unseasonal counter-weight to the hegemony of identity politics. Anderson's trenchant commitment to Enlightenment tenets might be considered reminiscent of the New Left's socialist humanism, with its adhesion to a vision of the 'good society' beyond class, nation and ethnicity. Surely, Anderson's universalist aspiration is not some form of cosmopolitan imperialism as Nairn, for example, has supposed, or a form of totalitarianism as the majority voice of recent postmodernist critique has maintained. Rather, it might be said to constitute the human alternative to a politics whose ultimate foundation rests on supposed 'facts' of existence – 'nation', 'culture', 'ethnicity'. However, if national identity does constitute an aspect of human nature, the expression of a recurring need for a sense of self, then such universalism is hopelessly utopian.[256] Indeed, if nationalism constitutes the only habitable zone of politics and identity, and the only possible arc of community, and if solidarity cannot be imagined except as an effect of ethnicity, then Anderson's cosmopolitan vision constitutes not just an impossible future but also one that is inherently perverse.

Anderson's contemporary repudiation of identity-politics, whether ethnic or nationalist, has crystallised his conception of the proper territorial reach of socialist politics. In recent times, Anderson has been at pains to expose the foibles of a

---

253. Anderson 2005.
254. Anderson 2007.
255. See Halliday 1992, pp. 483–9, for the need for such a stance in contemporary times. See Smith 1995, pp. 23–4, for a critique of cosmopolitanism, the political terminus of anti-nationalism.
256. This is the position of Nairn 1997 – providing here scientific proof of this argument.

socialist politics whose horizon does not extend beyond the nation-state. Indeed, identifying the contemporary lacunae of socialist nationalisms – 'socialism (or social democracy) in one country' – constitutes one of the dominant signatures of Anderson's conception of the nexus between socialism and national identity. 'The politics of a rational Left', he has argued, 'needs to be international in a new and more radical way today: global in its conclusions'.[257] In short, socialism must track the planetary compass of capital. 'The future belongs to the set of forces that are overtaking the nation-state. So far, they have been captured or driven by capital – as in the past fifty years, internationalism has changed sides. So long as the Left fails to win back the initiative here, the current system will be secure'.[258] In circumstances where the 'reconstruction of the globe in the American image, *sans phrase*' was a reality,[259] effective resistance to capital's hegemony would have to assume a cosmopolitan shape. 'The arrogance of the "international community" and its rights of intervention across the globe are not a series of arbitrary events or disconnected episodes. They compose a system, which needs to be fought with a coherence not less than its own'.[260] Not only would socialism yield a strategy for social transformation that was global in intent. According to Anderson, it would also have to quit the recurring campaign to uncover a social agent for capitalist transformation outside the circuit of capital. 'Only in the evolution of this order', Anderson argued, 'could lie the secrets of another one'.[261]

Among Anderson's first contributions to *New Left Review* in the early 1960s was an article, co-authored with the journal's then editor, Stuart Hall, on European integration and its consequences for socialism in Britain. Anderson revisited the process of European supra-nationalism in the early 1990s, under the impetus of the Maastricht treaty, once again with an eye to potential repercussions and opportunities for an anti-capitalist politics. Although primarily intended to grease the wheels of capitalist globalisation, and perhaps even, paradoxically, to extend the life history of the classical nation-state, European integration, Anderson argued, nonetheless revealed the panorama of an alternative future disobedient to capitalism.[262] Indeed, so revolutionary were the potential consequences of European integration, Anderson suggested, that they posed 'the question of whether in practice it might unleash the contrary logic'.[263] 'Europe', Anderson

257. Anderson 1992b, p. 353. Note also the comments in Anderson 2004a, p. 77. This general position – what might be called socialist cosmopolitanism at the level of strategy – is supported in Harvey 2000, p. 33.
258. Anderson 1992b, p. 367. See Meiksins Wood 2003, pp. 10–25, for an alternative view from the Left.
259. Anderson 2002, p. 24.
260. Anderson 2003, p. 30. See also Anderson 1998, pp. 117–8.
261. Anderson 2000, p. 17.
262. See, in particular, Anderson 1992a.
263. Anderson 1992a, p. 131.

speculated, might turn the world upside-down. Grasping Europe's contrary logic, socialists, Anderson recommended, should not oppose integration, as sections of the New Left had in the past. Rather, their task was 'to press towards the completion of a genuine federal state in the community with a sovereign authority over its constituent parts',[264] the reinstatement of social democracy 'at a supranational level'.[265]

Such notes have assumed a minor key in Anderson's more recent reflections on Europe.[266] Prominent, here, has been the characterisation of Europe as 'oligarchic', a 'counting-house' for international capital and as co-extensive with America's global interests. In short, 'social Europe' and 'democratic Europe' have been sacrificed to 'market Europe'. Anderson now scoffed at those who believed that there was any correspondence between the vision of Monnet or Delors and the reality of Sarkozy and Merkel. Europe's boosters – Habermas, Grass, Rifkin and Judt – were fairly deluded. The European Parliament, in Anderson's judgment, was 'a Merovingian legislature', unresponsive to popular pressure, resembling more the world of secret diplomacy rather than parliamentary democracy. Europe's social record had been no better. Indeed, hope, however slim, for a European social democracy had devolved into the actuality of the 'nightwatchman state', Brussels accepting widespread unemployment and gross social inequality now greater than in the United States. Matching this, in the region of international affairs, Europe had been reduced to a cipher of Washington, despite European politicians' breast-beating over Iraq. No alternative logic was in sight.

That judgment now stands for the globe. If there is one stance that Anderson has embodied at the beginning of the new century, it is one of 'uncompromising realism' – sober assessment of the extent of socialism's defeat and recognition of the Everest that must be climbed if that defeat is to be reversed.[267] 'The case against capitalism', Anderson argued, 'is strongest on the plane where the reach of socialism is weakest – at the level of the world system as a whole'.[268] Rather than preparing the field for its gravedigger, capitalism, at the millennium, was in historic good health, busy constructing a world-system least hospitable to socialism. 'The new reality', Anderson suggested at New Left Review's rebirth in 2000, 'is a massive asymmetry between the international mobility and organisation of capital, and the dispersal and fragmentation of labour that has no historical precedent. The globalisation of capitalism has not drawn the resistances to it

---

264. Anderson 1992b, pp. 364–5.
265. Anderson 1992b, p. 365. See Bonefield 2002, pp. 117–44, for an alternative account of European integration from a Marxist perspective.
266. See now the collection of essays in Anderson 2009.
267. Anderson 2000, p. 14.
268. Anderson 1992b, p. 366.

together, but scattered and outflanked them'.[269] The aggrandisement of identity politics was a reflection of these developments, leaving the field of universalism clear for capital. Socialism, whether manifest as social democracy or communism, whether understood as the reality of Monnet's European dream or as entryway of colonial peoples to history, was dead. 'No collective agency able to match the power of capital is yet on the horizon'.[270]

In the 'Foreword' to *English Questions*, Anderson, recalling the initial theoretical inspiration for the Anderson-Nairn theses, measured that 'Gramsci's strength of mind was to bring moral resistance and political innovation together'.[271] Judged by this criteria – 'moral resistance' and 'political innovation' – Anderson's thought since 1989 has been lopsided. On the question of 'moral resistance' to the forces of capital and national particularism, Anderson has remained steadfast to principles of socialist internationalism in circumstances uniquely weighed against any such commitment. Argument against war in Afghanistan and Iraq, illumination of the fate of Palestine, corrosive accounts of the banalities of democratic politics in Germany, Italy and Turkey, acerbic updates on the immoralities of power in the United States and punctual reminders of the growing disparity in material wealth within and across societies – all this has been in line with a socialist internationalism whose first principle has been the rejection of national identity and ethnicity as brakes on the achievement of human emancipation.[272] He has, in short, been a 'stubborn defender' of the 'causes of rationality and internationalism'.[273] However, alongside this intellectual practice has stood a telescopic assessment of the instantiation of socialism whose end-point has been a 'nightmare Marxism' – the view that socialism is impossible. This *has* had intellectual benefits. However, on balance, Anderson's moral resistance to capital's hegemony has not been matched by any sense of political innovation. No-one could dispute the historical nature of socialism's defeat. But having done so – what then? Anderson has been good at registering defeat, less good at imagining ways in which socialist internationalism could go on beyond it.

VIII

Tom Nairn's deliberately iconoclastic animus toward internationalists and internationalism is well known. In *Faces of Nationalism* – a book Anderson has often

---

269. Anderson 2000, p. 14.
270. Anderson 2000, p. 16. See Anderson 1998, p. 66, for an earlier instance of this argument.
271. Anderson 1992a p. 11.
272. Anderson 1992b, p. 353; Anderson 2001, pp. 5–22; Anderson 2001, pp. 5–30; Anderson 2003, pp. 5–30.
273. See E.P. Thompson 1991.

recommended, most recently, as one of the two or three most significant 'read-ings of the times'[274] – Nairn equates internationalism with the class-prejudice of metropolitan intellectual elites, those thinkers and activists who do not live in 'backyards', 'who convince themselves that the truth can be imported in con-tainers for home application, and . . . who end up substituting the "international struggle" for doing anything next door'.[275] Nairn claims this internationalist is familiar to him:

> Who does not know the internationalist sectarian, sternly weighing distant triumphs of the Movement against the humiliations of home? His national proletariat is a permanent disappointment and reproach. Unable to dismiss it, he is compelled nonetheless to make the situation more palatable by an exag-geration of the distant view. The Revolution is always in better form some-where else. Remote peasant peoples are doing more for the Emancipation of the Human Being than the (so-called) 'advanced' workers. Not many take this road to its logical conclusion: national nihilism at home and the romantici-sation of everywhere else (roughly in proportion to increasing psychological distance).[276]

The intended target of Nairn's animus, here, was undoubtedly his earlier socialist internationalist self. But might the criticism also apply to Anderson?

Descended from the Anglo-Irish elite, educated at public school and Oxford, versed in at least nine European languages, employed at University of Califor-nia, with international intellectual contacts that few could match, Anderson is undoubtedly a card-carrying member of the Anglo-American metropolitan elite in a way that Thompson, whose contacts were equally widespread, was not. Anderson, too, had once imagined that the truth – in the form of Western Marxism – could be imported almost without mediation into English intellectual culture as a means of effecting its 'internationalization'. He had also remained mostly distant from British political struggles, a constant critic of the English working class's revolutionary socialist credentials, believing that Revolution was being better served in Cuba, Vietnam or Portugal than in Battersea, Glasgow or Halifax. National nihilism was precisely the charge of Isaac Deutscher in response to 'Origins of the Present Crisis',[277] and if by the early 1980s Anderson had left behind the concrete romanticisms of his youth (Castro, Mao, Guevara and Debray), he had replaced them with an invented revolutionary tradition descended from Trotsky that had the barest relation to concrete Trotskyism.

---

274. Anderson 2007, pp. 31–6.
275. Nairn 1997, p. 32.
276. Nairn 1997, p. 36.
277. See Anderson 1992a, pp. 4–5 for Deutscher's judgment.

Anderson might well be the target in Nairn's sight, here, but although half right, as the *final* word on Anderson's internationalism it is wholly wrong.

Even in Nairn's most nationalist of tempers, he has been prepared to admit that there are other, more positive, aspects to internationalism. Internationalism, he suggested, 'can simply be a way of taking other peoples and their experiences seriously', involving 'a systematic outward-looking and inquiring attitude, an imaginative search into the meaning of other experiences',[278] which is the very basis of any adequate account of one's own culture: 'People can only comprehend their backyards properly through some degree of comparison and intercultural perspective'.[279] These aspects of internationalism have been preeminent in Anderson's contributions to New Left political thought. Sweden was the subject of his first contribution to the Hall-led *New Left Review*, while Angola was the focus of three essays that appeared in the earliest years of Anderson's editorship of the New Left journal. Since the mid-1960s, the number of 'other' cultures which have attracted Anderson's attention has grown exponentially. Russia, Turkey, Germany, Italy, Korea, Taiwan and Cyprus are just among the more recent examples of Anderson's long-standing commitment to the education of internationalist desire.[280] When he returned as editor of *New Left Review* at the turn of the new century, it was precisely a concern with other cultures that most exercised his vision for a future journal of the New Left, an appropriate stance, he considered, for a 'cosmopolitan' review which placed itself within the framework of capitalist globalisation.[281] Internationalism, of the sort practiced by Anderson, has had other benefits. Among those benefits might be counted an aversion to imperialism and chauvinism of any sort, a strongly felt and imagined regard for those who have been able to simultaneously transcend their own national contexts, but remain committed to ways of thinking which transform that context in socialist directions, and a strength of intellectual vision practiced on the long-distance view. But the last among these benefits has not come without its cost, particularly with regard to the national question.

In order to say anything at all, Stuart Hall has suggested, 'you have to position yourself *somewhere*'.[282] This, as Nairn has reminded us, is as true of internationalists as it is of nationalists.[283] Where is the 'somewhere' from which Anderson has written? 'Roots', as Darko Suvin has argued, 'can be sought in a projected better

---

278. Nairn 1997, p. 32.
279. Ibid.
280. See Anderson 2004; Anderson 2007; Anderson 2008; Anderson 2008; Anderson 2008; Anderson 2009; Anderson 2009; and Anderson 2009.
281. Anderson 2000, p. 24.
282. Hall 1996, p. 347.
283. Nairn 1996, p. 268.

world, one worked towards by applying the tools of the intellectual profession'.[284]
Here, we might find Perry Anderson's 'country'. His homeland has been consistently imagined as a future post-capitalist society free of class, nation and
ethnicity. Anderson has imagined loyalty to this homeland in exacting terms.
It has involved, for the most part, dismissal of other socialisms that have not
met its standards – more 'class against class' than 'popular front'. It has most
often involved a studied distance from practical politics – more Trotsky in exile
than Trotsky in Petersburg. It has involved unsentimental valuations of ideas and
cultures – more Kant than Herder. Lately, it has involved refusal of consolation
and acceptance of its fate as vanquished – more Roman Empire than British
Commonwealth. It has refused to settle. In the absence of global socialism, like
Anderson himself, it is a politics out of place.

284. Sukin 2005, p. 120.

Chapter Seven
Tom Nairn on Hating Britain Properly

I

Tom Nairn is a great hater. Though he has demonstrated little regard for the British working class and its institutions, and even less for the British middle-class and theirs, the prime object of his hate has been Britain, something he believes championed by both. Thus, Nairn proves that identity is more a function of what we are against rather than what we are for. In his case, hatred of Britain has been the only constant in what postmodernists have informed us is a contingent and never-ending project of identification. More so than his early association with socialist internationalism or his later, more enduring, fondness for Scotland, hatred of Britain has constituted the defining feature of his contribution to New Left political thought. Indeed, amid an intellectual career characterised by sometimes-abrupt shifts, Nairn's enmity toward Britain stands out like a headland resistant to disintegration.[1]

Nairn, though, has always sought to hate Britain properly: because it is a premodern, anti-democratic and imperial state resistant to modernisation whose obdurate presence has involved the suppression of ethnicity. But the wellsprings of his hatred have, nonetheless, changed over time. The reversals in his reasoning will constitute the subject of what follows. After a brief exploration of Nairn's 'identity problems', the remaining sections of the

---

1. For a compressed overview of what he has called his 'embarrassingly long trail of "identity decisions"' – including Italy, France, the Netherlands, Scotland, Ireland and Australia – see Nairn 2004a, p. 129, n. 10.

chapter will consider Nairn's contributions to New Left political thought from the angle of the nexus between socialism and national identity. The first of these sections will interrogate the Nairn-Anderson theses and Nairn's consequent socialist internationalism, manifest most clearly in *The Left against Europe?*. *The Break-Up of Britain: Crisis and Neo-Nationalism*, and the shifts signalled in that book, will provide the focus of the chapter's next section. Here, the touchstone will be as much Nairn's attempt to marry nationalism and socialism as his continuing, if deepening, distaste for the British state. The last of these sections will provide an analysis of Nairn's recent interventions into discussions of national identity. The chapter will conclude with a brief assessment of Nairn's contribution to New Left thought in relation to the national question via brief comparison with other New Left thinkers' identity-problems.

II

What is Tom Nairn's country? At least initially, Nairn pledged allegiance to a non-country, international socialism. From this extra-territorial perspective, Nairn launched a number of sorties against the British state and its satrapies, including British socialism, and also against various British nationalisms. Indeed, at this time, Nairn defined himself against other New Left thinkers, particularly E.P. Thompson, whose supposed populism Nairn interpreted as a mirror of Britain's outdated national culture. Eventually, however, Nairn repudiated his own rejection of roots and came to view socialist internationalism as a reflection of metropolitan hubris designed to suffocate 'backwaters' like Scotland, the country of Nairn's birth and childhood. His repudiation of socialist internationalism did not involve any substantial revision of his view of Britain. Still primarily constructed against 'old-hat' Britain, Nairn's country became a 'born-again Scotland' – a projected political community based on the resurrection of a historic nation to statehood. Socialism remained an aspect of this community, though subordinate to national liberation. Scotland, if not any sort of socialism, has remained his country, although not in any parochial sense. Indeed, like the late Raymond Williams, Nairn's homeland might be a 'nation', but it is an ordinary nation, his identity constituted by what Williams called 'anti-nationalist nationalism'.[2]

Nairn was born in Kirkcaldy, a small town on the east coast of Scotland, in 1932. A minor centre of industrial production, initially floorcloth, later coal-mining and printing, Kirkcaldy was subject to the modernisation common to north Britain in the Victorian period.[3] However Kirkcaldy was not just a centre of heavy industry,

---

2. Williams 2003, p. 24.
3. Devine 1999, p. 251.

populated only by what the Victorians Marx and Engels called proletarians and capitalists. It also contained a 'service intelligentsia' or the 'institutional middle class',[4] men like Nairn's father who was a headmaster at Kirkcaldy's local school. Despite being numerically dwarfed by the working class, it was this 'culturally dominant stratum', according to Willie Thompson, who acted as the 'transmitter of [Scotland's] peculiar national traits'.[5] Like most sons of this class – E.P. Thompson came from a similar background – Nairn was destined for neither factory nor pits. Social advancement through education was his sociologically decided fate. For Nairn, as for Raymond Williams a decade before, this meant not only university education, but also migration to the metropolis, which in the case of Britain has always included Cambridge and Oxford.

This was a common theme of Scottish intellectual history in the nineteenth and twentieth centuries. Afflicted with what Nairn later called 'a typical form of "provincialization"',[6] and having graduated from Edinburgh University with a Masters degree in 1956, he travelled to Oxford to undertake further study with Iris Murdoch. Shortly after, he won a British Council scholarship that facilitated study in Italy and France, where he became immersed in the unpublished writings of Antonio Gramsci.[7] Returning to Britain at the beginning of the 1960s, Nairn maintained established links with Italian communism, becoming the British correspondent for the Italian Communist Party's newspaper, *l'Unità* while assuming a fellowship at Birmingham University.[8]

Thus, up until the 1960s Nairn's career was typical of the upwardly mobile middle-class of the hinterland, in form if not content. He received a metropolitan education and encountered no national barrier to social advancement – his fate was not that of Creole elites in Latin America whose social being, according to Benedict Anderson, provided the basis for some of the earliest nationalist movements.[9] Nairn, no doubt, felt his distance from the southern English elites who dominated Oxbridge, though his alienation did not take a nationalist turn.[10] Rather, his lived experience of marginality – he later referred to it as the

---

4. W. Thompson 1992, p. 308.
5. W. Thompson 1992, p. 308. Nairn would later provide his own characterisation of this social stratum's social consciousness: 'evil mélange of decrepit Presbyterianism and imperialist thuggery'. For him, the Scottish middle class was discernible by virtue of its 'heavy, gritty stylelessness', its deafness to 'allusion and the subtler sorts of humour', and by its 'exasperating pedantry and solemn formalism'. See Nairn 1968a, p. 15. On the role of intellectuals in nationalist movements, see Hobsbawm 1962, pp. 133–5.
6. Nairn 1977, p. 125.
7. Ozkirimli 2000, p. 87.
8. W. Thompson 1992, pp. 308–10.
9. See B. Anderson 2006, pp. 47–66.
10. See Nairn 1977, p. 266, for an example of Nairn's invective against the English establishment.

'shame of inexistence'[11] – was sublimated in a cosmopolitan milieu of theory and politics.[12] Like many other young intellectuals from the periphery of European development at that time, Nairn found a home with other rootless individuals whose attachment was to socialist revolution rather than to any country. As a reflection of this, Nairn became involved, alongside Perry Anderson and Robin Blackburn, in the editorship of *New Left Review*, and with the movement known as the 'second' New Left.[13]

The New Left in Britain was distinguished by its thoroughgoing internationalism. This outward-looking impulse was maintained following the transition to a 'new' *New Left Review* from 1962 to 1964, a 'usurpation' that signalled, no matter how incompletely, the genesis of a 'second' New Left. The 'second' New Left announced a plague on British socialism, particularly the socialism of the original New Left, and turned *New Left Review*'s focus toward two very different traditions of Marxism: the theoretical Marxism of continental Europe,[14] and the 'Third World' Marxism of Latin America, Africa and Asia. The editors' commitment to the free trade in ideas in one sense echoed the internationalism of the 'first' New Left – after all, it had been no less concerned than its successor with global developments in socialist theory or with national liberation movements in the Third World.[15] But the *New Left Review* captained by Anderson and Nairn swapped the 'first' New Left's socialist humanism for a supposedly more rigorous continental Marxism. Put another way, where the 'first' *New Left Review* favoured the poetry of Adam Wazyk and the internationalism of the early Sartre, the second New Left favoured the structuralism of Louis Althusser and the 'Third Worldism' of Fanon's *The Wretched of the Earth*.

Since a review of Antonio Gramsci's translated work had appeared in *New Reasoner*, as well as translations of a number of his prison letters – he, too, might be considered another link connecting the two New Lefts.[16] Here, Nairn was crucial, since he possessed greater familiarity with the work of the Sardinian Marxist than almost anyone in Britain in the early 1960s. However, it was the Nairn-Anderson theses that drove a wedge through the New Left, and interpretation of the Sardinian's theoretical insights provided one point of conflict between Thompson and the editors of *New Left Review*. Indeed, it was Nairn who first set out those ideas that became collectively known as the Nairn-Anderson theses

---

11. Nairn 2000, p. 103.

12. See Calhoun 1997, p. 109, on the cosmopolitanism of 'colonials' in the metropolis.

13. The 'second' New Left is building up an impressive historiography, including Elliott 1997.

14. For a collection expressive of this influence, see *New Left Review*, ed., 1978.

15. See Palmer 2002, pp. 187–216, for the prehistory of this tendency in the 'first' New Left.

16. Hill 1958, pp. 107–13; Gramsci 1959, pp. 141–4; Gramsci 1959, pp. 123–7.

in an article that appeared in the Italian Communist Party's theoretical journal, *Il Contemporaneo*, in 1964.[17]

The 'second' New Left's internationalist impulse found expression in support for two political movements that were gathering strength throughout the 1960s – anti-colonial nationalisms and student-rebellion. Nairn's relation to the latter was clearer than to the former, despite his later interest in nationalism. Both, though, were 'foreign' to classical Marxist politics: anti-colonial nationalism because its social base was peasant, student rebellion because its social base was predominantly middle-class. But Marxists had long been used to accommodating social-classes other than the proletariat into their political imaginary. This was particularly necessary given the European, and above all the British, working class's supposed integration into both capitalist economics and national, if not nationalist, politics – the key around which Nairn's analysis of British labourism turned. Nairn was certainly not immune to the general Western Marxist search for the promise of Utopia in the Mountains of the Moon and Paris's Latin Quarter.[18] Indeed, as the reverberations of imperialism politicised another generation of New Left thinkers and activists, Nairn imagined the beginning of a new global epoch of revolutionary history. 'May 1968', according to him, 'was the precursor of the first revolution in history which can be right'.[19]

Nairn's concern with student-insurrection in Paris, however, did not involve the neglect of his own hinterland; the constant danger, he was later to complain, of internationalist impulses.[20] In fact, Nairn would explicitly link student revolt in Paris with the emergence of nationalist furies in Scotland:

> I for one am enough of a nationalist, and have enough faith in the students and young workers of Glasgow and Edinburgh to believe that these forces [for revolutionary change] are also present in them. I will not admit that the great dreams of May 1968 are foreign to us, that the great words on the Sorbonne walls would not be home on the walls of Aberdeen or St. Andrews, or that Liniwood and Dundee could not be Flins and Nantes. Nor will I admit that, faced with a choice between the Mouvement du 22 Mars and Mrs. Ewing, we owe it to 'Scotland' to choose the latter.[21]

17. Foragcs 1985, p. 75.
18. See Stedman Jones 1969, p. 25, for the conjunction of student-revolt and national liberation. Willie Thompson's suggestion that 'Nairn did not participate in these ecstasies (student rebellion)' is questionable. See W. Thompson 1992, p. 312, for Thompson's view.
19. Nairn and Quattrocchi 1968, p. 153.
20. Nairn 1997, pp. 300–1.
21. Nairn 1970a, pp. 53–4.

This was a great distance away from Nairn's later Scottish nationalism, when the politics of Mrs. Ewing became his own. Yet, as early as the late 1960s, he was maintaining that nationalist passions in Scotland were a manifestation of a global shift toward decentralisation – a view that mirrored opinion among 'old' New Left figures such as Raymond Williams.

Shortly after being dismissed from Hornsey College of Art (where he had been employed from 1966) over his support for student rebels,[22] Nairn accepted a position with Eqbal Ahmad's Transnational Institute in Amsterdam.[23] Logically enough, his connection with the Institute sparked an interest in the politics of European supra-nationalism. In the 1960s, Britain had twice failed to gain admission to the European Economic Community, frustrated on each occasion by a combination of Gallic obstruction and domestic parochialism.[24] While Nairn was stationed in Amsterdam, Britain again sought entry, this time with the vocal support of its own bourgeoisie. Commensurate with his conception of socialist internationalism, Nairn, as shall be shown at greater depth in the next section, embraced a dialectical understanding of European integration, providing at the same time a characteristically acerbic critique of the British Left's nationalism.

His return to Scotland, however, involved a reassessment of his socialist internationalism. Nairn's homecoming dovetailed with a rise in Scottish nationalism's fortunes.[25] Despite initial setbacks, the Scottish National Party (SNP) had become by 1974 'a real parliamentary force'.[26] Indeed, by the mid-1970s both major all-British parties had accepted some sort of Home Rule or Devolution on Britain's northern periphery as a *fait accompli*. Back in Edinburgh, Nairn established the Scottish International Institute with support from Michael Spens, Neal Ascherson and Peter Chiene. Based on Nairn's experiences in Amsterdam, the Scottish International Institute was a research organisation that sought to place the rise of nationalist fervour in Scotland within the context of international developments, something characteristic of Nairn's future analyses of nationalism.[27] The Institute was designed to illuminate Scotland's Enlightenment heritage, and to undermine the majority sector of the nationalist electorate's obsession with what Nairn derisively called 'tartanry'.[28]

Nairn's rejection of internationalism did not immediately involve a revision of his socialism. Nairn's socialism did, however, become nationalist, embodied in his membership of the Scottish Labour Party (SLP), which was established in

---

22. Nairn 1968b, pp. 3–15.
23. See W. Thompson 1992, p. 313.
24. See Milward 2000, pp. 345–424, for an account.
25. For a brief overview, consider Devine 2000, pp. 574–90.
26. Devine 2000, p. 574.
27. See Nairn 1977, p. 93, for an expression of the Institute's goals.
28. See Nairn 1968a, p. 18.

1976 in the wake of Jim Sellars and John Robertson's breakaway from the Labour Party.[29] A response to the march that the SNP had stolen on working-class politics during the proceeding decade, and an explicit repudiation of the Unionism of the all-British Labour Party, the SLP sought to hitch nationalism's horse to a socialist wagon. According to Willie Thompson, Nairn believed 'that the SLP corresponded to the sort of political force he [Nairn] regarded as necessary to accomplish the model of political change which he had developed theoretically and as potentially combining the strengths of both nationalism and socialism'.[30] However, following the aborted bid for Scottish devolution in 1979, and the eventual decline of the SLP, Nairn would increasingly question the partnership between social transformation and national sentiment.

The 1979 referendum on Scottish home rule resulted in a historic nationalist triumph, at least in some nationalist opinion.[31] Nationalist triumph, however, was soon deflated by Unionist perfidy – an assessment Nairn provided shortly after. The election of Thatcher did nothing to raise the nationalists' post-referendum gloom, particularly as it resulted in a decline in the SNP's vote. An ascending New Right extinguished any immediate prospect of a swift transition to Home Rule in Scotland, to say nothing of independence. With a hegemonic Thatcherism having obliterated any immediate expectation of Scottish self-determination, Nairn soon after had another foundation for his politics taken from under his feet. In the early 1980s, he resigned from the editorial board of *New Left Review* following a difference of opinion with Anderson and Blackburn over questions of procedure and politics.[32] His drift from the main political interests of the journal over the preceding decade had been obvious enough, in any case. Although

---

29. W. Thompson 1992, p. 317; Devine 2006, p. 586.

30. W. Thompson 1992, p. 317. See Nairn 1981b, pp. 365–404, for his own assessment of this politics.

31. See Finlay 2004, pp. 332–41, for an account of the 1979 referendum.

32. Rather ungenerously, in a later interview with Willie Thompson, Nairn claimed that 'it is by no means accidental that so many of the dominant figures on the Review originate in the traditional ruling class and possess as a result the self-confidence and effortless superiority derived from that background' (the quote is a précis of Nairn's words by Thompson). Nairn also maintained, according to Thompson, that the dispute that led to him severing ties with the journal could be described 'as a revolt of the middle class against the ruling class ending, as usual, with the former defeated'. See Thompson, 'Tom Nairn and the Crisis of the British State', p. 320. According to Neil Davidson, the dispute was over 'the question of whether the decline of Stalinism, both as state power in the East and working-class organization in the West, could herald the revival of a genuine revolutionary movement. Anderson and the editor, Robin Blackburn, were at this stage still committed . . . to a perspective which saw such a development as being possible. Nairn sided with the faction which held that it was not, and after they lost the fight, he resigned in solidarity with them'. See Davidson, 'Tom Nairn: In Perspective'. Like much else to do with *NLR*, this split is shrouded in mystery. But see the accounts in Elliott 1998, pp. 183–91; D. Thompson 2003, pp. 123–6.

without any institutional medium for the politics that had sustained his work over the proceeding two decades, the Union's preservation ensured an outlet for his nationalist fury. Far from a 'dreamland', a future independent Scotland was now his homeland, something he believed inevitable thanks to Ernest Gellner's *Nation and Nationalism*.

If anything, Nairn's hatred of Britain intensified during the 1980s.[33] *The Enchanted Glass* confirmed not just his hatred of Britain and British national identity, but also his long-held republicanism and his commitment to separatist nationalism. However, in this polemic against King & Country there was much less evidence of the socialism which had initially fired his political imagination. His republican-nationalist politics was given partial shape by his close connection with Charter 88.[34] Established on the tercentenary of the Glorious Revolution, Charter 88 constituted a broad church whose aim was the constitutional reform of Britain's polity.[35] Its principal objectives matched well Nairn's decades-long condemnation of the British state. The Charter's goals of a written constitution, a bill of rights, regional parliaments and the abolition of the House of Lords sought to finish Britain's original bourgeois revolution – the very modernising project that had animated the Nairn-Anderson theses in the early 1960s.

Events in Scotland, however, were soon outrunning Charter demands. In the late 1980s the nationalist beast awoke from its Thatcherite slumber to claim a famous electoral victory in formerly socialist Glasgow. Nationalism's fortunes rose even higher on the continent, ethnicity's revival seeming to spell the final doom of the now shop-soiled dreams of socialist internationalism.[36] Nairn was on hand to celebrate these nationalist triumphs. *Faces of Nationalism* cheered the course of events against the pessimism of metropolitan doomsayers who, Nairn argued, could not see the democratic prospect for the fog of ethnic atavism. The book, of course, also included a now-standard lament for Britain's backwardness (once in relation to France, now in relation to Andorra). In a polity that Nairn claimed was unchanged since William of Orange, nationalities remained trapped beneath a premodern political roof. Despite an overwhelming endorsement of Scottish independence in the late 1990s, and the establishment of a Scottish parliament, Nairn, now back teaching in Edinburgh, remained suspicious of the course of events in Ukania (Nairn's derogatory title for the UK, borrowed from Robert Musil). He found little joy in New Labour's plans for devolution, remark-

---

33. Nairn 1994.
34. See Howe 2009, pp. 552–67, for Charter 88. Charter 88 included a number of figures who had been associated with *New Left Review*, including, in addition to Barnett, Fred Halliday and Mike Rustin.
35. See Nairn 2001, p. 68. For an earlier view, consider Nairn 1979, pp. 43–69.
36. See Gellner 1991, pp. 127–34, on 1989 and nationalism.

able, according to him, only as evidence of the latest means to keep the old ship Britain safe from modernity.

Nairn has always worn his identity-problems on his sleeve.[37] These identity-problems have been various, but they have always been defined in relation to Britain and have always had their wellsprings in the 'Scottish question', the failure of Scotland, despite being a 'nation', to develop an adequate nationalism capable of challenging the British state. In different ways the Scottish question, sometimes self-reflexively, has informed all of his theoretical and political writings, from 'The Nature of the Labour Party' to *Global Matrix*. Perhaps because of this he has turned out to be his most fierce critic. The socialist internationalism of the young Tom Nairn found its most effective interlocutor in the writings of the late Tom Nairn. The most complete critique of *The Break-up of Britain* is perhaps *Faces of Nationalism*, though *Faces of Nationalism* can be read with value through the lens of *The Left against Europe?* as well. But Nairn's work has had other readers too, many from within the New Left. It is to these encounters that the remaining sections of this chapter will turn.

III

Nairn made his *entrée* into New Left political thought through contributions to the Nairn-Anderson theses.[38] Those theses were an attempt to understand why the British working class, an overwhelming numerical majority, since Victorian times, had failed to 'overthrow capital and fashion the new society that material conditions long ago made possible'.[39] Nairn, who provided the original impetus for the Nairn-Anderson theses, found an explanation in England's 'incomplete' bourgeois revolution. Instead of realising their sociological destiny – nation-state, democracy and republic – Britain's bourgeoisie had submitted to a social alliance with the aristocracy and accepted its characteristic forms of political power – Crown, unwritten Constitution and House of Lords.[40] Here, Nairn's first reasons for hating Britain can be found. The British bourgeoisie had abjured 'liberty, equality, fraternity' in favour of the 'shamanism of the British Constitution, an assorted repertoire of (largely false) antiquities, the poisonous remains of the once revolutionary ideology of Puritanism, and the anti-revolutionary invective of Edmund Burke'.[41]

---

37. As Nairn suggests in Nairn 1997, p. 180: 'I have never hidden the fact that my own dilemmas and oddities emanate from those of my country, Scotland'.

38. See Nairn 1964a, pp. 19–25; Nairn 1964b, pp. 43–57; Nairn 1964c, pp. 38–65; Nairn 1964d, pp. 33–62.

39. Nairn 1964c, p. 52.

40. Nairn 1964c, p. 56.

41. Nairn 1964c, p. 47.

The outcome – the paucity of Britain's intellectual traditions – explained the British working class's 'docility',[42] and the 'profound empiricism' of its characteristic industrial and political institutions.[43] After the downfall of Chartism, the working-class, according to Nairn, 'embraced one species of moderate reformism after another', becoming 'a consciously subordinate part of bourgeois society', and remaining 'wedded to the narrowest and greyest of bourgeois ideologies in its principal movements'.[44] The working class's failure to adopt Marxism, signpost of its corporative, anti-hegemonic nature, was not just a result of the bourgeoisie's 'instinctive distrust of reason'. It was also a result of the absence of a 'radical, disaffected intelligentsia', the only social stratum capable of scything through 'the immense, mystifying burden of false and stultifying consciousness imposed on [the working class] by English bourgeois civilization'.[45] The result: Britain's working-class party had become a 'mere trade-union party',[46] and, like the class it represented, was conservative and bereft of theory and hegemonic ambition. 'The history of Labourism', Nairn concluded, 'has demonstrated the inadequate character of indigenous socialist traditions only too well'.[47]

At first glance, there might appear little separating Nairn's view of Labourism from that of other New Left thinkers. Contributors to *Universities and Left Review* and *New Reasoner* had often enough bemoaned the effect of imperialism on working-class politics in Britain, and had repeatedly regretted the reformism of the Labour Party, hardly remarkable in a group of political thinkers who had spent so much time in the CPGB.[48] Nairn's anti-labourist anger certainly foreshadowed some of the animus against Labourism on display in *May Day Manifesto*. Indeed, Nairn's argument showed little sign of the 'continental Marxism' that supposedly typified the Nairn-Anderson theses, preferring instead to draw upon the work of G.D.H. Cole, Ralph Miliband and Raymond Williams. However, no one could mistake 'The Nature of the Labour Party' or Nairn's critique of E.P. Thompson's *The Making of the English Working Class* for contributions to the original impetus of the New Left. Williams had hymned trade-unionism and the Labour Party as the key contributions of the working class to culture; Nairn supposed them diseased fragments of bourgeois unreason. Thompson celebrated the revolutionary self-agency of working-class experience; Nairn characterised the English working class as docile and the

---

42. Nairn 1964c, p. 44.
43. Ibid.
44. Ibid.
45. Nairn 1964c, p. 57.
46. Nairn 1964a, p. 53.
47. Nairn 1964a, p. 56.
48. Including, most obviously, Miliband 1961.

fractured mirror of bourgeois 'structures of feeling'. It was to the width of this gap that Thompson responded in 'The Peculiarities of the English'.

The ground of Thompson's critique was his view that, alongside all the bad things, from imperialism to the reformism of the Labour Party, 'there are at the same time certain strengths and humane traditions in British life which Other Countries, including those whose airports are superb, whose Marxism is mature, and whose salesmanship is high powered, do not always display'.[49] Thompson countered that British socialists and the British working class had been far less parochial and provincial than Nairn supposed. In particular, Thompson pointed to a vigorous tradition of internationalism on the British Left. In the unpublished 'Where are we Now?', Thompson suggested that, 'So far from being peculiarly insular, the British labour-movement has always been fairly sensitive to international pressures'.[50] Indeed, he went on, 'far from our left having no internationalist traditions, I would say that next to "Spain" and anti-fascism itself, there was no issue which so seized the imagination and claimed the attention of British socialists as India'.[51] He also directed Nairn's attention to the busy traffic between Marxist ideas and the British working class, from the late nineteenth century onwards. 'So far from living in an island culture blissfully unaware of Marxism', he claimed, 'our culture is sensitized to Marxist concepts in a hundred ways'.[52] The nexus between Marxism and British politics, Thompson argued, went back to the 1880s, although he recognised both that Marxism did not become a 'significant force' until the 1920s, and that its force was partly registered, negatively, in the polemics of reaction.[53] Still, it had been a force, and this in England *and* Scotland. It is perhaps ironic, that it was the supposedly parochial Englishman who pointed out to the Scotsman the value of Scottish intellectual traditions, including Marxist ones.[54]

Thompson's search for a common thread in Nairn's evasions fixed on what he called a '*déracinée* element' in Nairn's writings, a conclusion that Nairn would later agree with. In effect, Thompson charged Nairn with purveying an 'abstract internationalism' far removed from the 'effective, active internationalism' evident either in the British Left's past – India, Spain, Korea – or in Campaign for Nuclear Disarmament (CND). Thompson, however, did not see Nairn's deracination as descending from a denial of national identity, as Nairn would later see it. Rather, Thompson compared Nairn to rootless communists in the 1930s, and

---

49. E.P. Thompson 1978, p. 266.
50. E.P. Thompson, 'Where Are We Now?', Unpublished Memo, 1962, DJS/109, University of Hull Archives, University of Hull.
51. Ibid.
52. Ibid.
53. E.P. Thompson 1978, pp. 286–7.
54. E.P. Thompson 1978, p. 269.

saw Nairn's deracination as an outcome of his remove from Britain's tradition of socialist internationalism. This remove, Thompson charged, led to a 'lack of any real sense of the possibilities and growing-points within the British scene'.[55] In effect, what Nairn was doing, Thompson argued, was 'impoverishing the creative impulse of the Marxist tradition';[56] a tradition, which, at its best, had always been rooted in *particular* places and had submitted its 'theory' to the control of empirical fact.

No more were these infelicities in evidence, Thompson believed, than in Nairn's interpretation of mid-Victorian working-class reformism. Thompson argued that it was in this period that 'the workers... proceeded to warren [capitalist society] from end to end'.[57] The result, he pointed out, was the 'characteristic class institutions of the labour movement' – those institutions that Williams counted among the highest achievements of working-class culture. If a defensive reformism still characterised those institutions, this was less because of some inherent corporatism than a result of the majority labour-movement's active rejection of communism, whose influence on the development of British labour-history Nairn had completely overlooked. Here, Thompson supposed, could be found the source of British socialism's crisis: the Cold War.

Though illuminating, Thompson's response could be blinding as well. He took umbrage at the 'hectoring tone of the Marxist Kirk Elder' and compared Nairn to *déracinée* elements in the CPGB in the 1930s.[58] This was not only misjudged. It also allowed Thompson's opponents to score a free goal, since they could paint him as the parochial defender of national traditions. Nairn continued to hunt the romantic-nationalist fox over the succeeding years, and he was encouraged to do so by some of the polemical exaggerations of 'The Peculiarities of the English' – exaggerations whose absence would have done no harm to Thompson's argument. For example, there was no need for Thompson to equate England with the 'empirical idiom' since Bloch and Marx his own examples, had also employed this idiom; while Paine, as Thompson would demonstrate in *The Making of English Working Class*, appeared no less *déracinée*, no less in thrall to abstraction, in the 1790s, than Anderson or Nairn did in the 1960s. Again, Thompson's exaggerations occluded his valid point that contrary to Nairn (and Anderson), there are no 'hermetic divisions between national cultures'.[59] As he made gestures of Englishry, Thompson's patient argument about the importance of 'the Protestant

---

55. E.P. Thompson, 'Where Are We Now?', Unpublished Memo, 1962, DJS/109, University of Hull Archives, University of Hull.
56. Ibid.
57. E.P. Thompson 1978, p. 281.
58. E.P. Thompson 1978, p. 275.
59. E.P. Thompson 1978, p. 267.

and bourgeois-democratic inheritance',[60] the tradition of political economy and natural science, and his defence of a methodology distinguished by a dialectic between theory and 'the facts', though not beyond criticism, could be ignored. National identity had something to do with the exaggerations and occlusions on both sides. In the case of Thompson, it was the 'Englishness' that was shorthand for his anti-Stalinism; in the case of Nairn, it was his hatred of all things British.

There was one further, more serious, shortcoming of Thompson's response. He was right to point to a strong tradition of internationalism in Britain, one indeed he had lived. There was also value in his argument that a valid internationalism constituted a dialogue between peoples rather than the submission of one people to the concerns of another, and to give the traffic between British socialism and Indian independence as a prime example of that internationalism at work. And Thompson was right to argue for the complexity of the history of decolonisation and the role that the labour-movement had played in simply 'making it unfeasible to fight a colonial war upon the sub-continent'.[61] But his justified, if heavily qualified, defence of the Left's internationalism became injurious when he went so far as to suggest that 'By and large, the emergence of those areas under Anglo-Saxon domination has been less marked with the extreme bitterness, torture and dehumanisation seen in Algeria or Angola'.[62] To believe as much was to imagine that Britain played no role in the outcome of Partition in India, to overlook the torture and inhumanity of Britain's role in Kenya, and to fail to imagine the possibility of Rhodesia, to say nothing of British imperialism's part in creating the conditions that led to the establishment of apartheid in South Africa. If Britain's role in decolonisation was an example of the 'humane traditions' which supposedly constituted Britain's true nature, then Nairn was right to suggest that there was not much to be said for Britain.

And, after all, Nairn *did* have a point – a point perhaps that could only be made by someone 'outside' the compass of those traditions under examination. It was not hard, in the 1950s and early 1960s, to make Nairn's sort of argument about Britain, and especially about the British Labour Party. Britain's intellectual well did seem dry, reflected not just in an uncharacteristic insularity, about which historians have now written numerous books, but also within dominant trends in political and social thought and history. Traditional*ism* had become an aspect of Britain's national culture, regenerated now more in the service of American imperialism rather than the British kind. The distance between the 1930s and the 1950s, especially in relation to what Thompson called a 'creative

---

60. Ibid.
61. E.P. Thompson, 'Where Are We Now?', Unpublished Memo, 1962, DJS/109, University of Hull Archives, University of Hull.
62. Ibid.

Marxism', was indeed great. Thompson himself pointed to the fracture in socialist internationalism in the 1950s, the breakdown of a tradition that had been
sustained through Europe's darkest years. The Labour Party and the trade unions
could be seen as cesspools of bureaucratic conservatism, as well as being among
the few places where socialist ideas might be put into practice. Yet, liberalism
rather than the emancipation of labour was the Labour Party's future, and much
of that future was presaged in Nairn's analysis.

The Left Against Europe?, published first as a special issue of *New Left Review*
(1972), shortly after as a Penguin book (1974), took the Nairn-Anderson theses
on to new, if related ground. In this book, Nairn directed his anti-British animus
toward the nationalist myopia of British socialism, from Labour Party to Marxist
sect, in relation to European integration.[63] The book's touchstone was 'the real
historical relationship between Marxism and nationalism which has characterised European history during the century now enduring'.[64] According to Nairn,
the debate over Europe in the early 1970s had precipitated an overturning of the
relationship between ideology and nation. In short, the Left had swapped class
for nation, while the Right had swapped nation for class. Nairn believed that
the reversal, evident just as clearly in social democracy's response to Europe as
the New Left's, constituted a disaster for British socialism. Rather than comprise
a nationalist vanguard defending the integrity of British sovereignty, socialists,
he argued, needed to abandon their 'narrow national limits' and embrace European integration as the foundation stone of a (potential) continent-wide socialist
society. Indeed, by endorsing European integration, the British Left, Nairn
believed, would be redeeming the 'most precious inheritance of the European
working-class: the traditions of Marxist internationalism'.[65]

The Left against Europe? reached many of the conclusions about nationalism and the nation-state that *May Day Manifesto* had. For example, Nairn's
view that 'capitalist forces of production long ago outstripped the confines of
nation-states' would not have been out of place in the 'old' New Left manifesto,[66]
while both Nairn and the *May Day Manifesto*'s authors dismissed chauvinism
and imperialism, and called into question the value of working-class nationalism. *The Left against Europe?* also mimed the deliberate vacillations of the New
Left's response to nationalism. But Nairn's book was clearly directed against the
'Euroscepticism' of many New Left thinkers.[67] Thompson fairly straightforwardly

---

63. Nairn 1972, pp. 5–120 and Nairn 1974b. The book contained an 'Introduction', not
included in the original essay, which situated the book within the context of the Nairn-
Anderson theses.
64. Nairn 1972, p. 6. This sentence did not appear in the book.
65. Nairn 1974b, p. 71.
66. Nairn 1974b, p. 152.
67. See, for example, Barratt Brown and Hughes 1961.

interpreted Europe as an anti-socialist 'capitalist club', while Williams pitched his Eurosceptic tent somewhere between acceptance of the Common Market and the 'left-wing nationalism' of the mainstream labour-movement. Nairn believed that Williams and Thompson were both 'national left-wing romantics',[68] and berated each for their 'warm embrace of the national *Gemeinschaft*'.[69] Left-wing nationalism, according to Nairn, was a useless passion at best, a dangerous one at worst, since neither the nation-state nor nationalism would survive the forces of multinational capitalism. British socialists, Nairn believed, should especially avoid association with nationalism because in Britain national sentiment 'was so heavily weighed down by bourgeois triumph'.[70] 'It is so massively conservative', Nairn continued, 'that all opposition to it which stays couched in national terms is doomed from the outset'.[71] In this light, oppositional Englishness was oxymoronic.

This was an unfair characterisation of Williams and Thompson, perhaps even of 'left-wing nationalism'. Both New Left thinkers had shown a commitment to socialist internationalism, Thompson to an internationalism of 'the people' against 'the elite', inspired as much by the 'spirit of Europe' created in 1944 as that evident in Hungary in 1956, Williams to a vision of socialist Europe built on the common interests of socialists from Scandinavia to Sicily. Both argued for an internationalism that opposed the Common Market's capitalist internationalism, what Thompson called 'introverted white bourgeois nationalism'.[72] But, for Nairn, this was precisely the problem. Such internationalism, he argued, was utopian, moralistic, one-sided and removed from the real movement of things. In opposition to this 'abstract' internationalism, an internationalism, he argued, sustained by the fantastic view that capital was no longer a progressive force, *The Left against Europe?* argued for a dialectical view of European integration. The Common Market, Nairn suggested, is 'intended to strengthen the sinews and the world-position of European capitalism', but 'it may *also* strengthen the position and enlarge the real possibilities of the European working classes and European social revolutionaries'.[73] Europe was a means of 'going beyond the nation', and, no matter which forces were driving it, the Common Market promised socialism the opportunity of putting into practice a 'concrete internationalism'.[74]

Nairn would later characterise the 'concrete internationalism' of *The Left against Europe?* as a form of metropolitan imperialism. Writing in 1979, he argued

---

68. Nairn 1974b, p. 111.
69. Nairn 1974b, p. 120.
70. Nairn 1974b, p. 60.
71. Ibid.
72. E.P. Thompson 1980a, p. 86.
73. Nairn 1974b, p. 147.
74. Nairn 1974b, p. 137.

that nationalism not internationalism, certainly not socialist internationalism, was the 'by-product of modern internationality'.[75] Far from being doomed, reactionary and antiquarian, nationalism was 'the process [internationality] itself', 'the necessary, inevitable translation of all those miles of railway line and business machine salesman'.[76] The type of internationalism that he had advocated in *The Left against Europe?*, he now considered wrongheaded, a result of that wayward internationalist belief that your 'national proletariat is a permanent disappointment and reproach' and that the real politics – the real revolution – is going on elsewhere.[77] Internationalism not nationalism, he believed, was the real form of modern false consciousness. Indeed, he now explained internationalism as a defect of personal psychology, a 'defence mechanism' of identity-deniers desperate to repress the truth of their own identity-problems. The distance travelled between 1974 and 1979 can be rendered this way: Whereas in *The Left against Europe?* Nairn could herald 'Marxism's Jewish grandeur' as the frontline opponent of nationalism and imperialism,[78] just five years later he was complaining that it was only 'Jewish intellectuals' who provided any sociological basis for socialist cosmopolitanism (they didn't live in 'backyards'),[79] or what he now discovered was 'thinly-veiled or occasionally full-frontal metropolitan self-interest and aggression'.[80] What remained unchanged was his hatred of Britain.

Thompson and Williams would have provided a different reading of *The Left against Europe?*. In one sense, Williams would eventually agree with Nairn. He would come to see Europe as the most likely terrain of socialist advance, and as both an answer to the 'break-up of Britain' and a response to residual big-state nationalisms. Like Perry Anderson much later, Williams would credit European integration with offering the potential of genuine international self-determination and socialist democracy. Thompson would have counted both *The Left against Europe?* and Nairn's auto-critique of that book as moonshine. Unlike Williams, he never saw much socialist hope in the Europe of Mollett, preferring to establish his internationalism on the ground of anti-war protest (it might be added that Thompson's own version of 'Europeanism' included both capitalist and socialist societies).[81] Like Anderson's most recent analysis of Europe, Thompson always believed that the Europe of European integration was a way of denying democracy and self-government – and also of ignoring much

---

75. Nairn 1997, p. 27.
76. Ibid.
77. Nairn 1997, p. 36.
78. Nairn 1974b, p. 157.
79. Nairn 1997, p. 29.
80. Nairn 1997, p. 42.
81. E.P. Thompson 1980a.

wider associations with Asia, Africa and Latin America.[82] Nairn would consider Thompson's view the *camera obscura* of British imperialism.

Responding to Nairn's claim that he was a 'romantic populist', Thompson defended his own politics as that of 'socialist internationalism'.[83] He did not deny that socialist internationalism had become far removed from the real movement of things, but he did not count this as a reason for turning on it. Far from capitulating to the British *Gemeinschaft*, he suspected that his defence of socialist internationalism had turned him into an 'alien'. Weirdly, he would pre-empt some of Nairn's own criticisms of internationalism. 'Internationalism', Thompson suggested, 'ought not to consist in lying prostrate before the ("Western Marxist") theorist of our choice, or in seeking to imitate their modes of discourse'.[84] He went on to argue, and here again pre-empting Nairn, that this kind of internationalism was a way of '[evacuating] ... the real places of conflict within our intellectual culture, as well as the loss of real political relations with our own people'.[85] This might have stood as a masthead over Nairn's writings from the late 1970s onwards. But Thompson still defended his own brand of socialist internationalism, that kind which consisted in 'listening attentively to an international discourse, but in contributing to it on our own account'.[86]

The Left against Europe? was not Nairn's first encounter with nationalism. Published three years before, 'The Three Dreams of Scottish Nationalism' had attended to the rise of nationalism in Scotland. In effect, Nairn's article grafted the Nairn-Anderson theses onto the peculiar case of Scotland. Scotland's history, Nairn claimed, could be characterised by the continuous dissociation between 'intellectual movements' and 'material realities'.[87] At each important moment of its history – Reformation, Enlightenment, Romanticism – the Scottish head had been removed from material preconditions. The emergence of nationalism in the 1960s, Nairn argued, was another example of this typical Scottish disjuncture between ideas and reality. In such circumstances, nationalism could only be the latest 'abstract, millennial dream' of Scottish history since the material conditions of nationalism's original emergence in world history – either as an escape from feudalism or from imperialism – no longer obtained in north Britain.[88] Consequently, Scottish nationalism was inherently reactionary, even bourgeois, based either on a populist 'complex of ideas' – 'Sporrany, alcoholism, and the

---

82. See E.P. Thompson, 'Where Are We Now?', Unpublished Memo, 1962, DJS/109, University of Hull Archives, University of Hull.
83. See E.P. Thompson 1978, p. iii.
84. E.P. Thompson 1978, p. iv.
85. Ibid.
86. Ibid.
87. Nairn 1968a, pp. 4–5.
88. Nairn 1968a, p. 5.

264 • Chapter Seven

ludicrous appropriation of the remains of Scotland's Celtic fringe' – or, as with the Scottish intelligentsia,[89] a repudiation of 'the trash-image of Scotland' which devolved into a 'complacent narcissism'.[90]

Not only did Nairn attempt to historicise Scottish nationalism and place it within world-history, he also sought to relate it to uneven capitalist development, characteristic manoeuvres of Nairn's later investigations of the national question. He also judged the political implications of separatist nationalism for the British state: 'In the slow, festering decay of British state and society', he wrote, 'they [Welsh and Scottish nationalisms] are the most important forces of disintegration to have appeared yet'.[91] It was for this reason that Nairn could not simply recommend that Scottish socialists reject nationalism, despite nationalism's 'impossible dissociation from the realities of history',[92] and despite its reactionary and bourgeois nature. In fact, despite its dream-like quality, Nairn was clear that nationalism '[prefigured] the dismemberment of the united British society which built up the imperial system itself'.[93] For this reason, Nairn recommended that Scottish socialists build up their own 'revolutionary nationalism' to oppose the nationalism of the SNP.[94] Only a revolutionary nationalism, Nairn concluded, could give Scotland a real identity.

The compass of Nairn's analysis of Scottish nationalism was 'outside' of Scotland. This 'out of country' perspective was characteristic of Nairn's contributions to the Nairn-Anderson theses, and might be described as 'an escape from [his] peculiar destiny, onto the plane of abstract reason'.[95] Where Thompson had seen resources from history that could be used in the present, Nairn saw only a record of proletarian quiescence, burked radicalism and socialist defeat. To be a socialist, Nairn argued, it was imperative to shed the skin of socialism's past, particularly its past association with the national intellectual culture. By arguing this, however, Nairn had arguably shed his own skin. This, at any rate, was Nairn's diagnosis two decades later. 'In my personal case this outward-bound neurosis led to frankly nihilistic excesses about strangling Kirk Ministers and mowing down be-kilted landowners with a Marxist machine gun'.[96] The Nairn-Anderson theses were undertaken from the God's-eye view of what Nairn would later call 'cosmological universalism'. It was, by definition, abstract and anti-nationalist. But it was not without value, despite Nairn's later claims. Nonetheless, following

---

89. Nairn 1968a, p. 9.
90. Ibid.
91. Nairn 1968a, p. 4.
92. Ibid.
93. Ibid.
94. Ibid.
95. Nairn 1968a, p. 7.
96. Nairn 2000, p. 104.

the disappointments of 1968, and the rise of Scottish nationalism, there was a perceptible shift within Nairn's work toward the view that nationalism, at least peripheral nationalisms, represented not just the end of all things British, but a necessary stepping-stone toward socialism. Indeed, from the mid-1970s Nairn would have new reasons, less *déracinée* than nationalist, for hating Britain.

IV

' "National" Marxism has always been a joke in doubtful taste'.[97] This was Nairn's view of the nexus between socialism and national sentiment in *The Left against Europe?*. 'The Three Dreams of Scottish Nationalism', published prior to *The Left against Europe?*, would have added the caveat that some socialist nationalisms are desirable, but only those which promise to be revolutionary, to devolve power and to break up imperial states.[98] British nationalism could not be counted among these, not just because its history was a chronicle of bourgeois conquest, but also because it was paradoxically parochial and imperialist. But Nairn's caveat could not hide his general negative assessment of nationalism, something not even absent from his account of Scottish nationalism. *The Left against Europe?* had described the nation-state as a 'spirit-whore' and nationalism as some sort of Nietzschean Dionysian that 'has run berserk and drunk with blood through the pages of history'.[99] By the time *The Break-Up in Britain* was published in 1977, Nairn had mostly dismissed this rhetoric. With *The Break-Up of Britain*, Nairn was now operating in a different paradigm, one shaped by the work of Ernest Gellner and Miroslav Hroch.[100] In this paradigm, nationalism was considered an inevitable, and inevitably positive product of, modernity, nation-states were considered *the* future, and the 'national experience' the only experience possible, except in those unlucky cases, such as Scotland and Wales, where the experience had been snuffed out by 'the peculiarities of the British'.

One measure of the paradigm shift can be gauged from *The Break-up of Britain*'s assessment of the 'first' New Left's political project. *The Left against Europe?* rebuked the 'first' New Left for its supposed 'cultural nationalism' and populism. *The Break-up of Britain*, however, lauded the very same cultural nationalism as an exemplar of 'socialist culture'. According to Nairn, the 'populist socialism', which had emerged out of the work of E.P. Thompson, Raymond Williams, and others, offered 'a much more concrete hope in the British political future'.[101]

---

97. Nairn 1974b, p. 157.
98. Nairn 1968a, p. 16.
99. Nairn 1974b, pp. 51, 69, 4.
100. See, in particular, Gellner 1964; Hroch 1968.
101. Nairn 1977, p. 304.

In the 'history from below' movement, England, Nairn believed, '[has] at least part of what corresponds to the usual mode of nationalist revival – the attempt to find strength for a better, more democratic future by re-examining (on occasion re-inventing) a mythic past'.[102] This 'left-nationalist popular culture', so recently condemned as self-deluding anti-Europeanist nonsense, Nairn now considered a correlate of Scottish and Welsh nationalism, as the basis for a progressive version of nationalism in England, and as the key to Britain's political future.

Nairn's appreciation for the original New Left must have come as a surprise to the co-author of the Nairn-Anderson theses. However, *Arguments within English Marxism*, published shortly after *The Break-up of Britain*, made no mention of Nairn's argument as apostasy, even going so far as to applaud its generosity.[103] Anderson did revisit the New Left's 'populism' in that book, he affirmed his earlier characterisation of the movement, though he also apologised for his earlier dismissal of the internationalist dimensions of the early New Left.[104] The apology was sincere. However, in reality Anderson's reversal was a means by which his and Nairn's original 'socialist internationalism' could be defended against Thompson's charges in 'The Peculiarities of the English'. He still thought Thompson populist, but he now maintained that this populism was commensurate with a certain type of socialist internationalism.[105] Though *The Break-up of Britain* replicated the hatred of Britain that had inspired the Nairn-Anderson theses, Anderson made no mention of the fact that Nairn now dismissed the socialist internationalism that had originally inspired his and Nairn's anti-British project in the mid-1960s.

Thompson, of course, dismissed Nairn's suggestion that the politics of the original New Left could be described as 'socialist populism'.[106] Raymond Williams had a different take on all this. Against the abstract internationalism of the Nairn-Anderson led *New Left Review*, he argued that if 'populism' meant sticking with 'the people' and trying to shift them in socialist directions then he found no dishonour in the description.[107] Much of the dispute, of course, turned around the definition of that notoriously elusive term 'populism'.[108] For Thompson and Williams, it had always constituted something like a political strategy or stance, designed as a way of entering political debate on the ground, and as shorthand for the rejection of democratic centralism and intellectualist elitism. For Anderson and Nairn, in the early 1960s, it was a word coterminous with nationalism,

---

102. Ibid.
103. Anderson 1980, pp. 140–1.
104. Anderson 1980, p. 141.
105. Anderson 1980, pp. 142–3.
106. E.P. Thompson 1978, pp. iii–iv.
107. Williams 1980e, pp. 241–2.
108. See Canovan 2004 for a recent discussion of 'populism',

and, discovered in the rhetoric of the original New Left, evidence of socialist apostasy. *The Break-up of Britain* saw the New Left's supposed populism in more hopeful terms. Nairn still equated populism with nationalism, but now the equation was deemed salutary. Anderson considered the original confusion a result of political context – specifically that moment of the Second World-War when internationalism and nationalism pulled in the same direction – and suggested that his and Nairn's original dismissal of populism was equally rooted in the contingencies of history – specifically the resurrection of a conservative nationalism in the context of Cold War.[109] He saw no reason for apology in this. What was unmistakable was that he believed that *The Break-up of Britain* closely shadowed Thompson's marriage of nationalism and internationalism, and that he was still willing to defend the original socialist internationalism of the Nairn-Anderson theses against both.[110]

Journeying across nationality-politics in Scotland, Wales, England and Ulster, the wretched state of Britain's polity and the general theory of nationalism, *The Break-up of Britain* was home to Nairn's most distinctive arguments concerning the nexus between socialism and national identity.[111] The book was in many ways an extension of the Nairn-Anderson theses, although it was devoted to explaining how Britain had escaped 'normal nationalist development' rather than the absence of socialist revolution in Britain.[112] Britain – 'the grandfather of the contemporary political world' – was still considered a backward polity,[113] but its backwardness was now expressed in the absence of nationalism – popular sovereignty, democracy and equality.[114] In these terms, there had been 'no second bourgeois revolution' in Britain,[115] no full Gellnerian transition from premodern to industrial society. Instead of 'real nationalism' based on 'the virtuous power of popular protest and action', Britain gave birth to a 'powerful inter-class nationalism', a 'peculiar' nationalism which worked against rule of the people.[116] The absence of a normal nationalism, according to Nairn, went far toward explaining the crisis of British society and economy. The British state was now at an

---

109. Anderson 1980, pp. 142–7.
110. Anderson 1980, p. 156.
111. The book was made up of a series of essays, some of which had appeared previously in *NLR*. *The Break-up of Britain* has been the subject of almost universal praise among nationalism scholars, including in Anderson 2006. See Gellner 1979; Orridge 1981, pp. 1–15; Blaut 1987, pp. 76–100; and Cocks 1998, for other assessments.
112. Nairn 1977, p. 141.
113. Nairn 1977, p. 19.
114. Nairn 1977, p. 30.
115. Nairn 1977, pp. 20–2, 31.
116. Nairn 1977, pp. 42–3.

advanced stage of disintegration, and the form this took, Nairn argued, was not social revolution but nationalist revolt.[117]

Unlike the original Nairn-Anderson theses, then, the foremost antagonist of *The Break-up of Britain* was not the cultural nationalism of British socialism and the 'old' New Left. Rather, Nairn's central interlocutor was 'proletarian internationalism' and a romantic 'anti-imperialist nationalism' – both features of *New Left Review* after 1962. A good deal of *The Break-up of Britain* was directed against socialist internationalists who rejected peripheral nationalisms, like those in Scotland and Wales, as evidence of 'regression'.[118] According to Nairn, 'if one perceives the United Kingdom as an *ancien régime* with no particular title to survival or endless allegiance, then the breakaway movements',[119] would appear less as 'destructive forces' and more as harbingers of 'the most modern, democratic, and decentralizable form of organization that current development permits'.[120] But, in face of the growing evidence of British decrepitude, socialist internationalists, Nairn lamented, continued to pledge allegiance to Britain, in the mistaken view that it represented either a 'viable state' or was a defence against atavistic nationalism.[121] They were wrong, he charged, on both counts. Far from viable, Nairn suggested that Britain was actually pre-modern and archaic, propped up by a nineteenth century economy and a seventeenth century polity, and that Scottish and Welsh nationalisms were more internationalist and progressive than the 'Great-British chauvinism' upheld by conservatism and labourism alike.[122]

The Break-up of Britain did not only challenge the politics of socialist internationalism; it questioned 'the very essence of the Marxist world-view'.[123] According to Nairn, nationalism represented 'Marxism's great historical failure'.[124] The source of this lacuna, he suggested, was philosophical: Marxism's emphasis on class-struggle and its inadequate account of capitalist development. The 'real history', Nairn believed, disproved both.[125] The truth of capitalist development was 'uneven development', that is the 'unforeseeable, antagonistic reality of capitalism's growth'.[126] Consequently, the contradiction at the heart of capitalist development was not conflict between capital and labour – 'two cosmopolitan classes,

---

117. Nairn 1977, pp. 14, 90.
118. Nairn 1977, p. 73.
119. Ibid.
120. Nairn 1977, pp. 73, 77.
121. Nairn 1977, pp. 80–1.
122. Nairn 1977, pp. 77–8.
123. Nairn 1977, p. 88.
124. Nairn 1977, p. 329. A widely-held view, there are nonetheless many who would disagree. See, for example, Forman 1998. See Cocks 1996, pp. 521–6, for the argument that Luxemburg, in particular, should be taken seriously by nationalism scholars. Eric Benner has disputed Nairn's view in relation to scientific socialism's founders in Benner 1995.
125. Nairn 1977, p. 331.
126. Nairn 1977, p. 337.

as it were, locked in the same battle from Birmingham to Shanghai'[127] – but the conflict between 'core-area nationalist' development (or imperialism) and those, on the periphery, who wanted development on their own terms.[128] The result was the unification of humanity 'at the cost of fantastic disequilibria, through near-catastrophic antagonisms and a process of socio-political fragmentation... still far from complete'.[129] In the end, it was 'atavistic urges' and nationality, impelled by uneven development, rather than class-consciousness, Nairn concluded, which was the 'motor of historical change'.[130] 'As a means of mobilization, nationalism was simply incomparably superior to what was contained in a still rudimentary... class consciousness'.[131] Like Williams, Nairn believed that nationalism offered 'something that class consciousness postulated in a narrowly intellectualist mode could never have furnished, a culture which however deplorable was larger, more accessible, and more relevant to mass realities than the rationalism of our Enlightenment inheritance'.[132]

In one sense, *The Break-up of Britain* was preaching to the converted. The 'old' New Left's *May Day Manifesto* had offered support, though guarded, for peripheral nationalisms in Britain – though in its encouragement for Scottish and Welsh nationalism it left unsaid what might happen to the English, as though the English did not have identity-problems. Still, the authors of *May Day Manifesto* were no friends of the British state, and they did acknowledge the democratic and disruptive potential of hinterland nationalism. Indeed, the authors looked on the Welsh and the Scots with some envy, since they, unlike the English, could use national identity to overturn the status quo.[133] *May Day Manifesto*, in addition to acknowledging the reality of 'uneven development', also recognised the Janus-like nature of nationalism, warning that peripheral nationalisms were 'in danger of the wrong kind of emphasis on what "national" feeling is'.[134] After 1968, Raymond Williams's support for peripheral nationalisms deepened, and he, like Nairn, believed that such nationalisms offered a stiff rebuke to stale British socialism. Stuart Hall devoted much of the 1970s to explaining the inherent racism of the British state, alerting the New Left to the progressive potential of anti-racist

---

127. Nairn 1977, p. 341.
128. Nairn 1977, pp. 337–41. The language of 'core' and 'periphery' owed much to Nairn's reading of Immanuel Wallerstein's *The Modern World System*, a debt he acknowledges in Nairn 1977, p. 361. Alongside this debt, he also draws on the work of Perry Anderson, and, at other places in the book, the work of Andre Gunder Frank, Samir Amin, and Arghiri Emmanuel.
129. Nairn 1977, p. 356.
130. Nairn 1977, p. 351.
131. Nairn 1977, p. 353.
132. Nairn 1977, p. 354.
133. Williams ed. 1968, p. 163.
134. Ibid.

politics among Britain's minority-ethnicities. Throughout this period, Thompson generated a sustained critique of the British state, drawing on a long-standing antipathy to 'Old Corruption', though he was less likely than either Williams or Nairn to hold out much hope for peripheral nationalisms. Moreover, Thompson would have found much to like in Nairn's critique of 'Marxism' – he had been saying much the same about this sort of Marxism since 1956 – though he would have had little time for Nairn's version of 'historical materialism', and none at all for his 'real history'.

In fact, the primary target of Nairn's critique of 'proletarian internationalism' was not the 'old' New Left, but his comrades on *New Left Review*.[135] The editors of *New Left Review* sponsored Eric Hobsbawm to respond to Nairn's call for separatist nationalism. In his critique of *The Break-up of Britain*, Hobsbawm repeated Lenin's warning about socialists painting nationalism red, arguing that socialists should not be nationalists, because 'nationalism by definition subordinates all other interests to those of its specific nation'.[136] Although not completely unsympathetic to national feeling, Hobsbawm suggested that there was no justification for supporting separatist nationalisms in Britain, particularly as they promised to establish states out of Britain's wreckage that could not hope to be viable. In short, peripheral nationalisms, Hobsbawm believed, would not promote the cause of international socialism. More likely, Hobsbawm argued, they would result in the subordination of socialism to nationalism, as had happened most often in such a marriage in the past. In such circumstances, Hobsbawm concluded, 'the Luxemburgist case is not entirely unrealistic'.[137]

But, arguably, Hobsbawm was not the primary target of *The Break-up of Britain*, though Nairn was no friend of Hobsbawm's anti-nationalism. In fact, at this time, the staunchest defender of 'proletarian internationalism' was actually Perry Anderson. In *Arguments within English Marxism*, Anderson, ostensibly with E.P. Thompson and the 'first' New Left in mind, gestured to Trotsky, and the tradition of socialist internationalism descended from Trotsky, as a counterpoint to the original New Left's marriage of nationalism and internationalism. 'Throughout his life', Anderson wrote, 'Trotsky was an unremitting adversary of every form of social patriotism or great-power chauvinism: no revolutionary ever preached or practiced so long and so consistently proletarian internationalism, in his own politics'.[138] Indeed, Anderson pointed to the Trotskyist tradition as offering an

---

135. Appropriately, according to Elliott, the publication of 'The Modern Janus' in *NLR* – cornerstone of *The Break-up of Britain* – caused much dispute among members on *NLR*'s editorial board. See Elliott 1998, p. 271, n. 19. Anderson later criticised the overestimation of the 'national revolts' in *The Break-up of Britain*. See D. Thompson 2007, pp. 98–9.

136. Hobsbawm 1977, p. 9.

137. Hobsbawm 1977, p. 13.

138. Anderson 1980, p. 155.

exemplary contemporary socialist internationalism. According to Anderson, the tradition's 'moral and intellectual grandeur has only grown with the passage of time, and the unfolding of other strands in the labour movement. So far, it is this tradition alone that has proved capable of an adult view of socialism on a world scale, as anyone who reads Mandel's recent *Revolutionary Marxism Today* may see for themselves'.[139] Anderson pointed to Trotskyism as a gulf separating the 'first' from the 'second' New Left. Arguably, however, it divided Anderson from Nairn, too.

A further difference, potentially of greater consequence, between Nairn and Anderson was also signaled in *The Break-up of Britain*. A key component of *New Left Review*'s politics in the 1970s and early 1980s was the contention that prospects for socialism in the West were dependent on the reform of socialism in the East. Indeed, Anderson argued that communist societies in the East could still be considered post-capitalist, and should be defended against American imperialism.[140] *The Break-up of Britain* took leave of these positions, and not just in suggesting that nationalism, rather than a reformed communism, offered the greatest potential benefit to British socialism. Nairn also argued that communism was 'an ideology of development or industrialization, rather than one of post-capitalist society'.[141] According to Nairn, socialism's triumph east of the Elbe, under the shadow of 'unbalanced development', was a condition of nationalism's victory to the west. 'Nationalism defeated socialism in the zone of high development, forcing it outwards into successive areas of backwardness where it was bound to become part of their compensatory drive to catch-up'.[142] Socialism, in other words, was really nationalism, at least when viewed through a world-historical telescope, and socialists' belief in the reality of global socialism could only appear the latest form of (internationalist) false consciousness. The Nairn-Anderson theses might have lived on in *The Break-up of Britain*, but the hyphen linking Nairn to Anderson had been undone.

In addition to 'proletarian internationalism', *The Break-up of Britain* also took umbrage at 'Third Worldism', a characteristic shibboleth of *New Left Review* in the immediate period after 1962. Nairn acknowledged that there was 'much truth' in the 'progressive myth of anti-imperialism', which characterised nationalism 'as a justified struggle of the repressed poor against the wealthy oppressors'.[143] However, he argued that this 'myth' failed to recognise that nationalism 'is a general fact of modern history, rooted in the development of the great powers as well

---

139. Ibid.
140. See Elliott 1998, pp. 143–63, for a good overview of Anderson's politics during this period.
141. Nairn 1977, p. 357.
142. Ibid.
143. Nairn 1977, p. 248.

as the under-privileged'.[144] Even anti-imperialist nationalism, Nairn claimed, was not immune to the appropriate general view of nationalism – the view that all nationalisms were 'spotted'.[145] There were not two nationalisms, one 'good' and one 'bad', as many, including many within the original New Left and its immediate successor, had believed. Rather 'all nationalism is both healthy and morbid', although this fact about nationalism, Nairn argued, did not imply 'that all forms of nationalism are as good, or as bad, as one another'.[146] What determined whether a nationalism was progressive or lunatic was not the nature of the thing itself but structural forces, the position, that is, of the particular nationalist movement in the process of uneven capitalist development.

Directed at adherents of 'Third Worldism', Nairn's critique of anti-imperialist nationalism mimicked Thompson's earlier salvo against *New Left Review*'s uncritical endorsement of national liberation in the Third World. In response to *New Left Review*'s embrace of 'Third Worldism' in the early 1960s, Thompson argued that even anti-imperialist nationalisms 'can become a source of mystification and chauvinism'.[147] Pointing to Maoism, Thompson argued that 'Every great liberating impulse is in danger of reproducing, out of the very conditions of its struggle, the vices of its antagonist in inverted form'.[148] What better description of Nairn's assessment of nationalism! Like Nairn, Thompson was aware that all nationalisms were spotted, containing the potential for both 'progress and regress'. His particular worry though, and here he diverged from Nairn, was that nationalism in the Third World could become a means whereby a nationalist bourgeoisie diverted attention away from what Thompson called 'internal contradictions' – in other words, class.[149] Nairn would have responded that subsuming such 'internal contradictions' under nationalism was necessary, and inevitable if 'backward' countries were to have development on their own terms.

The Break-up of Britain, despite the giant strides that the book made advancing the modernist theory of nationalism, was marked by a number of hesitations, not least surrounding Nairn's view of relations between socialism and national identity. Such hesitations were much less in evidence in Nairn's next major contribution to the analysis of Britain's national question, *The Enchanted Glass* (1988), a text which took the British state's central taboo, the monarchy, as the object of its anti-British optic.[150] Like *The Break-up of Britain*, *The Enchanted Glass* argued

---

144. Nairn 1977, p. 250.
145. Nairn 1977, p. 348.
146. Nairn 1977, p. 349.
147. E.P. Thompson, 'Where Are We Now?', Unpublished Memo, 1962, DJS/109, University of Hull Archives, University of Hull.
148. Ibid.
149. Ibid.
150. Nairn 1994.

that Britain was ruled by the wrong sort of nationalism – a nationalism intimately tied up with the monarchy, conservatism, and the British constitution.[151] But the earlier book was confident both that the break-up of Britain was imminent and that peripheral nationalisms would constitute both the precipitant cause and new nation-states the inevitable result, with socialism to benefit. *The Enchanted Glass*, written at the high point of Thatcherism, was much less optimistic, offering less hope about separatist nationalism, and none about socialism.

The Enchanted Glass took Nairn's hatred of Britain to a new pitch of intensity. Based now squarely in the corner of Gellner's 'modernization theory', the book traced the basis of Britain's backwardness to its developmental priority, to a 'pre-bourgeois revolution',[152] to the predominance of a premodern political-economy, and to a Constitution and Crown mystique buttressed by imperialism, all of which overdetermined a conservative, backward-looking, though resilient, version of national identity.[153] In such circumstances, Nairn lamented, nationalism, in the sense of popular sovereignty and democracy, never stood a chance. 'Originally the myth of Monarchy', Nairn explained, 'was employed to build up national-popular identity, in the time of George III – a safely anti-Republican nationalism which would keep the spirit of democracy at bay even when democratic forms of government had become inescapable. Now the myth is amplified and diffused in order to rally this same identity, to preserve a national self-image (and the old power reality it serves) against the greater tensions of a polity in disintegration'.[154]

Predictably, in the course of his exposition of British decrepitude, Nairn took pot shots at Thompson, on this occasion associating his defence of the national idiom in *The Poverty of Theory* – the image Thompson used was that of the bustard – with a defence of the Anglo-British identity associated with Monarchy's 'glamour of backwardness'.[155] 'As Edward Thompson has so often reminded his fellow-subjects, to the "empirical idiom" all such things [a written constitution, Enlightenment, republicanism] are a damned nuisance – abrasive reminders of how, since 1789, foreign importers have been ruining politics with their impossibly abstract demands'.[156] Ridiculing 'the Thompsonian left's' defence of 'customary freedoms',[157] at one point he also compared Thompson's vision of international relations to that of Winston Churchill.[158]

---

151. Nairn 1994, p. 97.
152. Nairn 1994, p. 239.
153. Nairn 1994, p. 236.
154. Nairn 1994, p. 215.
155. Nairn 1994, p. 214.
156. Nairn 1994, p. 233.
157. Nairn 1994, p. 260.
158. Nairn 1994, p. 253.

In addition to *The Poverty of Theory*, Nairn chose a 1987 *Independent* article by Thompson to prove his case, an article in which Thompson had argued that Britain, because of its connections with America, the Commonwealth and Europe, might be able to effect a break in Cold War tensions.[159] That is, not Thompson's articles on the jury-system, not his damning analysis of British authoritarianism, not the republican values of his historiography and not his solidarity with peaceniks who took to the streets against nuclear weapons. And not, of course, his hunting of Old Corruption, with the King or Queen at its apex, that constant antagonist of Thompson's historical and political writing. In other words, *contra The Enchanted Glass*, Thompson never wrote one word that would have given comfort to Nairn's 'Anglo-British identity'. The point of the *Independent* article, as indeed it had been of Thompson's politics since the late 1950s, was to take things from Britain's past and use them against Britain. This, for Thompson, was the proper way to hate Britain. He did not hate Britain any less than Nairn for finding in Britain's past things of value, including Painite republicanism, socialism and internationalism.

In one sense, *The Enchanted Glass* was an extension of the Nairn-Anderson theses. Anderson himself had recently revisited those theses, deciding that his and Nairn's argument required no significant emendation. However, Anderson did review his assessment of the national culture, concluding that the British 1980s generated 'the liveliest republic of letters in European socialism', a republic that owed its vive to many New Left thinkers including Williams, Thompson, Raphael Samuel and Stuart Hall. No such commendation of the original New Left appeared in *The Enchanted Glass*, however (despite the view of *The Break-Up of Britain*). Indeed, Nairn could not see much value in Anderson's republic at all, concluding that 'In modern England the world of Letters has laboured to serve the Royal-communitarian *Weltanschauung*'.[160] He was right to note that 'the British Monarchy, Europe's greatest living fossil, the enchanted glass of an early modernity which has otherwise vanished from the globe, had received next to no attention from British social theory'.[161] But, British social and political thought had not been as 'blind' to nationalism as Nairn claimed and it was not quite true that the British Left had simply ignored monarchy. This is especially so if we consider the tradition of British Marxist historiography – stretching from Christopher Hill's work on the English Revolution through Thompson's work on the Black Acts and nineteenth-century Jacobinism. 'Culture', a fairly central organising concept of *The Enchanted Glass*, had been perhaps more worked over in Britain than in any other 'national' intellectual tradition. But this would have

---

159. Nairn 1994, pp. 252–3.
160. Nairn 1994, p. 147.
161. Nairn 1994, p. 115.

meant recognition of the early New Left's achievements in ways foreign to *The Enchanted Glass*'s purpose and tone.

The distance between Nairn and Anderson's view of the national intellectual culture can be partly explained by the absence of socialism in *The Enchanted Glass*. Anderson had pointed to a *socialist* republic of letters, but Nairn had little interest in that sort of republic any more. Indeed, he left socialism to some indeterminate future, as something that could only be considered after constitutional reform and the rebuilding of Britain's political roof. 'Republicanism', he argued in *The Enchanted Glass*, 'is a proposed revolution of national identity, as a precondition of any imaginable set of feasible programmes or socio-economic policies'.[162] His aim was the revolution before The Revolution, that is, the reconstitution of 'nationhood', the 'most significant "social relation"', and of national identity, that essential 'cultural prerequisite of modernity'.[163] Britain had denied nationalism in the cause of a pseudo-nationalism (Royalism) and Monarchy had encouraged a national identity set as a barrier against ethnicity and democracy. According to Nairn, socialism could only be a product of modernity – and anachronistic, nationalism- and national-identity-less Britain could not be considered modern.[164]

As a mark of distinction, the New Left had set its face against the economic reductionism characteristic of 'mechanical' conceptions of Marxism. Nairn had taken this grimace to new lengths in *The Enchanted Glass*, arguing for the dominance of the political over the economic, something, for all the book's professed iconoclasm, that had already become a shibboleth of post-Marxist – better, anti-Marxist – argument. Indeed, *The Enchanted Glass* completed a repudiation of Marxism that Nairn had begun in *The Break-up of Britain*. It might, indeed, also be considered strange that this rejection reached its terminus at the high point of Thatcherism – one aspect of a global-class project against organised labour. But Nairn was not alone among New Left figures in casting off their socialism. Even Anderson had mostly left his radical past behind. Some, like Williams and Thompson, could still find a residual place for class in their political imaginary, and even for some sort of alternative to capitalism. But, for others, the political future would constitute a struggle over the meaning of identity. That struggle would become the point around which Nairn's future analysis of nationalism would turn, both in the context of his Scottish nationalism and in the substance of a general commitment to human diversity.

---

162. Nairn 1994, p. 387.
163. Nairn 1994, p. 181.
164. Nairn 1994, p. 137.

V

Returning to the themes of *The Enchanted Glass* in a new introduction to the book in 1994, Nairn argued that British identity and Britain had advanced beyond decrepitude. Drawing again on Gellnerian insights, Nairn argued that the break-up of Britain would definitely take national form, just as the break-up of communism in Eastern Europe had, since there was no other, especially no other of 'comparable collective attraction'.[165] 'Britain' would need to be reinvented just as much as 'Yugoslavia' or 'Czechoslovakia' in these circumstances. 'Nationality-politics are beginning to look like the salty shadow of this ever-continuing process [of uneven capitalist development], as distinct from the blueprints of the economists – a permanent reality rather than a phase, modernity's forced tribute to inextinguishable variation and discord'.[166] Ethnicity, Nairn in other words argued, could ultimately be explained by 'social history'.[167] However, in *Faces of Nationalism*, published just three years later, Nairn began to doubt the veracity of this Gellnerian claim. This book announced another paradigm change in Nairn's thinking, and provided new reasons for hating Britain.

Faces of Nationalism was composed within two contexts – one theoretical, the other political and historical.[168] The theoretical context were debates within nationalism studies that followed the publication of Benedict Anderson's *Imagined Communities* and Ernest Gellner's *Nations and Nationalism*.[169] Both examples of the predominant 'modernist' theory of nationalism, a theory to which Nairn himself had contributed in *The Break-up of Britain*, these books nonetheless increasingly came under challenge from 'primordialism' – the view that nations are the product of *ethnies* that long pre-exist 'industrialisation' or 'modernisation'.[170] That dispute – between 'modernists' and 'primordialists' – constituted the theoretical white noise behind *Faces of Nationalism*. The other background to the book was the course of world-events since 1989 – the break-up of communism, the rise of separatist nationalisms in Britain and the world-historical economic transformation dubbed 'globalisation'. In the terms of these two contexts, *Faces of Nationalism* professed Nairn's discontent with 'modernization theory' – it could explain much about nationalism, but not its 'spell' – and suggested that '1989' had, nonetheless, confirmed his view that nationality was

---

165. Nairn 1994, p. xxxi.

166. Nairn 1994, p. xxxvi.

167. Nairn 1994, p. xxvii.

168. *Faces of Nationalism* was made up of articles that Nairn had published in the two decades after *The Break-up of Britain*.

169. B. Anderson 2006; Gellner 1983. In addition, also see Breuilly 1982. See Eley and Suny 1996, for a good overview of nationalism-studies in the last half of the twentieth century. See Lawrence 2005, for a more recent overview.

170. Armstrong 1982; Smith 1986.

an unavoidable, and unavoidably good, product of capitalism's (uneven) colonisation of the globe. The concept which drew these two arguments together, and which has continued to define Nairn's work on national identity until the present, was 'human nature'.

Written from a professed 'nationalist point of view',[171] *Faces of Nationalism* sought to dispute two claims asserted in the aftermath of the 'nationalist disasters' that followed 1989 – on the one hand the deliberately paradoxical allegation, famously made by Hobsbawm, that nationalism was a declining vector of historical development;[172] and, on the other, the view that ethnic and nationalist discord, like that manifest in the Balkans, augured the atavistic Abyss.[173] Each claim, Nairn suggested, was wrongheaded. Far from being on the way out, nationalism, according to him, constituted the tracks along which all posthistory development would travel, as certain in Britain as in Yugoslavia or the former USSR. According to *Faces of Nationalism*, capitalist globalisation implied ethnic dissonance rather than universalised homogeneity, forcing the planet 'to fold up into a previously unimaginable and still escalating number of different ethno-political units'.[174] This, Nairn claimed, was an unambiguously good thing, despite the ambiguity surrounding some of those 'ethno-political units'. But this ambiguity was far more acceptable than what it replaced: the possible extinction of the human species.[175] Not only was nationalism 'the universal condition of modernity'.[176] This universal condition, Nairn argued, was also closest to human nature, promoting a 'more conscious and humane development lying (we have to hope) beyond primitive industrialization'.[177]

Nairn has always enjoyed appearing iconoclastic. There was no doubt, in the context of civil war in Yugoslavia and continued ethnic discord in many of the republics of the former Soviet Union, that Nairn's views did appear to rub against the grain of received wisdom. But, from another angle, *Faces of Nationalism* drifted with the tide. It certainly drifted with the tide of 'identity politics', the new received wisdom of modern politics. After all, nationalism was perhaps the original model of 'identity politics' and 'mere being' had become the sacred framework for any sort of politics in advanced capitalist countries, and many 'backward' ones as well. *Faces of Nationalism* also drifted with the tide of antisocialism, the rejection of class and the repudiation of historical materialism. Nairn could no doubt claim to have been in on this drift from the beginning,

---

171. Nairn 1997, p. 25.
172. Hobsbawm 1990, p. 163.
173. See Nairn 1995, pp. 91–103.
174. Nairn 1997, p. 63. See Mann 1996, pp. 295–316, for a similar argument.
175. Nairn 1997, p. 61.
176. Nairn 1997, p. 25.
177. Nairn 1997, p. 55.

but the intellectual stampede away from materialism since *The Break-up of Britain* marked further evidence of *Faces of Nationalism*'s conformity. Finally, in its political imaginary – its vision of a post-1989 'globalised' world characterised by small-scale nation-states, democracy, free markets and nationality – *Faces of Nationalism* conformed to that general political taboo that surrounded capitalism in any discussion of politics and political economy. Indeed, in a summation of the conformity *Faces of Nationalism* pretended to upset: Nairn could announce that there was no alternative to (uneven) capitalist development.[178]

In short-term retrospect, *Faces of Nationalism* had 'real history' on its side. Nationality has not gone away and nationalism, especially in its meaning dimension, shows no sign of loosening its grip on identity. Yet Nairn's 'anarchic optimism' was liable to overlook other aspects of the post-Cold War world, not least, Hobsbawm's view, that the end of communism constituted a 'human catastrophe',[179] characterised by a growing gap between rich and poor and renewed descent into barbarism.[180] 1989, according to Hobsbawm, was far from another 'spring-time of the nations'. Perry Anderson was no less convinced than Hobsbawm that the post-communist world was deserving of celebration: 'the salient feature of the present', he wrote in 1997, 'is not that the world at large is out of control, but that it has never been subject to such an extent of control by one power [the United States], acting to diffuse and enforce one system [neo-liberalism], as we see today'.[181] Anderson was no less sanguine about the prospects of democracy, arguing that its widespread dissemination after 1989 was coalescent with a reduction in its substance. Nairn, of course, would (eventually) see in the hegemony of neo-liberalism the breakdown of his original hopes. It is nonetheless remarkable that *Faces of Nationalism* contained no analysis of the United States, and the prospect that the break-up of communism resulted not in improved prospects for democracy and nationality but for capital accumulation and capitalism.

However, by the end of the twentieth century, there was much that Hobsbawm, Anderson and Nairn could agree on (indeed they would all agree that nationalism had come to an end in 1989, with Nairn perhaps adding the caveat that he would call it national-*ism*). They could all agree that, as Hobsbawm put it, nationalism constituted the 'inescapable' ground of modern politics, and that nationalist consciousness 'constituted the soil in which all other political sentiments grow'.[182] Even Anderson admitted the necessarily national framework

---

178. See Nairn 1997, p. 61. In addition, see Nairn 1996, p. 274.
179. Hobsbawm 2000, p. 74.
180. Hobsbawm 1998, pp. 580–5.
181. Anderson 2005, p. 318.
182. Hobsbawm 1993, p. 145.

of all future politics, even of anti-capitalist politics.[183] Indeed, Hobsbawm like Nairn, could argue that the only appropriate response to ethnic nationalism was 'citizen nationalism' – 'the only foundation for all the aspirations to build societies fit for all human beings to live anywhere on the Earth'.[184] *Faces of Nationalism* also argued that 'civic' nationalism provided the only sane response to the sometime-exuberance of 'ethnic' nationalism – gone was Nairn's view that all nationalisms were spotted. However, the differences, between Anderson and Nairn in particular, outweighed these similarities. Nairn and Anderson could agree that Gellner had failed to explain everything about nationalism, especially what was most important about it – namely, 'the overpowering dimension of collective meaning that modern nationalism has involved', its 'fulfilment of identity'.[185] But Anderson was unlikely to have agreed that the key to this answer would be found in the results of the Human Genome Project, in an analytic return to 'the blood' and the persistence of 'rurality' as *Faces of Nationalism* argued.[186]

The most important argument of *Faces of Nationalism* was the suggestion that it was 'human nature', the 'raw material of rurality', or 'custom' that explained what was most important about nationalism. This is what modernisation theory had overlooked, according to Nairn. Gellner had explained everything one needed to know about nationalism except what one needed most to know about it – that is, what Anderson had called its 'spell'. 'Events since 1989', Nairn believed, 'have returned us squarely to the problem of "blood" – the inherent and irreconcilable diversity of "human nature"'.[187] A new paradigm, Nairn argued, was required and he saw its most likely emergence in 'a more plausible link between biology and kinship on the one hand, and the world of political nation-states and resurgent nationality on the other'.[188] It was not that Nairn was calling for a return to socio-biology; he claimed that developments in genetics had defeated social Darwinism and racism for good.[189] What he argued was that the complex of things denoted by "nationalism" 'did not become so central and commanding by accident and disaster'.[190] There was more to nationalism, in other words, than social history. What that more was, *Faces of Nationalism* decided, was human nature, the unalterable fact of human diversity. Capitalist globalisation, according to Nairn, did not induce 'subordination to common standards and values',

183. Anderson 1992, p. 353.
184. Hobsbawm 1994, pp. 46–7.
185. Anderson 1992b, p. 205.
186. Nairn 1997, pp. 11, 7.
187. Nairn 1997, p. 11.
188. Nairn 1997, p. 13.
189. Nairn 1997, pp. 113–21. See Nairn and James 2005, p. 189, for a later argument along the same lines.
190. Nairn 1997, p. 16.

but 'the reproduction and the reinvention of diversity'.[191] And the point of all this, *the* point of national identity, was something like 'the government of one's own affairs'.[192] That – the need for democracy and ethnicity – was what human nature was all about. 'An authentic Internationale', *Faces of Nationalism* proclaimed, 'can only be based upon the liberation of human nature; which means (in the first instance) nationalities, the precondition for democracy and individual emancipation'.[193]

Human nature, and the effects on human nature of modernisation, had, of course, been a key concern of E.P. Thompson's. In *Customs in Common*, Thompson argued that 'capitalism (or "the market") made over human nature and human need'.[194] As indeed in *The Making of the English Working Class* and *Whigs and Hunters*, the chief concern of *Customs in Common* was to remind readers that, while a return to 'pre-capitalist human nature' was impossible, a reminder of that human nature's 'needs, expectations, and codes may renew our sense of nature's range of possibility'.[195] Thompson was also a great hater, and the prime object of his hate, perhaps alongside war, was capitalism – particularly the way capitalism made over 'human nature' to render it detached from what he believed was its mainsprings, creativity, cooperation and love. Much the same argument had constituted Raymond Williams's *The Country and the City*. As Thompson, reviewing Williams's book, put it: 'For if capitalism is the basic economic process of four centuries of history, there has been evidence throughout (and this is the challenge which socialist theory makes) of human processes that are alternatives to capitalism. We have to go on to ask: what form could a human protest take against an ongoing, all-triumphant economic process unless as "retrospect"'?[196] This was a view, of course, that Nairn had rejected in *The Enchanted Glass* as the 'immemorial custom' of Thompsonian nonsense, but this was much in accord with the spirit behind *Faces of Nationalism*. However, unlike Nairn, both Williams and Thompson had imagined capitalism as antithetical to human nature.

Faces of Nationalism concluded with Nairn's standard lament for the backwardness of Britain, and with the hope that 'identity angst', particularly Scottish 'identity angst', in the context of Labour's 1997 return to office, would become a prominent feature of Britain's political landscape in the new century.[197] He now

---

191. Ibid.
192. Nairn 1997, p. 53.
193. Nairn 1997, p. 134.
194. E.P. Thompson 1991, p. 15.
195. Ibid.
196. E.P. Thompson 1994, p. 249. Compare this with Nairn and James 2005, p. 178.
197. See, in particular, Nairn 1997, pp. 210–24. Reference to 'identity angst' can be found at p. 212.

had new reasons for hating Britain. Not only was it 'out of place' in any 'small-state world', and alone among states for its 'refusal of ethnicity',[198] it was also an affront to 'human nature'. Nonetheless, Nairn was confident of the further break-up of Britain and confident that the break-up would take a 'civic' rather than an 'ethnic' turn. At the beginning of the new millennium, back now in the fold of *New Left Review*, Nairn returned to these questions in two books, *After Britain* and *Pariah*, in the context of what he was still describing as the crisis of the British state. *Pariah* constituted an updated version of Nairn's long and tenaciously held thesis that Britain was a premodern relic overdue for nationalist reconstruction, while *After Britain* contained his most insistent argument after *The Break-up of Britain* for the realisation of national separatism in the British Isles. Indeed, *After Britain*, published in 2000, was constructed as a validation of the 'break-up of Britain' thesis and a celebration, though partly muted, of the reemergence of Scottish nationhood following the majority vote on devolution. In the romantic rhetoric favoured by Nairn, the Scottish vote for devolution had brought 'the underground river up to the surface'.[199] The ascent spelt the 'end of Britain', that is, the final demise of a state that had based itself on a denial of nationalism and ethnicity. Yet *Pariah* offered a significant caveat to this view, since, with a renewed hatred of Britain, it claimed that Labour's neo-liberal 'third way' was actually a form of 'Britishism' designed to keep the United Kingdom intact.[200]

In truth, these books offered little new.[201] However, there was a crucial absence in the roundabout of Nairn's writing on Britain. That absence was any conception of the socio-economic order that might emerge from Britain's demise. *After Britain* and *Pariah* were equally silent about the social and economic order that would replace the existing multi-national state. Nairn, of course, would have considered this an 'old-hat' argument which consistently missed the point of the need for constitutional change and reform of the state *now*. However, given that *Faces of Nationalism* had asserted that capitalism constituted 'the sole matrix of further evolution', it was clear that an independent Scotland or a new England would not be socialist. A critique of 'Great British Socialism' had consistently accompanied Nairn's comment on Britain since 'The Nature of the Labour Party'. But, whereas those early essays had critiqued this version of socialism from the perspective of another sort, that other sort had been absent from *The Enchanted Glass* onwards. Nairn essentially abandoned socialism to an indeterminate

---

198. Nairn 2009.
199. Nairn 2000, p. 111.
200. Nairn 2000, p. 72 and Nairn 2002, p. 56. Nairn made the somewhat startling comment that New Labour was more interested in British nationalism than capitalism.
201. Nairn 2002, pp. 16, 70.

future, arguing that socialism was a way of not 'facing real conditions of life' and abandoning 'real relations' with people.[202] If there were some, including some in the 'second' New Left, who found his analysis wanting in this respect,[203] there were others who had different reasons for rejecting his post-Britain vision.

Conditioned perhaps by his biography, Hobsbawm had been a long-time critic of the break-up of existing multi-national states, suggesting that separatist nationalists had overlooked 'the enormous difficulties and cruelties to which the attempt to divide Europe [and by extension every other part of the world] into homogeneous nation-states had led in this century (including separation, partition, mass expulsion and genocide)'.[204] Nairn would have considered such rumination hysterical in the case of Britain, but more ordinary every-day forms of racism were overlooked in *After Britain* and *Pariah*. This everyday racism was Stuart Hall's principal concern. A non-ethnic nationality like Britishness, according to him, was potentially more inclusive than an ethnic identity on which separate states in Britain would necessarily be founded. For Hall, there was no contradiction in being 'black' and 'British', but the identity composite Black-English was unimaginable. As Hall put it in his contribution to *The Future of Multi-Ethnic Britain: The Parekh Report*, 'Britishness is not ideal, but at least appears acceptable, particularly when suitably qualified – Black British, Indian British, British Muslim, and so on'.[205]

The difference between Nairn and Hall, of course, was that Nairn could not imagine Britishness meaning anything else than imperialism, monarchy, 'class' and the House of Lords.[206] Hall had a more dialectical conception of ethnicity and nationality, predicting that its meaning was open to interpretation and re-interpretation, an 'empty signifier' that could be filled by any number of political ideologies. For Nairn, however, 'Britishness' was always a way of avoiding ordinary nationality and ethnicity, since 'Britishness lies in being far too big for tiresomely national boots'.[207] The source of this – here repeating an early argument of the original Nairn-Anderson theses – was the historical dominance of finance capital over industrial capital. 'Only industrial capitalism had ever been guilty of democracy and conspiracy with the plebs. By contrast, finance capital was either tolerant of or positively favourable to the pomp and circumstance of monarchy, populist pantomimes and pageantry'.[208] This was the point of his critique of Blairism. According to him, it was a survival-kit, designed to patch up greatness,

---

202. Nairn 2001, pp. 70–1.
203. See, in particular, Mulhern 2000b, pp. 53–66.
204. Hobsbawm 1977, p. 4.
205. Hall, cited in Nairn 2002, p. 105.
206. Nairn 2002, p. 109.
207. Nairn and James 2005, p. 166.
208. Ibid.

monarchy and British identity.[209] The alternative to all this, according to Nairn, was Scandinavia and Ireland. Nairn looked forward to an 'archipelago of British-Irish variety and dissonance', 'with all kinds of family quarrels still going on, but in a democratic and outward-looking manner, from which the claustrophobia of Great Britain will have disappeared alongside its false security, its hegemonic conceit and its be-Crowned stultification'.[210]

Many of the themes outlined in *Faces of Nationalism*, were expanded upon in a series of essays that Nairn wrote for *London Review of Books, New Left Review, Open Democracy* and contributions to *Global Matrix*, a co-authored book with Paul James. A synthesis of these ideas has been promised in a forthcoming work, *Global Nations*, though the direction that synthesis will take is now fairly clear. Central to that synthesis, no doubt, will be the distinction between nationality politics and national-*ism*.[211] The last, according to Nairn, was hegemonic between the 1860s and 1989, and has had a ghoulish after-life in the 'war on terror', no less in Britain than in the United States. 'The ism of nationality', Nairn explained, 'was not rooted in nations or societal diversity, but had been grafted onto them from the 1860s onwards, had led to two world wars, and was congealed in place for a further generation by the Cold War'.[212] But this phase had ended in 1989. Indeed, globalisation 'implies that something like the victory promised in 1848 may also become possible, a century and a half late: the generalization and deepening of democracy, as a precondition of whatever social forms the ocean ahead may then make possible'.[213] Globalisation – at least in that warped American-dominated form that emerged after 1989 – was a 'boundary-less world',[214] but its death-throes in Mesopotamia signal 'the reality of globalization, as an emergent, multiform, diversifying pattern of open and more democratic nations'.[215]

It is perhaps ironic that Nairn now proclaims the 'peculiarities' that formed the shorthand of Thompson's original critique of the Nairn-Anderson theses. Indeed, Nairn's idea that nationality would have to be saved from super-powered globalisation run by great-power nationalisms was a replica of Thompson's view that the USA and USSR were the principal enemies of freedom of expression and national independence. 'Let Poland be Polish and let Greece be Greek!' had been END's clarion call.[216] Stuart Hall, of course, was an early advocate of the idea of hybridity as a bulwark against ethnicity in the bad sense, and he was as likely as

---

209. Nairn 2000, p. 72.
210. Nairn 2001, p. 74.
211. See Nairn 1995, p. 95, for an early example of this distinction. See Nairn and James 2005, p. 248, for the same argument.
212. Nairn 2005b. In addition, see Nairn 2008.
213. Nairn 2006.
214. Nairn 2004; Nairn 2005b, pp. 44–5.
215. Nairn 2004. See also Nairn 2007, pp. 5–7.
216. E.P. Thompson 1985b, p. 186.

Nairn to see the future as some sort of rooted cosmopolitanism.[217] Like Nairn, Williams believed that boundaries were crucial signposts of humanity's species-being, and he, like Nairn and Thompson, favoured small over big. This is not to suggest that Williams, Thompson and Hall would have seen a mirror of their own political imaginaries in the late writings of Nairn. But it is to suggest that Nairn's late writings have drawn on a fund of ideas that had been thought before in the context of New Left political discourse.

Indeed, Williams and Thompson would have each provided important caveats to Nairn's reflections on globalisation. Anderson tentatively voiced some quali-fications. Commenting on Nairn's recent work, Anderson has suggested: 'Fresh nation-states have risen, but nearly all the newcomers are weak or marginal. Boundaries of some kind may be an anthropological a priori, but why should these be national, rather than civilizational, regional, cantonal or other'?[218] Wil-liams would certainly have agreed with this, since he had always envisaged 'self-governing societies' at the regional level. Thompson, like Anderson, may have raised that 'old' question of class, and might have suggested that wher-ever nationalities were formed, and no matter how small, there was always the problem that they might paper over social divisions. Nairn always considered Thompson a bore, and when talking about class Thompson sometimes felt him-self as much. But boring or not, and no matter that Thompson considered it 'long past its sell-by date',[219] class still haunts the age, providing perhaps *the* barrier to generalised human emancipation. As Thompson once recorded, 'it is capital – now insecure and supra-national, but still with an imperative inertia – which is daily dismantling...historic England over our heads: inexorably destroying old landscapes, old buildings, old cultural modes, old institutions, and striving to compact us conveniently into a modernised and managed circuit of conditioned need and consonant supply'.[220] 'It is money', he concluded, 'which seeks to make over society as its organ'.[221] Nairn would have agreed with this, but still asked, 'yes, but *whose* money'?

VI

Tom Nairn has hated Britain now for almost half a century. The persistence and depth of this hatred has been the product of a specific field of force, descend-

217. See Nairn 2003, p. 124, for his vision of cosmopolis.
218. Anderson 2005.
219. E.P. Thompson 1994, p. 326.
220. E.P. Thompson 1994, p. 331.
221. Ibid.

ing from the 'Scottish' dilemma.[222] A nation without nationhood that had willing given up sovereignty to another state, Scotland, according to Nairn, was a 'suppressed state' that had deviated from the common trajectory of modernity.[223] These facts of history constituted Nairn's identity-problems. Initially, his hatred derived from an 'out of country' perspective, subsuming his Sottish dilemma within the thought-world of socialist internationalism. This was common enough, as Nairn later recognised. 'From their earliest bookish encounters', he once wrote, 'Scottish intellectuals imbibe a form of national nihilism, the sense of a Heimat lovable yet incurably divorced from the modern'.[224] The result of Nairn's national nihilism was a specific form of socialist internationalism, deliberately abstract and theoretical. But in the wake of Empire, socialism and de-industrialisation – that crisis of Anderson's 'Origins of the Present Crisis' – Nairn repudiated 'departure-lounge internationalism' and returned to the problems of Scotland,[225] a return from what Nairn would later characterise as a 'self-exile'. Britain could be hated for better reasons, including the reason that it denied Scotland's self-determination. But there was nothing necessarily parochial about this. It denied other forms of self-determination in Britain, too, and, prostrate before the United States, many others outside Britain as well.

Nairn's contribution to New Left thought has combined a number of peculiar qualities. He has an unmatched hatred for Britain, possible perhaps only in a Scot, though it should be remembered that Anderson's assessment of Britain, and that of Hall and the late Williams, from the perspective of their own identity-problems, has been no less forgiving. Thompson might have been more inclined to see some good in Britain, but he was no less dismissive of the British state or British imperialism. Like Thompson and Williams, in particular, Nairn has been an unswerving advocate of self-determination. His love of country though has often manifested itself as a hatred of the way his country is, but, like Thompson, he has often argued that patriotism must sometimes be revolutionary. Nairn's fortitude has been sustained by the hope, not yet lost, that there might be something imaginable other than Britain, inured in traditionalism, bewitched by monarchy and hierarchy, and constrained by the imperial ties of the past and the present. Nations are ordinary, and Nairn's hope has always been that Britain might become ordinary, too, but as four – perhaps even eight or nine – rather than one.[226]

---

222. See Nairn 2005c, p. 131, for a recent elucidation of this dilemma.
223. Nairn 2000, p. 227.
224. Nairn 1997, p. 185.
225. Nairn 2000, p. 103.
226. Nairn 2002, p. 135.

Conclusion

> Ideas generated by a social movement do not present themselves in an orderly manner. They are thrown up by circumstances, shaken by destinies and left-hanging in mid-air. Expressive of political tensions within the fabric of society, they are raw with interests.[1]

I

A recurrent theme of this book has been that New Left thinkers wrestled with the national and anti-national tendencies constitutive of twentieth-century social reality, a unity of opposites structured by cosmopolitan flows of finance, commodities and ideas and the perseverance of nation-states and national sentiment. A further theme has been that interests, sometimes raw interests, associated with place, belonging and national identity have inflected their encounter. Dilemmas indicative of the nexus between socialism and national identity have framed New Left thought in a number of diverse ways, often providing points of tension and contest between New Left thinkers, connected as much with Britain's national and nationalist questions as with recurrent crises of socialism.

Responses to Gramsci's concept of the 'national-popular' illuminate many of these contests within New Left thought.[2] The early New Left sought to represent what Raphael Samuel called 'Radical England': 'real

---

1. Rowbotham 1989, p. 294.
2. See Forgacs 1984 on Gramsci's concept of the 'national-popular'.

living, breathing, thinking, feeling people: Tredegar steel workers and Cannock miners, Kentish town mothers and Wythenshawe clerks: the common people'.[3] 'Radical England' was 'an alternative democratic view of the nation',[4] rooted in a political sociology characterised by the division between the 'common people' ('the nation') and 'an exclusive and competitive elite'.[5] It was an 'ideal' class-alliance between the organised working class and a series of other social-groups who, the New Left believed, were vulnerable to the appeal of socialism as an alternative way of life. 'Alongside the industrial workers', E.P. Thompson wrote, 'we should see the teachers who want better schools, scientists who wish to advance research, welfare workers who want hospitals, actors who want a National Theatre, technicians impatient to improve industrial organization'.[6]

This interpretation of 'radical England' was challenged (although it seems nobody questioned Samuel's inclusion of 'Tredegar steel workers' among 'the people' of 'Radical England'). For a start, Stuart Hall worried that 'the people' were parochial and racist, intolerant towards not just other national cultures, but socialist militancy, too.[7] Perry Anderson echoed these concerns, adding that 'the people' were also not sufficiently schooled in socialist theory.[8] These concerns built on earlier assessments of 'the people' found in *New Reasoner* and *Universities and Left Review*. At least part of 'the people', according to Peter Worsley, had been so 'influenced by [Britain's] long imperialist history' that they had become 'chauvinist' and 'the least active on colonial issues'.[9] Ralph Miliband added that 'the people' had become 'nationalised' and reconciled to the British state. 'That trade union leaders now regularly clamour for State protection against employers', he wrote, 'suggests that they expect some protection from it; and get it'.[10] In this view, 'the people' were not so radical after all.

Raymond Williams and E.P. Thompson offered more hopeful and generous interpretations of 'the people'. Williams derived his understanding of the 'national-popular' principally from his early experience of working-class community in the border country. 'The people', according to him, were those men (Williams did not often think of 'the people' as women) who had been involved in the 1926 General Strike, joined by their common experience of exploitation and neighbourhood.[11] They were the quietly determined opponents of capital's

---

3. Samuel 1960, p. 9.
4. Ibid.
5. See Hall et al. 1958, p. 32. See also E.P. Thompson 1950b, p. 28.
6. E.P. Thompson 1960a, p. 8.
7. Hall 1958, p. 27.
8. Anderson 1961.
9. Worsley 1957, p. 15. See also Hanson 1958, p. 3; Miliband 1964, p. 103. Compare these views with Anderson 1964, pp. 35–6.
10. See Miliband 1958b, p. 42.
11. Williams 1977, p. 40.

imperatives whose commitment to a 'different human order' derived as much from their 'whole way of life' as their relation to the mode of production. For Thompson, 'the people' were anti-fascist, anti-militarist and anti-imperialist, inheritors of a long-tradition of democracy and liberty associated with 'the free-born Englishman'.[12] They were also 'the people' of working-class self-activity in Halifax, Fife, Hungary and Poland, those people, like Jim Roche, full-time organiser of the Leeds Communist Party whose formulation of 'the positions of socialist humanism [in 1956] meant getting out his tools and returning to the cutter's bench...'.[13]

The second New Left of Perry Anderson and Tom Nairn had little time for 'the people', a signal, for them, of the New Left's pre-socialist submission to populism.[14] They detached socialism from working-class self-activity, making it a product of 'socialist intellectuals' rather than 'the people'. If they had a vision of 'the people', it was peasant and urban guerrillas in Latin America and Vietnam and revolutionary students in the Latin Quarter – the last dialectically liberated by the first. These people were representatives of Nairn's new revolutionary epoch, 'real monsters, walking paragraphs from the *1844 Manuscripts* and the *Grundisse*'.[15] They were 'the people' of Anderson's 'small revolutionary groups', those who shook the citadels of bourgeois culture, and sometimes power, in Paris, Milan and elsewhere. They were 'the people', too, who protested against the Vietnam War in Grosvenor Square in 1968 – those who called not for peace, but for the victory of socialism in Vietnam.[16]

In the 1970s, Perry Anderson's notion of socialist agency shifted under the weight of his encounter with Trotskyism. Students, intellectuals and revolutionary guerrillas were swapped for the 'associated producers', a conception suitably distanced from any particular people. Tom Nairn's vision moved in an opposite direction. 'The people', for him, were neither proletarians nor intellectuals but national peoples, no matter how confused about their ethnic origins, who mobilised to demand progress on their own terms. Not yet a normative concept, 'the people' were necessarily nationalist, using whatever they had to hand – ethnos, skin colour, mythicised origins – in order to deflect the homogenising tendencies of capitalist globalisation. However, when Nairn's 'the people' became the 'Scottish people' in the 1980s, his conception of national identity became as much a matter of collective subjectivity as the impassive product of uneven development. In this vision, historical agency was associated with nationalism's

---

12. E.P. Thompson 1957, pp. 124, 140; E.P. Thompson 1960, p. 9.
13. E.P. Thompson 1978, p. 133.
14. Anderson 1965a; Anderson 1966.
15. *New Left Review* 1968, p. 5.
16. Anderson 1980, p. 145.

'self-determination of peoples' rather than socialism's 'self-determination of people'.[17]

This was not so far removed from Raymond Williams's sense of the 'Welsh people' in the 1970s. Williams, however, never severed his Welshness, as Nairn was to sever his Scottishness, from socialism. Welshness, according to Williams, was a sign of 'the people's' reach for control, the desire for self-government against the signatures of centralised, and distanced, power. National identity in this view, though not the national identity associated with big states such as Britain, was one aspect of people's search for effective modes of autonomy.[18] Autonomy, 'the people' governing themselves, and the overweening power of centralised states was a concern of E.P. Thompson's in the 1970s, too. He counter-posed the libertarian traditions of the 'free-born Briton' to this growing state-authoritarianism. For him, 'the people' were not so much associated with national identity but with a political culture, though one now under increasing threat. 'The freeborn Briton', he worried, 'has been bred out of the strain, and the stillborn Britperson has been bred in. The people have been drugged into an awe of office, and into that diminished reality-sense known as "normality".'[19] Dissent was now the uncommon culture of 'the people'. END reaffirmed Thompson's faith in a dissenting culture though, validating his long-held belief in the potential of voluntary association from below.

Stuart Hall had a different interpretation of 'the people' in the 1970s. No less opposed to the state's authoritarianism than Thompson, he nonetheless found it difficult to counter-pose 'the free-born Briton' to the state's culture of law and order. 'The people', for Hall, were a political subject without a given politics, a free-floating signifier, in terms he would later favour, whose meaning would be determined by discursive struggle. In the 1970s, he believed, 'the people' had been constructed against a number of 'internal enemies' including trade-unionists, socialists and Black Britons. Hall repeatedly emphasised the importance of this struggle around the meaning of 'the people', and he attempted to reclaim both 'Britishness' and 'the people' against Thatcherism. The idea, according to Hall, was to construct 'the people' in opposition to Thatcherism's association of the 'signifier' with a revenant imperial grandeur. 'In fact', Hall argued, 'what the nation "means" is an on-going project, under constant reconstruction'.[20] Unlike Williams and Nairn, Hall believed that Britain could be 're-imagined' in 'profoundly inclusive' ways that would work for rather than against socialism.[21]

---

17. See Eagleton 1999, for the distinction.
18. Williams 2003, p. 24.
19. E.P. Thompson 1980a, p. 255.
20. Hall 1999/2000, p. 5.
21. Hall 1999/2000, p. 10.

A further way contests between New Left thinkers can be rendered is through their encounter with Europe and European integration. E.P. Thompson and Raymond Williams's experience of Europe was initially mediated by war. Thompson's war was overwhelmingly political. The Europe he first experienced was anti-fascist and associated with partisan-struggle in Eastern Europe, with Red Army victories and with votes for Labour in 1945. It was this Europe which was 'intrigued against ceaselessly to restore "British interests in the East and near East, and capitalist enterprise in Europe; who sent missions into exposed positions in the field, and who then failed to give them support, or double-crossed them when in action...'.[22] But another Europe survived, even beyond the Cold War, which was rendered in Thompson's brothers' letters. 'How wonderful it would be to call Europe one's fatherland, and think of Krakov, Munich, Rome, Arles, Madrid as one's own cities.... Not only is this Union the only alternative to disaster. It is immeasurably more agreeable than any way of life we have known to date'.[23] Williams' war was much less political in this sense. Nonetheless, in his war-time journalism he recommended that we 'go on hating fascism which caused this destruction, and go on working for all that is true, all that is noble, all that is human, all that is opposed to the horror we hated...'.[24]

The early New Left established important relations with Europe, and not just through its support for communist dissent in Poland, Hungary and the Soviet Union. Relations were also established with socialist outriders on the fringes of Italian and French socialism. Despite this, the early New Left mostly rejected European integration. Stuart Hall and Perry Anderson believed that economic and political union would mean the end of British sovereignty and thus any hope of establishing a socialist Britain.[25] They agreed with Michael Barratt Brown and John Rex that the Rome Treaty was designed to subvert any prospective socialist control of Britain's national economy. 'Positive neutralism', Barratt Brown and Rex argued, 'demands in the first place action through the United Nations and its specialised and regional agencies. These are the true growing points of internationalism, not the narrow customs union in a part of a part of Europe'.[26] Hall and Anderson's repudiation was based on similar, internationalist, reasons. In opposition to 'capitalist Europe', they argued for a 'global reorientation' that would involve 'the pooling of world industrial, agricultural and capital resources' and a new 'world political system, an edging out of the new menacing homogeneity

22. E.P. Thompson 1980a, pp. 131–2.
23. Frank Thompson cited in E.P. Thompson 1997a, p. 102.
24. Williams cited in Smith 2008, p. 203.
25. Hall and Anderson 1960.
26. Barratt Brown and Rex 1960, pp. 42–3.

of the Western Alliance, and a turn towards non-alignment in the military and international power struggle'.[27]

Many of these objections to European integration were rehearsed in *May Day Manifesto*. This New Left consensus, however, was shortly after dynamited by Tom Nairn in *The Left against Europe?* – an intervention that Perry Anderson would later describe as 'the most powerful single argument ever made for support to European integration from the left'.[28] Later, Nairn admired Europe for different reasons, now more to do with the Union providing the appropriate 'political roof' for long-denied nationalities. Williams, perhaps uniquely among 'first' New Left thinkers, embraced European integration in the 1970s, though as a climate where regional socialisms might blossom, not nation-states. However, like Nairn, Williams embraced Europe as a way of giving up Britain. 'Any useful [socialist strategy]', he said, 'would involve a great building up of autonomy in such regions of Britain, but instead of orienting that to the British state, looking out for the connections which can be made to Western Europe'.[29] However, it would be Perry Anderson who would emerge as Europe's most consistent champion among New Left thinkers, and this even allowing for his recent transformation into the Union's most incisive critic.[30]

Thompson, though, argued against European integration till the end. He saw no socialist value in 'going into Europe', a community he associated with a 'stomach', 'the logical extension of the eating-out habits of Oxford and North London'.[31] He supposed official Europe a matter of 'capitalist convenience' that had nothing to do, whether as preparation or otherwise, with socialist internationalism. 'The lines of British culture', Thompson supposed in 1975, 'still run vigorously towards the point of change where our traditions and organisations cease to be defensive and become affirmative forces: the country becomes our own'.[32] This, in hindsight, was utopian, though if Thompson rejected official Europe, he certainly did not repudiate 'Europeanism', evidenced by his role in END, or suggest that Britain was anything else but European. Stuart Hall also drew attention to Europe's limitations. Hall's late reflections on Europe were premised on unseasonal reminders, amid much European idealism, of Europe's colonial past and present. Europe's value, he suggested, would be revealed in the Union's negotiation of multi-cultural issues. 'The problem is the "barbarians" are

---

27. Hall and Anderson 1960, p. 14.
28. Anderson 2009, p. xv.
29. Williams 2003, p. 214.
30. Anderson 2009, p. xv.
31. E.P. Thompson 1975, p. 85.
32. E.P. Thompson 1975, p. 88.

already inside the gate; and face-to-face with them, European cosmopolitanism does not stand up well to the test'.[33]

Contests around Europe and 'the people' demonstrate some of the tensions that existed among New Left thinkers. They provide evidence, too, of those opposing tendencies constitutive of New Left thought. These tendencies cannot be simply rendered as 'nationalism' and 'internationalism'. European integration could be rejected for internationalist reasons, just as 'the people' could be defined against other nationalist-inflected definitions. National identity could be marshalled against nationalism, just as internationalism could be based on respect for national difference. Internationalism could be associated with voluntary movements from below or endorsed as a project from above. Like all ideological traditions, intersecting tensions and oppositions constituted the New Left.

II

New Left thinkers engaged many of Britain's national questions and that engagement, as this book has demonstrated, was influenced by their own loyalties and allegiances. There were some outstanding instances of neglect, though. The most obvious, perhaps, was Ireland and Northern Ireland. Indeed, neglect of Ireland sometimes seems pervasive in New Left political thought. Burke or Shaw's 'Irishness' went unremarked in *Culture and Society*. When Anderson referred to the value of 'small revolutionary groups' in the late 1960s, he certainly did not have the IRA in mind. Hall and his co-authors paid no attention to the Irish as a former, perhaps still residual, reserve army of labour in *Policing the Crisis*. Instances could be multiplied. Williams' account of the 1840s in *The Long Revolution* made no mention of the Irish Famine, just as his forward-looking 'Britain in the 1960s' provided no premonition of gathering troubles in Ulster. *May Day Manifesto* did not mention Ireland or Northern Ireland, and this despite the contribution of Terry Eagleton. *New Left Review* devoted barely an article to Northern Ireland in the 1970s.

There were two exceptions to this general neglect. The most obvious exception was Tom Nairn. *The Break-Up of Britain* provided an explanation for 'the troubles' that built on Nairn's general theory of nationalism. He rejected suggestions that the conflict was primarily a matter of religion or ethnicity and linked national tensions in Northern Ireland with the general fragmentation of 'old nation-state frameworks'.[34] He refused, too, the suggestion – common within

---

33. Hall 1991, p. 19.
34. Nairn 1977, p. 218.

Britain's extra-parliamentary Left – that the Irish Catholic struggle was a type of 'anti-imperialism'. Uneven development rather than lingering colonialism, according to Nairn, was the underlying cause of conflict in Ulster. 'Multinational corporations and state subsidies', Nairn argued, 'reanimated the nationality struggle, not the shade of Finn MacCool'.[35] Nairn did not just offer a unique explanation for nationalist tension in the Six Counties. He also offered, at that time at least, a unique solution: Ulster independence. Nairn has upheld this solution, though later he was more inclined to view nationalist tension a product of 'modernity as well as ... ethnos and inheritance'.[36] His hope was, and is, that civic nationalism, in Northern Ireland as elsewhere in Britain and Europe, would constitute the only viable future for Ulster.

Ireland and Northern Ireland also figured in the thought of E.P. Thompson. The Irish played more than a bit part in his account of proletarian formation. Bernadette Devlin was invited to Thompson's Centre for Social History at Warwick. The Ulster conflict also figured in Thompson's more general analysis of the rise of the 'secret state' in the 1970s. Here he argued – and this in opposition to some sections of Britain's ultra-Left, including some associated with *New Left Review* – that 'Provisional terrorism, and its Loyalist counterpart, are a symptom of the present malaise [the rise of authoritarianism] and point towards no kind of solution'.[37] He agreed with Nairn that imperialism was not the source of Ulster's problems. Unlike Nairn, though, he argued that Ulster's furies descended from 'a historic conflict within Ireland itself, and *within the Irish working class*'.[38] And he recommended internationalism, rather than separatist nationalism, as a solution. 'In such circumstances', he concluded, 'the duties of internationalism should be met, not by giving equivocal rhetorical support, from positions of English safety, to the Provisionals, but by throwing our arguments, and if need be our bodies, in between'.[39]

Perry Anderson was no more sympathetic to the Irish Republican struggle, or its political strategy, in Ulster than Thompson. However, one would search in vain for any substantial comment on Ireland in his oeuvre, the more surprising, perhaps, given Anderson's Anglo-Irish background – or perhaps not, since he once used his residual connection to the Protestant Ascendancy as reason for his aversion to both national struggles and the study of popular nationalism.[40] It is nonetheless surprising that *New Left Review* refused to engage Irish questions. The reason, it seems, was political differences within the *New Left Review*

---

35. Nairn 1977, p. 227.
36. Nairn 1997, p. 164.
37. E.P. Thompson 1980a, p. 171.
38. E.P. Thompson 1980a, p. 172.
39. Ibid.
40. Anderson 1992, p. 7.

collective – some, particularly those associated with the International Marxist Group provided rhetorical support for the IRA, the majority, including Nairn and Anderson, did not.[41] Adherents of opposed positions agreed not to raise the issue in the journal.

The relative neglect of Irish issues in New Left thought is difficult to explain. Residual 'Britishness' might be one explanation, though New Left thinkers demonstrated no residual imperial feeling when it came to India, Kenya or Cyprus. Another reason might be found in the political tactics of the Irish republican struggle, and the relative removal of the Ulster question from general Cold War conflicts of the time. The early civil-rights movement might be assimilated to New Left politics; the military struggle of the IRA, given the movement's reliance on terrorism, could not. A final reason might be found in the political orientation of the majority, Protestant, labour-movement in Northern Ireland. It was obviously difficult for any socialist to associate with the Ulster Workers' Council's general strike in 1974. If evidence were needed that capitalism creates workers and not a socialist working class, then much of this evidence could be found in Irish history. In this sense, perhaps, Northern Ireland rather than being a throwback to an atavistic past was a portent of a future – our future – antagonistic to the New Left's 'international of the imagination'.[42]

III

Ellen Meiksins Wood has argued that 'the forces tending to prolong the historic connection between capitalism and the nation-state are very powerful, indeed rooted in the very nature of capitalism'.[43] This constituted a useful rebuke to some contemporary interpretations of globalisation. But what Wood left unsaid was socialism's relation to the nation-state. In fact, this relationship has been no less historic and no less powerful. Indeed, the nation-state was the 'unavoidable medium' of socialist politics too.[44] All the instruments of socialist policy, whether social-democratic or communist, have been bound to the nation-state, no less planning than welfare, nationalisation than trade-union rights. However, if capitalism has been dependent on the nation-state, it has never been constrained by it. In contrast, socialism has remained dependent on the nation-state and has been continually constrained, and defeated, by the international reach of capital.

---

41. D. Thompson 2007, p. 95.
42. See Nairn 1977 – this was his suggestion, too.
43. Wood 2002, p. 29.
44. Wood 2002, p. 24.

Dilemmas associated with a world governed by global capitalism, *and* an international system of nation-states, were a common theme in New Left thought. 'The Insiders' speculated that in the post-war period, 'giant capitalist corporations' had replaced national economies as the key actors in the world economy.[45] According to Anderson and Hall, writing in 1960, capitalism's transnational development had enervating consequences for national economics in both hemispheres of the world-economy: in the 'north' European integration was facilitating a process whereby 'all barriers to trade and to the free movement of goods, labour, capital and services are to be removed',[46] while in the 'south' the national independence of newly-established states had been subverted by the global reach of Adam Smith's invisible hand. *May Day Manifesto* replayed this song, too. 'Giant multi-territorial firms', according to *Manifesto*, traverse the globe, investing 'not according to national interest, but where profit opportunities are brightest on the international market'.[47] This instantiated a new internationalism: 'the overriding of all other interests for the creation of a market in which the giant international companies can operate'.[48]

One socialist response to this situation was to fill the national void vacated by capital. 'The Insiders', for example, argued for a 'socialist national plan' and the 'public ownership of large firms in order to obtain maximum efficiency in the interests of our country's welfare'.[49] In response to Britain's proposed entry to the Common Market, Michael Barratt Brown argued that 'socialists had every reason to demand the retention of sovereignty over our national economy'.[50] A capitalist Europe, according to Hall and Anderson, would not only 'make nationalization of key sectors [of the economy] extremely difficult', but would 'rob' socialism 'of those very devices – selective quotas, export licenses and exchange controls – which even the modest programme of the 1945 Labour government required'.[51] This commitment to nationhood and national economics was no less a feature of the early New Left's support for national self-determination in Algeria or Kenya.

However, despite the apparent antinomy, the New Left also argued for what Ralph Miliband in the first volume of *Socialist Register* called 'socialism without frontiers'.[52] This conception of socialism was built on a philosophical anthropology associated with Marx's idea of species-being. The essence of humanity, the

---

45. Hall et al. 1958, p. 61.
46. Hall and Anderson 1960, p. 7.
47. Williams (ed.) 1968, p. 100.
48. Williams (ed.) 1968, p. 134.
49. Hall et al. 1958, p. 61.
50. B. Brown 1958, p. 44.
51. Hall and Anderson 1960, p. 10.
52. Miliband 1964, p. 95.

New Left presumed, was social – 'no single man can ever fully realise himself except united with all other men who hold the missing parts of his humanity'.[53] This theory of human nature issued in a conception of socialism of proportionate scope. Hence, New Left support for anti-imperialist movements and communist dissent in Eastern Europe. Hence, the centrality of the struggle against war and nuclear weapons in New Left rhetoric: 'In fighting anywhere', *May Day Manifesto* claimed, 'we are fighting anywhere'.[54]

This socialist internationalism remained rooted in the traditional nation-state framework. However, once the prospect of going beyond the nation-state became a reality some New Left thinkers, most obviously Tom Nairn, Perry Anderson and Raymond Williams saw Europe as the appropriate means of surmounting socialism's national dilemmas. This explains why *The Left against Europe?* was so scathing about the early New Left's supposed socialist nationalism. The nation-state, according to Nairn, was the framework of counter-revolution, not socialism. Rather than oppose European integration, he argued, socialists should embrace Europe because 'it *may* also strengthen the position and enlarge the real possibilities of the European working classes and European social revolutionaries'.[55] 'Such a Union', Anderson suggested much later, 'is the only kind of general will that can contest the new power of the invisible hand as the arbiter of collective destinies'.[56] Raymond Williams took a different perspective. He embraced European integration, but as means of creating a political framework for socialism constituted by forms of representation below (Wales or the Basque Country) the nation-state.

Europe has proved fallow ground for the development of international socialism. But this is not the primary reason socialists have provided for their 'experience of defeat'. Indeed, most thinkers have blamed that real movement of things which was once supposedly a platform for socialised humanity. A combination of the nation-state's decline and capital's intensified globalisation has provided the most popular explanation for socialism's historic defeat. This was certainly Perry Anderson's view. He has imagined the increasing transnationalisation of capitalist productive forces as the principal solvent of the socialist vision, though intimations of the view can be found in the work of Williams, Hall and Nairn too. According to Anderson, 'increasingly, as the twentieth century advanced, the movement that prided itself on having overcome national boundaries fell ever further behind the system it set out to replace, as the civilisation became steadily more international, not just in its economic mechanisms – with the arrival of

---

53. Anderson 1961b, p. 35.
54. Williams (ed.) 1968, p. 100.
55. Nairn 1974, p. 147.
56. Anderson 1992d, p. 365.

the multinational corporation – but also in its political arrangements, with the machinery of NATO and the G-7'.[57] This belief has given rise to Anderson's 'historic pessimism': 'What moves is only the market...'[58] The pessimism is not Anderson's alone nor has he been alone in drawing a link between the decline of the nation-state and the cooling fortunes of socialism.

Nairn put the question in abeyance. He was clear that capitalist globalisation produced new ethnicities, a view shared by Hall, which formed the subjective basis for new nation-states. Whether socialism suffered or not as a result of globalisation's production of cultural diversity was irrelevant since, for Nairn at least, nationality politics was a pre-condition of any new social order. As much as capitalist globalisation has encouraged processes of nationalist separatism, Nairn has nonetheless maintained that nationality politics remains the only means of resisting the uniformity and power associated with capital's hegemony. This view is not that distanced from Anderson's suggestion that 'national differences, however relative compared with conditions outside the metropolitan zone, continue to count for those who fall under them'. Although calling for a reinvigoration of socialist internationalism, Anderson has argued that the Left 'has not yet ceased to be national in its conditions'.[59]

In this sense, the initial historical conditions of the New Left remain operative, what Wood has called 'the contradiction between the global sweep of capitalism and the persistence of national entities...'.[60] In such circumstances politics is necessarily national, if not necessarily nationalist, because the nation-state constitutes the only viable framework for social solidarity. But this viability remains constrained, and increasingly constrained, by footloose capital's ability to transcend national borders. The dilemma might be put this way: socialist politics must be national, but to be successful socialism must match the inter-national reach of capital. This insight was central to New Left thought, even if New Left thinkers provided different ideas of relations between 'the national' and 'the international', and nothing at all like a final solution to that unity of opposites that constitute our world.

---

57. Anderson 1992d, p. 367.
58. Anderson 1998, p. 114.
59. Anderson 1992, p. 353.
60. Wood 2002, p. 17.

References

Aaronovitch, Sam 1950, 'The American Threat to British Culture', *Arena*, 8: 2–23.

Ahmad, Aijaz 1992, *In Theory: Classes, Nations, Literatures*, London: Verso.

Ali, Tariq 1972, *The Coming British Revolution*, London: Random House.

—— 2005 [1987], *Street Fighting Years: An Autobiography of the Sixties*, London: Verso.

Ali, Tariq and Quintin Hoare 1982, 'Socialists and the Crisis of Labourism', *New Left Review*, I/132: 59–81.

Alexander, Ken and John Hughes 1958, *A Socialist Wages Plan: The Politics of the Pay Packet*, London: New Left Pamphlet.

—— 1966, 'A Defence of the Incomes Policy Strategy', *New Left Review*, I/36: 92–4.

Anderson, J.A. 1982, *Nations before Nationalism*, Chapel Hill, NC: University of North Carolina Press.

Anderson, Benedict 1990, *Language and Power: Exploring Political Cultures in Indonesia*, Ithaca, NY: Cornell University Press.

—— 1996, 'Introduction', in *Mapping the Nation*, edited by Gopal Balakrishnan, London: Verso.

—— 1998, *The Spectre of Comparisons: Nationalism, Southeast Asia, and the World*, London: Verso.

—— 2006 [1983], *Imagined Communities: Reflections on the Origins and Spread of Nationalism*, London: Verso.

Anderson, Perry 1961a, 'Sweden: Mr. Crosland's Dreamland (Part I)', *New Left Review*, I/9: 34–45.

—— 1961b, 'Sweden: Mr. Crosland's Dreamland (Part II)', *New Left Review*, I/7: 4–12.

—— 1962a, 'Portugal and the End of Ultra-Colonialism, Part I', *New Left Review*, I/5: 83–102.

—— 1962b, 'Portugal and the End of Ultra-Colonialism, Part II', *New Left Review*, I/16: 88–123.

—— 1962c, 'Portugal and the End of Ultra-Colonialism, Part III', *New Left Review*, I/17: 85–114.

—— 1964a, 'Origins of the Present Crisis', *New Left Review*, I/23: 26–53.

—— 1964b, 'Critique of Wilsonism', *New Left Review*, I/27: 3–27.

—— 1965a, 'Problems of Socialist Strategy', in *Towards Socialism*, edited by Perry Anderson and Robin Blackburn, London: Fontana.

—— 1965b, 'The Left in the Fifties', *New Left Review*, I/29: 3–18.

—— 1965c [1964], 'Origins of the Present Crisis', in *Towards Socialism*, edited by Perry Anderson and Robin Blackburn, London: Fontana.

—— 1966, 'Socialism and Pseudo-Empiricism', *New Left Review*, I/35: 2–42.

—— 1967, 'The Limits and Possibilities of Trade Union Action', in *The Incompatibles: Trade Union Militancy and the Consensus*, edited by Robin Blackburn and Alexander Cockburn, Harmondsworth: Penguin.

—— 1968, 'Components of the National Culture', *New Left Review*, I/50: 3–57.

—— 1974a, *Lineages of the Absolutist State*, London: New Left Books.

—— 1974b, *Passages from Antiquity to Feudalism*, London: New Left Books.

—— 1976, *Considerations on Western Marxism*, London: Verso.

—— 1976-7, 'Antinomies of Antonio Gramsci', *New Left Review*, I/100: 5–78.

—— 1978, 'The Strategic Option: Some Questions', *The Future of Socialism in Europe?*, edited by André Liebich, Montreal: Interuniversity Centre for European Studies.

—— 1980, *Arguments within English Marxism*, London: Verso.

—— 1981, 'Communist Party History', in *People's History and Socialist Theory*, edited by Raphael Samuel, London: Routledge.

—— 1983a, *In the Tracks of Historical Materialism*, London: Verso.

—— 1983b, 'Trotsky's Interpretation of Stalinism', *New Left Review* I/139, pp. 49–58.

—— 1992a, *English Questions*, London: Verso.

—— 1992b, *A Zone of Engagement*, London: Verso.

—— 1997 [1996], 'The Sign of the Interim', in *The Question of Europe*, London: Verso.

—— 1998, *The Origins of Postmodernity*, London: Verso.

—— 1999, 'Reflections on the Left from the Left: A Conversation with Perry Anderson', available at: <http://globetrotter.berkeley.edu/Elberg/Anderson/Anderson-cono.html>.

—— 2000, 'Renewals', *New Left Review*, II/1: 1–20.

—— 2001, 'The Oslo Accords', in *New Left Review*, II/10: 5–30.

—— 2002, 'Internationalism: A Breviary', *New Left Review*, II/14: 5–25.

—— 2003, 'Force and Consent', in *New Left Review*, II/17: 5–30.

—— 2004a, 'The River of Time', in *New Left Review*, II/26: 67–77.

—— 2004b, 'Revolution without End', in *New Statesman*, 22 November.

—— 2005 [1993], *Spectrum*, London: Verso.

—— 2007, 'Jottings on the Conjuncture', in *New Left Review*, II/48: 5–37.

—— 2009, *The New Old World*, London: Verso.

Anderson, Perry and Patrick Camiller (eds.) 1994, 'Introduction', in *Mapping the West European Left*, London: Verso.

Andrews, Geoff 2004, *Endgames and New Times: The Final Years of British Communism, 1964–1991*, London: Lawrence and Wishart.

Arblaster, Anthony 1985, 'Labour's Future and the Coalition Debate', *New Left Review*, I/157: 45–60.

Arendt, Hannah 1968, *Between Past and Future*, New York: Viking Press.

Ascherson, Neal 2009, 'Wedgism', *London Review of Books*, 31, 4.

Avineri, Shlomo 1991, 'Marxism and Nationalism', *Journal of Contemporary History*, 26, 3/4: 637–57.

Balakrishnan, Gopal 1995, 'The National Imagination', *New Left Review*, I/211: 56–69.

Barke, James 1936, 'The Scottish National Question', *Left Review*, 2, 14.

Barnett, Anthony 1969, 'A Revolutionary Student Movement', *New Left Review*, I/53: 43–53.

Barratt Brown, Michael 1958, 'A New Foreign Economic Policy?', *New Reasoner*, 4: 39–57.

—— 1959, *Who are the Tories? What is the Election About?*, London: New Left Pamphlet.

—— (ed.) 1960a, 'Imperial Retreat', in *Out of Apathy*, London: New Left Books.

—— 1960b, 'Imperialism Yesterday and Today', *New Left Review*, I/5: 42–9.

—— 1963, 'Third World or Third Force?', *New Left Review*, I/20: 32–6.

—— 1988, 'Away with all the Great Arches: Anderson's History of Capitalism', *New Left Review*, I/167: 21–51.

Barratt Brown, Michael and John Hughes 1961, *Britain's Crisis and the Common Market*, London: New Left Review.

Barratt Brown, Michael and Royden Harrison 1966, 'Incomes Policy: A Reply', *New Left Review*, I/137, 86–94.

Baxendale, John 2001, '"I Had Seen a Lot of Englands": J.B. Priestley, Englishness and the People', *History Workshop Journal*, 51: 87–111.

Bentley, Nick 2005, 'The Young Ones: A Reassessment of the British New Left's Representation of 1950s Youth Subcultures', *European Journal of Cultural Studies*, 8: 65–83.

Benn, Tony 1982, *Parliament, People and Power: Agenda for a Free Society – Interviews with New Left Review*, London: Verso.

Benner, Erica 1995, *Really Existing Nationalism: A Post-Communism View of Marx* and Engels, Oxford: Oxford University Press.

Berger, Mark T. 2004, 'After the Third World? History, Destiny and the Fate of Third Worldism', *Third World Quarterly*, 25: 9–39.

Berger, Stefan 2000, 'Class vs. Nation, Class and the Nation, between Class and Nation? Labour's Response to the National Question, c.1870–1939 with Special Reference to Britain and Germany', *Histoire Sociale/Social History*, 33, 66: 291–305.

Berman, Marshall 1999 [1985], 'Signs in the Street', in *Adventures in Marxism*, London: Verso.

Berman, Sheri 2006, *The Primacy of Politics: Social Democracy and the Making of Europe's Twentieth Century*, Cambridge: Cambridge University Press.

Bess, Michael 1993a, *Realism, Utopia and the Mushroom Cloud: Four Activist Intellectuals and their Strategies for Peace*, Chicago: University of Chicago Press.

Best, Geoffrey 1965, 'The Making of the English Working Class', *Historical Journal*, 8: 271–81.

Black, Lawrence 2001, '"The Bitterest Enemies of Communism": Labour Revisionists, Atlanticism and the Cold War', *Contemporary British History*, 15, 3: 26–62.

—— 2003, *The Political Culture of the Left in Affluent Britain, 1951–1964: Old Labour, New Britain?*, London: Palgrave.

Blackburn, Robin 1963, 'Prologue to the Cuban Revolution', *New Left Review*, I/21: 52–91.

—— 1988, 'Raymond Williams and the New Left', *New Left Review*, I/168: 12–21.

—— 1992, 'A Brief History of *New Left Review*, 1960–1990', in *Thirty Years of New Left Review: Index to Numbers 1–184 [1960-1990]*, London: NLR.

Blackledge, Paul 2004, *Perry Anderson, Marxism, and the New Left*, London: Merlin.

Blaut, J. 1987, *The National Question: De-Colonising the Theory of Nationhood*, London: Zed Books.

Bogues, Anthony 1997, *Caliban's Freedom: The Early Political Thought of C.L.R. James*, London: Pluto.

Bonefield, Werner 2002, 'European Integration: The Market, the Political and Class', *Capital and Class*, 77: 117–44.

Bonnett, Kevin, Simon Bromley, Bob Jessop and Tom Ling 1984, 'Authoritarian Populism, Two Nations and Thatcherism', *New Left Review*, I/147: 32–60.

Brenkman, J. 1995, 'Raymond Williams and Marxism', in *Cultural Materialism: On Raymond Williams*, edited by Christopher Prendergast, Minnesota: University of Minnesota.

Brenner, Robert 2003, *The Economics of Global Turbulence*, London: Verso.

Breuilly, John 1993, *Nationalism and the State*, Manchester: Manchester University Press.

Brewster, Ben 1967, 'Presentation of Althusser', *New Left Review*, I/41: 11–4.

Briggs, Asa and John Saville (eds.) 1960, *Essays in Labour History*, London: MacMillan.

Brooke, Stephen 1992, *Labour's War*, Oxford: Oxford University Press.

—— 1996, 'Evan Durbin: Reassessing a Labour "Revisionist"', *Twentieth Century British History*, 7, 1, 27–52.

Brubaker, Rogers 1992, *Citizenship and Nationhood in France and Germany*, Cambridge, MA: Harvard University Press.

Brunsdon, C. 1996, 'A Thief in the Night: Stories of Feminism in the 1970s at CCCS', *Stuart Hall: Critical Dialogues in Cultural Studies*, edited by David Morley and Kuan-Hsing Chen, London: Routledge.

Buchanan, Keith 1963a, 'The Third World – Its Emergence and its Contours', *New Left Review*, I/18: 5–23.

—— 1963b, 'Bingo or UN', *New Left Review*, I/21: 21–9.

Calhoun, Craig 1997, *Nationalism*, Buckingham: Open University Press.

—— 2007, *Nations Matter: Culture, History and the Cosmopolitan Dream*, London: Routledge.

Callinicos, Alex 1988, 'Exception or Symptom? The British Crisis and the World System', *New Left Review*, I/169: 97–106.

Canovan, Margaret 2004, 'Populism for Political Theorists', *Journal of Political Ideologies*, 9, 3: 241–52.

Carpenter, L.P. 1973, *G.D.H. Cole: An Intellectual Biography*, Cambridge: Cambridge University Press.

Chandavarkar, Rajnarayan 1997, '"The Making of the Working Class": E.P. Thompson and Indian History', *History Workshop Journal*, 43: 177–97.

Chun, Lin 1993, *The British New Left*, Edinburgh: Edinburgh University Press.

Claeys, Gregory 1985, '"The Lion and the Unicorn", Patriotism, and Orwell's Politics', *The Review of Politics*, 47, 2, 186–211.

Cocks, Joan 1996, 'From Politics to Paralysis: Critical Intellectuals answer the National Question', *Political Theory*, 24, 3: 518–37.

—— 1998, 'Fetishizing Ethnicity, Locality, and Nationality: The Curious Case of Tom Nairn', *Arena Journal*, 10: 129–50.

—— 2002, *Passion and Paradox: Intellectuals Confront the National Question*, New Haven: Princeton University Press.

Cohen, G.A. 1988, *History, Labour, Freedom*, Oxford: Oxford University Press.

Cole, G.D.H. 1913, *The World of Labour: A Discussion of the Present and Future of Trade Unionism*, London: G. Bell & Sons.

—— 1915, *Labour in Wartime*, London: G. Bell & Sons.

—— 1933, 'Guild Socialism', in *The Intelligent Man's Way to Prevent War*, London: Victor Gollancz.

—— 1935, *The Simple Case for Socialism*, London: Victor Gollancz.

—— 1937, *The People's Front*, London: Victor Gollancz.

—— 1939, *War Aims*, London: New Statesman Pamphlet.

—— 1941, *Europe, Russia and the Future*, London: Victor Gollancz.

—— 1944, *Money: Its Present and Future*, London: Cassell.

—— 1947, *The Intelligent Man's Guide to the Post-War World*, London: Victor Gollancz.

—— 1955a, 'The Future of Socialism', *New Statesman*, 15:22 January.

—— 1955b, 'The World Socialist Movement News Bulletin', 4, October.

—— 1956, *World Socialism Restated*, London: New Statesman Pamphlet.

—— 1958, *A History of Socialist Thought, Volume 4, Part. II: Communism and Social Democracy 1914–31*, London: Macmillan.

Colley, Linda 1994, *Britons: Forging the Nation, 1707–1837*, New Haven: Yale University Press.

Collini, Stefan 1999, *English Pasts: Essays in History and Culture*, Oxford: Oxford University Press.

—— 2006, *Absent Minds: Intellectuals in Britain*, Oxford: Oxford University Press.

—— 2008, *Common Reading: Critics, Historians, Publics*, Oxford: Oxford University Press.

Coombes, John 1980, 'British Intellectuals and the Popular Front', in *Class Structure and Social Change: A New View of the 1930s*, edited by Frank Gloversmith, Sussex: Harvester.

Conradi, Peter, *Iris Murdoch: A Life*, New York: Harper Collins.

Coppard Kit, Paddy Whannel, Raymond Williams and Tony Higgins 1961, 'Television Supplement', *New Left Review*, I/7: 28–48.

Crawfurd, Helen 1933, 'The Scottish National Movement', *Communist Review*, 5: 84–7.

Crossley, Nick 2006, *Contesting Psychiatry: Social Movements in Mental Health*, London: Routledge.

Crossman, Richard Howard Stafford 1940, 'Nationalism and Social Democracy', in *Where Stands Democracy?*, edited by Harold Laski et al., London: Macmillan.

—— 1952, *New Fabian Essays*, London.

—— 1973, 'Review of H. Thomas, *John Strachey*', *The Listener*, 3.

Cunningham, Hugh 1989, 'The Language of Patriotism', in *Patriotism: The Making and Unmaking of British National Identity, I: History and Politics*, London, Routledge.

Curran James, Julian Petley and Ivo Gaber 2005, *Culture Wars: The Media and the British Left*, Edinburgh: Edinburgh University Press.

Davies, Ioan 1991, 'British Cultural Marxism', *International Journal of Politics, Culture, and Society*, 4, 3: 323–44.

Davis, Madelaine 2006, 'The Marxism of the British New Left', *Journal of Political Ideologies*, 11: 335–58.

Day Lewis, C. 1936, 'English Writers and a People's Front', *Left Review*, 2, 13: 671–4.

Debray, Régis 1965, 'Latin America – The Long March', *New Left Review*, I/33: 17–58.

—— 1977, 'Marxism and the National Question', *New Left Review*, I/105: 25–41.

Denning, Michael 2004, *Culture in the Age of Three Worlds*, London: Verso.

Deutsch, Karl 1953, *Nationalism and Social Communication*, Cambridge, MA: MIT Press.

Deutscher, Isaac 1957, 'Russia in Transition', *Universities and Left Review*, 1: 1, 4–12.

Devine, Tom 2006, *The Scottish Nation: A History, 1700–2000*, Harmondsworth: Penguin.

Di Michele, Laura 1993, 'Autobiography and the "Structure of Feeling" in Border Country', in *Views from the Border Country: Raymond Williams and Cultural Politics*, London: Routledge.

Dickinson, Harry Thomas (ed.) 1989, *Britain and the French Revolution*, London: Palgrave.

Dunn, John 1985, 'Unimagined Community: The Deceptions of Socialist Internationalism', in *Rethinking Modern Political Theory*, Cambridge: Cambridge University Press.

Durbin, Evan Frank Mottram. 1940, *The Politics of Democratic Socialism*, London: Routledge.

Dutt, Rajani Palme 1936, *World Politics, 1918–1936*, London: Random House.

—— 1940, *India Today*, London: Random House.

—— 1943, *Britain in the World Front*, London: Lawrence and Wishart.

Douglas, Ray 2004, *The Labour Party, Nationalism and Internationalism, 1919–1951*, London: Routledge.

Dworkin, Dennis 1997, *Cultural Marxism in Postwar Britain: History, the New Left and Origins of Cultural Studies*, Durham: Duke University Press.

Eagleton, Terry 1976, 'Criticism and Politics: The Work of Raymond Williams', *New Left Review*, I/95: 3–23.

—— 1981, *Walter Benjamin, or Towards a Revolutionary Criticism*, London: Verso.

—— 1988, 'Resources of a Journey of Hope: The Significance of Raymond Williams', *New Left Review*, I/168: 3–11.

—— (ed.) 1989, 'Introduction', in *Raymond Williams*, Chicago: Northeastern University Press.

—— (ed.) 1990, 'Nationalism, Irony, and Commitment', in *Nationalism, Colonialism and Literature*, Minnesota: University of Minnesota Press.

—— 1992, *On Ideology*, London: Verso.

—— 1998 [1976], *Criticism and Ideology: A Study in Marxist Literary Theory*, London: Verso.

—— 1999, 'Nationalism and the Case of Ireland', *New Left Review*, I/234: 41–66.

—— 2003a, 'Stuart Hall' in *Figures of Dissent: Critical Essays on Fish, Spivak, Zizek and Others*, London: Verso.

—— 2003b, *After Theory*, London: Basic Books.

Ehrenreich, John 1983, 'Socialism, Nationalism and Capitalist Development', *Review of Radical Political Economists*, 15, 1: 1–42.

Eley, Geoff and Ronald Grigor Suny (eds.) 1996, *Becoming National*, Oxford: Oxford University Press.

—— 2002, *Forging Democracy: The History of the Left in Europe, 1850–2000*, Oxford: Oxford University Press.

Elliott, Gregory 1998, *Perry Anderson: The Merciless Laboratory of History*, Minneapolis: University of Minnesota Press.

Fagan, Hymie 1938, *Nine Days That Shook England*, London: Victor Gollancz.

Farrar, Max 1989, 'The Liberation Movements of the 1970s', *Edinburgh Review*, 82: 58–79.

Farred, Grant 1996, 'You Can Go Home Again, You Just Can't Stay: Stuart Hall and the Cultural Diaspora', *Research in African Literature*, 27, 4: 28–48.

Fernbach, David 1969, 'Strategy and Struggle', *New Left Review*, I/53: 37–42.

—— 1982, 'Tom Wintringham and Socialist Defense Strategy', *History Workshop*, 14: 63–91.

Field, Geoffrey 1992, 'Social Patriotism and the British Working Class: Appearance and Disappearance of a Tradition', *International Labor and Working Class History*, 42: 20–39.

Fieldhouse, Roger 1985, *Adult Education and the Cold War*, Leeds: University of

Leeds, Department of Adult and Continuing Education.

Fine, Robert 1994, 'The Rule of Law and Muggletonian Marxism: The Perplexities of Edward Thompson', *Journal of Law and Society*, 21, 2: 193–213.

Forgacs, David 1989a, 'Gramsci and Marxism in Britain', *New Left Review*, I/176: 70–88.

—— 1989b [1984], 'National-Popular: Genealogy of a Concept', *Cultural Studies: A Reader*, London: Routledge.

Forman, Michael 1998, *Nationalism and the International Labor Movement: The Idea of the Nation in Socialist and Anarchist Thought*, University Park: Pennsylvania State University Press.

Fountain, Nigel 1988, *Underground: The London Alternative Press, 1966–1974*, London: Routledge.

Fox, Ralph 1933a, 'Review of *The Coming Struggle for Power*', *Daily Worker*, 27 September.

—— 1933b, *The Colonial Policy of British Imperialism*, London: International Publishers.

—— 1935, *Communism and a Changing Civilisation*, London: John Lane the Bodley Head.

—— 1937, *Ralph Fox: A Writer in Arms*, edited by John Lehmann, T.A. Jackson, and Cecil Day Lewis, London: International Publishers.

Francis, Martin 1995, 'Economics and Ethics: The Nature of Labour's Socialism, 1945–1951', *Twentieth Century British History*, 6, 2: 220–43.

Freeden, Michael 1998, 'Is Nationalism a Distinct Ideology?', *Political Studies*, 46: 748–65.

Freedman, Carl 1983, 'Overdeterminations: On Black Marxism', *Social Text*, 8: 142–50.

Freud, Sigmund 1964 [1932], 'New Introductory Lectures', in *The Standard Edition of the Complete Psychological Works of Sigmund Freud*, edited by John Strachey and Anna Freud, Volume XXII, London: W.W. Norton & Company.

Fulbrook, Mary and Theda Skocpol, 'Destined Pathways: The Historical Sociology of Perry Anderson', in *Vision and Method in Historical Sociology*, edited by Theda Skocpol, Cambridge: Cambridge University Press.

Gaitskell, Hugh 1960, 'At Oxford in the Twenties', *Essays in Labour History in Honour of G.D.H. Cole*, edited by Asa Briggs and John Saville, London: Macmillan.

Gellner, Ernest 1964, *Thought and Change*, Chicago: University of Chicago Press.

—— 1979, *Spectacles and Predicaments: Essays in Social Theory*, Cambridge: Cambridge University Press.

—— 1983, *Nations and Nationalism*, Ithaca, NY: Cornell University Press.

Gibson, Mark and John Hartley, 'Forty Years of Cultural Studies: An Interview with Richard Hoggart', *International Journal of Cultural Studies*, 1, 1: 5–9.

Gilroy, Paul 1991 [1987], *There Ain't No Black in the Union Jack: The Cultural Politics of Race and Nation*, Chicago: University of Chicago Press.

Gorak, Jan 1988, *The Alien Mind of Raymond Williams*, Columbia, MS: University of Missouri Press.

Greenberger, Allen 1969, *The British Image of India: A Study in the Literature of Imperialism, 1880–1960*, Oxford: Oxford University Press.

Greenfeld, Liah 1992, *Nationalism: Five Roads to Modernity*, Cambridge, MA: Harvard University Press.

Gregg, Robert 1998, 'Class, Culture, and Empire: E.P. Thompson and the Making of Social History', *Journal of Historical Sociology*, 11, 4: 419–60.

Grossberg, Lawrence 1996, 'On Postmodernism and Articulation: An Interview with Stuart Hall', *Stuart Hall: Critical Dialogues in Cultural Studies*, edited by David Morley and Kuan-Hsing Chen, London: Routledge.

Guevara, Che 1967, 'Vietnam Must Not Stand Alone', *New Left Review*, I/43: 79–91.

Guess, Raymond 2001, *History and Illusion in Politics*, Cambridge: Cambridge University Press.

—— 2005, *Outside Ethics*, Princeton and London: Princeton University Press.

Guibernau, M. 1997, 'Marx and Durkheim on Nationalism', in *Rethinking Nationalism and Ethnicity: The Struggle for Meaning and Order in Europe*, edited by H.R. Wicker, Oxford: Berg.

Gunn, Neil M. 1936, 'Scotland a Nation', *Left Review*, 2, 14.

Hanson, Harry 1960, 'Socialism and Affluence', *New Left Review*, I/5: 10–16.

Hall, Stuart 1957a, 'The New Conservatism and the Old', *Universities and Left Review*, 1, 1.

—— 1958a, 'In the No Man's Land', *Universities and Left Review*, 3.

—— 1958b, 'A Sense of Classlessness', *Universities and Left Review*, 5: 26–32.

—— 1959, 'The Big Swipe', *Universities and Left Review*, 7: 50–2.

—— 1960a, 'Crosland Territory', *New Left Review*, I/2: 1–3.

—— 1960b, 'The Supply of Demand', in *Out of Apathy*, edited by *New Left Review*, London: New Left Books.

—— 1967, *The Young Englanders*, London: National Committee of Commonwealth Immigrants.

—— 1972 [1970], 'Black Britons', in *Social Problems of Modern Britain*, edited by E. Butterworth and D. Weir, London: Fontana.

—— 1973a, 'Encoding and Decoding in the Media Discourse', *Working Papers in Cultural Studies*, Birmingham: Centre for Contemprary Cultural Studies.

—— 1973b, 'Deviancy, Politics, and the Media', in *Deviance and Social Control*, edited by P. Rock and M. McIntosh, London: Tavistock.

—— 1977, 'Rethinking the "Base and Superstructure" Metaphor', in *Class, Hegemony, and Party*, edited by J. Bloomfield, London: Lawrence and Wishart.

—— 1978a, 'Racism and Reaction', in *Five Views of Multi-Racial Britain*, London: Commission on Racial Equality.

—— 1978b, 'The "Economic" and the "Political" in Marxist Theory of Classes', in *Class and Class Structure*, edited by Alan Hunt, London: Lawrence and Wishart.

—— 1979, 'The Great Moving Right Show', *Marxism Today*, January: 14–20.

—— 1980a (ed.), *Culture, Media, Language: Working Papers in Cultural Studies (1972–1979)*, Birmingham: Centre for Contemporary Cultural Studies.

—— 1980b, 'Race, Articulation, and Societies Structured in Dominance', in *Sociological Theories: Race and Colonialism*, Paris: UNESCO.

—— 1980c, 'Popular-Democratic vs Authoritarian Populism: Two Ways of "Taking Democracy Seriously"', in *Marxism and Democracy*, edited by Alan Hunt, London: Lawrence and Wishart.

—— 1980d, 'Thatcherism – A New Stage?', *Marxism Today*, 22–7.

—— 1981, 'In Defence of Theory', in *People's History and Socialist History*, edited by Raphael Samuel, London: Routledge.

—— 1982, 'A Long Haul', *Marxism Today*, 25: 11, 16–21.

—— 1984a, 'The Crisis of Labourism', in *The Future of the Left*, edited by J. Curran, Cambridge: Polity Press.

—— 1984b, 'The Culture Gap', *Marxism Today*, 28, 1: 18–23.

—— 1985a, 'Signification, Representation, Ideology: Althusser and the Post-Structuralist Debates', *Critical Studies in Mass Communication*, 2, 2: 91–114.

—— 1985b, 'Realignment – For What?', *Marxism Today*, 29:12, 12–17.

—— 1985c, 'Faith, Hope or Clarity', *Marxism Today*, 29, 1: 15–19.

—— 1985d, 'Reply to Jessop et al.', *New Left Review*, I/151: 115–24.

—— 1986, 'Gramsci's Relevance for the Study of Race and Ethnicity', *Journal of Communication Inquiry*, 10, 2: 5–27.

—— 1987, 'Gramsci and Us', *Marxism Today*, 31: 6, 16–21.

—— 1988a, 'Brave New World', *Marxism Today*, 32: 11, 24–29.

—— 1988b, 'Migration from English-Speaking Caribbean to the UK, 1950–1980', in *International Migration Today 1: Trends and Prospects*, edited by R. Appleyard, Paris: UNESCO.

—— 1988c, 'The Toad in the Garden: Thatcherism among the Theorists', in *Marxism and the Interpretation of Culture*, edited by Carey Nelson and Lawrence Grossberg, Urbana: University of Illinois Press.

—— 1988d [1982], 'The Battle for Socialist Ideas in the 1980s', in *The Hard Road to Renewal: Thatcherism and the Crisis of the Left*, London: Verso.

—— 1988e, 'Minimal Selves', in *Identity: The Real Me*, ICA Documents, 6, London: Institute of Contemporary Arts.

—— 1989a, 'Ethnicity: Identity and Difference', *Radical America*, 23, 4: 9–20.

—— 1989b, 'The "First" New Left: Life and Times', in *Out of Apathy: Voices of the New Left Thirty Years On*, edited by

Oxford University Socialist Group, London: Verso.

—— 1990a, 'Cultural Identity and Diaspora', in *Identity: Community, Culture, Difference*, edited by Jonathan Rutherford, London: Lawrence and Wishart.

—— 1990b, 'The Emergence of Cultural Studies and the Crisis of Humanities', *October*, 53: 11–23.

—— 1991a, 'Politics and Letters', in *Raymond Williams: Critical Perspectives*, edited by Terry Eagleton, Oxford: Blackwell.

—— 1991b, 'The Local and the Global', in *Culture, Globalization and the World System*, edited by A.D. King, Minneapolis: University of Minnesota Press.

—— 1991c, 'Europe's Other Self', *Marxism Today*, 35: 8, 18–19.

—— 1991d, 'Old and New Identities, Old and New Ethnicities', in *Culture, Globalization and the World System*, edited by A.D. King, Minneapolis: University of Minnesota Press.

—— 1992, 'Race, Culture and Communications: Looking Backward and Forward at Cultural Studies', *Rethinking Marxism*, 5: 1, 11–18.

—— 1993, 'Culture, Community, Nation', *Cultural Studies*, 7, 3: 349–63

—— 1995a, 'Parties on the Verge of a Nervous Breakdown', *Soundings*, 1: 19–33.

—— 1995b, 'Negotiating Caribbean Identities', *New Left Review*, I/209: 3–14.

—— 1996a, Morley, David and Kuan-Hsing Chen (eds.), *Stuart Hall: Critical Dialogues in Cultural Studies*, London: Routledge.

—— 1996b, 'When was "The Post-Colonial"? Thinking the Limit', in *The Postcolonial Question: Common Skies, Divided Horizons*, London: Routledge.

—— 1997, 'Culture and Power: An Interview with Stuart Hall', *Radical Philosophy*, 86.

—— 1998a, 'The Windrush Issue: Postscript', *Soundings*, 10: 188-191.

—— 1998b, 'The Great Moving Nowhere Show', *Marxism Today*, 42: 11 9–14.

—— 1998c, 'Aspiration and Attitude: Reflections on Black Britain in Nineties', *New Formations*, 33: 38–46.

—— 1999a, 'Cultural Composition: Stuart Hall on Ethnicity and the Discursive Turn. Interview with Julie Drew', in *Race, Rhetoric and the Postcolonial*, edited by Gary A. Olson and Lynn Worsham, Albany, NY: SUNY Press.

—— 1999b, 'Closing Remarks to Reinventing Britain: A Forum', *Wasafiri*, 14, 29: 43–4.

—— 1999c, 'From Scarman to Stephen Lawrence', *History Workshop*, 48: 187–97.

—— 1999/2000, 'Whose Heritage? Unsettling "The Heritage", Reimagining the Post-Nation', *Third Text*, 49: 3–13.

—— 2000, 'Conclusion: The Multi-Cultural Question', *Un/Settled Multiculturalisms: Diasporas, Entanglements, "Transruptions"*, London: Zed Books.

—— 2002, 'Reflections on "Race, Articulation, and Societies Structured in Dominance"', *Race Critical Theories*, edited by Philomena Essed and David Theo Goldberg, Oxford: Blackwell.

—— 2003 [1974], 'Marx's Notes on Method: A "Reading" of the "1857 Introduction"', *Cultural Studies*, 17, 2: 113–49.

—— 2006, 'Black Diaspora Artists in Britain: Three "Moments" in Post-War History', *History Workshop*, 61, 1: 1–24.

—— 2007, 'An Intellectual Life', *Culture, Politics, Race and Diaspora: The Thought of Stuart Hall*, edited by Brian Meeks, London: Lawrence and Wishart.

—— 2009a, 'At Home and Not at Home: Stuart Hall and Les Black in Conversation', *Cultural Studies*, 23, 4: 658–88.

—— 2009b, 'Richard Hoggart, *The Uses of Literacy* and the Cultural Turn', *International Journal of Cultural Studies*, 10, 1: 39–49.

—— 2010, 'Life and Times of the First New Left', *New Left Review*, I/61: 177–96.

Hall, Stuart et al. 1957a, 'The Insiders', *Universities and Left Review*, 3.

—— 1957b, 'Algeria', *Universities and Left Review*, 1, 2.

—— 1958, 'The Habit of Violence', *Universities and Left Review*, 5.

—— 1978, *Policing the Crisis: "Mugging", the State, and Law and Order*, London: Macmillan.

Hall, Stuart and Norman Fruchter 1961a, 'Notes on the Cuban Dilemma', *New Left Review*, I/9: 2–12.

Hall, Stuart and Perry Anderson 1961b, 'The Politics of the Common Market', *New Left Review*, I/10: 1–15.

Hall, Stuart and Martin Jacques 1989, 'Introduction', in *New Times: The Changing Face of Politics*, edited by Stuart Hall and Martin Jacques, London: Lawrence and Wishart.

Halliday, Fred 1992, 'Bringing the "Economic" Back In: The Case of Nationalism', *Economy and Society*, 21: 483–9.

Hanson, Harry 1960, 'Socialism and Affluence', *New Left Review*, I/5: 10–16.

Harvey, David 2000, *Spaces of Hope*, Edinburgh: University of Edinburgh Press.

Hastings, Adrian 1997, *The Construction of Nationhood: Ethnicity, Religion and Nationalism*, Cambridge: Cambridge University Press.

Haupt, George 1972, *Socialism and the Great War: The Collapse of the Second International*, Oxford: Clarendon Press.

Heller, Agnes 1977, 'Review of *Passages from Antiquity to Feudalism* and *Lineages of the Absolutist State*', *Telos*, 33: 202–10.

Hennessy, Peter 1999, *Never Again: Britain 1945–1951*, London: Cape.

Hill, Christopher, Margaret James, and Edgell Rickword, *The English Revolution, 1640: Three Essays*, London: Lawrence & Wishart.

Hilton, Rodney 1954, 'The British Tradition', *Our History*.

—— 1957, 'Socialism and the Intellectuals', *Universities and Left Review*, 1, 2: 19–20.

—— 1977, 'Christopher Hill: Some Reminiscences', in *Puritans and Revolutionaries: Essays in Seventeenth-Century History Presented to Christopher Hill*, edited by D. Pennington and Keith Thomas, Oxford: Clarendon Press.

Hilton, Rodney et al. 1976, *The Transition from Feudalism to Capitalism*, London: New Left Books.

Hindess, Barry and Paul Q. Hirst 1975, *Pre-Capitalist Modes of Production*, London: Routledge.

Hinton, James 1995, 'Voluntarism versus Jacobinism: Labor, Nation, and Citizenship in Britain, 1850–1950', *International Labor and Working-Class History*, 48: 68–90.

—— 1997, '1945 and the Apathy School', *History Workshop Journal* 43: 266–72.

Hirst, Paul 1985, 'The Uniqueness of the West – Perry Anderson's Analysis of Absolutism', in Paul Hirst, *Marxism and Historical Writing*, London: Routledge.

History Workshop Journal 2006, 'Document: Minutes of the Oxford University Socialist Club Executive Committee, 17 October 1956–27 February 1957', *History Workshop Journal*, 62: 205–13.

Hoare, Quintin 1967, 'Discussion on "Women: The Longest Revolution"', *New Left Review*, I/41: 78–81.

Hobsbawm, Eric 1977, 'Some Reflections on "The Break-Up of Britain"', *New Left Review*, I/105: 3–23.

—— 1984, 'What is the Workers' Country?', in Eric Hobsbawm, *Worlds of Labour*, London: Abacus.

—— 1990, *Nations and Nationalism since 1780: Programme, Myth, Reality*, Cambridge: Cambridge University Press.

—— 1994, 'Barbarism: A Users Guide', *New Left Review*, I/206: 44–54.

—— 1995a [1994], *The Age of Extremes: The Short Twentieth Century*, London: Abacus.

—— 1995b, 'Edward Palmer Thompson', *Proceedings of the British Academy*, 90: 521–39.

—— 1998, *Uncommon People: Resistance, Rebellion and Jazz*, London: Abacus.

—— 1999 [1973], 'Problems of Communist History', in Eric Hobsbawm, *Revolutionaries*, London: Weidenfeld and Nicolson.

—— 2006, *Interesting Times: A Twentieth Century Life*, London: Penguin.

—— 2011, *How to Change the World: Marx and Marxism 1840–2011*, London: Little Brown:

Holorenshaw, Henry 1939, *The Levellers and the English Revolution*, London: Victor Gollancz.

Hopkins, James 1998 *Into the Heart of the Fire: The British in the Spanish Civil War*, Stanford: Stanford University Press.

Howe, Stephen 1993, *Anti-Colonialism in British Politics: The Left and the End of Empire, 1918–1964*, Oxford: Oxford University Press.

Hutt, Allen 1937, *The Post-War History of the British Working Class*, London: Victor Gollancz.

Inglis, Fred 1995, *Raymond Williams*, London: Polity.

Ingram, Geoff 1988, 'Commerical Capital and British Development: A Reply to

Michael Barratt Brown', *New Left Review*, I/172: 45–65.

Jackson, Ben 2005, 'Revisionism Reconsidered: "Property-Owning Democracy" and Egalitarian Strategy in Post-War Britain', *Twentieth Century British History*, 16, 4: 416–40.

Jackson, Thomas Alfred 1929, 'Self-Criticism', *Communist Review*, 1, 2: 132–6.

—— 1937, 'Dickens, the Radical', *Left Review*, 3, 2: 88–95.

Jacques, Martin 1988, 'New Times', *Marxism Today*, 32: 10.

Jaggi, M. 2000, 'Prophet at the Margins', *The Guardian*, 8, 07.

James, Cyril Lionel Robert 1936, ' "Civilising" the "Blacks": Why Britain Needs to Maintain Her African Possessions', *New Leader*, 29, available at http://www.marxists.org/archive/james-clr/works/1936/civilising-blacks.htm.

—— 1963 [1938], *The Black Jacobins: Toussaint L'Ouverture and the San Domingo Revolution*, New York: Random House.

—— 2003, *Letters from London*, London: Signal.

Jameson, Fredric 1993, 'On Cultural Studies', *Social Text*, 34: 17–52.

—— 2008, *Valences of the Dialectic*, London: Verso.

JanMohamed, Abdul 1992, 'Worldiness-without-World, Homelessness-at-Home', in *Edward Said: A Critical Reader*, edited by Michael Sprinker, Oxford: Oxford University Press.

Jay, Martin 1984, *Marxism and Totality*, Cambridge: Cambridge University Press.

Johnson, Richard 1978, 'Edward Thompson, Eugene Genovese and Socialist-Humanist History', *History Workshop Journal*, 6: 79–100.

—— 1980, 'Barrington Moore, Perry Anderson and English Social development', in *Culture, Media, Language*, edited by Centre for Contemporary Cultural Studies, Birmingham: Centre for Contemporary Cultural Studies.

Jones, Douglas 2010, 'The Communist Party of Great Britain and the National Question in Wales, 1920–1991', Unpublished PhD thesis, University of Wales: Aberystwyth.

Jones, Gareth Stedman 1979 [1971], *Outcast London: A Study in the Relationship between Classes in Victorian Society*, London: Clarendon Press.

—— 1982, *Languages of Class: Studies in English Working-Class History 1832–1982*, Cambridge: Cambridge University Press.

Jones, P. 1994, 'The Myth of "Richard Hoggart": On "Founding Fathers" and Cultural Policy', *Cultural Studies*, 8: 395–418.

Kahn, Derek 1936, 'What is Culture?', *Left Review*, 2, 14.

Kedourie, Elie 1993 [1960], *Nationalism*, Oxford: Blackwell.

Kenny, Michael 1995, *The First New Left: British Intellectuals after Stalin*, London: Lawrence and Wishart.

—— 2000, 'Socialism and the Romantic Self: The Case of Edward Thompson', *Journal of Political Ideologies*, 5, 1: 104–26.

Kiernan, Victor 1959, 'Culture and Society', *New Reasoner*, 9, 10: 74–83.

—— 1970, 'The Peasant Revolution', *Socialist Register*, London: Merlin.

Kohn, Hans 1968 [1962], *The Age of Nationalism*, New York: Harper and Row.

Kozak, Marion 1995, 'How it all Began: A Footnote to History', *Socialist Register 1995*, London: Merlin.

Kramnick, Isaac and Barry Sheerman 1993, *Harold Laski: A Life on the Left*, London: Penguin.

Laclau, Ernesto 1979, *Politics and Ideology in Marxist Theory: Capitalism, Fascism, Populism*, London: Verso.

—— 2005, *On Populist Reason*, London: Verso.

Lago, Mary, *'India's Prisoner': A Biography of Edward John Thompson, 1886–1946*, New York: Columbia University Press.

Lamb, Peter 1997, 'Laski on Sovereignty: Removing the mask from Class Dominance', *History of Political Thought*, 28, 2: 326–42.

Larrain, Jorge 1991, 'Stuart Hall and the Marxist Concept of Ideology', *Theory, Culture and Society*, 8: 1–28.

Laski, Harold 1919, *Authority in the Modern State*, Oxford: Oxford University Press.

—— 1921, *The Foundations of Sovereignty and Other Essays*, Harcourt: Brace & Co.

—— 1925, *A Grammar of Politics*, New Haven: Yale University Press.

—— 1932, 'Nationalism and the Future of Civilization', in *The Danger of Being a Gentleman and Other Essays*, London: Allen & Unwin.

—— 1933, 'The Economic Foundations of Peace', in *The Intelligent Man's Way to Prevent War*, edited by Leonard Woolf, London: Victor Gollancz.

—— 1934, 'A Leningrad Letter', *The Nation*, 18 July.

—— 1935, *The State in Theory and Practice*, London: Allen & Unwin.

—— 1940, *Where Do We Go From Here?*, London: Penguin.

—— 1941, *The Strategy of Freedom: An Open Letter to American Youth*, New York: Harper.

—— 1942, *Reflections on the Revolution of Our Times*, London: Allen & Unwin.

—— 1947, 'The Crisis in our Civilization', *Foreign Affairs*, 26.

—— 1948 [1930], *Liberty in the Modern State*, London: Allen and Unwin.

Lawrence, Paul 2005, *Nationalism: History and Theory*, Harlow: Unwin.

Leopold, David 2007, *The Young Marx: German Philosophy, Modern Politics and Human Flourishing*, Cambridge: Cambridge University Press.

Left Review 1936a, 'Editorial', *Left Review*, 2, 14: 729–30.

Left Review 1936b, 'Editorial: National Identities', *Left Review*, 2, 12.

Leys, Colin 1985, 'Thatcherism and British Manufacturing', *New Left Review*, I/151: 115–24.

—— 1989 [1983], *Politics in Britain: From Labourism to Thatcherism*, London: Verso.

Lichtheim, George 1974, *Imperialism*, Harmondsworth: Penguin.

Lindsay, Jack 1936, 'not english? A Reminder for May Day', *Left Review*, 2, 8: 353–7.

Löwy, Michael 1989, 'Fatherland or Mother Earth? Nationalism and Internationalism from a Socialist Perspective', *Socialist Register 1989*, London: Merlin.

Löwy, Michael and Robert Sayre 2002, *Romanticism against the Tide of Modernity*, Durham: Duke University Press.

MacEwen, Malcolm 1958, 'The Two-Camps', *New Reasoner*, 4: 11–19.

Macintyre, Stuart 1975, 'Imperialism and the British Labour Movement in the 1920's', *Our History*, 64.

—— 1980a, *A Proletarian Science: Marxism in Britain 1917–1933*, Cambridge: Cambridge University Press.

—— 1980b, *Little Moscows: Communism and Working-Class Militancy in Inter-War Britain*, London: Croom Helm.

Mackenzie, Norman (ed.) 1958, *Conviction*, London: Mackibbon and Kee.

Mais, Stuart Petre Brodie 1946, 'Culture and Craft in the Countryside', *Our Time*, 5, 11.

Mandel, Ernest 1995, *Trotsky as Alternative*, London: Verso.

Mandler, Peter 2006, *The English National Character: The History of an Idea from Edmund Burke to Tony Blair*, New Haven: Yale University Press.

Mann, Michael 1992, 'The Emergence of European Nationalism', in *Transition to Modernity*, edited by John A. Hall and I.C. Jarvie, Cambridge: Cambridge University Press.

—— 1996, 'Nation-States in Europe and Other Continents: Diversifying, Developing, Not Dying', in *Mapping the Nation*, edited by Gopal Balakrishnan, London: Verso.

Mao, Zedong 1969, 'Talk on Strategic Dispositions', *New Left Review*, I/54: 83–96.

Marr, Gordon 1959, 'Postscript on Cyprus', *Universities and Left Review*, 6: 56–7.

Marshall, Thomas Humphrey 1950, *Citizenship and Social Class*, Cambridge: Cambridge University Press.

Marx, Anthony 2003, *Faith in Nation: Exclusionary Origins of Nationalism*, Oxford: Oxford University Press.

McAllister, Laura 2001, *Plaid Cymru: The Emergence of a Political Party 1945–2001*, Bridgend: Seren.

McCabe, Colin 2005, 'An Interview with Stuart Hall', *Critical Quarterly*, 50: 1–2.

McIlroy, John 1993, 'Border Country: Raymond Williams in Adult Education', in *Raymond Williams in Adult Education*, edited by John McIlroy and Sallie Westwood, Leicester: National Institute of Adult Continuing Education.

—— 2006, 'The Establishment of Intellectual Orthodoxy and the Stalinization of British Communism: 1928–1933,' *Past and Present*, 192: 187–230.

McLennan, R. 1932, 'The National Question in Scotland', *Communist Review*, 4: 505–10.

McRobbie, Angela 1996, 'Looking Back at New Times and its Critics', in *Stuart Hall: Critical Dialogues in Cultural Studies*, edited by David Morely and Kuan-Hsing Chen, London: Routledge.

Merrill, Michael 1981, 'Interview with E.P. Thompson', *Visions of History*, Manchester: Manchester University Press.

Miliband, Ralph 1958a, 'The Transition to the Transition', *New Reasoner*, 6: 35–48.

—— 1958b, 'The Politics of Contemporary Capitalism', *New Reasoner*, 5: 39–52.

—— 1961, *Parliamentary Socialism: A Study of the Politics of Labour*, London: Allen and Unwin.

—— 1975, 'Political Forms and Historical Materialism', *Socialist Register 1975*, London: Merlin.

—— 1985, 'The New Revisionism in Britain', *New Left Review*, I/150: 5–26.

—— 1995, 'Harold Laski's Socialism', *Socialist Register 1995*, London: Merlin.

Miles, Andy 1984, 'Workers' Education: The Communist Party and the Plebs League in the 1920s', *History Workshop*, 18, 102–14.

Mill, Samuel 1937, 'The Rebellious Neddleman', *Left Review*, 3, 4: 203–7.

Mitchell, Juliet 1966, 'Women: The Longest Revolution', *New Left Review*, I/40: 11–37.

—— 1971, *Women's Estate*, Harmondsworth, Penguin.

Morgan, Kenneth 1985, *Labour in Power 1945–1951*, Oxford: Oxford University Press.

Morgan, Kevin 1989, *Against Fascism and War: Ruptures and Continuities in British Communist Politics 1935–1941*, Manchester: Manchester University Press.

Morton, A.L. 1940, *A People's History of England*, London: Victor Gollancz.

Mulhern, Francis 1981, 'Introduction: Preliminaries and Two Contrasts', in *Teachers, Writers, Celebrities – The Intellectuals of Modern France*, edited by Régis Debray, London: Verso.

—— 1996, 'A Welfare Culture? Hoggart and Williams in the Fifties', *Radical Philosophy*, 77.

—— 2000a, *Culture/MetaCulture*, London: Routledge.

—— 2000b, 'Britain after Nairn', *New Left Review*, II/5: 53–66.

Nairn, Tom 1964a, 'The British Political Elite', *New Left Review*, I/23: 19–25.

—— 1964b, 'The English Working Class', *New Left Review*, I/24: 43–57.

—— 1964c, 'The Nature of the Labour Party (Part I)', *New Left Review*, I/27: 38–65.

—— 1964d, 'The Nature of the Labour Party (Part II)', *New Left Review*, I/28: 33–62.

—— 1965, 'Labour Imperialism', *New Left Review*, I/32: 3–15.

—— 1968a, 'The Three Dreams of Scottish Nationalism', *New Left Review*, I/49: 3–18.

—— 1968b, 'Hornsey', *New Left Review*, I/49: 3–15.

—— 1970a, 'The Three Dreams of Scottish Nationalism', in *Memoirs of a Modern Scotland*, London: Faber and Faber.

—— 1970b, 'The Fateful Meridian', *New Left Review*, I/60: 3–35.

—— 1970c, 'Enoch Powell: The New Right', *New Left Review*, I/61: 3–27.

—— 1971, 'British Nationalism and the EEC', *New Left Review*, I/69: 3–28.

—— 1972, 'The Left against Europe?' *New Left Review*, I/75: 5–120.

—— 1973, 'Immigration under Capitalism', *New Left Review*, I/80: 111–12.

—— 1974a, 'Scotland and Europe', *New Left Review*, I/83: 57–82.

—— 1974b, *The Left against Europe?*, Harmondsworth: Penguin.

—— 1975, 'The Modern Janus', *New Left Review*, I/94: 3–27.

—— 1977, *The Break-Up of Britain: Crisis and Neo-Nationalism*, London: New Left Books.

—— 1979, 'The Future of Britain's Crisis', *New Left Review*, I/113/114: 43–69.

—— 1981a, 'The Crisis of the British State', *New Left Review*, I/130: 37–44.

—— 1981b, 'Into the Emergency', in *The Break-Up of Britain: Crisis and Neo-Nationalism*, Second Edition, London: Verso.

—— 1989, 'Britain's Royal Romance', *Patriotism – The Making and Unmaking of British National Identity, Volume 3, National Fictions*, London: Routledge.

—— 1994 [1988], *The Enchanted Glass: Britain and its Monarchy*, London: Random House.

—— 1995, 'Breakwaters of 2000: From Ethnic to Civic Nationalism', *New Left Review*, I/214: 91–103.

—— 1996, 'Internationalism and the Second Coming', in *Mapping the Nation*, edited by Gopal Balakrishnan, London: Verso.

—— 1997 [1979], *Faces of Nationalism: Janus Revisited*, London: Verso.

—— 1998 [1968], *The Beginning of the End: France, May 1968*, London: Verso.

—— 2000, *After Britain: New Labour and the Return of Scotland*, London: Granta Books.

—— 2001, 'Farewell Brittania: Break-Up of Britain or New Union?', *New Left Review*, II/7: 55–74.

—— 2002, *Pariah: Misfortunes of the British Kingdom*, London: Verso.

—— 2003, 'A Myriad of Byzantiums', *New Left Review*, II/23: 115–34.

—— 2004a, 'Out of the Cage', *London Review of Books*, 26, 12.

—— 2004b, 'Ambiguous Nationalism: A Reply to Joan Cocks', *Arena Journal*, 22: 119–35.

—— 2005a, 'Make for the Boondocks', *London Review of Books*, 27, 9: 11–14.

—— 2005b, 'Finishing the Story: Reflections at a Distance', in *Spirits of the Age: Scottish Self Portraits*, edited by Paul Henderson Scott, Edinburgh: Saltire Society.

—— 2006, 'History's Postman', *London Review of Books*, 28, 2: 11–13.

—— 2007, 'The Enabling Boundary', *London Review of Books*, 29, 20: 5–7.

—— 2008, 'Globalization and Nationalism: The New Deal?', available at <http://www.opendemocracy.net/article/globalisation/institutions_government/nationalism_the_new_deal>.

—— 2009, 'The English Postman', available at <http://www.opendemocracy.net/ourkingdom/tom_nairn/english_postman>.

Nairn, Tom and Paul James, 2005, *Global Matrix: Nationalism, Globalism and State-Terrorism*, London: Pluto Press.

New Left Review 1960a, 'Editorial', *New Left Review*, I/1: 1–3.

—— 1960b, *Out of Apathy*, edited by E.P. Thompson et al., London: New Left Books.

—— 1960c, 'Editorial', *New Left Review*, I/1: 2–3.

—— 1961, 'Television Supplement: Kit Coppard, Paddy Whannel, Raymond Williams, and Tony Higgins', *New Left Review*, I/7: 28–48.

—— 1963, 'On Internationalism', *New Left Review*, I/18: 3–4.

—— 1967, 'The Marxism of Régis Debray', *New Left Review*, I/45: 8–12.

—— 1968a, 'Introduction to Gramsci 1920-1921', *New Left Review*, I/51: 53–4.

—— 1968b, 'Introduction to Special Issue on France, May 1968', *New Left Review*, I/58: 1–8.

—— 1969, 'Introduction to Tuchachevsky', *New Left Review*, I/55: 74–89.

—— 1971, 'Themes', *New Left Review*, I/68.

—— 1977, *Western Marxism: A Reader*, London: New Left Books.

—— 1982, *Exterminism and Cold War*, London: Verso.

New Reasoner 1958, 'Can We Have a Neutral Britain', 4.

—— 1959, 'Letter to our Readers', 10.

Newman, Gerald 1987, *The Rise of English Nationalism*, London: Weidenfeld and Nicolson.

Newman, Michael 1993, *Harold Laski: A Political Biography*, London: Macmillan.

—— 2004, *Ralph Miliband and the New Left*, London: Merlin.

Norris, Christopher 1993, 'Old Themes for New Times: Basildon Revisited', *Socialist Register 1993*, London: Merlin.

O'Connor, Alan 1989, *Raymond Williams: Writing, Culture, Politics*, Oxford: Blackwell.

Orridge, A.W. 1981, 'Uneven Development and Nationalism I', *Political Studies*, 29, 1: 1–15.

Orwell, George 2000 [1941], 'The Lion and the Unicorn: Socialism and the English Genius', in *Essays*, London: Penguin.

—— 2001 [1947], 'The English People', in *Orwell's England*, London: Penguin.

Our Time 1942, 'Editorial', *Our Time*, 2, 7.

—— 1945, 'Editorial', 5, 2.

Padmore, George 1931, *The Life and Struggles of Negro Toilers*, London: Wildside Press.

—— 1936, *How Britain Rules Africa*, London: Wishart.

—— 1940, 'Hands Off the Soviet Union', *Left Forum*, 41, available at <http://www.marxists.org/archive/padmore/1940/hands-off-soviets.htm>.

—— 1941, 'Empire, "Gauleiters" Greet Each Other', *Left Forum*, 52, available at <http://www.marxists.org/archive/padmore/1941/gauleiters.htm>.

Palmer, Bryan 1981, *The Making of E.P. Thompson: Marxism, Humanism, and History*, Toronto: New Hogtown Press.

—— 1994, *E.P. Thompson: Objections and Oppositions*, London: Verso.

—— 2002, 'Reasoning Rebellion: E.P. Thompson, British Marxist Historians and the Making of Dissident Political Mobilization', *Labour/Le Travail*, 50: 187–216.

Panitch, Leo and Sam Gindin 2005, 'Finance and American Empire', *Socialist Register 2005*, London: Merlin.

Parekh Report 2000, *The Future of Multi-Cultural Britain*, London: Profile Books Ltd.

Parry, Benita 1998 [1972], *Delusions and Discoveries: Studies on India and the British Imagination, 1880–1930*, London: Verso.

Pimlott, Ben 1977, *Labour and the Left in the 1930s*, Cambridge: Cambridge University Press.

Pinkey, Tony 1989, 'Raymond Williams and the "Two Faces of Modernism"', in *Raymond Williams*, edited by Terry Eagleton, Chicago: Northeastern University Press.

Purvis, Trevor 1999, 'Marxism and Nationalism', in *Marxism and Social Science*, edited by Andrew Gamble et al., London: Macmillan.

Rattenbury, Arnold 1997, 'Convenient Death of a Hero', *London Review of Books*, 19, 9: 12–14.

Redfern, Neil 2004, 'British Communists, the British Empire and the Second World War', *International Labor and Working Class History*, 65: 117–35.

—— 2005, *Class or Nation: Communists, Imperialism and Two World Wars*, London: I.B. Taurus.

Rée, Jonathan 1984, *Proletarian Philosophers: Problems in Socialist Culture in Britain, 1900–1940*, Oxford: Clarendon Press.

Reid, Alastair J. 2011, 'The Dialectic of Liberation: The Old Left, the New Left and the Counter-Culture', in *Structure and Transformations in Modern British History*, edited by David Feldman and Jon Lawrence, Cambridge: Cambridge University Press.

Revolutionary Socialist Students' Federation 1969, 'RSSF Manifesto', *New Left Review*, I/53: 21–2.

Rex, John 1957, 'Africa's National Congresses and the British Left', *New Reasoner*, 2: 56–64.

—— 1959, 'Labour's Task in Central Africa', *Universities and Left Review*, 6: 7–12.

Rickword, Edgell 1936, 'Stalin on the National Question', *Left Review*, 2, 14: 746–9.

—— 1978 [1937], 'Culture, Progress, and English Tradition', in *Literature in Society: Essays and Opinions (II) 1931–1978*, edited by Alan Young, Manchester: Carcanet.

—— 1941, 'Introduction on English Freedom', in *Spokesman for Liberty: A Record of English Democracy through Twelve Centuries*, edited by Jack Lindsay and Edgell Rickword, London: Lawrence & Wishart.

Riddell, Neil 1995, 'The Age of Cole'? G.D.H. Cole and the British Labour Movement 1929–1933', *The Historical Journal*, 38, 4: 933–57.

Roberts, Geoffrey 1997, 'The Limits of Popular Radicalism: British Communism and the People's War, 1941–45', *Chronicon*, 3: 1–92.

Rojeck, Chris 1998, 'Stuart Hall and the Antinomian Tradition', *International Journal of Cultural Studies*, 1, 1: 45–65.

—— 2003, *Stuart Hall*, Cambridge: Polity Press.

Rose, Hilary and Steven Rose 1978, 'Radical Science and its Enemies', *Socialist Register 1978*, London: Merlin.

Rous, Jean 1957, 'Last Chances of Negotiation in Algeria', *Universities and Left Review*, 1, 2: 4–8.

Rowbotham, Sheila 1979, 'The Woman's Movement and Organising for Socialism', in *Beyond the Fragments: Feminism and* the Making of Socialism, edited by Sheila Rowbotham, Lynne Segal and Hilary Wainwright, London: Merlin Press.

—— 1989, The Past is Before Us: Feminism in Action since the 1960s, London: Penguin.

—— 1993, 'E.P. Thompson: A Life of Radical Dissent', New Statesman and Society, 6, 268.

—— 1999, Threads through Time: Writings on History and Autobiography, Harmondswoth: Penguin.

Rowthorn, Bob 1965, 'The Trap of an Incomes Policy', New Left Review, I/24, 3–11.

Rustin, Michael 1985, For a Pluralist Socialism, London: Verso.

—— 1989a, 'The Politics of Post-Fordism: Or, The Trouble with New Times', New Left Review, I/175: 54–77.

—— 1989b, 'The New Left as a Social Movement', in Out of Apathy, edited by Oxford University Socialist Discussion Group, London: Verso.

Said, Edward 1994, Culture and Imperialism, New York: Random House.

Samuel, Ralph 1958a, 'New Authoritarianism – New Left', Universities and Left Review, 5: 67–9.

—— 1958b, 'Class and Classlessness', Universities and Left Review, 5: 44–50.

—— 1960, 'Bastard Capitalism', Out of Apathy, edited by New Left Review, London, New Left Books.

—— 1980, 'The British Marxist Historians: Part One', New Left Review, I/120: 21–96.

—— 1981, 'History Workshop, 1966–80', in People's History and Socialist Theory, edited by Raphael Samuel, London: Routledge.

—— 1989, '"Philosophy teaching by example": Past and Present in Raymond Williams', History Workshop Journal, 27: 141–53.

—— 1991, History Workshop: A Collectanea, 1967–1991, London: Routledge.

Sassoon, Donald 1996, One Hundred Years of Socialism: The West European Left in the Twentieth Century, New York: The New Press.

Saville, John 1976, 'The Twentieth Congress and the British Communist Party', Socialist Register 1976, London: Merlin.

—— 1990, 'Marxism Today: An Anatomy', Socialist Register 1990, London: Merlin.

—— 1991, 'The Communist Experience: A Personal Appraisal', Socialist Register 1991, London: Merlin.

—— 2004, Memoirs from the Left, London: Merlin.

Schneer, Jonathan 1984, 'Hopes Deferred or Shattered: The British Labour Left and the Third Force Movement, 1945–49', Journal of Modern History, 56, 2: 197–226.

Schwarz, Bill 2003, 'George Padmore', in West Indian Intellectuals in Britain, edited by Bill Schwarz, Manchester: Manchester University Press.

—— 2005, 'Stuart Hall', Cultural Studies, 19, 2: 176–202.

—— 2007, 'Disorderly Politics: Reading with the Grain', in Caribbean Reasonings: Culture, Politics, Race and Diaspora: The Thought of Stuart Hall, edited by Brian Meeks, Kingston: University of West Indies Press.

Searby, Peter, Robert Malcolmson and John Rule 1993, 'E.P. Thompson as a Teacher: Yorkshire and Warwick', in Protest and Survive, edited by Robert W. Malcolmson and John Rule, London: Merlin Press.

Sedgwick, Peter 1976 [1964], 'The Two New Lefts', in The Left in Britain, 1956–1968, edited by David Widgery, Harmondsworth: Penguin.

Segal, Lynne 2003, 'Lost Worlds: Political Memoirs of the Left in Britain', Radical Philosophy: A Journal of Socialist and Feminist Philosophy, 121.

Skidelsky, Edward 1999, 'Perry Anderson', New Statesman, 19 March.

Slater, Monty 1935, 'Writers' International', Left Review, 4.

Smith, Anthony 1986, The Ethnic Origins of Nations, Oxford: Blackwell.

—— 1995, Nations and Nationalism in a Global Era, Cambridge: Cambridge University Press.

Smith, Dai 1989, 'Relating to Wales', in Raymond Williams: Critical Perspectives, edited by Terry Eagleton, Boston: Northeastern University Press.

—— 2008, Raymond Williams: A Warrior's Tale, Cardigan: Parthian.

Smith, Mike 1977, The Underground and Education: A Guide to the Alternative Press, London: Meuthen.

Solomos, John et al. 1982, 'The Organic Crisis of British Capitalism and Race: The Experience of the Seventies in CCS Race and Politics Group', in *The Empire Strikes Back: Race and Racism in '70s Britain*, London: Centre for Contemporary Cultural Studies.

Sparks, Colin 1996, 'Stuart Hall, Cultural Studies and Marxism', in *Stuart Hall: Critical Dialogues in Cultural Studies*, edited by David Morley and Kuan-Hsing Chen, London: Routledge.

Spender, Stephen 1937, *Forward from Liberalism*, London: Victor Gollancz.

Strachey, John 1932, *The Coming Struggle for Power*, London: Victor Gollancz.

—— 1933, *The Menace of Fascism*, London: Victor Gollancz.

—— 1934, 'Why I Became a Communist', *Left Review*, 3, 1.

—— 1935, *The Nature of Capitalist Crisis*, London: Victor Gollancz.

—— 1936, *The Theory and Practice of Socialism*, London: Victor Gollancz.

—— 1955, *Contemporary Capitalism*, London: Victor Gollancz.

—— 1959, *The End of Empire*, London: Victor Gollancz.

Stapleton, Julia 1994, *Englishness and the Study of Politics: The Social and Political Thought of Ernest Baker*, Cambridge: Cambridge University Press.

—— 2006, *Sir Arthur Bryant and National History in Twentieth-Century Britain*, Lanham, MD: Lexington Books.

Steele, Tom 1997, *The Emergence of Cultural Studies, 1945–65: Cultural Politics, Adult Education and the English Question*, London: Lawrence and Wishart.

Stevens, Thomas 1941, 'A New Model in Army Education', *Our Time*, 1, 7: 8–15.

Survin, Darko 2005, 'Displaced Persons', *New Left Review*, II/31: 107–23.

Swingler, Randall 1937, 'The Imputation of Madness: A Study of William Blake and Literary Tradition', *Left Review*, 3, 1: 21–8.

Szporluk, Roman 1988, *Communism and Nationalism: Karl Marx versus Friedrich List*, New York: Oxford University Press.

Taylor, Charles 1957a, 'Marxism and Humanism', *New Reasoner*, 2: 92–8.

—— 1957b, 'Socialism and the Intellectuals: Three', *Universities and Left Review*, 1, 2: 18–19.

—— 1958, 'Alienation and Community', *Universities and Left Review*, 5: 11–18.

—— 1960, 'Changes of Quality', *New Left Review*, I/3: 3–5.

—— 1994, 'The Politics of Recognition', in *Multiculturalism: Examining the Politics of Recognition*, Princeton: Princeton University Press.

—— 1998, 'Nationalism and Modernity', in *The State of the Nation*, edited by John A. Hall, Cambridge: Cambridge University Press.

Taylor, Miles 1990, 'Patriotism, History and the Left in Twentieth Century Britain', *Historical Journal*, 33: 971–87.

Taylor, Richard 1988, *Against the Bomb: The British Peace Movement, 1958–1965*, Oxford: Oxford University Press.

Therborn, Goran, 1968, 'From Petrograd to Saigon', *New Left Review*, I/48: 3–11.

Thompson, Dorothy Katharine Gane 1993, 'The Personal is Political', *New Left Review*, I/ 200: 87–100.

—— 1996, 'On the Trail of the New Left', *New Left Review*, I/215: 93–100.

Thompson, Duncan 2007, *Pessimism of the Intellect? A History of the New Left Review*, London: Merlin Press.

Thompson, Edward Palmer 1947, *The Fascist Threat to Britain*, London: Communist Party of Great Britain.

—— 1951a, 'William Morris and the Moral Issues of Today', *Arena*, 2.

—— 1951b, 'Note', *Arena*, 2.

—— 1952, *The Struggle for a Free Press*, London: Communist Party of Great Britain.

—— 1956, 'Reply to George Matthews', *The Reasoner*, 1.

—— 1957a, 'Socialist Humanism: An Epistle to the Philistines', *New Reasoner*, 1: 105–43.

—— 1957b, 'Socialism and the Intellectuals – A Reply', *Universities and Left Review*, 1, 2: 20–2.

—— 1957c, 'Socialism and the Intellectuals', *Universities and Left Review*, 1, 1: 31–6.

—— 1958a, 'N.A.T.O., Neutralism and Survival', *Universities and Left Review*, 4: 49–51.

—— 1958b, 'Commitment in Politics', *Universities and Left Review*, 6: 50–5.

—— 1958c, 'Agency and Choice – I', *New Reasoner*, 5: 89–106.

—— 1959a, 'The New Left', *New Reasoner*, 9.

—— 1959b, 'A Psessay in Ephology', *New Reasoner*, 10: 1–8.

—— 1960a, 'Revolution Again! Shut Your Ears and Run', *New Left Review*, I/6: 18–31.

—— 1960b, 'Revolution', *New Left Review*, I/3: 3–9.

—— 1961a, 'The Long Revolution (Part 1)', *New Left Review*, I/9: 24–33.

—— 1961b, 'The Long Revolution (Part 2)', *New Left Review*, I/10: 34–9.

—— 1965, 'The Peculiarities of the English', *Socialist Register 1965*, London: Merlin.

—— 1967, 'Time, Work-Discipline and Industrial Capitalism', *Past and Present*, 38: 56–97.

—— 1968 [1963], *The Making of the English Working Class*, London.

—— 1970, *Warwick University Ltd: industry, management and the universities*, Harmondsworth: Penguin.

—— 1971a, 'The Moral Economy of the English Crowd in the Eighteenth Century', *Past and Present*, 50: 76–136.

—— 1971b, 'An Open Letter to Leszek Kolakowski', *Socialist Register 1971*, London: Merlin.

—— 1972, '"Rough Music": Le Charivari Anglais', *Annales: Economies, Societies, Civilisations*, 27, 2.

—— 1974, 'Patrician Society, Plebian Culture', *Journal of Social History*, 7, 4: 382–405.

—— 1975a, *Whigs and Hunters: The Origins of the Black Act*, London: Penguin Books.

—— 1975b, 'The Crime of Anonymity', in *Albion's Fatal Tree: Crime and Society in Eighteenth-Century England*, edited by E.P. Thompson et al., New York: Pantheon.

—— 1976a [1955], *William Morris: Romantic to Revolutionary*, London: Merlin.

—— 1976b, 'The Marx Claimants', *Guardian*, 16 September.

—— 1977, 'Caudwell', *Socialist Register 1977*, London: Merlin.

—— 1978, *The Poverty of Theory and Other Essays*, New York: Monthly Review Press.

—— 1980a, 'The Great Fear of Marxism', *Writing by Candlelight*, London: Merlin.

—— 1980b, 'Protest and Survive', in *Protest and Survive*, edited by E.P. Thompson and Dan Smith, London: Monthly Review Press.

—— 1980c, 'Notes on Exterminism: The Last Stage of Civilization, *New Left Review*, I/121: 3–31.

—— 1981, 'The Politics of Theory', in *People's History and Socialist Theory*, edited by Raphael Samuel, London: Routledge.

—— 1982, *Beyond the Cold War*, New York: Pantheon.

—— 1985 [1983], *The Heavy Dancers*, London: Merlin.

—— 1987, 'Diary', *London Review of Books*, 9, 9: 20–1.

—— 1989, 'Ends and Histories', in *Europe from Below*, edited by Mary Kaldor, London: Verso.

—— 1990, 'The Ends of the Cold War', *New Left Review*, I/182: 139–46.

—— 1991, *Customs in Culture: Studies in Traditional Popular Culture*, New York: New Press.

—— 1992, *Witness against the Beast: William Blake and the Moral Law*, Cambridge: Cambridge University Press.

—— 1993, *Alien Homage: Edward Thompson and Rabindranath Tagore*, New Delhi: Oxford University Press.

—— 1994, *Making History: Writings on History and Culture*, New York: The New Press.

—— 1997a, *The Romantics: England in a Revolutionary Age*, edited by Dorothy Thompson, London: Merlin.

—— 1997b, *Beyond the Frontier: The Politics of a failed Mission, Bulgaria, 1944*, Stanford: Stanford University Press.

Thompson, Edward Palmer and John Saville 1958–9, 'John Stuart Mill and E.O.K.A.', *New Reasoner*, 7: 1–11.

Thompson, Noel 1993, *John Strachey: An Intellectual Biography*, London: Macmillan.

—— 2006, *Political Economy and the Labour Party, 1884–2005*, London: Routledge.

Thompson, Willie 1992, 'Tom Nairn and the Crisis of the British State', *Contemporary Record*, 6, 2: 306–25.

Tilly, Charles 1992, 'States and Nationalism in Europe, 1492–1992', in *Perspectives* on *Nationalism and War*, edited by J.L. Comaroff and P.C. Stern, Amsterdam: Gordon and Breach.

Tiratsoo, Nick 1993, 'Labour and its Critics: The Case of the May Day Manifesto', in *The Wilson Labour Governments 1964–1970*, edited by Nick Taratsoo et al., London: Pinter.

Turner, Graeme 1990, *British Cultural Studies: An Introduction*, London: Routledge.

Universities and Left Review 1957, 'ULR Club' 1957, *Universities and Left Review*, 1, 2.

—— 1958, 'Editorial', *Universities and Left Review*, 2.

Veldman, Meredith 1994, *Fantasy, the Bomb and the Greening of Britain: Romantic Protest, 1945–1980*, Cambridge: University of Cambridge Press.

Verdery, Katherine 1996 [1993], 'Whither "Nation" and "Nationalism"?', *Mapping the Nation*, edited by Gopal Balakrishnan, London: Verso.

Visawanathan, Gauri. 1993, 'Raymond Williams and British Colonialism: The limits of Metropolitan Cultural Theory', in *Views beyond the Border Country: Raymond Williams and Cultural Politics*, edited by Dennis D. Dworkin and Leslie G. Roman, London: Routledge.

Walker, Pamela 2000, 'Interview with Dorothy Thompson', *Radical History Review*, 77: 4–19.

Wallerstein, Immanuel 1991, 'The Myrdal Legacy: Racism and Underdevelopment as Dilemmas', in *Unthinking Social Science: The Limits of Nineteenth Century Paradigms*, Cambridge: Polity.

Wallerstein, Immanuel and Etienne Balibar 1991, 'The Ideological Tensions of Capitalism: Universalism versus Racism and Sexism', in *Race, Nation, Class: Ambiguous Identities*, London: Verso.

Ward, Paul 1998, *Red Flag and Union Jack: Englishness, Patriotism and the British Left, 1881–1924*, London: The Boydell Press.

—— 2002, 'Preparing for the People's War: Labour and Patriotism in the 1930s', *Labour History Review*, 67, 2: 171–85.

Warner, Rex 1937, 'Jonathan Swift', *Left Review*, 3, 5: 266–72.

Webb, Beatrice and Sidney Webb 1913, 'What is Socialism?', *New Statesman*, 26 July.

Webb, William Larkin 1994, 'A Thoroughly English Dissent', *Radical History Review* 58, 160–4.

Wilcox, James 1969, 'Two Tactics', *New Left Review*, I/53: 23–32.

Williams, Raymond 1952, *Drama from Ibsen to Eliot*, London: Chatto and Windus.

—— 1957, 'Working-Class Culture', *Universities and Left Review*, 1, 1: 29–32.

—— 1960, *Border Country*, London: Chatto and Windus.

—— 1961, *The Long Revolution*, Harmondsworth: Penguin.

—— 1962, *Communications*, Harmondsworth: Penguin.

—— 1965a, 'Towards a Socialist Society', in *Towards Socialism*, edited by Perry Anderson and Robin Blackburn, London: Fontana.

—— 1965b, 'The British Left', *New Left Review*, I/30: 18–26.

—— 1966, *Modern Tragedy*, London: Chatto and Windus.

—— (ed.) 1967, *May Day Manifesto*, London: May Day Manifesto Committee.

—— (ed.) 1968, *May Day Manifesto*, London: Penguin.

—— 1970a, *The English Novel from Dickens to Lawrence*, London: Hogarth Press.

—— 1970b, 'On Reading Marcuse', in *The Cambridge Mind: Ninety Years of the Cambridge Review 1879–1969*, edited by Eric Homberger, William Janeway and Simon Schama, London: Allen and Unwin.

—— 1973, *The Country and the City*, New York: Oxford University Press.

—— 1976, 'Notes on Marxism in Britain since 1945', *New Left Review*, I/100: 81–94.

—— 1977, *Marxism and Literature*, London: Oxford University Press.

—— 1979a, *Politics and Letters: Interview with New Left Review*, London: Verso.

—— 1979b, *The Fight for Manod*, London: Chatto and Windus.

—— 1980a, 'The Politics of Nuclear Disarmament', *New Left Review*, I/124: 25–42.

—— 1980b, *Culture and Materialism: Selected Essays*, London: Verso.

—— 1983a, [1958] *Culture and Society: 1780–1950*, New York: Colombia University Press.

—— 1983b, *Towards 2000*, Harmondsworth, Penguin.

—— 1985 [1981], 'Crisis in English Studies', in *Writing in Society*, Verso: London.

—— 1989a [1970], *What I Came to Say*, London: Hutchinson.

—— 1989b, *Resources of Hope*, London: Verso.

—— 2003, *Who Speaks for Wales?: Nation, Culture, Identity*, Cardiff: University of Wales Press.

Wintringham, Tom 1935, 'Who is for Liberty?', *Left Review*, 1, 12.

—— 1941, *The Politics of Victory*, London: Routledge.

—— 1942, *People's War*, London: Penguin.

Wood, Ellen Meiksins 2002, 'Global Capital, National States', in *Historical Materialism and Globalization*, edited by Mark Rupert and Hazel Smith, London: Routledge.

—— 2003, *Empire of Capital*, London: Verso.

Wood, Neal 1959, *Communism and British Intellectuals*, New York: Columbia University Press.

Woodhams, Stephen 2002, *History in the Making: Raymond Williams, Edward Thompson and the Radical Intellectuals 1935–1956*, London: Merlin.

Woolf, Leonard (ed.) 1933, *The Intelligent Man's Way to Prevent War*, London: Victor Gollancz.

Worsley, Peter 1957, 'The Anatomy of Mau Mau', *New Reasoner*, 1.

—— 1960, 'Imperial Retreat', *Out of Apathy*, edited by E.P. Thompson et al. London: New Left Books.

—— 1961, 'The Revolution in the Third World', *New Left Review*, I/12: 18–25.

—— 2008, *An Academic Skating on Thin Ice*, New York: Berghahn Books.

Wright, A.W. 1979, *G.D.H. Cole and Socialist Democracy*, Oxford: Clarendon Press.

—— 1981, 'Socialism and Nationalism', in *The Nation State*, edited by L. Tivey, Oxford: Robinson.

Yeo, Stephen 1977, 'A New Life: The Religion of Socialism in Britain', *History Workshop*, 4, 5–56.

—— 1986, 'Socialism, the State and Some Oppositional Englishness', in *Englishness: Politics and Culture 1880–1920*, edited by Robert Colls and Philip Dodd, London: Croom Helm.

—— 1989, 'Intellectual versus Cultural Producers: Mainly from Raymond William's Fiction', *Journal of Historical Sociology*, 2, 3: 243–57.

Young, James D. 1983, 'Marxism and the Scottish National Question', *Journal of Contemporary History*, 18, 1: 141–63.

—— 1985, 'Nationalism, "Marxism" and Scottish History', *Journal of Contemporary History*, 20, 2: 337–59.

Index

CPSIA information can be obtained at www.ICGtesting.com
Printed in the USA
LVOW07s1959031115

460986LV00009B/41/P

9 781608 463770